Handbook of Infant Perception

Volume 2
From Perception to Cognition

DEVELOPMENTAL PSYCHOLOGY SERIES

SERIES EDITOR
Harry Beilin

Developmental Psychology Program
City University of New York Graduate School
New York, New York

A complete list of titles in this series is available from the publisher.

Handbook of Infant Perception
Volume 2
From Perception to Cognition

Edited by

Philip Salapatek

Institute of Child Development
University of Minnesota
Minneapolis, Minnesota

Leslie Cohen

Department of Psychology
The University of Texas at Austin
Austin, Texas

1987

ACADEMIC PRESS, INC.
Harcourt Brace Jovanovich, Publishers
Orlando   San Diego   New York   Austin
Boston   London   Sydney   Tokyo   Toronto

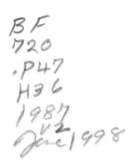

ACADEMIC PRESS, INC.
Orlando, Florida 32887

United Kingdom Edition published by
ACADEMIC PRESS INC. (LONDON) LTD.
24–28 Oval Road, London NW1 7DX

Library of Congress Cataloging in Publication Data
(Revised for vol. 2)

Handbook of infant perception.

Includes bibliographies and indexes.
Contents: v. 1. From sensation to perception —
v. 2. From perception to cognition.
1. Perception in infants. I. Salapatek, Philip.
II. Cohen, Leslie B. [DNLM: 1. Perception—in infancy &
childhood. WS 105.5.D2 H236]
BF720.P47H36 1987   155.4'22   86-10788
ISBN 0-12-615152-0 (v. 2 : alk. paper)

PRINTED IN THE UNITED STATES OF AMERICA

86 87 88 89   9 8 7 6 5 4 3 2 1

Contents

Preface

It has been more than a decade since the publication of Cohen and Salapatek's two-volume compendium on infant perception. At that time research in the area of infant sensory and cognitive processes had proliferated to such an extent that a unified summary appeared both timely and necessary. Yet, the proliferation of knowledge was uneven. Individual investigators and laboratories had made remarkable strides in limited domains of inquiry, while many equally important areas of infant perception remained unexplored. Thus, the original *Infant Perception* books emerged as a collection of in-depth summaries of work of individual investigators, with some obvious substantive omissions, such as developmental anatomy, effector mechanisms in vision, the other senses, visual psychophysics, color perception, event perception, and cross-modal integration.

We felt in 1975 that while many of the foregoing omissions were important areas of infant perception, research on these topics was either scant or outdated. The field of infant perception had indeed grown at that time, but in an ungainly, adolescent fashion. Such is not the case at the present time. While new topics undoubtedly will be developed in infant perception, it is currently possible to draft two new volumes in which topics ranging from sensory to cognitive processes are treated systematically without many glaring omissions. Hence, the title, *Handbook of Infant Perception*.

In both current volumes, each contributor summarizes research in his/her area, and in addition introduces his/her most relevant findings. We believe the two volumes together provide a coherent picture of the current status of knowledge about infant perception, and while we had some reservations about splitting the handbook into separate volumes, the sheer quantity of information made it necessary. A convenient, although arbitrary distinction was made between the more sensory and psychophysical topics (Volume 1) and those that deal more with the relationship between perception and cognition (Volume 2).

Hickey and Peduzzi introduce Volume 1 with a rigorous account of the anatomical development of the human visual system and the relationship of its development to that of other species. The human data are of recent vintage, and a chapter such as this could not have been written in our earlier volume.

Aslin provides the bridge between anatomy and psychophysics in his chapter on effector mechanisms in infant vision. In this chapter the current wealth of data, much of it very recent, on visual accommodation, pupillary adjustments, and the various eye movement systems (saccadic, pursuit, vergence) are treated in a way that emphasizes the importance of these systems to visual intake.

On the more sensory side, Banks and Dannemiller consider the methodologies used to determine thresholds for pattern during human infancy. In addition to threshold techniques, spatial frequency analysis is outlined as a tool by which some aspects of both threshold and suprathreshold pattern detection may be understood.

Teller and Bornstein bridge the gap between sensory and more perceptual processes. On the one hand, they carefully outline the brightness and wavelength sensitivities of the infant. On the other hand, what is known about the categorical perception of color is also treated.

The volume concludes with chapters by Crook and by Reisman. Crook lays out the data on taste and smell in infants, while Reisman does the same for the other senses, namely, proprioception, vestibular sensitivity, touch, and pain.

Volume 2 begins with Dodwell, Humphrey, and Muir's treatment of infant shape and pattern perception. They discuss primarily two-dimensional shape from both a theoretical and an empirical point of view. There is a careful blending of traditional and current theory and data on the topic.

Yonas and Owsley extend the perception of shape to the third dimension, rigorously examining the nature of infant binocular vision and a variety of the other cues to depth. Nelson and Horowitz continue this extension in their chapter on infant visual motion perception.

Infant perception is advanced to a more cognitive level in the chapters by Harris and by Huttenlocher and Smyth-Burke. Harris considers various theoretical and empirical approaches to the question of how infants perceive the permanence of objects. The perception of objects is extended to the perception of simple and complex events by Huttenlocher and Smyth-Burke. They begin with the infant's simplest imitation acts and move toward the meaning of the first utterances.

Evidence for the integration of the senses is considered by Spelke in her contribution on cross-modal perception. She provides data indicating that from the earliest months, transfer of information takes place between the senses, and some perceptual attributes appear to be amodal.

Finally, Kuhl departs from visual perception to deal with infants' perception of speech and sound. She provides thorough treatment of speech-like sounds both cross species and cross culturally. The chapter covers everything from basic sensory processes to the perception of categorical information.

Because of our attempt to produce a comprehensive work on infant perception, these volumes were long in the making. However, it is with a good deal of satisfaction that we view the outcome in terms of both depth and scope. For this, of course, we must thank the dedication and patience of the contributors, whose manuscripts were a pleasure to read and to edit. We would also like to thank Michael Kuskowski and Linda Oakes for their help in preparing the final manuscripts. A special thanks goes to Linda, Phil's wife, for her love and support.

Memorial

Phil Salapatek died in March 1984, while the *Handbook of Infant Perception* was still in preparation. He was a good colleague and a close friend. Over the years we had occasion to teach together, room together, and play together. Phil had been ill for some time, but his death still came as a shock to those of us who knew him well and cared about him. Although we first became acquainted in the late 1960s, our close association and friendship really began with our joint editorship of *Infant Perception: From Sensation to Cognition,* which appeared in 1975. Phil's seminal contribution on infant pattern perception still stands as a model of scientific ingenuity and comprehensiveness. It clearly illustrated both his encyclopedic knowledge of infant perception and his dedication to furthering that knowledge. From Phil's earliest work on the precise measurement of infant scanning patterns to his latest investigations of event-related potentials to unexpected events, he has always been at the forefront of the field. His collection of superb graduate students at the University of Minnesota, who are now making their own major contributions to the understanding of infant perception, is another indication of his lasting contribution. In fact, four of his former students have contributed chapters to this handbook. Two of them, in particular, Dick Aslin and Marty Banks, deserve a special note of thanks for their aid in bringing these two volumes to completion. In a very real sense the *Handbook of Infant Perception* stands as a tribute to Phil; to his scientific contribution, his dedication to knowledge, and his ability to instill in others the same excitement he felt about the study of infant perception.

Leslie B. Cohen

Phil Salapatek died unexpectedly at the age of 43. To his students, Phil was more like a colleague than a senior professor. We learned and worked together, and his death caused each of us to ponder what we had lost. Shortly after his death, we gathered informally at a restaurant in New York City, during the biennial Infancy Conference, to attempt to understand what happened to Phil and to share our experiences as his students. Three days later, at a memorial service in Minneapolis, we joined Phil's family and colleagues in expressing more formally our feelings about his impact on our careers. While the intellectual contributions Phil made to the field of infant perception are numerous and profound (see his obituary in *Infant Behavior and Development,* 1984, *7,* 383–385), we all agreed that Phil's influence on our lives went beyond his role as scholar and mentor. From our collective impressions, covering over 15 years of graduate student supervision, we each volunteered the opinion that Phil's integrity, both professional and personal, was his most salient characteristic. Phil consistently went out of his way to support his students in ways we have since learned are very rare in the academic world. Despite his specific research interests, he was willing to embrace new ideas if convinced of their merit. Yet his support was not superficial or gratuitous. He made us work hard and think clearly until we were absolutely certain that our findings and interpretations were as solid as we could possibly make them. Reaching the correct conclusion was more important than collecting publishable data or protecting a former position. What we will miss most is the sage counsel, the reflective pauses, the good-natured joking, and the sailboat rides. As the major force in our professional careers, Phil gave us a gift we will value always. We can only hope to repay this gift by attempting to live up to his level of commitment as a scholar.

Phil Salapatek's students

Handbook of
Infant Perception

Volume 2
From Perception to Cognition

1

Shape and Pattern Perception*

PETER C. DODWELL
Department of Psychology
Queen's University
Kingston, Ontario, Canada K7L 3N6

G. KEITH HUMPHREY
Department of Psychology
University of Western Ontario
London, Ontario, Canada N6A 5C2

DARWIN W. MUIR
Department of Psychology
Queen's University
Kingston, Ontario, Canada K7L 3N6

I. GENERAL INTRODUCTION

In 1960 J. A. Deutsch wrote

> . . . it is unlikely that any hypothesis in Psychology can at present be of more than a provisional nature. It should be sufficient that a theory leads to further predictions concerning the outcome of experiments which have not been performed. In this way it will be possible to establish precisely in what way the present theories do not fit the facts and to use experiment to narrow the range of theoretical possibility. It is difficult to envisage an ordered scientific advance in any other way. The number of possible experiments that can be performed is infinite. Without some sort of policy which leads to a narrowing of theoretical possibilities, experiments proliferate chaotically. Of facts there is already too much in psychology, of evidence too little.

The guiding principle of our chapter is embodied in this quotation. In a relatively new field like the study of infant perception there are obviously

---

* Order of authorship is alphabetical as authors contributed equally to the preparation of the chapter.

a great many facts to be discovered, but it is also true that some of these facts will be far more telling than others.

The old methods of merely cataloging the achievement of infants and young children at different ages, while of great value in the early days of child study, have clearly been superseded in the modern era of experimental research. Researchers vary enormously in their theoretical predilections, and in the extent to which their experiments are guided by hypotheses strictly derived from theory, but it is true that virtually every experimenter is influenced by theoretical considerations of some sort and is sensitive to their pervasive influence. The influence affects the sort of experimental question posed, to some degree the methods employed and paradigms used, and certainly is generally a major factor in the interpretation of results. That being so, it is appropriate to start the chapter with a cursory review of the major theoretical positions which have influenced recent research on shape and pattern perception in infants.

A. Theories

Although it may seem almost totally banal to say so, it is nevertheless true that the majority of child and infant researchers are most easily and recognizably ordered along the nativism–empiricism dimension. It must be borne in mind, however, that this *is* a dimension and not two mutually incompatible points of view. There is probably not a researcher in the field today who will deny the importance of a genetically determined physiological substrate which constrains many features of development, and likewise there can be few who will deny the importance of environmental influence, specifically of experience and learning, on perceptual development. Nearly every contemporary experiment can be seen as an attempt to understand how elements from these two groups of factors interact to further processes of development.

The roots of nativism and empiricism of course lie in philosophical traditions that go back many centuries. There have always been influential individuals and schools of thought to argue the importance of one set of factors over the other, and historically the pendulum has tended to swing from one extreme to the other over time. Starting perhaps with those giants of the late 19th century Hering and Helmholtz, the battle has been joined on these issues, specifically on the nature of human knowledge, its origins and acquisition. Questions about pattern and shape perception in infancy are of scientific interest because they rest squarely within this epistemological context.

The modern form of the empiricist tradition is most prominently represented by the ideas of D. O. Hebb and by the research and theory which have flowed from his seminal work (Hebb, 1949). It must be stressed that this is not a pure form of empiricism. Hebb's theory, as is so well known, is certainly constructivist; while accepting that certain primitive features of the perceptual world have Gestalt-like properties, in Hebb's view the major psychological event of early development is the construction of neurological counterparts or models (cell assemblies) of the features of the external world, by an associationistic process of perceptual learning. Specifically, he postulated that certain primitive pattern elements (perhaps lines, edges, or—his guess—*corners*) are innately coded. True pattern representation, which he labeled a "superordinate activity," is built up by the contiguous firing in space and time of the neurons, or neural assemblies, representing the primitive elements. Such contiguous firing was held to lead to the strengthening of synaptic connections, and thus the development of neural structures that model properties of the environment. The coherent sequencing of eye movements, from one pattern element to another, was held to be the generator of relevant contiguities and, hence, correct structures. In some respects Hebb's identification of certain primitive stimulus features which had to be integrated into true patterns brilliantly anticipated the electrophysiological discoveries of Hubel and Wiesel on contour-coding mechanisms at the single cell level. At the same time it must be stated that no satisfactory theory (including Hebb's own) has as yet become generally accepted on how the integration of such stimulus elements might occur. This is true both at the level of psychological theory and at the level of speculation among physiologists (Dodwell, 1978).

Hebb's ideas have been immensely influential in psychology, and in particular have spawned a good deal of developmental work with animals. As we shall see, one prominent branch of perceptual research with infants also manifests the Hebbian tradition, particularly with regard to feature detection (pattern elements), recognition of feature configurations or Gestalts (patterns), and the role that eye movements may play in bridging the gap between the two.

Despite Hebb's influence, there has been a fairly strong swing in recent years towards the nativist position so far as infant perceptual abilities are concerned. We think there are three main reasons for this, reasons which are of quite disparate character. They are, first, the emergence of the ethological approach to the study of behavior; second, recent developments in the fields of electrophysiology and metabolic image-processing techniques such as autoradiography; and third, the theoretical contributions of J. J. Gibson.

The influence of ethological ideas on psychology has been quite pervasive, for instance in the field of animal learning, in which the importance of biological constraints on learning is now widely recognized and studied; in the field of infant perception the influence has been present at least from the time of Spitz and Wolf's study (1946) of smiling as a stimulus to social communication and action. Generally, one may characterize the ethological approach as one which asks the questions: what are the *biologically* important stimuli in the organism's environment, and what behavioral mechanisms have developed to detect and respond to those objects and events? In conformity with Lorenz's (1965) identification of the importance of behavioral systems both as the outcome of evolution and the tools of further evolutionary change, one asks not simply about the responses of the young organism which satisfy primitive needs for food, warmth, and shelter, but also about the development of social and other more complex behaviors which are species-typical and further the survival of both the individual and its group. As we mentioned, the work of Spitz and Wolf was an early example of the ethological influence; study of the importance of the human face as a stimulus object for the infant remains a major interest that is nourished theoretically for ethological reasons. More generally, it is true to say that there is now a sharp awareness of the biological nature of the young human organism, and of the need to take into account evolutionary and other biological constraints when studying its behavior, including the ways in which it perceives.

The spectacular advances in electrophysiology of the past two decades, and specifically those which have allowed the recording of responses from individual neurons of the visual system, have certainly had a profound influence on psychological thought, including the thought of infant investigators. The now classical work of Hubel and Wiesel (1962), for example, finally laid to rest the notion of the cortex of the brain as a bowl of porridge. More especially, the demonstration, through electrophysiological and metabolic image-processing techniques, of a high degree of innate structure to the visual system have certainly led us to accept the fact of "hard wiring;" it is a form of innate structure that is both species-typical and also in certain respects—at least among mammals—fairly universal.

The persuasively argued and consistently maintained theoretical position of J. J. Gibson constitutes the third element in the swing towards nativism which we have identified. Although Gibson himself always claimed that he was not a nativist, that his theory cut across the nativism–empiricism controversies, it is nevertheless true that in certain respects his views are highly nativistic and definitely inimical to some of the favorite tenets of the traditional empiricism, as we shall shortly discuss (J. J. Gibson & Gibson, 1955; Postman, 1955). It is not our intention to outline the Gibsonian position in any great detail (see J. J. Gibson, 1966, 1979). Our aim here is simply to show how the Gibsonian influence has shaped many aspects of recent work on the perception of pattern and object in infancy. Perhaps the first researcher to attempt to bring the Gibsonian viewpoint to bear on problems of infant perception was Bower (1966c); more recently, a more exact formulation of the Gibsonian point of view with respect to infancy has been propounded by E. J. Gibson (1969, 1977, 1982; see also Butterworth, 1981).

As is well known, the major tenet of Gibson's theory is that the stimulation falling on the retina of the normal observer contains a far richer array of information than was ever considered in the traditional empiricist view. Rather than being a patchwork of elementary "sense data," or as we should now say "local features," which in some sense had to be glued together or integrated to form a coherent visual world, J. J. Gibson argued that the whole "stimulus array" contained within itself information both necessary and sufficient to specify the veridical properties of the world. Thus *surfaces* are well specified by textures and texture and movement gradients, *objects* by edges, perspective, and interposition cues (both static and dynamic), and so on. Perceptual development from this point of view, at least as interpreted by E. J. Gibson (1969), consists of learning to discriminate ever finer and *more general* features of stimulation, which is an immensely complex array under most natural conditions. On this view perceptual learning consists solely of processes of discrimination, for all the organization, and all the higher levels of potential information, are already carried in the external stimulus source. J. J. Gibson characterized as being "invariances" or "higher order invariants" of the stimulus array.

There is no doubt that J. J. Gibson made a major contribution to perceptual theory by identifying for us the poverty of the traditional view of the sensory field. By pointing to sources of information in the stimulus array which no one had discussed or investigated before, Gibson certainly brought a new level of sophistication to perceptual theorizing, and his work has been very influential in a number of respects. Nevertheless there are some problems with the concept of "invariance" and its detection, which we shall address at the end of the chapter. For the moment it is noteworthy that the Gibsonian point of view has led researchers on infant perception to ask questions about sensitivity to many different properties of stimulation, and—in a more traditional sense—to ask at what stage of development the infant becomes sensitive to specific cues or types of cue. Investigation of sensitivity to depth cues in general (E. J. Gibson & Walk, 1960) and to looming objects in particular (Ball & Tronick, 1971; Yonas, Pettersen, & Lockman, 1979) are good examples of this. In general one might say that Gibsonian researchers tend to stress the importance of complex and dynamic properties of a stimulus display

(E. J. Gibson, 1982; Ruff, 1980; Spelke, Chapter 6, this volume) rather than individual features on the one hand, or categorization, as this was classically understood, on the other (Postman, 1955).

We recognize the importance of discovering the time at which infants become sensitive to a particular cue or set of cues, but there is nonetheless a certain danger in restricting one's enquiry to this question. What is surely required is not just knowledge of when a particular cue becomes effective, but rather an understanding of how that cue plays a role in the general process of perceptual development. That is to say, one wants to understand how perceptual ability changes or grows over time as a function of age-related events (maturation, experience). This point holds true independently of one's preference for nativism or empiricism as a theoretical orientation.

In certain important respects the questions that a neo-Hebbian might ask are not really different from those of interest to a Gibsonian. In both cases one will be interested in questions concerning which cues are effectively used in making discriminations, the role which experience may play in the development of cue utilization, the extent to which configurations are important, and, again, the role that experience may play in determining how configurational properties are responded to. It is certainly true that much post-Hebbian research has been devoted to the question of how specific experiences may affect perception, and this point of view receives comfort and support from the electrophysiological work on the biasing of neural codes by specific stimulus exposure (for example, Blakemore & Cooper, 1970; Hirsch & Spinelli, 1970; Spinelli & Jensen, 1979). We should emphasize, however, that this work has all been done with subhuman mammals, and the extent to which their plasticity is similar to that of the human infant remains unknown. Also, we note again that the general problem of integration of stimulus elements remains unresolved for the neoempiricist. The effects of particular experiences, especially of sensory deprivation, have been emphasized by some researchers (e.g., White & Held, 1966) and the possibility of sensitive periods in perceptual development has been raised from time to time (e.g., Banks, Aslin, & Letson, 1975; von Noorden & Maumenee, 1968). The level of evidence and debate, however, have been quite general and certainly not precise enough to bear in any real sense on the Hebbian question of what motivates and guides perceptual development.

We have thus two modern epistemological viewpoints. One leans toward nativism and the other toward empiricism as these have classically been defined, but neither one is an extreme form of theory in denying the importance either of innate structures or of the role of experience and learning in perceptual development. We shall see, however, that the sorts of research commonly undertaken, and particularly its interpretation, are heavily influenced by the viewpoint a particular researcher espouses. We have already indicated the sorts of difference to expect: The neoempiricist is likely to ask whether the infant perceives patterns, or only pattern elements. He will be interested in how and when the infant progresses from the latter to the former, if indeed there is a progression, and what specific behaviors and/or experiences are conducive to the change. A neonativist, on the other hand, will be likely to investigate more complex, more dynamic, and very probably more natural stimulus situations. She will seek to show both the inbuilt character of much of the responding and its biologically useful function.

These categories of research are not, of course, sharply bounded or mutually exclusive. Nevertheless they serve to give shape to a remarkably large amount of the research on pattern and object recognition in infancy. We shall illustrate our chapter by considering in detail three areas of research. These are (1) research on "abstract" pattern processing and recognition, (2) research on the constancies in infancy, and (3) research on face perception.

B. Methodologies

Before discussing substantive research issues, a brief survey of the methodologies common to the field is in order. We shall give no detailed compilation, for others have done this admirably (e.g., Greenberg, 1977; Maurer, 1975; McGurk, 1974; Olson & Sherman, 1983).

The modern era of research into infant perception really started with the nearly simultaneous publication of two papers in 1958, both reporting a highly similar method, and indeed quite compatible findings, over different age ranges, on the perceptual activity of infants (Berlyne, 1958; Fantz, 1958). The technique employed by both these authors was that of "preferential looking." Berlyne's interest in epistemic behaviour and the effects of stimulus complexity on arousal, following the lead of the Russian school's work on the orienting reflex (Sokolov, 1963) led him to ask if infants (3–9 months of age) would show preference for different stimuli as a function of their complexity, and if so, whether such preferences change with age. Fantz's initial interest was to discover whether the newborn infant (about 48 hr old), showed *any* evidence of ability to discriminate between grossly different patterns. Both researchers used a simple preferential looking technique; the infant, lying supine and comfortable, was presented with two patterns, one to the left of midline and one to the right, at a supposedly convenient viewing distance. A peephole in the screen on which the patterns were displayed, and between them, allowed the investigator to estimate to which side the infant turned its gaze. Suffice it to say that both researchers found clear evidence of preferential looking and demonstrated its sensitivity to stimulus variation; some patterns were clearly preferred (looked at longer) over others.

The preferential looking technique is still used today (e.g., Fantz & Yeh, 1979) and some modifications have been made to make it methodologically comparable to some psychophysical procedures (Teller, 1979). A pair of techniques which are directly derived from the preference method have gained considerable prominence. Berlyne's particular theoretical concern in 1958 was with arousal and the orienting reflex; it is not surprising, therefore, that the question of habituation should soon have arisen. One of the first individuals specifically to use a habituation paradigm with young infants was Bartoshuk (1962), although he worked with cardiac acceleration and deceleration to specific stimuli rather than with looking as a response measure. He used a full habituation paradigm, namely, a period of habituation in which the original stimulus was presented repeatedly at constant intervals, followed by dishabituation to a new stimulus, just as in the classical work (Sokolov, 1963).

The central idea in this paradigm is that any organism will be aroused by, or orient to, a novel stimulus. The fact that babies will look at (orient to) a visual stimulus suggests that they are "exploring" it as something novel. If this is true, repeated presentation of the stimulus should lead to a decrease in orienting or exploration, and eventually to cessation of any response to that stimulus. However, a change of stimulation of any sort should by definition be novel or at least relatively novel and should lead to the reappearance of orienting behavior. Fantz (1964) was the first to show that young babies will detect novel displays, while Saayman, Ames, and Moffett (1964) showed that after habituation they will subsequently orient to novel displays, thus demonstrating both that infants are active information seekers, and also that they are subject to the vicissitudes of arousal by things new. That being so, it is possible to use the adaptation paradigm to assess the *extent* to which two displays are perceived as different from one another. The infant is habituated to stimulus A, and subsequently presented with stimulus B. The degree of recovery of response (orienting) is used as a measure of the perceived difference between A and B. There are some possible difficulties with this paradigm, as we shall discuss later, but it has been very widely used in infant research, and generally with great success.

The second paradigm derivative from preferential looking is that of visual scanning. If infants will look at a display, one may naturally ask what exactly they are looking at. Except for very small displays, one may reasonably propose that different parts of the display will attract the gaze at different times, and that at least rudimentary scanning should be observed. It is of course well known that adults scan fairly systematically over complex displays and typically show rather consistent patterns of scanning (Noton & Stark, 1971; Yarbus, 1967). The scanning paradigm is again simple in conception, although in this case the measurement technology can be quite complicated. (For examples of recent use and a critical evaluation of the scanning technique used in infant research the interested reader is referred to Bronson, 1982, Hainline, 1981, and Haith, 1980). The first investigation of scanning in young infants was reported by Salapatek and Kessen (1966).

To investigate scanning behavior, one needs a reasonably accurate measure of the actual direction of gaze at any instant. This is usually done by photographing reflections from the front surface (cornea) of the eyeball, either the actual pattern at which the infant is gazing or, more usually, the reflection of one or more infrared reference beams, which are invisible to the human eye. This was the method used by Salapatek and Kessen (1966). They studied the scanning responses of newborn infants to a triangle (a shape given classical prominence in the developmental theory of Hebb), and their reference beams marked the corners of the triangle. They therefore had a reasonably accurate estimate of where the infants gaze was centered at any instant within about 3° of visual angle, although somewhat better accuracy is now possible.

Two other procedures which have been used to assess pattern vision in infants should also be described briefly. The first is a "conditioning" procedure, in which the infant is rewarded for responding to some eliciting stimulus. The typical use of this paradigm has been to attempt to condition a baby to turn its head to one side when a particular stimulus is presented, this being reinforced with a "peek-a-boo." Subsequent generalization tests should be able to establish what aspect of the stimulus had been conditioned to elicit the head turning. The sucking response has also been employed as a response in this paradigm, and also in conjunction with the habituation paradigm. Like head-turning (orienting), sucking is a "natural" response of the young infant, one which adapts and can be conditioned. Its use in pattern recognition research has been comparatively rare, but it has occasionally been successfully employed.

II. RESEARCH ON 'ABSTRACT' PATTERNS AND PATTERN ELEMENTS

Some years ago Bond (1972) summarized our state of knowledge about the perceptual abilities of the infant as follows:

"The data indicate that the early responses of the infant can be accounted for largely by his attraction to relatively simple characteristics of stimulation, such as contours, angles, and stimulus change. This contention is based primarily on data showing visual scanning patterns, and responses to stimuli with differential change and contour. At least part of the explanation for the selection of this kind of information may be found in the presence of neural coding mechanisms optimally responsive to certain types of stimulation."

Bond's summary of the position would still be considered quite accurate today, in spite of much new evidence. A good account of our knowledge of infant pattern perception up to the mid-1970s is contained in a review chapter by Salapatek (1975). Most of the researchers in this area (abstract patterns and pattern elements) can be described as post-Hebbian in their general theoretical orientation. This is evident in the sorts of questions they have addressed, the sorts of stimuli they have used, and the explanations they have offered for their findings.

There is much evidence that the perceptual abilities of the infant undergo considerable change around the second month of life, as we shall discuss below. It is not unreasonable to suppose that many of these changes are intimately connected with the fact that the visual system is quite immature at birth and develops very rapidly over the first few weeks (Amigo, 1972; Bronson, 1974; Parmelee & Sigman, 1976). There has been intense speculation about the anatomical structures and neurophysiological mechanisms which may control behavior at this time, and as we shall see, although most models fall short of the task, they have nevertheless played an important role in guiding thinking and research on early perceptual development.

A. Two Visual Systems Model

Some theorists (Bronson, 1974; Karmel & Maisel, 1975; Salapatek, 1975) have argued for a "two systems" view of perceptual development. It is now well known that many different parts of the brain are involved in visual processing, but there are at least two major ascending pathways which have come to be known as the primary and secondary visual systems. The phylogenetically older of these two (see Diamond & Hall, 1969) is the secondary or midbrain system centered on the superior colliculus. The primary system is the phylogenetically newer geniculostriate system. The idea propounded by Bronson and others is that the older system is more highly developed at birth and therefore is functional before the primary or neocortical system.

It is proposed that subcortical mechanisms control visual behavior up to 2 months of age. At this time the neocortical system comes into operation, and subsequently, both systems can mediate different aspects of visual behavior.

What functions are the two systems supposed to mediate? In a well-known paper Schneider (1969) argued, on the basis of somewhat slim evidence, that the two systems have quite distinct functions, which can be experimentally separated. On the basis of ablation studies, Schneider concluded that the secondary system is mainly involved with visual orientation and guidance, but that the primary system is necessary for the analysis of patterns. Although this division of function may not be as clear cut as Schneider implied (see Weiskrantz, 1974), it has nevertheless become influential. If in fact the primary system were nonfunctional in infants younger than 2 months of age, and if indeed Schneider's interpretation of its function is correct, then there should be little or no response to pattern or shape in the very young infant.

Three main lines of evidence have been used to support the view that the young infant's visual behavior is controlled by the midbrain system: (1) the visual cortex is relatively immature at birth; (2) visual evoked potentials (VEPs) appear to be controlled by subcortical mechanisms prior to about 2 months of age; and (3) some of the visual behavior of infants under 2 months of age resembles that of destriate animals.

The first line of evidence rests primarily on anatomical and histological evidence. (See Hickey and Peduzzi, Chapter 1, Volume 1.) The components of the VEP are known to be generated in different parts of the visual system. Based on the results of recording VEPs in cats with various ablations, G. Rose and Lindsley (1968) showed that the late negative component is controlled by subcortical systems, while the early positive component is primarily a function of neocortical activity. Analysis of infant VEP patterns indicates that the amplitude of the late negative component reflects response to checkerboard patterns in infants below 6 weeks of age, while the early positive component is more closely related to the response in infants over 6 weeks of age (R. F. Hoffman, 1978; Karmel & Maisel, 1975). On the basis of this and similar evidence, Karmel and Maisel (1975) have argued that although the visual cortex of the infant below 6 weeks of age is intact, it may not be processing patterns.

Salapatek (1975, pp. 204–207) drew attention to a similarity in the visual behavior of destriate animals and very young infants, a comparison which has subsequently been re-evaluated by Maurer and Lewis (1979), as we shall discuss below. Of particular interest is a longitudinal study of a destriate rhesus monkey reported by N. K. Humphrey (1974). This animal showed for a considerable length of time very little evidence of postoperative visual behavior. Eventually, some vision was recovered but it was of a fairly unusual kind, characterized by Humphrey as responding to "salience," but with no ability to analyze patterns and objects or to compare them on any specific dimension. Although the monkey might detect and reach for small objects, this ability was destroyed by placing the object within a visual frame of some sort. Salapatek (1975) reported on experiments in which 1-month-olds scanned a limited portion of an external contour when presented with patterns containing both such a contour and internal detail. The scanning of 2-month-olds, however, was more thorough and seemed to concentrate on the internal detail in a more systematic fashion. Infants in both age groups could fixate the small elements when they were presented without the surround.

The analogy is clear; 1-month-old infants, like the destriate monkey, do not notice internal detail, but older infants do. Milewski (1976) provided some converging evidence for such a shift in processing abilities. One-month-old infants dishabituated to changes in the shape of an external contour surrounding an internal pattern element, or to changes in the internal *and* external contour, but not to changes in the internal detail alone. Four-month-olds, however, dishabituated to all of these changes. However, this "enclosure" effect found with very young infants can be overcome if relative movement is introduced into the stimulus array, as I. W. R. Bushnell (1979) has demonstrated. His 5-week-old infants detected a change in the shape of a small element surrounded by an external contour when the former was flashed or oscillated. Whether the small element was inside or outside the larger contour was irrelevant. Moreover, a change in the shape of the external contour was not detected when the internal element was modulated but not itself changed in shape. Bushnell attributes these effects to an attentional change, rather than to an information-processing limitation. The fact that static internal details are not scanned or apparently detected may be due to their lack of salience.

If simple manipulations like introducing movement can enhance the saliency or "attention-getting properties" of a stimulus, then it would be difficult to maintain that failure to scan or detect internal detail tells us anything very profound about the infant's information-processing capabilities. In fact, an experiment by Ganon and Swartz (1980) has capitalized on young infants' preferences for certain types of patterns such as bull's-eyes and checkerboards. These authors demonstrated that 1-month-olds detected changes in internal detail when such salient stimuli were surrounded by frames. There may well be limits to the young infant's ability to process compound forms or patterns, but there is nothing in the presently available evidence to show that this must be the result of a nonfunctioning cortex. On the other hand the "saliency" or "attention-getting" hypothesis is not incompatible with the notion of a nonfunctional cortex, since Humphrey found saliency to be the one characteristic which was relevant to the visual abilities of his decorticate monkey. Our point is that until exploration of a number of pattern dimensions has been undertaken, it would be premature to pronounce on the general question of cortical–subcortical functioning of the visual system in early life. One can quite plausibly argue, as Haith (1978) has done, that the cortex functions in early life but is not very efficient.

Some other evidence suggests that the "nonfunctional cortex" hypothesis is too simple. For example, newborns can distinguish curved shapes from straight ones (Fantz, Fagan, & Miranda, 1975) and horizontal from vertical stripes (Slater & Sykes, 1977). By 1 month, at least, infants can discriminate between right and left oblique stripe patterns (Maurer & Martello, 1980). Such pattern discriminations are presumably mediated by cortical processes, rather than by the less acute collicular system.

B. Model Based on Two Types of Visual Neuron

Although it is possible that there would be a sudden change in function and control just at 2 months of age, it is much more likely that there is a steady (if rapid) period of physiological development, a point of view espoused by Maurer and Lewis (1979). In attempting to reconcile the evidence that the cortex is nonfunctional at birth with the contrary evidence that in certain respects it is, they have proposed an alternative model of early visual development, based on knowledge gained from electrophysiological recordings in the primary and secondary visual systems. Their model is based not on that distinction, but on the fact that two separate classes of visual neurons have been identified within the two systems. The two classes have different functions and develop at different rates (for detailed review of this literature, see Maurer & Lewis, 1979; Stone, Dreher, & Leventhal, 1979).

The two classes of cells are commonly called X-cells and Y-cells and have generally well-defined different properties both anatomically and physiologically, although some work (Lennie, 1980) challenges the absolute distinction between the two types. These cell types have been extensively studied in the kitten and monkey, and there is psychophysical evidence to suggest that a similar classification of cell types exists in the human visual system. X-cells can be classed as "spatial detail detectors," and Y-cells as "movement and temporal detail detectors." This is perhaps an oversimplification but captures the essence of the difference. X-cells tend to have small receptive fields, to be tuned to high spatial frequency (they respond well to spatial detail), and to have poor temporal resolution; their fibers also conduct slowly. In contrast Y-cells prefer targets of low spatial frequency and respond well to temporal changes; they have fast-conducting fibers. X- and Y-cells in the retina project through the thalamus to X- and Y-cells in the cortex, thereby maintaining two apparently separate sets of visual channels, but Y-cells also project directly to the midbrain structures, the superior colliculus and pretectum. There is also a projection down from the cortex in the Y system to these midbrain structures. The X and Y systems (at least in kittens) have different degrees of plasticity and, as we mentioned, develop at different rates. The evidence suggests that the X-cells are functional before the Y-cells, but that the latter are more susceptible to change of function as a result of deprivation or selective exposure (e.g., Sherman, Hoffman, & Stone, 1972), although the issue is still controversial (see Shapley & So, 1980; Sherman & Spear, 1982).

Maurer and Lewis present quite a suggestive argument to show that the changes in visual behavior in the neonate can be explained on the hypothesis that the X-cell channels are functional before 2 months of age, and probably from birth (although not necessarily at full efficiency) but that the Y-cell cortical system develops more slowly and becomes functional at about 2 months of age. Table 1, taken from their 1979 article, is their summary of the abilities of the very young infant. They are able to show quite good agreement between the items listed in this table and the functions supposedly mediated by the X and Y systems, although there are a few anomalies. We discussed above the question of ''saliency'' and how this complicates the interpretation of evidence of pattern recognition. The discovery that young infants do not discriminate shapes inside identical frames has been challenged but this is not supposedly a function of differential X- and Y-cell activity. Although some behavioral findings are consistent with the proposal of Maurer and Lewis, a model based just on single cell activity is bound to be too simple (Banks & Salapatek, 1983; Dodwell, 1970). There is no doubt that a specific model of this sort, based on solid anatomical and neurophysiological data, will lead to further investigations and insight into the very early development of pattern recognition. Insofar as this work seeks to relate perception to its neurological substrate, we may characterize it, in terms of our earlier scheme, as being definitely in the neo-Hebbian tradition.

C. Spatial Frequency Analysis Model

Another, somewhat different, approach to understanding the operations of the visual system as a pattern recognizer has been postulated, partly on neurophysiological grounds, partly on psychophysical (Campbell, 1974; Campbell & Robson, 1968; J. G. Robson, 1975). Campbell and

TABLE 1
Visual Capacities of Infants under 2 Months Old[a]

Clearly present	Poorly developed
Discriminations	
Moving from stationary	
Flickering from nonflickering	Mature critical flicker fusion frequency
Intensity	
Contour	
Orientation	
Shape	Shapes inside identical frames
Arrangement of features	Arrangement of features inside identical frames
Eye movements	
Fixation on stationary stimulus	Thorough scanning
Eye movements in various directions	
Localization of temporal stimuli	Localization of nasal stimuli
Tracking of moving stimulus	Smooth pursuit
OKN when stimuli move temporally to nasally	OKN when stimuli move nasally to temporally

[a] Before 2 months infants are able to make a variety of discriminations which suggest that the cortex is functional. However, the eye movements infants are capable of suggest that the Y-pathway to the cortex is nonfunctional but becomes so at approximately 2 months of age. (Adapted from Maurer & Lewis, 1979.)

Robson demonstrated that individual cells in the cat's visual system display the characteristics of a tuned frequency filter. (Indeed, it was this work that led to the classification of X and Y types of cell described above.) That is to say, a single cell within the visual system typically responds best to a pattern of stripes at a particular position, orientation, and of a particular spatial frequency. This leads naturally to the idea that spatial frequency filtering is the basis for image processing in the visual system, and to the postulate that patterns are described and stored in terms of their spatial frequency components. It has even been proposed that the visual system performs a form of Fourier analysis (e.g., Pollen, Lee, & Taylor, 1971), although there are many reasons for supposing that this cannot in general be true (Dodwell, 1978; Julesz & Caelli, 1979; Robson, 1975).

A related approach has been applied in the study of infant vision. This approach uses spatial frequency concepts but does not claim that spatial frequency analysis is the basis for pattern recognition (Banks & Salapatek, 1981, 1983). If the human visual system did indeed operate as a spatial freqency analyzer, it would be of interest to know how the infant system compares with that of the adult, and what the developmental sequence is.

The spatial frequency response of the human visual system has been measured as a function of the contrast necessary for detection at a variety of spatial frequencies (for a review, see Braddick, Campbell, & Atkinson, 1978), the resulting function being known as a contrast sensitivity function. Under certain fairly restrictive assumptions it could theoretically be used to predict the response of the visual system to any spatially extended input pattern. That there are difficulties with this approach as a general model of pattern recognition we have already stated; nevertheless, some insight into the nature of the visual processing of which the infant is capable can be attained by measuring its contrast sensitivity function. This has been done (Atkinson, Braddick, & Moar, 1977; Banks & Salapatek, 1978, 1981). Infants have a much higher contrast threshold than adults and display especially poor resolution for high spatial frequencies. What this means in common-sense terms is that they are incapable of resolving, and hence detecting, patterns with low contrast, or fine detail, or both (something, incidentally, that was already known from less sophisticated experimental work). Infants under 2 months of age also fail to show the reduced sensitivity at very low frequencies that is characteristic of older infants and adults. The contrast sensitivity function of the very young infant rapidly improves with age, and after a few months approaches the typical adult form, although not reaching full sensitivity until much later.

How much insight do such findings give us into the nature of the infant's visual world? It could be argued that the contrast sensitivity function defines the basic characteristics of infant pattern vision. However, it is also possible to argue that the contrast sensitivity function is merely a convenient (but precise) way of measuring one particular limitation on vision, namely, the limitation of its ability to detect spatial contrast of different grains and amplitudes. One can only make the former strong claim if one is already committed to the theory that the visual system operates by spatial frequency analysis; measuring the function in infants makes it neither more nor less plausible. As we have already pointed out, the spatial frequency model is not plausible as a general model of visual pattern analysis, but this does not mean that measurement of spatial frequency response in the infant is unimportant. At the very least it will characterize some of the system's linear or quasilinear properties precisely (Cornsweet, 1970); knowing the contrast sensitivity function of the infant might allow one to predict and explain some of the factors that determine visual pattern preferences in young infants, as Banks and Salapatek (1981) and Gayl, Roberts, and Werner (1983) have shown. These authors also discuss some of the limitations of the approach; we are far from understanding pattern and shape perception in infancy or at any other time of life from this point of view alone.

D. The Perception of Two-Dimensional Shapes

Although there are notable exceptions to this rule (e.g., Fantz & Yeh, 1979), it is generally true to say that our attempts to understand pattern perception in the very young infant are limited to questions of detection, the immaturity of the system, and the relationship of neurological changes to perceptual development. The older the infant becomes, the less are our concerns dominated by such considerations. One of us has argued elsewhere (Dodwell, 1975, 1978) that there are three logically rather distinct levels at which the visual system is studied, namely, the levels of (1) "detection," (2) pattern organization, and (3) cognitive use. Although we are far from having a complete understanding of how these three levels relate to each other, it nevertheless seems to be a fairly natural division, both for the ways in which the visual system itself operates and as a convenience for its study and analysis.

We turn now to the question of pattern organization (level 2) and consider the findings and implications of work with neonates and older infants. At this level one has to address the question of what Lashley called "stimulus equivalence." In our case, this is the question of how it is that a particular pattern or shape can be recognized independently of position, size (to some extent), or orientation, and so on. There is an interesting history to the development of ideas about stimulus equivalence (see Dodwell, 1970, Chap. 1, for a resume). The ideas and debates of physiologists, biophysicists, and psychologists led gradually to a sharpening of the notion of a sensory code. Something of a landmark in this development was the shape recognition system proposed by J. A. Deutsch in 1955; without going into details one may characterize his approach as being an attempt to answer the question, "What sort of sensory code would map a highly variable stimulus input into a few relevant categories of shape?" Rather than taking the sort of transformational approach of Pitts and McCulloch (1947) or Lashley (1942), Deutsch proposed that a simple mechanism for analyzing the internal properties of a shape, in his case the distances between its contours, would fit the bill. He designed such a system and showed that it was internally consistent and moderately in agreement with the facts of pattern recognition as they were then known. Others entered the debate, notably Sutherland (1957) and Dodwell (1957), with other ideas about how the shape coding might be accomplished. The main difference between these sorts of models and Hebb's ideas was that whereas Hebb proposed that simple elements had to be integrated into patterns (and classes of patterns) with the aid of the motor system, these shape-coding models generated a form of simple stimulus equivalence by their very internal structure and mode of operation. Although the ontological status of these models was never discussed explicitly by their authors, they were clearly thought of as innately determined coding mechanisms and not affected in any important way by specific experience. Dodwell (1961) later considered the question of perceptual learning in relation to his model, postulating that its outputs could be made inputs to a "conditional probability computer" (Uttley, 1954), thereby producing an analog of associationistic perceptual learning. Such a dual mechanism, a rather mechanistic, but well-specified, Hebbian perceptual system, predicts that there should be two quite different forms of "stimulus equivalence:" that which could be due to coding (innately programmed) and that to be attributed to "conditional probability computation" (perceptual learning). There is evidence in the animal literature (e.g., Tees, 1968) for such a distinction.

Although these ideas about coding generated a good deal of research with animals, they had not been seriously applied to the question of infant vision until fairly recently. The question of whether there is an innate code for simple patterns (conglomerations of elements) is certainly worth asking, and if the answer were positive, it would be important to know if one of the "Deutsch type" models correctly predicts the infant's generalizations. Along these lines, Schwartz and Day (1979) report a series of experiments in which shape coding in the young infant was investigated. Using the habituation paradigm, they presented a display repeatedly until the infant habituated, then presented a series of novel displays varying systematically from the original, for instance in rotation or angular properties. By measuring the degree of recovery of interest or otherwise, they tried to assess what the coding processes of the infant might be. Figure 1 shows some of their typical stimuli and results indicating that infants recovered looking to figural changes but not to rotations of the habituation stimulus. From this work it becomes clear that even in the very young infant coding goes beyond the simple detection of line elements *à la* Hubel and Wiesel. One can argue, as Schwartz and Day do, that these results occur in organisms so young that no appreciable degree of perceptual learning could have occurred; it seems more plausible to suppose that they are generated by some internal, "prewired," coding process. This, so far as we are aware, is the first attempt to look systematically at the coding of patterns of young infants from such a theoretical point of view. Schwartz and Day do not confirm predictions from any of the models

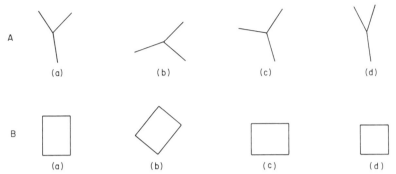

Figure 1. The habituation stimuli (a) and novel stimuli (b, c and d) used in two experiments reported in Schwartz and Day (1979). In (A) infants did not recover looking to (b) a rotation of the adapting stimulus, but did so to (c) and (d). Similarly, in (B) infants did not recover looking to (b) and (c), both rotations of the adapting stimulus, but did so to (d), a figural change.

mentioned earlier, but that is perhaps not surprising nor the main point of their contribution. They have shown that at a very early age infants consistently will discriminate some configurational properties of extremely simple figures and show a degree of generalization to variations on the original shape. Whether these results can be integrated into a constructionist model of pattern recognition, as Cohen (1979) has suggested, will only be shown by further research.

A large proportion of the research with infants over 2 months of age is directed towards the question of configurational perception. Fantz showed in some of his early studies, and has extended the demonstration quite convincingly in subsequent work (Fantz & Yeh, 1979), not only that infants will prefer to look at some patterns over others, but that the type of pattern they prefer changes consistently with age. Figure 2, taken from the 1979 paper, is an example of how preference changes from the simple to the more complex. Figure 2A illustrates an increase in preference, as a function of age, for a more complex organization of identical elements. Infants also show an increasing preference for a pattern composed of complex elements (Figure 2B). Fantz has argued that this increasing preference for looking at subtle and complex patterns is what distinguishes the developing human visual system from other species.

A more specific question about configuration has to do with whether infants can detect differences in the arrangement of sets of identical pattern elements. The question is, "Does the infant respond to configuration as such?" That is, does the infant respond to the structure in the pattern, rather than to the elements in isolation or some lower-level aspect of the pattern such as its contour density? This is closely related to the questions

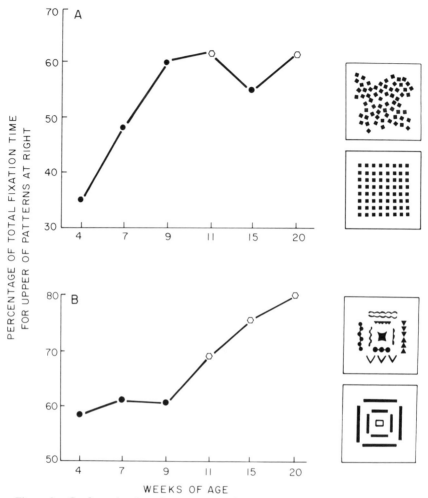

Figure 2. Configurational preference curves from Fantz and Yeh (1979) showing increases in relative attention to more intricate or subtle patterning as a function of age. The curves give the percent of fixation time that was directed to the upper pattern of each figure. The hexagonal symbols indicate results significantly above 50%. (A) illustrates an increase in preference for a more complex organization of identical elements, while (B) shows an increasing preference for a pattern composed of complex elements.

posed by Schwartz and Day, although the emphasis is different. They pitted one figural feature against another (angle, line, orientation), whereas the present emphasis is on the perception of configuration *versus* the perception of elements.

Bower (1966a) was one of the first to ask whether infants respond to the features of a compound stimulus or to the overall configuration. Specifically, he was interested in whether infants operate according to the Law of Heterogeneous Summation, which states that the total "strength of reponse" to the separate parts presented in isolation is equal to the "strength of response" to the whole figure. Such responding implies that principles of grouping or figural unity are not operating. On the other hand, if the "strength of response" to the whole figure is greater than the sum of the responses to the parts, it is inferred that the figure is perceived as a whole.

Bower (1966a) tested infants at 2, 3, 4, and 5 months of age who were trained to make a leftward head movement as a conditioned response. Reinforcement was a "peek-a-boo" from the experimenter. The compound stimulus consisted of a flecked disc with two intersecting diagonals and two dots near the center (see Figure 3A). The whole figure was placed 10 cm in front of a flecked screen. When training was completed, responsiveness to the parts of the figure and to the whole figure was assessed. The Law of Heterogeneous Summation was clearly operative at 2 and 3 months of age. That is, the sum of the responses to the parts was equal to the responses to the whole figure. It should be noted that the greatest number of responses was given to the disc alone at these two ages. The increased retinal size of the fleck, relative to the screen, and the parallax differences between it and the rest of the screen could be very salient to these young infants. It was not until 5 months of age that the infants responded more to the figure than to its parts.

Miller (1972) has presented evidence that 4-month-old infants process a compound pattern sequentially, proceeding from the most to least salient features. The relative saliency of each part of a three-element pattern (see Figure 3A and B) was first determined for each infant. The infants were then habituated to the whole pattern and tested for recovery to the individual features. Responding to the component initially "rated" most salient by magnitude of responding dropped significantly. Responding remained at about the same level for the next most salient compound but increased to the component which was least salient initially. Stimulus processing had been occurring to the stimulus components in order of their saliency (but see Lasky, 1979). This result again suggests that infants at 4 months of age are not processing the pattern as a whole but are rather more responsive to the elements.

Cohen (1973) has reported an experiment which also supports such a view. Four-month-old infants were habituated to color–shape compounds (e.g. red circle, green square) and subsequently tested with new compounds containing the same components (e.g., green circle, red square) or novel compounds containing new shapes and colors. Rearrangement of

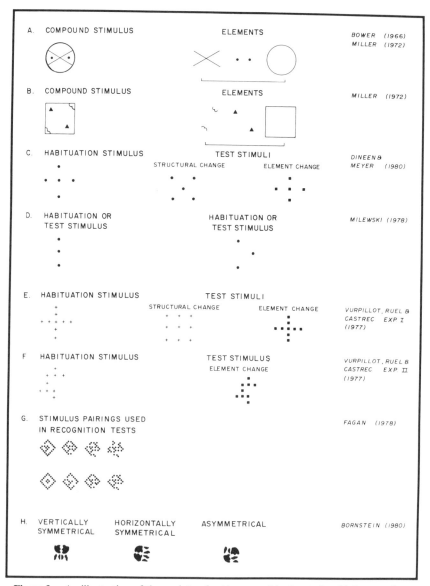

Figure 3. An illustration of the variety of patterns used in the study of infant configuration perception (see text for details).

familiar components into new combinations did not evoke renewed interest, whereas completely novel compounds did. This suggests that the infants made discriminations on the basis of components (elements of the stimulus) rather than the compounds, or total configuration (see also Younger & Cohen, 1983).

E. W. Bushnell and Roder (1985) have questioned the generality of Cohen's (1973) findings. They used a paired comparison procedure in which the infants were habituated to two color–form compounds. On test trials the infants were presented with one of the familiar stimuli and a novel stimulus composed of a familiar color and familiar shape in a new combination. The infants looked reliably longer at the new color–form compound. E. W. Bushnell and Roder (1985) argue that the only possible basis for differential looking would be that the new compound represented an unfamiliar pairing of color and shape. They suggest that their procedure is largely responsible for the differences between their results and those of Cohen (1973). The paired comparison procedure may provoke the infant, during habituation, to attend to ways in which the stimuli are both similar and different and thus assist in encoding aspects of the patterns which could be relevant on test trials (see also Ruff, 1978). E. W. Bushnell and Roder (1985) go on to argue that the simultaneous presentation on test trials may also be relevant. Perhaps, as they suggest, when presented with two stimuli simultaneously the infant might compare the stimuli to one another as well as to memories of previously presented stimuli. The infant might then decide which of the two stimuli is more similar (or different) to those presented before. If presented with just one stimulus, as in Cohen's (1973) study, the infant may just note whether the stimulus is in any way similar to memories of stimuli presented previously. Just how simultaneous habituation and testing affect encoding and recognition could be investigated using combinations of single and double presentations during habituation and recovery trials. Such an investigation could not only sort out the reasons for the different results of Cohen (1973) and E. W. Bushnell and Roder (1985) but could help to specify more sensitive research designs.

The *most* precise form of evidence on Gestalt perception occurs when sets of identical pattern elements are organized into different configurations. For example, Dineen and Meyer (1980) tested 3- to 4-month-olds and 6- to 7-month-olds in the usual habituation paradigm. After habituation to five black round dots in a "cross" pattern the infants were shown either the same dots in a new configuration (the original "cross" pattern rotated 45° to make it an "X" pattern), or five small squares in the original "cross" pattern (Figure 3C). The results were quite clear; 3- to 4-month-olds showed greatest dishabituation to change in the features rather than to a change in the configuration. The 6- to 7-month-olds, however, dishabituated equally to both transformations. Features are apparently more salient for the younger child, but the 7-month-olds showed evidence of recognizing the larger configuration as well. This change in perceptual behavior has no absolute significance with respect to age, however. For example, Milewski (1979) has found that 3-month-old infants will responde to very simple configurations (Figure 3D), whereas Vurpillot, Ruel, and Castrec (1977) have shown that 2- and 4-month-olds also are sensitive to configuration when the individual elements of the visual array are small but are more responsive to the elements making up the configuration when those elements are large (Figure 3E). Obviously, one should expect the size of the elements and of the configuration to affect visual processing, but the visual angles of the small stimuli used by Vurpillot et al. (1977) and those of Dineen and Meyer (1980) were not greatly different. Possibly the configurational change in the Dineen and Meyer study was more subtle than that of Vurpillot et al. The former configurational change was a 45° rotation of the test stimulus (from a "cross" to "X"), whereas Vurpillot et al. used a configurational change from a cross composed of five horizontal and five vertical elements to a three-by-three matrix. Once again we come up against a problem we have seen before: until more systematic work is done varying element size and type as well as configurational factors over a somewhat wider range, it will be impossible to state with confidence at what age infants become sensitive to configuration, or what the developmental story is. It seems likely that sensitivity to configuration as such appears at around 2 to 3 months of age depending on the stimulus arrays used; more evidence is clearly needed. (But see also the work of Schwartz and Day, described above, and some of our own results with Garner's patterns described below.)

Our point is reinforced by a further study by Vurpillot et al. (1977). Using stimuli containing the same type of elements as before, but in more complicated configurations (the pattern was more complex because it lacked symmetry) (Figure 3F) Vurpillot et al. showed that 4-month-olds responded to a change in the elements, suggesting that with a more complex pattern the elements again become salient. In a rather more systematic experiment, Fagan (1978b) found a clear relationship between figural complexity and the age at which it was discriminated by infants. He used a black and white display of 24 small diamond-shaped elements arranged in an overall diamond pattern (Figure 3G). The discrimination task (using a familiarization–novelty paradigm) was to detect the difference between the regular overall diamond pattern and the same pattern but with some of the elements displaced. Five-month-olds detected the difference between the intact overall pattern and one with two displaced elements, between the patterns with two and four displaced, and between the patterns with four and six elements displaced. However there was no evidence of discrimination between the patterns when six and eight element displacements were compared. It is likely, as Fagan suggests, that the main stimulus factor which alters as a function of displacement of the elements is the regular, compact, and symmetrical form of the original pattern. With six or eight elements displaced the pattern appears essentially as a random arrangement of small diamonds, with no obvious configuration; in other words, it is a "bad" form. More systematic and quantitative evidence along these lines is required if we are to give a reasonable account of how the perception of configuration develops in the infant.

Research with adults has demonstrated that symmetry, especially in patterns with vertical symmetry, can be detected in an "immediate" manner (Barlow & Reeves, 1979; Royer, 1981). It has been suggested that the extraction of symmetry information is processed very early in the nervous system (Royer, 1981) and precedes the extraction of shape or form information (Corballis & Beale, 1976; Howe, 1980). If symmetry is so readily detected by adults, perhaps young infants are also sensitive to this pattern property.

Bornstein (1981; Bornstein, Ferdinandsen, & Gross, 1981) has recently emphasized the importance of symmetry, and especially vertical symmetry, in the infant's pattern perception. The processing of vertically symmetrical, horizontally symmetrical, and asymmetrical patterns by 4-month-old infants was assessed by comparing the rate and amount of habituation to each type of pattern. Bornstein's patterns consisted of three sets of two identical elements (Figure 3H). The sets differed from each other, each being a fairly complex form. Habituation to vertically symmetrical patterns was faster than to horizontally symmetrical or asymmetrical patterns, while the rates of habituation to horizontal and asymmetrical patterns did not differ.

Fisher, Ferdinandsen, and Bornstein (1981) went on to show that 4-month-old infants who were habituated to vertically symmetrical figures dishabituated to novel patterns but did not do so if habituated to horizontally symmetrical or asymmetrical patterns.

Both Bornstein et al. (1981) and G. K. Humphrey, Humphrey, Muir, and Dodwell (1986) found that infants did not show a preference for patterns differing in the type or amount of symmetry when successive presentation was used. Bornstein (1981) suggested that choice might be a more sensitive measure of symmetry preference. G. K. Humphrey and Humphrey (1985) tested this notion. They presented 4- to 5-month-old and 7- to 8-month-old infants with the patterns shown in Figure 4. These patterns allowed much more flexibility in producing variations in the

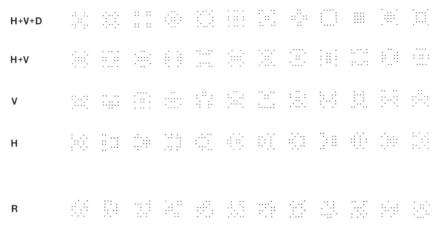

Figure 4. Patterns used in the study of symmetry preference. The top row shows patterns with four axes of symmetry; horizontal, vertical, and the two diagonals (H + V + D). Patterns with vertical and horizontal symmetry are shown in the next row (H + V). The next two rows show patterns with only a single axis of symmetry, either vertical (V) or horizontal (H). Random patterns (R), without any axis of symmetry, are illustrated in the bottom row.

amount and type of symmetry than did the amorphic forms used by Bornstein and his colleagues. The patterns were created by placing 16 dots in an imaginary six-by-six matrix with the restriction, to prevent pattern clumping, that four dots were placed in each three-by-three quadrant.

Four types of symmetry were created; horizontal (H), vertical (V), horizontal plus vertical (H + V), and horizontal plus vertical plus the two diagonals (H + V +D). The infants were presented, on each trial, a symmetrical pattern paired with a random (R) pattern without any axis of symmetry. For each infant only four of the twelve symmetrical patterns, of each type, were presented along with a random pattern (48 in all) for a total of 16 10-sec trials. The 4 patterns of each type were chosen at random, without replacement, for each infant. Thus the actual patterns chosen for each infant varied widely, but the pattern properties were held constant.

The results, illustrated in Figure 5, showed a reliable preference for both of the mulitply symmetric pattern types in the 4- to 5-month-olds, and for the horizontal plus vertical patterns in the 7- to 8-month-olds. Neither age group showed a reliable preference for the patterns with a single axis of symmetry. The results of the 7- to 8-month-olds diverged from those of the 4- to 5-month-olds in that they did now show a preference for the patterns with the most symmetry (i.e., H + V + D). Presumably, they can detect this symmetry, given that the younger infants did.

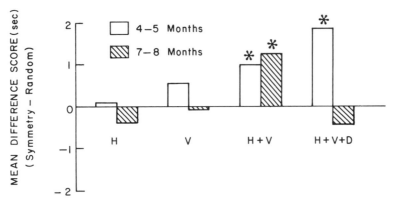

Figure 5. Preference for symmetry expressed as the mean amount of time spent looking at the symmetrical patterns minus the looking time to the random patterns.

This result could be interpreted to suggest that the 7- to 8-month-olds prefer a "moderate level" of symmetry, given the stimulus set. That is, perhaps the patterns with four axes of symmetry are too simple, or too low in information content (Attneave, 1955). Such preferences are well known in the literature on aesthetic perception (e.g., Berlyne, 1971). G. K. Humphrey and Humphrey (1985) presented these same patterns to adults and asked them to rank order the patterns in terms of how "interesting" they were. The adults showed the same pattern of responding as the 7- to 8-month-old infants but shifted to the vertically symmetrical patterns as being the most interesting. The results of this study suggest that preference for symmetry might be shown in a choice situation, although no preferences were shown among vertically symmetrical, horizontally symmetrical, and asymmetrical patterns.

The results reviewed above certainly show that symmetry and horizontality–verticality are important factors in the encodability of patterns for young infants, as indeed some of the early shape coding systems (e.g., Dodwell, 1957; Sutherland, 1957) had suggested (see also Rudel & Teuber, 1964). Be that as it may, Bornstein (1981) argues that vertical symmetry is a prototypical characteristic of pattern organization in young infants although such symmetry may not be immediately preferred over a random pattern (G. K. Humphrey & Humphrey, 1985). It is certainly true that symmetries of all sorts strongly affect pattern perception in human adults, but what the developmental sequence from the early detection of simple symmetries to the subtleties of the adult situation may be is undetermined.

An unusual slant on the configuration question is contained in a report by Bertenthal and his colleagues (Bertenthal, Campos, & Haith, 1980; see also Treiber & Wilcox, 1980). These authors were interested in whether young infants can detect "subjective" or "gradient-free" contours. A subjective contour is defined by Kanizsa (1955) as a contour perceived in the absence of any physical gradient of change in the display. Figure 6A illustrates the point. This figure is taken from Bertenthal et al. (1980); the second and third parts (Figure 6B and C) show rearrangements of the identical stimulus elements in such a way as not to form subjective contours. The authors demonstrated that infants of at least 7 months of age are sensitive to the arrangement which, for an adult, generates subjective contours, and on this basis argued that the same phenomenon was present in the young child. This is a fascinating area for further research, but the findings need to be amplified and generalized.

We can conclude that at some time during the first 6 months of life infants develop sensitivity to configurations as well as to the elements of which they are composed. In particular, they respond well to regular and symmetrical patterns, in a word, to "good form" (Garner, 1974). More research is clearly needed to examine the ways in which responses to configuration develop with age. Current evidence is fragmentary, although reasonably consistent so far as it goes. We suggest that two lines of research could be particularly fruitful if we are to further our understanding of the processing of abstract two-dimensional patterns and their component parts.

One approach would be to employ some well-understood group of patterns such as those developed by Garner (1974), in which the degree of structure has been quantified. The tremendous advantage of such an approach is that, rather than letting the infant tell us how similar two patterns are in terms of dishabituation, and then defining differences between patterns in those terms, we start with an *a priori* metric and then ask the infant to tell us whether it is one to which his perceptual system is attuned. To put it another way, we would ask the infant whether he scales

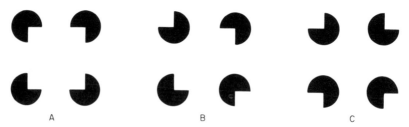

A   B   C

Figure 6. Stimuli used by Bertenthal, Campos, and Haith (1980) demonstrating that infants can perceive subjective contour. (A) An example of a subjective contour; (B) and (C) were nonillusory stimuli.

the patterns in terms of "figural goodness," in terms of their structure and informational content, as measured by an independent set of criteria.

For example, Garner proposed that the number of different figures generated by rotating five-element dot patterns (see Figure 7A) by 90, 180, and 270° and reflecting them about their horizontal, vertical, and diagonal axes is a measure of their figural goodness. The fewer figures generated, the better the pattern. Figure 7B shows a unique pattern such that it is reproduced if reflected or rotated about any axis in 90° steps. This pattern is very good, forming a rotation and reflection (R and R) subset of size one. An R and R subset of size four is illustrated in Figure 7C. Each of these patterns form any of the others by the appropriate reflections and rotations. Similarly, each of the patterns in Figure 7D can form any of the others by the appropriate reflections and/or 90° rotations. They form an R and R subset of eight patterns.

Given this independent set of criteria we would ask whether infants scale the patterns in terms of "figural goodness." Results from our laboratory (G. K. Humphrey et al., 1986) indicate that 4-month-old infants are sensitive to the structure of these patterns. Humphrey et al. demonstrated

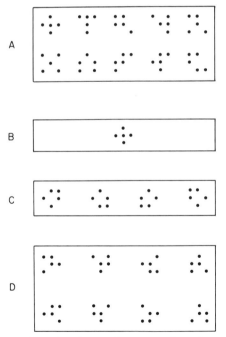

Figure 7. A selection of the five-element dot patterns from Garner (1974). For details of their "information" value see text.

a processing advantage for "good" patterns relative to "poor" patterns in terms of both the rate of habituation and recovery. The patterns used are shown in Figure 8. The top two patterns [A (1) and (2)] are very good, coming from R and R subsets of size one. The next two [B (1) and (2)] are from an R and R subset of size four and the last two are poor, coming from R and R subsets of size eight. Six groups of infants were presented with one of the patterns on habituation trials, using a fixed trial procedure with eight 20-sec trials.

The results of the habituation phase are presented in Figure 9 collapsed across patterns from the same-sized R and R subsets, as there were no pattern differences within the R and R subsets. Only infants presented with patterns from R and R subsets of size one or four showed a reliable decrement in looking time from the first trial block (mean of the first two habituation trials) to the last trial block (mean of last two trials). Furthermore, only infants habituated to R and R subsets of size one and four showed renewed looking on recovery trials, and this was shown most consistently to a change in the orientation of the habituation pattern, rather than to a configuration change. It is perhaps not surprising that infants presented with patterns from R and R subsets of size eight did not recover looking as they did not habituate. There is reason to suspect, however, that infants of this age would not recover looking to changes in such poorly structured patterns even if they had habituated. Others have found that infants of this age have great difficulty in perceiving differences between patterns if they have first been habituated to poorly structured patterns composed of identical elements (see Bertenthal, Proffitt, & Cutting, 1984; D. W. Muir, Humphrey, Dodwell, & Humphrey, in preparation; Strauss & Curtiss, 1981; all discussed below; and Vurpillot et al., 1977, discussed above).

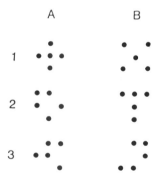

Figure 8. Garner patterns used by G. K. Humphrey, Humphrey, Muir, and Dodwell (1986) to study the effects of pattern goodness on visual pattern encoding in 4-month-old infants.

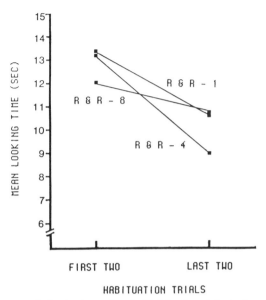

Figure 9. Between the beginning and end of habituation, infants decreased their looking time to patterns of R and R subset sizes of one or four, but not to size eight. (The patterns used are shown in Figure 8.)

Strauss and Curtiss (1981) have shown that the ability to integrate nine-element dot patterns varying in goodness of form as defined by Garner's metric is dependent upon the age of the subject. In their study 3-month-olds only discriminated between good forms; 5-month-olds discriminated between one good form and another and between two intermediate patterns; while 7-month-old infants discriminated between examples of all three patterns (good, intermediate, and poor). This result again emphasizes the importance of pattern goodness in investigating the infant's developing perceptual abilities.

The second approach would be to use patterns derived from the Lie Transformation Group Model of Neuropsychology (LTG/NP) of W. C. Hoffman (1966, 1978). This is an approach to visual processing that derives from a mathematical theory of the action of continuous transformation groups. It has been explained in relatively nontechnical langugae and given a particular psychological interpretation by Dodwell (1983). The patterns in question are the so-called orbits of the basic Lie Transformation Groups. These orbits, some of which are shown in Figure 10, have particularly simple mathematical properties and as Dodwell (1983) shows—and Hoffman certainly realized—they must be generated in a simple and consistent way in the processing system of the human brain as

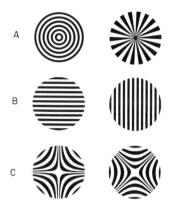

Figure 10. The three pairs of elementary Lie orbits for (A) rotation (left) and dilation (right), (B) horizontal (left) and vertical (right) translations, and (C) operations in binocular space which, in its pure form, is hyperbolic.

a result of the evolutionary and ecological conditions under which it develops.

Basically LTG/NP claims that certain visual forms are "primitives," easy to encode and easy to remember, because a visual organism has to operate continually with certain transformations that generate those forms. The orbits resulting from the first two pairs of transformations are shown in Figure 10A: expansions–contractions and rotations in the frontal plane represented by a radial pattern and concentric circles; and in Figure 10B: translations (horizontal and vertical) represented by sets of parallel horizontal and vertical lines. The orbits for the third pair, shown in Figure 10C, are represented by sets of rectangular hyperbolae asymptotic to the horizontal/vertical axis in one case, and to perpendicular lines oriented at 45° to those axes in the other. The first two pairs of transformations and resulting orbits can be given a fairly obvious "ecological" interpretation (see Dodwell, 1983). As an organism locomotes in a normal environment the visual field undergoes transformations of expansion–contraction and rotation as well as translations. Such an ecological interpretation is not so obvious for the last pair, which can be considered as frontal projections of the hyperbolic lines of simple binocular space (Luneberg, 1947). The LTG/NP considers these three pairs of transformations as being generated by the iterative action of local vector processes, thereby tracing out orbits across the visual field. These transformations are always being applied to visual input because the organism locomotes; visual patterns sweep across the retina, but pattern recognition remains invariant. Thus, the processors for these orbits should be embedded in the visual system, either by evolution, or through perceptual learning, or both.

LTG/NP has a detailed account of how the relevant structures operate in the visual system. For our purposes it is sufficient to note that, according to this model, the processing occurs in cortical vector fields that embody the orbits of the transformation groups. Partial representations of some of these vector fields is contained in the vector patterns of Figure 11A and B. If LTG/NP is correct in identifying these as primitives, they should be easy for infants to encode and recognize, but Figure 11C should not, as it is not a well-defined vector pattern according to the model. Caelli and Dodwell (1982) and Dodwell and Caelli (1984) have shown that similar sets of vector patterns have highly salient perceptual properties for adults.

Muir et al. (in preparation) habituated three groups of 4-month-old infants to the vector patterns shown in Figure 11. The location of the centers of the elements were the same among the three patterns, but the orientation of the elements differed. The local orientation of the elements differed by 90° between patterns A and B but differed in a random amount

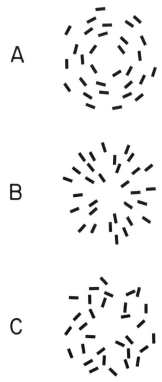

Figure 11. Vector patterns used to investigate infant perception of pattern structure according to the Lie transformation group model of visual perception.

between patterns A and C and between B and C. The global orientation of the patterns was randomly perturbed between habituation trials and between recovery trials to prevent the infants from recovering interest due to a shift in local features. Also, infants were only included in the analysis if they decreased their looking time from the beginning of the habituation phase to the end.

The three patterns shown in Figure 11 were used as habituation stimuli for three separate groups. Each group received the two remaining patterns on recovery trials. Only the infants receiving the structured vector patterns (Figure 11A or B) increased looking on recovery trials and then most reliably to the other structured pattern (see Figure 12). The group habituated to the random vector pattern did not recover looking to either of the structured vector patterns.

These results, along with those showing discrimination of patterns similar to those in Figure 10 by kittens (Dodwell, Wilkinson, & von Grünau, 1983; Wilkinson & Dodwell, 1980), suggest that such patterns, representing primitives of visual processing as identified by the LTG/NP, are readily perceived by young organisms. In addition, the lack of recovery in the infants habituated to the random vector pattern further demonstrates that

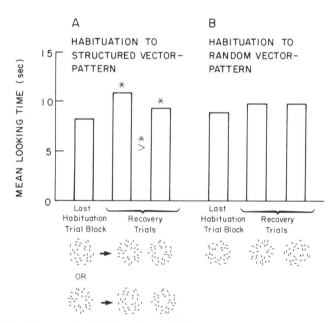

Figure 12.   Four-month-old infants show reliable recovery of looking to structured vector patterns after habituation to structured vector patterns, but not after habituation to random vector patterns.

infants of this age have difficulty encoding poorly structured patterns, as others have found (G. K. Humphrey et al., 1986; Strauss & Curtiss, 1981), but here structure has been defined by a different approach to pattern perception.

Although the approach of Garner (1974) and the LTG/NP are different in many respects, they are both concerned, at least at one level, with discovering metrics which will predict, in an *a priori* fashion, human perceptual response. Thus, stimuli derived from these approaches could prove to be important research tools in the study of infant perception of pattern structure. Furthermore, although the patterns used are static two-dimensional displays, it has been hypothesized that the reason for our ease in perceiving such patterns ultimately depends on a dynamic conception of perception, as is obvious in the case of the LTG/NP and has been suggested in the case of Garner patterns (Palmer, 1982; Shepard, 1981).

Rather than leave this section on what some may feel to be a rather abstract, not to say far-out, note, we would reiterate some points made earlier: research described in this section is mostly well grounded in the neo-Hebbian tradition, that is, it is research which seeks to relate the early pattern detection abilities of the infant to their neurological substrate, to ask about the origins of form and pattern perception, and (ideally, but not actually in practice) to ask under what conditions the perception of pattern, as opposed to pattern elements, actually develops. Although some of the authors we quote have acknowledged Gibson's influence (notably Fantz & Yeh, 1979), the constructivist bent of most of the work on pattern elements, components, and configurations is fairly obvious.

III. THE CONSTANCIES

Adults recognize the same object or person in different contexts, perspectives, and at different distances. Clearly any adequate theory of pattern perception and object recognition must account for these so-called constancies, which permit us to perceive a stable visual world despite continuous variation in retinal stimulation. It should be noted that the constancies have nearly always been studied with respect to vision, and the infant work likewise is restricted to this modality. In a review of the literature on the development of perceptual constancies, Day and Mc-Kenzie (1977) identified three general classes. The most commonly recognized type is object constancy: objects are judged to maintain the same physical properties as they change position or context, and as their retinal images vary in size, shape, orientation, color, or brightness. The second type, egocentric constancy, refers to the perception of stable locations in a general spatial framework as the position of the perceiver changes. Identity–existence, the third class, refers to the recognition of the continuing existence of an object when it changes place over time, such as when it disappears from view. In this section we will discuss research on object constancy, the other two types being the subject matter of chapters in other volumes (e.g., Cohen, DeLoache, & Strauss, 1979; Day & McKenzie, 1977).

The question of object constancy and how it arises is central to the epistemological debate. What are the sources of our knowledge of the external world? What we know about the action of the sense organs, of optics and the laws of perspective (in the case of vision), and of the rules of physical measurement, tell us that there should be conflicts between the properties of the "proximal stimulus" (the immediate stimulation of the sense organs) on the one hand and the distal properties (the physically defined attributes such as length, mass, and volume) on the other. As is well known, the perceptual judgements of adults tend to compromise between these two sources of knowledge, so that judged constancy of shape, size, etc., is not exactly in conformity with physical attributes or retinal projections. It is an "irrational," but nonetheless quite successful, integration of knowledge from two apparently incompatible sources (Dodwell, 1975).

The dominant theoretical issue in discussions of object constancy in infant studies is, again, Nativism versus Empiricism. Are shape and size constancies learned, or are they in some sense innate? The empiricist will argue that the sense organs are subject only to proximal stimulation, and from this the observer must infer or construct external reality; the nativist, however, will claim that this elaboration is already "given" and requires no special "superordinate" activity of a constructivist kind. J. J. Gibson would say that the senses respond as perceptual systems from the beginning, that they are "tuned" to the distal properties and simply become more efficient with practice. E. J. Gibson's comment illustrates this latter position:

> I think objects and events and layout are perceived from the start, insofar as anything is, but with little differentiation. I am not persuaded by experiments that display line drawings of geometrical forms to neonates that perceiving begins with the pickup of a line, and then gradually more lines, welded together into cell assemblies by eye movements. (E. J. Gibson, 1977, p. 159)

This viewpoint was applied to infant work by Bower in the mid-1960s (see Bower, 1974a, 1974b, for his review of that work), who argues that human infants recognize certain object properties at birth. In 1978 he went beyond this position to propose the notion of an early amodal perceptual process which, in some unspecified way, operates independently of particular modalities, or at least is sensitive to perceptual properties which are not modality-specific. Although this position is difficult to evaluate empirically, several studies have attempted to demonstrate sensitivity to certain amodal dimensions (e.g., Lewkowicz & Turkewitz, 1980; Meltzoff & Borton, 1979; and see Spelke, Chapter 6, this volume).

Research has focused on attempts to identify the earliest age at which a particular constancy can be shown to operate, rather than the charting of developmental trends for changes in infants' responses to the same object undergoing different spatial transformations. This is what Bruner, Goodnow, and Austin (1956) in another context termed "focused gambling." If one could show the presence of perceptual constancy at or very near birth, one would have applied the *coup de grace* to the empiricist position. Nothing as simple as this has proved possible, of course; in fact to find reliable evidence of the constancies which is clearly interpretable in the very young child has proved to be surprisingly difficult (Dodwell, Muir, & DiFranco, 1976, 1979).

A. Size and Shape Constancy

The major problem for the researcher is to know how to ask the infant the appropriate question, "Is a familiar object recognized in an unfamiliar position or context?" Most experimental attempts to answer this question have involved the use of a discrimination paradigm. In one of the first experiments to investigate size constancy (Cruikshank, 1941) infants between $2\frac{1}{2}$ and 12 months of age were tested. Cruikshank recorded the frequency with which they reached for each of three rattles, a small one within graspable range, the same rattle at three times the distance, and a large rattle three times the size of the original at the greater distance (i.e., with the same retinal subtense as the original). If distal properties (object properties) control responding, then infants should reach only for the small close rattle. If proximal properties were important, however, they should reach for both the small near rattle and the distant large one with an equivalent retinal size. Cruikshank's results seem to support the innate size constancy position: her youngest infants made "approach" arm movements 52% of the time to the near object and only 5% of the time to each of the two distant objects. However, the interpretation of this finding was complicated by the performance of older infants. Reaching toward the distant object *increased* with age, until by about 5 months they were reaching for the large distant object 40% of the time and for the small distant object 27% of the time. In yet older infants reaching to both distant objects declined. How can one interpret such a result? A naturally occurring response such as reaching may be subject to motivational factors which change during development; possibly attention toward distant objects varies at different stages of development, as a finding of Day and McKenzie (reported below) seems to show. Also one is reminded of J. Field's (1976) report that the appreciation of distance in the near space of an infant develops around the middle of the first year: a possible interpretation of Cruikshank's results is that infants have some rudimentary appreciation of distance from a very early age (conceivably a function of their relatively inflexible accommodative mechanism) but that by 5 months they are learning to correlate perceived distance with the range of their grasp. Beyond 5 months they have learned what can be grasped and what cannot, so the grasping for distant objects declines. This is pure speculation, and clearly more research is required to resolve the issue. At least this early report by Cruikshank and its interpretation serve to demonstrate some of the problems with trying to get definitive results in this field.

Attempting to provide a stronger case for the early existence of size and shape constancy, Bower (1965, 1966b) used a conditioning paradigm and a greater number of control conditions than Cruikshank. He conditioned 2-month-olds to turn their heads in the presence of an object, the turn being reinforced with a "peek-a-boo." In subsequent generalization tests he presented the same object in the "old" and in a "new" position, and a new object designed to project the same retinal image as the conditioning stimulus in both the "old" and "new" position. In the size constancy experiment he used a 12-in cube at 3 ft as the conditioning stimulus and tested with the 12-in cube at 9 ft (same physical properties) and a 36-in cube at 9 ft (same retinal subtense). In the shape constancy experiment he used a rectangular piece of wood slanted 45° from the fronto-parallel plane for the conditioning stimulus and tested with the same rectangle in the fronto-parallel plane and a trapezoid (same retinal subtense as the conditioning stimulus), also in the frontal plane. In both cases Bower's evidence appears to favor the existence of constancy. Infants responded with approximately twice as many head turns to the old object in a position involving a novel retinal projection as they did to the new object with retinal subtense equal to that of the old object.

Although Bower's evidence seems to be clear-cut, closer inspection again reveals problems: responses were depressed for *all* novel test conditions, indicating that infants did not view the conditioning cube at a distance of 9 ft as equivalent to the same cube at 3 ft. Moreover, they responded as much to the large novel cube at 3 ft as they did to the original cube 9 ft away. Thus, infants evidently recognized that objects had changed either in size or distance; they simply turned less when the stimulus changed, being least responsive to the object which differed in both size and distance. A different pattern of results was obtained in the shape constancy experiment, however. There infants responded equally to the rectangle whether it was in the familiar rotated position used during conditioning or in the novel frontal position; it appeared that they "were responding to a true shape and displaying shape constancy without having discriminated between different orientations of the same object" (Bower, 1966c, p. 88).

Use of the conditioning paradigm to detect the presence of constancies seems straightforward enough. The infant is conditioned to a stimulus and then one looks for "generalization decrement" as stimulus conditions are changed. If there is little or no such decrement when the same object is repositioned, this seems to be rather good evidence that the infant is responding to its physical properties rather than to the proximal stimulation of the retina. However, as Harris and Allen (1974) have pointed out, this paradigm presents the infant (or more likely the experimenter) with a dilemma. Logically there are two distinct questions, and we do not know *a priori* which one the infant is responding to. One question is, "Do the two objects presented differ in size or orientation?" The other is, "Are they the same object in spite of these differences?" Harris and Allen maintain that, so long as only one respose measure is taken, one cannot decide which question is being asked, so the response is not interpretable. A positive result in such a discrimination experiment (i.e., decreased responding on the test trials) is evidence that the infant can detect a difference. If that occurs when the familiar object is shown in a new position, it is evidence against constancy. If the result is, however, negative (no response decrement to the object in a new position), this might imply constancy, but it might simply demonstrate the infant's inability to discriminate variations in the proximal stimulus, or even lack of interest in such variation.

Harris and Allen's recipe for overcoming this problem is to train infants to make two responses, one for object change and another for position (including orientation) change. In this case if infants were to show that they could detect changes in the object when they occur but also could recognize a familiar object in a new position, one would have much stronger eivdence for constancy. Although use of this paradigm would resolve the question, no studies have been reported which have clearly accomplished that feat.

No replication of Bower's results using the conditioning procedure have been reported, but several investigators have attempted to replicate his finding on constancy by using the visual orientation habituation paradigm. A similar logic applies. In this case, infants are repeatedly exposed to an object until they habituate, which is indexed by a decline in looking time. Subsequently they are presented either with the identical object in new positions or orientations, or with different objects having retinal projections equal to that of the original stimulus. If constancy is working, looking time should recover to the novel objects despite the unchanged retinal projections but remain at a low level for the familiar object in the new position. Notice, however, that Harris and Allen's caveat still applies: failure of recovery of interest in the second condition could mean either that the infants perceived the physical object as such, or that they failed to detect or react to changes in proximal stimulation.

McKenzie and Day (1972) used this paradigm in attempting to demonstrate size constancy in infants between 6 and 20 weeks of age. They found little visual interest in, and no habituation to, a large cube presented at 3 ft from the infant. However, they observed a marked increase in fixation when the cube was moved closer, to a distance of $1\frac{1}{2}$ ft. Likewise a small cube at the near distance evoked far more visual interest than the large cube at the far distance (same retinal subtense). In a second experiment they attempted to compare habituation rates when one and the same cube was presented at different distances, with rates for cubes of different sizes (but of equal retinal subtense) presented at different distances. There were no differences in the amount of fixation elicited by familiar or novel cubes; however, there was a simple decline in fixation time as distance increased. It appears that infants will fixate near objects, but their interest declines steadily with distance—itself evidence that they have some appreciation of visual depth.

It is conceivable that the cubes used by McKenzie and Day were not interesting enough to the infant to elicit a large enough number of fixations to manifest constancy; subsequently, McKenzie, Tootell, and Day (1980) used a more interesting object, namely, a life-sized colored model of an adult female human head. They also used an "infant control" procedure to ensure that each individual infant's looking time dropped by 50% during the familiarization period, thereby guaranteeing that a significant amount of habituation had occurred prior to testing. Both 4- and 6-month-old infants habituated to repeated presenations of the head; however, size constancy was demonstrated only by the 6-month-olds, who showed much less recovery of response when the original model's viewing distance was changed than when physical size was varied, or size and distance. Four-month-olds, on the other hand, showed renewed visual interest to all changes, in distance, physical size, or both. All of the work of this group of researchers on size constancy thus fails to confirm Bower's claims about size constancy using stationary objects or displays (but see below).

Day and McKenzie (1973), however, provide indirect support for Bower's conclusions concerning shape constancy. They reasoned that infants having shape constancy should habituate similarly to repeated exposures of a cube in one orientation or in different orientations but should not habituate when photographs of the cube in different orientations are presented. Their argument hinges on the assumption that the difference between a cube and a photograph of a cube can be detected by an infant capable of shape constancy—surely a not unreasonable assumption. The photographs should be seen by infants as two-dimensional patterns rather than as representations of the same three-dimensional object. Day and McKenzie reported a similar degree of habituation by 8- and 14-week-old infants for both cube conditions (constant orientation and changing orientation) but no habituation to the photographs of cubes in different orientations.

Cook, Field, and Griffiths (1978) have pointed out that Day and McKenzie's results might have little to do with shape constancy if the infants in fact failed to discriminate that a cube is being rotated from trial to trial (a special case of the Harris and Allen criticism mentioned earlier.) Cook et al. replicated Day and McKenzie's experiment with 12-week-old infants; they found a significant decline in fixation times when the same cube was presented in different orientations but no reduction to successive presentations of photographs of the cubes in different orientations, thus replicating the main result. However, they also found that habituation rates to presentation of a cube alternated with a wedge, or a truncated pyramid, were not different from the cube-alone condition. Does this mean that three-dimensional objects are simply less interesting to the 12-week-old than pictures, or that all solid geometrical objects are seen as equivalent or are too complex to process? The first two possibilities seem unlikely, but the result poses an unresolved puzzle and certainly lessens one's faith in this paradigm for demonstrating true shape constancy.

More elaborate attempts to demonstrate shape constancy in infants using the same visual habituation paradigm have been reported by A. J. Caron, Caron, and Carlson (1978, 1979), and by R. F. Caron, Caron, Carlson, and Cobb (1979). Their results highlight the problems inherent in the use of any discrimination paradigm that were pointed out by Harris and Allen (1974). In the Carons' initial studies, different groups of 12-week-old infants were habituated, using the "infant control" procedure, to squares of various sizes or trapezoids tilted at different angles away from the fronto-parallel plane. Following such habituation all groups were subsequently tested with a square either in the upright position, or tilted. The habituation and test stimuli as well as the results are summarized in Figure 13A and B. Clearly, their results run counter to Bower's claims,

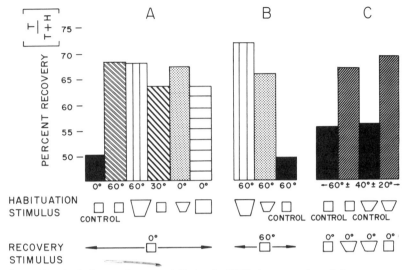

Figure 13. A. J. Caron, Caron, and Carlson's (1979) demonstration of shape constancy by 12-week-old infants. The percentage of recovery to the test stimulus (labeled "Recovery Stimulus") following habituation of fixation time to 50% of initial levels is shown in the columns above each habituation stimulus, along with its slant. Each column represents a different group while A, B, and C are from different studies. No recovery occurs in A and B when habituation and test stimuli are the same figures at the same slants, 0° or 60°. Recovery does occur when either slant or shape or both change in all conditions in A and B. In C, following habituation to a shape exposed at different slants from one trial to the next, infants recover interest to an altered shape but not to the same shape at a novel slant, indicating that constant real shape can be perceived across rotational transformations.

for any change from habituation to test stimuli in size, shape, degree of slant, or some combination of these was discriminated by the infants. (Remember that degree of recovery in this paradigm equals degree of discriminability.) Evidently, 12-week-olds do not view as equivalent either the same stimulus at a new slant or a new stimulus with a retinal projection equal to that of the habituated stimulus. (The results that would have been needed for a clear demonstration of shape constancy are outlined in the legend to Figure 13.) Infants will respond both to a change in the position of a familiar object and to a change of object, at least in the habituation procedure so far used; so, obviously, some alternative method is needed.

A report by G. K. Humphrey et al. (1986) is relevant in the present context. They habituated seven groups of 4-month-old infants to the habituation pattern shown in Figure 14. On recovery trials the recovery patterns illustrated in Figure 14 were presented separately, one to each group. The circle around the patterns represents the edge of the circular

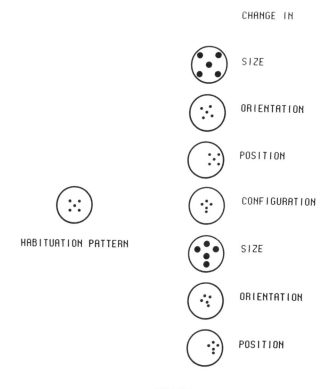

CHANGE IN

SIZE

ORIENTATION

POSITION

CONFIGURATION

SIZE

ORIENTATION

POSITION

HABITUATION PATTERN

RECOVERY PATTERNS

Figure 14. Stimuli used by G. K. Humphrey, Humphrey, Muir, and Dodwell (1984), demonstrating that 4-month-old infants recover looking to changes in the size, orientation, and position of a pattern whether these changes occur in the habituation pattern or in a novel pattern. The circle around the patterns represents the edge of the screen on which the patterns were projected.

projection screen. Infants showed reliable looking to changes in the size, orientation, and position of the habituation pattern whether the change was to the actual habituation pattern (top three patterns in Figure 14) or to a novel pattern (bottom three patterns in Figure 14). They did not show reliable recovery of looking to the configuration change alone.

This recovery to changes in size, orientation, and position of the habituation pattern indicates that infants detect these common global pattern changes and may seem to imply that 4-month-old infants lack pattern or shape constancy. Such recovery and the lack of recovery to a configuration change alone does not mean that the infants lacked any sensitivity to configuration. Humphrey et al. (1986) also report that infants showed differential habituation rates as a function of pattern structure (see Figure 9) indicating at least some perception of configuration. From a functional point of view, information about configuration and other spatial attributes can be significant depending on the perceptual task. For example, for activities such as reaching, registration of the size, position, and orientation of an object is important. For other purposes, however, the visual system must factor out the information concerning the size, position, and orientation of an object from that specifying the invariant shape of an object. The general point is that an adaptive organism must perceive information in several forms and it is the discrimination problem or memory task that determines what is relevant. Unless procedures such as those described below are used to make variations in size, orientation, position, or other spatial dimensions irrelevant, infants may respond to such changes.

A. J. Caron et al. (1979) and Day and McKenzie (1981) have used a habituation procedure which effectively instructs the infant to ignore simple spatial transformations associated with changes in an object's location. They habituated infants to an object which was placed at different positions on each trial. Day and McKenzie (1981) moved a model head during each trial, varying its starting position from one trial to the next, continuing until looking time per trial declined by 50%. During the test trials, two objects were presented—the familiar head, or another head differing in physical size. Again they were moved from novel starting positions within the range used during habituation and their projective shapes were similar to those seen during habituation. Infants showed greater response recovery to the head differing in physical size, thus apparently demonstrating size constancy by 4 months of age. Even this result, however, has to be treated with caution, as we shall discuss shortly.

A similar strategy was used by A. J. Caron et al. (1979). During the habituation phase they varied the slant of a square from one trial to the next between 69° backward and 40° forward; in the test phase infants viewed two stimuli in the novel (upright) position, the square and an equal-sized trapezoid. The infants showed a significant degree of recovery of fixation to the trapezoid but not to the square (see Figure 13C) despite the fact that the projected image of the slanted square was more like the upright trapezoid than the upright square. This is strong evidence that by 12 weeks of age infants can appreciate the constant, real shape of an object under certain conditions.

B. Object Recognition and Motion Perception

As many authors have pointed out, one of the most prominent and forceful being Bruner (1957), infants live in a world which is undergoing transformation, and their task in coming to terms with the enormous flux of stimulation is to categorize, to identify sources of stimulation that transcend the fluctuations, and generally to seek coherence in a chaotic world. The Gibsons put this another way by stating that the infant has to detect invariances in the stimulus array. However one expresses the point, it is clear that infants either have to learn (Bruner) or learn to detect (Gibsons) what used to be called "stimulus equivalence," surely a prerequisite for true object recognition. There is a surprising paucity of research on the perception of objects in infancy, except for that specifically concerned with shape and size constancy. Most of the research has been undertaken within the Gibsonian tradition of detecting the stable features of a dynamically changing array.

Ruff (1978) demonstrated in a series of studies that 9-month-old infants are capable of recognizing the form of three-dimensional objects despite changes in size, orientation, and color. Six-month-olds, on the other hand, were not able to achieve this generalization. The usual familiarization–novelty paradigm was used, and in this case during the familiarization period the "familiar" object was presented in a number of different versions. This variation during the familiarization period apparently helped, particularly with the recognition of more difficult objects, and the presentation of variations within trials rather than successively between trials seemed to be particularly beneficial. Under the within-trials condition it was found that infants frequently shifted fixation from one object to another, which, as Ruff suggests, probably facilitates the comparison of different forms. Young infants live in a world in which stimuli are continually transformed in a smooth fashion, so variation within trials seems to be a natural way to present transformations.

Although it seems to be possible to "instruct" infants as to how they should respond, simply shifting the position of a stationary object from one trial to the next is not effective in every case, as research by Owsley (1983) and Kellman (1984) shows. Owsley (1983) has made this point by comparing the recovery of visual fixation by 4-month-olds following habituation to one of three stimulus conditions: first, a stationary wedge monocularly viewed projecting an image equal to a cube rotated 45° from its frontal position; second, the stationary wedge, which was rotated from trial to trial, or third, a wedge which rotated around its vertical axis during each trial. She found no response recovery in the two stationary conditions to a wedge in new and old positions, or to a new object, namely a cube [cf. the experiment of Cook et al. (1978) cited earlier]. However, form constancy was demonstrated when the wedge was *moved during* habituation trials. In this condition, infants treated the cube as a novel object and failed to show response recovery to wedges in either position.

Kellman (1984) has assessed visual perception of three-dimensional shape using three kinds of two-dimensional displays, a kinetic condition and two static conditions. In the kinetic condition 4-month-old infants were presented with videotapes of objects (a wedge or an L-shaped solid) continuously rotating. Infants in the static conditions were shown slides of successive static views of the rotation sequences in either 60° steps (six views spaced 60° apart for 2 sec each with a 0.5-sec blank interval between slides) or in 15° steps (24 views 15 degrees apart for 1 sec each with a 0.5-sec blank interval). During habituation trials, infants in the kinetic condition were presented with the same object undergoing rotation around two different axes. Infants in the kinetic group were presented with the familiar object rotating about a new axis and a new object rotating around this same axis on recovery trials. Infants in the two static conditions were habituated and tested similarly. Only infants in the kinetic condition showed differential recovery of looking on the recovery trials with reliably greater looking to the new object. It is important to note that Kellman (1984) also found longer looking times to the kinetic than to the static displays.

J. J. Gibson (1966, 1979) demonstrated that a textured surface moving relative to a similarly textured background can, through covering (deletion) and uncovering (accretion) of the texture elements of the background, specify depth at an edge. The displacement of a textured object across a similarly textured background also can lead to recognition of the object's shape, which cannot be recognized or even detected under suitable static conditions. Kaufmann-Hayoz, Kaufmann, and Stucki (1986) have asked whether infants can perceive shape using this source of information. They placed white dots on black objects and a black background and videotaped the displays. The shape of the moving object could easily be detected by adults but could not be seen under static conditions. Three-month-old infants reliably dishabituated to a change in the shape of the textured object moving against a background of identical texture. Another group presented with the same shapes, but as static white forms on a completely black background, also showed evidence of discrimination. A third group of infants habituated to the moving textured shape showed more reliable recovery of looking to a new static white form than to the familiar static white form, suggesting that infants can perceive the shape of the moving textured surface. Kaufmann-Hayoz et al. (1986) also found that the infants looked longer at the moving than at the static displays.

The importance of dynamic variation, and particularly of smooth transformations, has also been borne out in experiments by E. J. Gibson and her colleagues. E. J. Gibson, Owsley, and Johnston (1978) showed that 5-

month-olds distinguish between rigid motion of objects and deformation. That is, infants habituated to three different rigid motions of an object showed greater dishabituation to a deformation than to a fourth rigid motion. Similarly E. J. Gibson, Owsley, Walker, and Megaw-Nyce (1979, Experiment 1) showed that 3-month-olds who were habituated to two objects undergoing rigid motion maintained habituation to a new rigid motion, but not to a deforming motion. Thus infants can perceive rigidity as an invariant property of an object that is different from nonrigid deformations.

E. J. Gibson et al. (1979) demonstrated that infants as young as 3 months old can recognize the form of an object (an invariant) that was presented undergoing continuous rigid motions. In one experiment they habituated infants to a shape undergoing two different motions. Subsequently, a new shape was shown undergoing the same motions. These infants showed a significant revival of interest compared to a group presented with the original shape (also moving) during the test trials. The same pattern of results occurred in a subsequent experiment even when the novel and familiar shapes (presented to separate groups of subjects) were motionless during the test trials. The authors argue that the shape of an object is specified by a family of transformations which can be generated only by that object. (That they can be so specified is a truism.) Furthermove, they argue that only continuous transformations provide sufficient information to define the shape of a solid object.

Finlay, Sacchetti, and Ivinskis (1982) have questioned the results of E. J. Gibson et al. (1978, 1979). Finlay et al. habituated 3- to 4-month-old infants to a shape undergoing, successively, one of two rigid motions or to two shapes presented successively undergoing the same rigid motion. The stimuli were videotaped two-dimensional patterns rotated around the vertical, horizontal, or depth axis. Measures of visual fixation and a cardiac measure were obtained. Finlay et al. (1982) found that the infants recovered interest following habituation to a single shape undergoing two rigid motions when either the shape *or* the motion transformation changed. The novel motion transformation was a rigid motion around a new axis and the shape change was to another simple two-dimensional shape. The infants presented with a mixed sequence of shapes undergoing the same transformation also showed recovery when either the shape or the transformation was changed. Recovery of interest was indicated quite reliably by both measures.

Finlay et al. (1982) argue that their results are at odds with those obtained by E. J. Gibson et al. (1978, 1979) and suggest that the results support the notion that the infants are responding to change *per se* rather than to some invariant property of a stimulus such as rigidity. A close comparison of Finlay et al. (1982) and E. J. Gibson et al. (1978, 1979) reveals many differences between their reports, perhaps one of the most important differences being in the stimuli used. Finlay et al. used computer-generated stimuli to gain control over all stimulus properties, whereas E. J. Gibson et al. used hand-held stimuli that would produce much variation from trial to trial. Although Finlay et al. criticize this lack of stimulus control, perhaps the greater variation in the E. J. Gibson et al. stimuli was important in that the infants would have seen a greater range of variation and hence would be less likely to recover looking unless the change was clearly outside the range presented on habituation trials. This speculation is obviously open to experimental test and again underscores the importance of even minor variations in the types of stimuli used in infant research.

Two further reports are important in the present context. Both Bertenthal et al. (1984) and Fox and McDaniel (1982) investigated infant perception of "biological motion" (see Johannson, 1973). Bertenthal et al. (1984) presented infants with dynamic point-light displays of human walkers, which are created by attaching lights to the head and major joints of a person and filming locomotion in the dark (Johannson, 1973) or by mimicking such a dynamic pattern through computer simulation. For an adult, any static frame from such a film record looks like a random, meaningless display of dots. Recognition of a walking human figure is perceived immediately, however, in moving displays (for a review, see Cutting & Proffitt, 1981).

Bertenthal et al. (1984) showed, using an habituation procedure, that infants 3 and 5 months of age discriminated between upright and inverted moving walkers, but not between upright and inverted static displays (Experiment 1). They also showed that infants discriminated between an upright "stationary" (treadmill) walker and an "anomalous" walker. This latter display consisted of point-lights that moved with the same motion as the stationary walker, but with the location of each point-light scrambled to create, for an adult, a swarming, random display. Infants did not discriminate between upright and inverted versions of the anomalous walker, or between static displays in which different and progressive static images of the walking cycle were presented during habituation (Experiment 2). Bertenthal et al. (1984) found that, generally, the infants looked more at the moving than static displays.

Fox and McDaniel (1982) used a forced-choice preferential looking technique (Teller, 1979) to assess the perception of biological motion by infants 2, 4, and 6 months of age. The infants saw, side by side, a biological motion pattern (a point-light display of the profile of a human running on the spot) and a pattern of the same number of dots, each moving in an independent, randomly determined direction. While 2-month-olds showed no preference, both 4- and 6-month-old infants preferred the biological motion pattern. In a second experiment, using only 4- and 6-month-olds, both age groups showed a preference for an upright over an inverted biological motion pattern of a stationary runner. In a third experiment, dots were placed on the joints of the fingers and wrist and the pattern was a pair of hands that, to an adult, appeared to grasp an invisible glass and then withdraw. A pattern not perceived by adults to indicate biological motion was created by placing the dots on off-joint positions. Infants of 6 months, but not 2 or 4 months showed a reliable preference for the biological motion pattern.

The research reviewed above clearly indicates that continuous object movement helps to specify the shape of an object for young infants whether the object is of a rigid or of a nonrigid or "biological" nature. Whether the movement makes an object more interesting and therefore better attended to or whether the movement itself leads to "extraction of invariant properties" in Gibson's terms is simply not known. Many of the reports reviewed above found that infants spend more time looking at the moving displays than at the static displays, as had been found previously by others (e.g., Volkman & Dodson, 1976). More formal theoretical work (Ullman, 1979) on "structure from motion" suggests that the form of a moving object, even one created by placing dots on a surface, can be uniquely determined from a small number of noncoplanar views. Perhaps our visual system has evolved to detect "structure from motion" and to accomplish this very early in life. Indeed, it may take some time after shape can be seen in continuously moving objects before shape information can be derived from a succession of static views.

In conclusion we may note that nearly all the work on the constancies has been done with shape and size constancy, to the neglect of other important properties of mature perception such as brightness and color constancy, to say nothing of constancies in other modalities. Not only is our knowledge incomplete, but it may be that shape and size constancy are special cases. The changes in shape and size that an object projects to the eye, as its position in space changes, are easily detectable for an adult. Changes in the apparent brightness and color of an object as illumination changes are not readily perceived, even if one pays particular attention to them. Brightness and hue constancy seem to have a more "automatic" character (Forgus, 1966). It may be that, whereas size and shape constancy require training, even in infancy (as in the habituation paradigm) to ignore shifts in object position, brightness and color constancy will be more immediately demonstrable in early life.

We have emphasized the fact that infants are extremely sensitive to the conditions under which the experiment occurs, and to the particular stimulus displays which are used. The interpretation of results is certainly not always straightforward. An analogy with Piagetian experiments on conservation may be illuminating here: children can be trained to make "conservation type" responses, and there may be a strong inclination to interpret such findings as demonstrating that conservation can be acquired through training. However there is always the possibility that correct responding is not the same as true understanding. Infants can be "instructed" to generalize along a particular dimension, such as viewing distance, and having done so may give constancylike responses; how are we to know that they *really* demonstrate shape or size constancies rather than a more superficial generalized response? Two points seem clear to us. The first is that conclusive results will not come from a single experiment or the use of a single method: converging evidence from a number of directions will be required for a definitive answer. Second, we emphasize again that what is important is an understanding of the developmental sequence rather than the attribution of "constancy processing" to one particular age. It should now be clear that whether or not constancy is demonstrated at a particular age depends very much on how the question is asked, as well as on the experimenter's willingness to interpret the findings in a particular way.

The question of constancy arises because it is a specific aspect of the general question of the infant's understanding of the world (our "level three" analysis). There are certainly other ways in which this question can be approached, for example by using stimuli which are ecologically valid and perhaps more interesting to the infant as the research using dynamic displays suggests.

C. Picture Perception

Picture perception is an abstract instance of the relationship between objects and their representations. Some of the same sorts of questions arise as with the constancies, although the emphasis is somewhat different. As one might expect, there have been two basic approaches to the study of picture perception (for a review and detailed discussion see Hagen, 1974). According to the "empiricist–cognitive" approach the relationship between pictures and objects is arbitrary and must be learned. For instance Goodman (1976) has argued that picture perception involves an act of interpretation which is dependent upon a knowledge of the "language" of pictorial representation. Similarly, Gregory (1972) has shown that very many pictures have a conventional or diagrammatic component (this can vary widely of course) and in such cases it is obvious that the conventions have to be learned. The other approach, which by now should come as no surprise, is J. J. Gibson's (the main ideas are contained in his 1971 publication). His viewpoint on picture perception is fairly easily predictable from his general theory: he emphasizes the structural similarity between pictures and the objects depicted. J. J. Gibson (1971, p. 31) expressed this position as follows: "a picture is a surface so treated that a delimited optic array to a point of observation is made available which contains the same kind of information that is found in the ambient optic arrays of an ordinary environment." In certain cases this is obviously true, a photograph being a trivial example. Pirenne (1970) has discussed extensively the conditions under which "trompe l'oeil" art is effective. It turns out that the conditions under which a photograph (or picture) is virtually indistinguishable from the real scene it depicts are the conditions in which the eye is held stationary at the point from which the original pictorial observation was made. Here indeed the optic array is in most respects identical to that of the real scene. However, we do not have to think long to realize that this is a very special case and is not true of the vast majority of pictorial representations. Further discussion of these points is to be found in Pirenne (1970) and in Gombrich (1960).

The question of picture perception in infancy has aroused some interest, and demonstrations that picture transfer occurs in infrahumans (e.g., Cabe, 1976) perhaps have a bearing on whether some aspects of picture perception are innately programmed. Similarly, experiments with human infants who have had little opportunity to learn associations between pictures and objects bear on the issue of whether picture perception is dependent on prior learning, or is more immediate, as Gibson maintains. Before discussing the evidence a word of caution is in order; there are two aspects to the question of whether representations of objects are recognized as such. On the one hand it may be that an organism recognizes the representational character and understands what the reference object is. On the other hand it is altogether possible, particularly in cases where the optic arrays for the two are highly similar, that the organism simply fails to discriminate between them. We would be hard put to justify the latter as a case of recognizing a pictorial representation, and it is only that question which has real interest so far as understanding the visual world of the infant is concerned. Our point is of course another instance of the caveat sounded by Harris and Allen (1974) in their discussion of constancy studies.

Using the now familiar familiarity–novelty paradigm, S. A. Rose (1977) investigated transfer between two- and three-dimensional arrays in which infants were first presented with a two- or three-dimensional pattern, and then tested with either the same pattern or a new one. Rose showed that 6-month-olds can discriminate between two- and three-dimensional representations of the same pattern, although transfer between two- and three-dimensional representations of the same pattern could also be demonstrated, thus indicating perception of some degree of equivalence. When both aspects of a pattern were changed (its configuration as well as its dimensionality) infants looked longer at the novel stimulus in which both aspects changed, compared to a stimulus in which only one was changed. This seems to demonstrate both a sensitivity to depth cues, although we do not know in this case exactly what the cues were, and also some evidence that two- and three-dimensional instances of a pattern are recognized as equivalent. On similar lines Deloache, Strauss, and Maynard (1979, Experiment 1) showed that 5-month-olds familiarized to a small doll showed greater recovery of looking to both color and black and white photographs of a novel doll compared to photographs of the original. Deloache et al. (1979, Experiment 3) also found that infants at this age can discriminate between the objects and their various representations, thereby showing that transfer in their Experiment 1 could not be attributed simply to a failure of discrimination between solid objects and their pictures.

A study by J. Field (1976), referred to earlier, is also relevant, since it demonstrates how important it may be to take multiple measures of the infant's behavior. Field found that infants 3 to 6 months old that would reach for solid objects would also reach for two-dimensional representations of them. As he points out, this may have been the result of indiscriminate reaching triggered by any patterned surface that is within reach, rather than a failure to discriminate between three-dimensional objects and two-dimensional representations of them. This seems likely, since he found the ability to discriminate between them. J. Field subsequently found (1977) that somewhat older infants demonstrate a better apprehension of depth by reaching only for objects that are within reach, and also by this same measure differentiate between solid and nonsolid displays. At the same time one can use two-dimensional displays to elicit reaching for the investigation of sensitivity to depth cues (see Chapter 2, this volume, by Yonas and Owsley). For example, McDonnell and Doyle (1980) have successfully employed the reaching response to examine the development of sensitivity to linear perspective, compression gradients, and the combination of these cues in two-dimensional displays in 6- through 17-month-old infants. Infants reached for the representation of the object at the appropriate "distance" as defined by these cues. Thus it seems unlikely that the question of whether infants detect three-dimensionality and respond to it appropriately can be answered in simple experiments with a single response measure and impoverished stimulus conditions. No doubt different cues become salient at different times and are utilized differently as the infant's response repertoire becomes larger and more refined.

The depth cues normally available and commonly discussed are motion parallax, binocular disparity, and information from interposition, texture gradients, and the like. Following Gibson, we now realize that there are also powerful depth cues in the stimulus array (both static and dynamic) that go beyond the simple concept of motion parallax, such as the dynamic gradients of change over time for moving textured surfaces. The studies reviewed above demonstrate that there is some transfer between two- and three-dimensional patterns which share certain similarities, but little is known about either the use of, or the failure to discriminate, the sorts of potential dynamic depth cue just mentioned (see Yonas and Owsley, Chapter 2, this volume).

Ruff, Kohler, and Haupt (1976) report on an experiment in which motion parallax may have played a role. Three- and $5\frac{1}{2}$-month-old infants were presented with three-dimensional objects and two-dimensional colored photographs of the objects. The infants were familiarized and subsequently tested with a three-dimensional object or with a photograph of the object. Only the $5\frac{1}{2}$ month-olds familiarized and tested with three-dimensional objects showed a consistent preference for a novel object. The authors suggest that the stimuli may have been too complex for the younger infants to process during the 10-sec familiarization period. They also speculate that the three-dimensional objects may have led to faster learning in the older infants because of the information provided through such cues as motion parallax. Whether this was the only cue or the most effective cue remains to be demonstrated.

Thus, although there have been a number of experiments and some intriguing findings, there is much to be done before we can specify the nature and limits of picture perception and its relation to object recognition in infancy. As Hagen (1974) had suggested, research is needed on the development of sensitivity to the many forms of pictorial information and representations. Some candidates for research with infants include linear perspective, superposition, texture gradients, aerial perspective, shadow and highlights, and color contrast (see Chapter 2, this volume, by Yonas and Owsley).

IV. FACE PERCEPTION

There are three broadly overlapping areas of research on the infant's developing perception of the human face. One body of research has emphasized components: that is, the face is treated as a configuration of elements or features, and investigators have been concerned with identifying responses to each one of them. Also, as one might expect, there has been investigation of the configuration of elements which define a "face": the second approach assumes that the face (for the infant) is a gestalt and is concerned with its detection under various transformations. In these two cases the study of face perception follows two of the general themes in infant perception which we identified earlier. A third approach emphasizes the communicative role of the face. The function of facial expression and its perception in the development of social bonds has been stressed in theories of attachment, studies of parent–infant interaction, and generally in ethological theorizing, the third of our themes (Freedman, 1974; K. Robson, 1967; Spitz & Wolf, 1946; Stern, 1974; Vine, 1973). According to this theoretical viewpoint, the face serves an important communicative function in early social interactions. We shall give a general review of these three areas; for more detailed reviews of the adult literature see Ellis (1975), and for a more comprehensive account of the infant literature, particularly in the 5- to 7-month age range, see Fagan (1978b).

A. Components

A number of investigators have suggested that there are important changes in the infant's processing of the face at 2 months of age, and again at 4 months of age. In line with the theorizing outlined earlier, it has been argued that prior to 2 months of age the infant does not respond to the inner features of faces. After 2 months of age it is argued that the infant begins to attend to the internal elements and eventually, at about 4 months of age, responds to the configuration of elements which define a face.

Scanning patterns have been measured in an attempt to isolate those aspects of the face to which the infant is responsive. Most research (Haith, Bergman, & Moore, 1977; Hainline, 1978; Maurer & Salapatek, 1976) has confirmed the results of earlier reports on the scanning of faces and other two-dimensional shapes (reviewed by Salapatek, 1975). Very young infants (under 2 months) execute most of their scans to the regions of the hairline and chin, while older infants (4 months) scan both external borders and internal features, concentrating on the eyes. Thus at an early stage of development infants achieve visual inspection strategies similar to those employed by adults, in which the eyes receive most attention (Zusne, 1970). These ideas about how infants scan (and hence—probably—perceive) faces may well need revision when a larger range of stimulus conditions has been investigated. We would remind the reader of our earlier comments about changes in saliency when stimulus movement is introduced (I. W. R. Bushnell, 1979; Girton, 1979).

A challenge to the view that infants do not perceive facial configurations at an early age was provided in two reports by Goren, Sarty, and Wu (1975) and Jirari (1970; reported in Freedman, 1974). They claimed to show more reliable head and eye turning in neonates to schematic faces than to scrambled faces and blanks (see Figure 15). Maurer and Young (1983) have not been able to obtain this result in a well-controlled attempt at replication. It should be noted, however, that their background contrast was high compared to that used by the original experimenters; this might have predisposed the infants to ignore the configurational properties of the internal features. Clearly, if the results of Goren et al. and Jirari stand we shall have to alter our ideas about the development of face perception. The weight of evidence at the moment, however, favors the view that at least for static features, the infant below 2 months of age does not make elaborate distinctions.

B. Configuration

Maurer and Barrera (1981) demonstrated (using the usual habituation methodology) that 2-month-old infants can discriminate among schematic drawings of a human face arranged naturally, symmetrically but scrambled, and asymmetrically. Two-month-olds also showed a preference for the natural arrangement of the facial features. However at 1 month of age the discriminations were not made, nor was the preference for the natural

Figure 15. Neonates show an increasing degree of responsiveness (eye and head turns) to stimuli A through D, with maximal response to D, the most facelike stimulus. (From Goren, Sarty, & Wu, 1975.) It should be noted that high background contrast was present in the Maurer and Young (1983) study, but not in the Goren, Sarty, and Wu (1975) study.

arrangement shown. The authors suggest that the 1-month-olds probably limited their visual inspection to the oval frame within which the features occurred, but this was not examined specifically. At all events, by 2 months of age infants appear to recognize the natural arrangement of static facial features and to be capable of generalizing that knowledge to schematic versions of the face.

Somewhat similar evidence, but with older subjects, has been reported by Haaf and his colleagues (Haaf, 1974; Haaf & Bell, 1967; Haaf & Brown, 1976). They showed that there is a change between 10 and 15 weeks of age in the stimulus dimensions underlying response to facelike patterns, namely, the dimensions of resemblance to face and stimulus complexity (Figure 16). "Complexity" refers to the total number of ele-

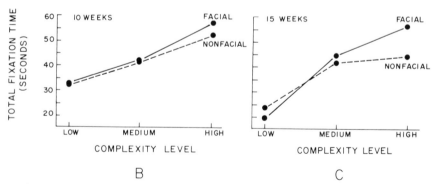

Figure 16. A comparison of infant preference at 10 and 15 weeks of age for facial and nonfacial stimuli varying in degree of complexity. By 15 weeks infants show a preference for the facial over the nonfacial stimulus, but only at the high complexity level. (From Haaf & Brown, 1976.)

ments in the stimulus, while "facial resemblance" refers to the number of appropriately positioned facial features. The results of Haaf and Brown (1976) demonstrate a preference for facial organization at 15 weeks that is absent at 10 weeks (Figure 16B and C). Two sets of patterns containing identical elements were used which differed only in terms of the organization of the elements, with symmetry held constant (Figure 16). This is probably important as earlier studies (e.g., Haaf & Bell, 1967) may have confounded symmetry with complexity in facial resemblance (see Haaf, 1977; Thomas, 1973). The discrepancy in age-related ability to detect facelike patterns between Maurer and Barrera on the one hand and Haaf and Brown on the other is somewhat disturbing and needs further investigation (see below), although some of the discrepancy could be a result of the different methodologies used. The view that perception of the configuration of the face occurs at about 4 months of age is consistent with earlier reviews of the literature (e.g., E. J. Gibson, 1969).

The research of Thomas (1973) and Thomas and Jones-Molfese (1977) has also challenged the traditional view about when infants begin responding to facial organization. Thomas (1973) argued that preference measures for individual infants, rather than averaged data for groups of infants, should be used in assessing visual preferences which may be controlled by some underlying dimensional factor. Two or more infants may show a different preference ordering for a set of stimuli, despite the fact that their responses are actually functions of the same underlying scale. It is possible to verify whether there is a single unidimensional scale underlying infant preferences, and it is also possible to estimate what the scale is. The techniques described by Thomas (1973; Hettmansperger & Thomas, 1973) are based on the unfolding theory of Coombs (1964). The theory assumes that a subject has a preferred location or "ideal point" on the continuum to which he is responding. The manifest preference ordering of the subject (the I scale) results from "folding" of the underlying continuum (the J scale) about that subject's ideal point. A given J scale may be consistent with a number of alternative I scales, but it is possible to estimate the most probable J scale given a number of different, but transitive, I scales. Thus examination of a set of transitive preferences, which appear different for different infants, may be misleading. Thomas (1973) reanalyzed data from a number of preference experiments and demonstrated preference for facelike stimuli as early as 5 weeks of age. In a later report (Thomas & Jones-Molfese, 1977), infants were tested with a blank oval, a face with scrambled parts, a schematic facelike drawing, and a black and white photograph of a real face. From their results the authors conclude that a single scale, agreeing with the "faceness" continuum, accounted for most of the pattern preferences of individual infants aged 2 through 9 months. There was little evidence of change in preference ordering with increasing age, and 42 of the 52 infants tested most preferred the facelike display.

It appears then that the infant at 2 months, and possibly younger, is responsive to some configurational aspects of the face. The suggestion that the perception of facial configuration only occurs at 4 months is probably incorrect, although direct comparison of results employing different displays and different methodologies has its dangers. The stimuli used in the studies so far described have been static, with the exception of the reports of Goren et al. (1975) and Maurer and Hutchinson (1980). The importance of exploring a wider range of stimulus variation, including particularly contrast and movement, is obvious. The importance of the dynamic components of a face has yet to be explored. Wider use of analyses based on the Coombs (1964) unfolding technique is also to be encouraged. Although there certainly will be problems of interpretation when the underlying scale is not unidimensional (see, for example, Sherrod, 1979), the very fact that the scale is not unidimensional would itself be informative. No one theoretical or methodological approach is totally adequate; we should be willing to keep an open mind and to experiment further.

C. Transformation and Invariance

Other studies of facial perception have been motivated by an interest in the infant's ability to recognize transformed versions of stimuli to which they have previously been exposed. That is, the research has focused on the perception of configuration under transformation, or invariance; in a sense this is an aspect of perceptual constancy. Bornstein, Gross, and Wolf (1978, Experiment 1) investigated responses to left- and right-facing profiles of familiar and novel male profiles in 4-month-old infants, finding that turning the familiar profile view through 180° did not cause dishabituation, whereas presentation of a new profile did.

Fagan and his colleagues have investigated many aspects of facial recognition by infants over orientational changes (reviewed in Fagan, 1978b). For instance, Fagan (1978a) has shown a good degree of abstraction of invariant features of the face with changes in orientation around the vertical axis. Infants of approximately 7 months of age were familiarized with a full profile together with a three-quarter profile and a full frontal photograph of the same face. Subsequently, they looked more at a novel full profile than at the familiar full profile. The same pattern of results occurred if the infants were presented with just the three-quarter and full profile during familiarization, but not if they were familiarized to only a frontal view and full profile. The latter group showed no preference for the novel face, hence no evidence of recognizing it as different from the original. It seems, as Fagan (1978a) suggests, that the three-quarter profile provides more facial features for encoding, although alternative explanations are possible. For example, the three-quarter to full facial view is a smaller transformation than from profile to frontal view. Conceivably, the 7-month-old infant can handle the former but not the latter.

Although this finding appears to contradict the results of Bornstein et al. (1978) it should be borne in mind that they used highly dissimilar faces, while Fagan used faces of high similarity. Once again we are reminded of the danger of generalizing about age-related abilities from a small stimulus set. In fact Fagan (1976, Experiment 1) has shown that 7-month-olds can discriminate dissimilar profiles. He also showed (1976, Experiment 2) that infants 7 months of age can discriminate between different orientations of the same face around the vertical axis but respond more to the novel face in a novel orientation, or to a novel face in the familiar orientation (Fagan, 1976, Experiment 3).

Fagan and Shepherd (1979) have examined the ability of infants to detect rotation of faces in the frontal plane. In general this ability is shown to follow Braine's (1978) description of the development of orientation perception for familiar objects. Fagan and Shepherd (1979) showed that 4- to 5-month-old infants can discriminate between an upright face and one rotated to 90° or 180°, but not between an upright and diagonally oriented face (45°), or between a 90° and 180° rotation. Infants at 5 to 6 months can make all the discriminations of the 4- to 5-month-old, but in addition can discriminate between upright and diagonally oriented faces and 90° and 180° rotations and do not discriminate between left and right diagonals. Thus, there is an increasing ability to detect invariance under rotational transformation over the first half-year of life or more.

Another aspect of the detection of invariance under transformation (constancy) is concerned with the infant's ability to detect similarities and differences between real objects (real live faces) on the one hand and representations (pictures) of those faces on the other. Dirks and Gibson (1977) habituated 5-month-olds to live people. In a test phase the infants were presented with high-fidelity colored photographs of these same people, or novel photographs of people who differed in sex, hair color, and hair style. The infants only dishabituated for the novel photographs. In the second experiment using the same procedure, but controlling for sex, hair color, and hair style between the novel and familiar photographs, infants did not recover interest to the "novel" photographs. The authors concluded that infants of this age do not need extended exposure to pictures in order to perceive both similarities and gross differences between individual people and high-fidelity photographs. Barrera and Maurer (1981b) have shown that infants even at 3 months of age can recognize a photograph of their mother; infants at this age preferred a colored photograph of their mother's face to that of a stranger, thus indicating transfer between three-dimensional objects and their two-dimensional representation, in this case a highly important "object" in the infant's environment. Similarly, Deloache et al., (1979) have found discriminations between familiarized and novel photographs in 5-month-old infants. After familiarization with colored photographs of faces, the infants were presented with novel and familiar photographs, black and white photographs, and line drawings of faces. In all cases there was more interest in the novel representations than the familiar. The authors argue that the infants extract "invariant cues" across the representations, but what those cues are we at present have no idea. Cohen and Strauss (1979; see also Fagan & Singer, 1979) have also investigated concept acquisition for faces in infants.

It appears from the still somewhat fragmentary evidence that between 4 and 7 months of age infants' perception of fairly salient characteristics of faces comes into operation. As was the case for perception of configuration in abstract forms, a great deal needs to be done before we can say with any firmness or generality what the real developmental pattern is. In particular we cannot yet say whether these responses to the human face are peculiar because it is a human face, or whether they reflect some more general stimulus attributes as yet unidentified. We do not know, for example, whether the responses to the human face are functions of a general perceptual–cognitive development, as some authors have suggested (Bornstein et al., 1978; Fagan, 1978a).

D. Communication

A number of studies designed to answer questions about auditory–visual coordination and early imitation of facial gestures suggest that, under appropriate testing conditions, infants respond very early in life to facial configurations. Should these results turn out to be reliable, they must be taken into account in any general description of the development of face perception. Much of this research also has direct implications for social–emotional development.

It has been demonstrated that infants 20–30 days old can discriminate between their mother's voice and the voice of other females (Mills & Melhuish, 1974). This is a source of information usually ignored in studies of face perception but obviously may be very important. For example

Bigelow (1977) showed that 1-month-olds do not reliably differentiate mother from stranger unless their faces are accompanied by a voice. However, it is clear that by 3 months of age the presence of the voice is not necessary (Barrera & Maurer, 1981).

Carpenter (1974) showed that infants 2 to 7 weeks old look more at their mother than at a stranger, regardless of the presence of her voice. Each face was examined longer if accompanied by a voice, and there was more turning away from direct regard when faces and voices were mismatched. Research by Spelke and Owsley (1979) also suggests a specific sensitivity to face–voice combinations in infants by $3\frac{1}{2}$ months of age.

Many aspects of facial configuration are known to be important in social intercourse. The direction of gaze (Argyle, 1972) and facial expressions such as smiling and frowning are important social signals, some of which occur in infancy (Ekman, 1972). Facial gestures play an important role in parent–infant attachment as well (see Fraiberg, 1977). It is natural to ask at what age human infants become responsive to facial expressions. Fagan (1978a) reported that during a familiarization period 5- to 1-month-old infants spend a greater proportion of their time looking at full frontal and three-quarter profile views of faces than the full profile. Furthermore, although not specifically examined, it appears that the full frontal view was always looked at longer than the three-quarter profile. It is known that even 3-week-old rhesus monkeys are sensitive to the direction of gaze of other monkeys (Mendelson, Haith, & Goldman, 1978) and appear to be upset by faces looking back at them; such staring may be interpreted as a hostile gesture. Fagan's results are suggestive, but clearly much more research is needed on gaze and expression in the perception of the human face by infants.

The importance of facial expression for early communication has been known, or assumed, for a long time (e.g., Darwin, 1872/1965). Controlled research is of recent origin, however, In general this research indicates that 3-month-olds can differentiate smiling from frowning (Barrera & Maurer, 1981a), happy from surprised faces (Young-Browne, Rosenfeld, & Horowitz, 1977) and, at 4 months, happy from angry faces (LaBarbera, Izard, Vietze, & Parisi, 1976). Again, the results are very preliminary and it would be interesting to employ Thomas's (1973) suggestions or scaling to see if infants ideed scale facial expressions on an identifiable continuum.

A particularly striking study of infant perception of facial expressions was reported by Meltzoff and Moore (1977). These researchers asked whether infants 12 to 21 days old would imitate the facial gestures of a live model. Tongue protrusion, mouth opening, and lip protrusion in the infants appears to be somewhat contingent upon similar gestures of the model. Their results suggest a remarkable ability to apprehend a dynamic facial gesture and to reproduce it. Whether this ability is an elaborate cognitive "mapping," as the authors suggest, or simply a species-specific innate response, as seems more likely, is unknown, and perhaps a question not worth asking at present, as the results have been seriously questioned on both methodological and theoretical grounds. The interested reader, and anyone contemplating such research, should examine the many critical reviews and failures to replicate this finding (Anisfield, 1979; Hayes & Watson, 1981; Jacobson, 1979; Jacobson & Kagan, 1979; Kleiner & Fagan, 1984; Koepke, Hamm, Legerstee, & Russell, 1983; Masters, 1979; McKenzie & Over, 1983) as well as some comments on these criticisms and replication failures (Meltzoff & Moore, 1979, 1983a, 1983b). Positive findings have also been reported (T. M. Field et al., 1983; T. M. Field, Woodson, Greenberg, & Cohen, 1982; Meltzoff & Moore, 1983c).

Although the results of Meltzoff and Moore (1977) are highly controversial, we would like to emphasize an aspect of their study which is often neglected in infant research, that is, the use of dynamic stimuli and responses. The structure of a totally rigid object or of an object with some rigid parts (e.g. a "biological object") can easily be detected under dynamic conditions (Johannson, 1973; Ullman, 1979). It is to be expected, and indeed research has shown, that infants are sensitive to various types of motion, including rigid and nonrigid transformation (E. J. Gibson et al., 1978, 1979). In an important study using 1-, 3-, and 5-month-old infants, Sherrod (1979) has shown that infants' ordering of stimuli was dependent on two factors relating to animation and complexity. The animation which characterizes the live person seemed to be of high attention value at all ages (Carpenter, 1974; Kaufmann & Kaufmann, 1980).

Bassili (1978) demonstrated that adults can discriminate between facial expressions using moving stimuli lacking in static features. The procedure was similar to the "biological motion" studies of Johannsen (1973) except that white dots or other small elements are placed on a blackened face and filmed or videotaped at high contrast. Movement of the face specifies a face to adults, despite the lack of facial features in a static frame, and some degree of emotional expression can be discerned.

Stucki and Kaufmann-Hayoz (1984) have shown that 3-month-old infants can discriminate between such a moving face and a rubber mask of the face which was deformed by hand. Discrimination between the face and mask was most reliable when the face was presented upright, rather than inverted, during habituation trials. Perhaps the face, like the human body, is best perceived in an upright orientation, this being the usual or natural orientation (see Bertenthal et al., 1984; Fox & McDaniel, 1982).

A most novel stimulus has been used by Nelson and Horowitz (1983) to investigate 1- and 5-month-olds' perception of faces. They used holographic stereograms that either moved or were stationary. Interestingly they found that 2-month-olds, but *not* 5-month-olds, detected a compound change in facial expression and pose using such stimuli. They suggest that the young infant's probable lack of stereopsis (e.g., see review in Aslin & Dumais, 1981) enabled it to attend to the relevant dimensions of expression and to exclude the dimension of depth. The older infants, they suggest, could not ignore the depth dimension because of their stereopsis and, consequently, they may not have habituated to the relevant dimensions. Whether this is a viable interpretation awaits further experimentation. Nelson and Horowitz (1983) also found in another study using only 5-month-olds that moving holograms were not looked at longer than stationary holograms, but contrast in movement was a significant factor. Specifically, infants habituated to a stationary hologram were much more likely to recover looking to a moving hologram than were infants who were habituated to a moving hologram and presented with a stationary hologram on recovery trials. Just how much this latter result depends on the use of holograms remains to be examined. Nelson and Horowitz (1983) clearly recognize the tentative nature of their interpretations, given the many unknowns in the use of such stimuli. Whether holographic stereograms will become a viable and valuable reserach tool remains to be seen. It is obvious that research needs to be done to evaluate the sensitivity of infants to the various aspects of dynamic stimulation, however presented.

In summary, then, we can say that there is considerable evidence of the infant's ability to detect static features of the face; we have some evidence on constancy of face perception, or the ability to detect its invariants under transformation; and there is also some evidence on the role of facial gestures and movements in communication. Although studies of the human face have been going on for two decades or more, it is still true to say that we are far from a complete understanding either of the features to which the infant is sensitive or an understanding of the ability to detect the face as a true sensitive Gestalt. The three areas we have reviewed cannot be seen as totally independent of each other, of course, although they are somewhat distinct in terms of the questions asked and their interpretation. Again the distinction between the neoempiricist and the neonativist points of view are fairly obvious: the work on abstract components derive from one tradition, while the work on constancy, transformation, and communication come from the other.

V. CONCLUSION

We started the chapter with a quotation from Deutsch on the importance of the theoretical relevance of experimental studies; we must end by admitting that his prescription, neat and logical though it is, is an ideal not closely approximated by most research on shape and pattern perception in infancy. We have tried to show that much of this research is motivated by a strong theoretical bent of one sort or another, but instances of a clear theoretical prediction to be decided definitively one way or the other by an *experimentum crucis* are fairly infrequent. That is not (or not always) because of lack of clear understanding of the issues at stake, or other forms of fuzzy thinking. It is rather because of the very complicated nature of the infant, its sensory and perceptual systems, and the variety and subtlety of the cues to which they may respond.

What has emerged from the 20 years of intensive study of pattern and object recognition in infancy is a general picture of some perceptual competency at birth that develops rapidly in the first year of life. While the visual acuity of newborn infants is poor, they are at least capable of discriminating between gross pattern features. Their interest in complex patterns develops rapidly, so that certainly by the second half of the first year of life, and perhaps much earlier, they can discriminate subtle cues, are sensitive to purely configurational factors in a display, and perceive such true *Gestalts* as the human face with remarkable competence. Infants at birth not only orient to sights, sounds, and touches (see Spelke, Chapter 6, this volume), they also show some rudimentary coordination between them. By 6 months of age their hand–eye coordination is good, and they show appreciation of depth and solidity; some degree of shape and size constancy is also present.

We have emphasized throughout the chapter the importance not just of discovering what infants of a particular age can (on average) perceive, or what they are sensitive to, but also of understanding the developmental sequence that leads to those particular abilities. Our knowledge on the first level is quite good, although far from complete. Our understanding of the second, developmental, story is still almost nonexistent. We know about the form of developmental functions in a few isolated instances (e.g., Fantz & Yeh, 1979; D. Muir, Abraham, Forbes, & Harris, 1979) but have no general picture. Here, surely, is the place where we should look for major new insights into pattern and object perception in infancy.

A second theme of the chapter has been our insistence that discoveries in this field are still too much a function of the methodologies employed, and even of the particular displays chosen for investigation, such as the size and shape of elements in a pattern and the actual configurations and transformations thereof that are studied. A robust scientific finding—not merely robust in the statistical sense—must remain stable under reasonable degrees of variation in measurement method and analysis. There are not too many findings in the literature on infant perception that stand up well to such variation, the findings on element versus configurational discrimination being a good case in point. We have mentioned before, and state again, that adequate sampling of element sizes and shapes, and of different configurations—to say nothing of adequate sampling of infant ages—will be required before a proper understanding of figural perception in infancy is attained. We think that quantitative and mathematical models of pattern structure will play an increasingly important role in such investigations. What is true of configurational perception is also obviously true in other areas: there is still much to learn.

We have noted, and applauded, the recent trend towards using more natural, and particularly dynamic, stimuli in infant studies. This has occurred largely as a result of J. J. Gibson's theorizing and thus has naturally led investigators to seek to explain their results in terms of the "invariants" of perceptual arrays. These invariants are, according to Gibsonian theory, what specify the veridical (and specifically the object) properties of the perceptual world. Yet no Gibsonian has ever successfully given an independent definition of what those invariants are. The line of reasoning is something like this: the infant (or other organism) is responding to an object; since many aspects of the stimulus array are changing (that is how a Gibsonian experiment is run) it must be that the infant is responding to some property of the array that is perceived *not* to change, that is, an invariant property. What does this buy us? Only the notion that, by definition, objects have some invariant properties (which of them may be *perceived* properties is another point worthy of investigation) and, since infants do respond to objects, they must therefore be responding to those invariant properties. Without better specification of the latter, this looks like a circular argument. Rigidity, rigid motion, perspective transformations with change of distance, etc., are object properties in the natural world, not abstract entities existing in some epistemological hall of mirrors. This is not to deprecate the Gibsonian line of empirical research with infants; on the contrary, we have commended it. Our point is that the tradition puts its theoretical emphasis in the wrong place. "Invariants" is now little more than a slogan; what we should be asking is what the invariants are, and how they are computed.

A great deal of contemporary research on infant perception uses the habituation paradigm, or some variant of it. Brilliant innovation though it was in the field of infant studies, the paradigm has some inherent weaknesses (it measures what *interests* the infant, not necessarily all that it is capable of *detecting*) and should at least be supplemented by other methods, including training methods. We have perhaps come to rely too much on this one approach to studying infant perception.

Finally, what have we learned about that fundamental *leitmotif* of research on infancy, nature versus nurture? Only, probably, that general assertions about the primacy of one or the other are likely to be unsupportable in the long run. One predominates with respect to certain aspects of pattern and object perception, the other is paramount in others. To return to our concept of the three levels of functioning of a perceptual system, namely, (1) detection, (2) organization, and (3) cognition, we have clear evidence of the predominance of inborn capacities in the formation and maturation of the sense organs and their simple detector functions; equally clearly , nurture is a dominant factor in the naming and recognition of perceptual objects. What of the middle level, of organization and transformation? There we face the greatest uncertainty, the most degrees of freedom, and hence, of course, the most challenging problems. As knowledge of the physiological basis of pattern element detection grows, and models of how the elements can be integrated into pattern representations develop on the one hand, and Gibsonian specifications of the properties of stimulus arrays become more refined on the other, we may hope for progress towards a deeper understanding of pattern and object recognition. At this level, of organization, inborn and experiential factors are recognized as being important by virtually every theorist. It is not a question of this or that, rather of when and how both sets of factors operate.

Researchers who investigate perception in infancy borrow most of their theoretical notions from the general field of perception; it is becoming increasingly common for tests of theories of pattern and object perception generally to be securely and conveniently made with infants. In this sense the field of infant perceptual study remains squarely within the context of experimental epistemology, which is where it should be.

ACKNOWLEDGMENTS

Preparation of this chapter was supported by grants from the Natural Science and Engineering Research Council (A-0044) of Canada to P. C. Dodwell and D. W. Muir and (A-8289) to G. K. Humphrey.

REFERENCES

Amigo, C. (1972). Visuo-sensory development of the child. *American Journal of Optometry and Archives of American Academy of Optometry, 49*, 991–1001.
Anisfield, M. (1979). Interpreting "imitative" responses in early infancy. *Science, 205*, 214–215.
Argyle, M. (1972). *The psychology of interpersonal behavior* (2nd ed.). London: Penguin Books.

Aslin, R. N., & Dumais, S. T. (1981). Binocular vision in infants: A review and theoretical framework. In H. W. Reese & L. P. Lipsitt (Eds.), *Advances in child development and behavior* (Vol./5). New York: Academic Press.

Atkinson, J., Braddick, O., & Moar, K. (1977). Contrast sensitivity of the human infant for moving and static patterns. *Vision Research, 17,* 1045–1047.

Attneave, F. (1955). Symmetry, information and memory for patterns. *American Journal of Psychology, 68,* 209–222.

Ball, W., & Tronick, E. (1971). Infant responses to impending collision: Optical and real. *Science, 171,* 818–820.

Banks, M. S., Alsin, R. N., & Letson, R. D. (1975). Sensitive period for the development of human binocular vision. *Science, 190,* 675–677.

Banks, M. S., & Salapatek, P. (1978). Acuity and contrast sensitivity in 1-, 2-, and 3-month-old human infants. *Investigative Ophthalmology and Visual Science, 17,* 361–365.

Banks, M. S., & Salapatek, P. (1981). Infant pattern vision: A new approach based on the contrast sensitivity function. *Journal of Experimental Child Psychology, 31,* 1–45.

Banks, M. S., & Salapatek, P. (1983). Infant visual perception. In M. M. Haith & J. J. Campos (Eds.), *Handbook of child psychology* (Vol. 2). New York: Wiley.

Barlow, H. B., & Reeves, B. C. (1979). The versatility and absolute efficiency of detecting mirror symmetry in random dot displays. *Vision Research, 19,* 783–793.

Barrera, M. E., & Maurer, D. (1981a). The perception of facial expressions by the three-month-old. *Child Development, 52,* 203–206.

Barrera, M. E., & Maurer, D. (1981b). Recognition of mother's photographed face by the three-month-old infant. *Child Development, 52,* 714–716.

Bartoshuk, A. K. (1962). Human neonatal cardiac acceleration to sound: Habituation and dishabituation. *Perceptual and Motor Skills, 15,* 15–27.

Bassili, J. N. (1978). Facial motion in the perception of faces and emotional expression. *Journal of Experimental Psychology: Human Perception and Performance, 4,* 373–379.

Berlyne, D. E. (1958). The influence of albedo and complexity of stimuli on visual fixation in the human infant. *British Journal of Psychology, 49,* 315–318.

Berlyne, D. E. (1971). *Aesthetics and psychobiology.* New York: Appleton-Century-Crofts.

Bertenthal, B. I., Campos, J. J., & Haith, M. M. (1980). Development of visual organization: The perception of subjective contours. *Child Development, 51,* 1072–1080.

Bertenthal, B. I., Proffitt, D. R., & Cutting, J. E. (1984). Infant sensitivity to figural coherence in biomechanical motions. *Journal of Experimental Child Psychology, 37,* 213–230.

Bigelow, A. (1977). *Infants' recognition of mother.* Paper presented at the Society for Research in Child Development, New Orleans.

Blakemore, C., & Cooper, G. F. (1970). Development of the brain depends on the visual environment. *Nature (London), 228,* 477–478.

Bond, E. K. (1972). Perception of form by the human infant. *Psychological Bulletin, 77,* 225–245.

Bornstein, M. H. (1981). Two kinds of perceptual organization near the beginning of life. In W. A. Collins (Ed.), *Minnesota symposia on child psychology* (Vol. 14). Hillsdale, NJ: Erlbaum.

Bornstein, M. H., Ferdinandsen, K., & Gross, C. (1981). Perception of symmetry in infancy. *Developmental Psychology, 17,* 82–86.

Bornstein, M. H., Gross, C. G., & Wolf, J. Z. (1978). Perceptual similarity of mirror images in infancy. *Cognition, 6,* 89–116.

Bower, T. G. R. (1965). Stimulus variables determining space perception in infants. *Science, 149,* 89–89.

Bower, T. G. R. (1966a). Heterogeneous summation in human infants. *Animal Behaviour,* *14,* 395–398.

Bower, T. G. R. (1966b). Slant perception and shape constancy in infants. *Science, 151,* 832–834.

Bower, T. G. R. (1966c). The visual world of infants. *Scientific American, 215,* 80–92.

Bower, T. G. R. (1974a). *Development in infancy.* San Francisco, CA: Freeman.

Bower, T. G. R. (1974b). The evolution of sensory systems. In R. B. MacLeod & H. L. Picks (Eds.), *Perception: Essays in honor of James J. Gibson.* Ithaca, NY: Cornell University Press.

Bower, T. G. R. (1978). Perceptual development: Object and space. In E. C. Carterette and M. P. Friedman (Eds.), *Handbook of perception: Vol. 8. Perceptual Coding.* New York: Academic Press.

Braddick, O., Campbell, F. W., & Atkinson, J. (1978). Channels in vision: Basic aspects. In R. Held, H. W. Leibowitz & H.-L. Teuber (Eds.), *Handbook of sensory physiology: Vol. 8. Perception.* Berlin & New York: Springer-Verlag.

Braine, L. G. (1978). Early stages in the perception of orientation. In M. Bortner (Ed.), *Cognitive growth and development: Essays in memory of Herbert G. Birch.* New York: Bruner & Mazel.

Bronson, G. W. (1974). The postnatal growth of visual capacity. *Child Development, 45,* 873–890.

Bronson, G. W. (1982). *The scanning patterns of human infants: Implications for visual learning.* Norwood, NJ: Ablex.

Bruner, J. S. (1957). On perceptual readiness. *Psychological Review, 69,* 123–152.

Bruner, J. S., Goodnow, J. J., & Austin, G. A. (1956). *A study of thinking.* New York: Wiley.

Bushnell, E. W., & Roder, B. J. (1985). Recognition of color-form compounds by 4-month-old infants. *Infant Behavior and Development, 8,* 255–268.

Bushnell, I. W. R. (1979). Modification of the externality effect in young infants. *Journal of Experimental Child Psychology, 28,* 211–229.

Butterworth, G. (1981). Object permanence and identity in Piaget's theory of infant cognition. In G. Butterworth (Ed.), *Infancy and epistemology: An evaluation of Piaget's theory.* Brighton: Harvester Press.

Cabe, P. A. (1976). Transfer of discrimination from solid objects to pictures by pigeons: A test of theoretical models of pictorial perception. *Perception and Psychophysics, 19,* 545–550.

Caelli, T. M., & Dodwell, P. C. (1982). The discrimination of structure in vectorgraphs: Local and global effects. *Perception and Psychophysics, 32,* 314–326.

Campbell, F. W. (1974). The transmission of spatial information through the visual system. In F. O. Schmitt (Ed.), *The neurosciences: Third study program.* Cambridge, MA: M.I.T. Press.

Campbell, F. W., & Robson, J. G. (1968). Application of fourier analysis to the visibility of gratings. *Journal of Physiology (London), 197,* 551–566.

Caron, A. J. Caron, R. F., & Carlson, V. R. (1978). Do infants see objects or retinal images? Shape constancy revisited. *Infant Behavior and Development, 1,* 229–243.

Caron, A. J., Caron, R. F., & Carlson, V. R. (1979). Infant perception of the invariant shape of objects varying in slant. *Child Development, 50,* 716–721.

Caron, R. F., Caron, A. J., Carlson, V. R., & Cobb, L. S. (1979). Perception of shape-at-a-slant in the young infant. *Bulletin of the Psychonomic Society, 13,* 105–107.

Carpenter, G. (1974). Mother's face and the newborn. *New Scientist, 61,* 742–744.

Cohen, L. B. (1973). A two process model of infant visual attention. *Merrill Palmer Quarterly, 19,* 157–180.

Cohen, L. B. (1979). Commentary on "Visual shape perception in early infancy" by M. Schwartz & R. H. Day. *Monographs of the Society for Research in Child Development, 44* (Serial No. 182).

Cohen, L. B., DeLoache, J. S., & Strauss, M. S. (1979). Infant visual perception. In J. D. Osofsky (Ed.), *Handbook of infancy.* New York: Wiley.

Cohen, L. B., & Strauss, M. S. (1979). Concept acquisition in the human infant. *Child Development, 50,* 419–424.

Cook, M., Field, J., & Griffiths, K. (1978). The perception of solid form in early infancy. *Child Development, 49,* 866–869.

Coombs, C. H. (1964). *Theory of data.* New York: Wiley.

Corballis, M. C., & Beale, I. L. (1976). *The psychology of left and right.* Hillsdale, NJ: Lawrence Erlbaum Associates.

Cornsweet, T. N. (1970). *Visual perception.* New York: Academic Press.

Cruikshank, R. M. (1941). The development of visual size constancy in early infancy. *Journal of Genetic Psychology, 58,* 327–351.

Cutting, J. E., & Proffitt, D. R. (1981). Gait perception as an example of how we may perceive events. In H. Pick & R. D. Walk (Eds.), *Perception and perceptual development* (Vol. 2). New York: Plenum.

Darwin, C. (1965). *The expression of emotions in man and animals.* Chicago, IL: University of Chicago Press. (Original work published 1872)

Day, R. H., & McKenzie, B. E. (1973). Perceptual shape constancy in early infancy. *Perception, 2,* 315–320.

Day, R. H., & McKenzie, B. E. (1977). Constancies in the perceptual world of the infant. In W. Epstein (Ed.), *Stability and constancy in visual perception: Mechanisms and processes.* New York: Wiley.

Day, R. H., & McKenzie, B. E. (1981). Infant perception of the invariant size of an approaching object. *Developmental Psychology, 17,* 670–677.

DeLoache, J., Strauss, M. S., & Maynard, J. (1979). Picture perception in infancy. *Infant Behavior and Development, 2,* 77–89.

Deutsch, J. A. (1955). A theory of shape recognition. *British Journal of Psychology, 46,* 30–37.

Deutsch, J. A. (1960). *The structural basis of behavior.* Chicago, IL: University of Chicago Press.

Diamond, I. T., & Hall, W. C. (1969). Evolution of neocortex. *Science, 164,* 251–262.

Dineen, I. T., & Meyer, W. J. (1980). Developmental changes in visual orienting behavior to featural versus structural information in the human infant. *Developmental Psychobiology, 13,* 123–130.

Dirks, J., & Gibson, E. (1977). Infants' perception of similarity between live people and their photographs. *Child Development, 48,* 124–130.

Dodwell, P. C. (1957). Shape recognition in rats. *British Journal of Psychology, 48,* 221–229.

Dodwell, P. C. (1961). Coding and learning in shape discrimination. *Psychological Review, 68,* 373–382.

Dodwell, P. C. (1970). *Visual pattern recognition.* New York: Holt, Rinehart & Winston.

Dodwell, P. C. (1975). Contemporary theoretical problems in seeing. In E. C. Carterette & M. P. Friedman (Eds.). *Handbook of perception: Vol. 5. Seeing.* New York: Academic Press.

Dodwell, P. C. (1978). Human perception of patterns and objects. In R. Held, H. W.

Leibowitz, & H. L. Teuber (Eds.), *Handbook of sensory physiology: Vol. 8. Perception*. Berlin & New York: Springer-Verlag.

Dodwell, P. C. (1983). The Lie transformation group model of visual perception. *Perception and Psychophysics, 34*, 1–16.

Dodwell, P. C., & Caelli, T. M. (1985). Recognition of vectorpatterns under transformations: Local and global determinants. *Quarterly Journal of Experimental Psychology, 37A*, 1–23.

Dodwell, P. C., Muir, D., & DiFranco, D. (1976). Responses of infants to visually presented objects. *Science, 194*, 209–211.

Dodwell, P. C., Muir, D., & DiFranco, D. (1979). Infant perception of visually presented objects. *Science, 203*, 1137–1139.

Dodwell, P. C., Wilkinson, F. E., & von Grünau, M. W. (1983). Pattern recognition in kittens: Performance on Lie patterns. *Perception, 12*, 393–410.

Ekman, P. (1972). Universals and cultural differences in facial expressions of emotion. In J. K. Cole (Ed.), *Nebraska symposium on motivation* (Vol. 19). Lincoln: University of Nebraska Press.

Ellis, H. (1975). Recognizing faces. *British Journal of Psychology, 66*, 409–426.

Fagan, J. F. III. (1976). Infants' recognition of invariant features of faces. *Child Development, 47*, 627–638.

Fagan, J. F. III. (1978a). Facilitation of infants' recognition memory. *Child Development, 48*, 1066–1075.

Fagan, J. F. III. (1978b). The origins of facial pattern recognition. In M. H. Bornstein & W. Kessen (Eds.). *Psychological development from infancy*. Hillsdale, NJ: Erlbaum.

Fagan, J. F. III, & Shepherd, P. A. (1979). Infants' perception of face orientation. *Infant Behavior and Development, 2*, 227–234.

Fagan, J. F., III, & Singer, L. T. (1979). The role of simple feature differences in infants' recognition of faces. *Infant Behavior and Development, 2*, 39–45.

Fantz, R. L. (1958). Pattern vision in young infants. *Psychological Record, 8*, 43–47.

Fantz, R. L. (1964). Visual experience in infants: Decreased attention to familiar patterns relative to novel ones. *Science, 146*, 668–670.

Fantz, R. L., Fagan, J. F., III, & Miranda, S. B. (1975). Early visual selectivity. In L. B. Cohen & P. Salapatek (Eds.), *Infant perception: From sensation to cognition* (Vol. 1). New York: Academic Press.

Fantz, R. L., & Yeh, J. (1979). Configurational selectivities: Critical for development of visual perception and attention. *Canadian Journal of Psychology, 33*, 277–287.

Field, J. (1976). Relation of young infants' reaching behavior to stimulus distance and solidity. *Developmental Psychology, 12*, 444–448.

Field, J. (1977). Coordination of vision and prehension in young infants. *Child Development, 48*, 97–103.

Field, T. M., Woodson, R., Cohen, D., Greenberg, R., Garcia, R., & Collings, K. (1983). Discrimination and imitation of facial expressions by term and preterm neonates. *Infant Behavior and Development, 6*, 485–489.

Field, T. M., Woodson, R., Greenberg, R., & Cohen, D. (1982). Discrimination and imitation of facial expressions by neonates. *Science, 218*, 179–181.

Finlay, D., Sacchetti, A., & Ivinskis, A. (1982). Perception of invariants, or "change," across transformations of shape and substance. *Australian Journal of Psychology, 34*, 281–288.

Fisher, C. B., Ferdinandsen, K., & Bornstein, M. H. (1981). The role of symmetry in infant form discrimination. *Child Development, 52*, 457–462.

Forgus, R. H. (1966). *Perception: The basic process in cognitive development*. New York: McGraw-Hill.

Fox, R., & McDaniel, C. (1982). The perception of biological motion by human infants. *Science, 218*, 486–487.

Fraiberg, S. (1977). *Insights from the blind: Comparative studies of blind and sighted infants.* New York: Basic Books.

Freedman, D. G. (1974). *Human infancy: An evolutionary perspective.* Hillsdale, NJ: Erlbaum.

Ganon, E. C., & Swartz, K. B. (1980). Perception of internal elements of compound figures by one-month-old infants. *Journal of Experimental Child Psychology, 30*, 159–170.

Garner, W. R. (1974). *The processing of information and structure.* Potomac, NJ: Erlbaum.

Gayl, I. E., Roberts, J. O., & Werner, J. S. (1983). Linear systems analysis of infant visual pattern preferences. *Journal of Experimental Child Psychology, 35*, 30–45.

Gibson, E. J. (1969). *Principles of perceptual learning and development.* New York: Appleton-Century-Crofts.

Gibson, E. J. (1977). How perception really develops: A view from outside the network. In D. LaBerge & S. J. Samuels (Eds.), *Basic processes in reading: Perception and comprehension.* Hillsdale, NJ: Erlbaum.

Gibson, E. J. (1982). The concept of affordances in development: The renascence of functionalism. In W. A. Collins (Ed.), *The concept of development: The Minnesota symposia on child development* (Vol. 15). Hillsdale, NJ: Erlbaum.

Gibson, E. J., Owsley, C. J., & Johnston, J. (1978). Perception of invariants by five-month-old infants: Differentiation of two types of motion. *Developmental Psychology, 14*, 407–415.

Gibson, E. J., Owlsey, C. J., Walker, A., & Megaw-Nyce, J. (1979). Development of the perception of invariants: Substance and shape. *Perception, 8*, 609–619.

Gibson, E. J., & Walk R. D. (1960). The visual cliff. *Scientific American, 202*, 64–71.

Gibson, J. J. (1966). *The senses considered as perceptual systems.* Boston, MA: Houghton-Mifflin.

Gibson, J. J. (1971). The information available in pictures. *Leonardo, 4*, 27–35.

Gibson, J. J. (1979). *The ecological approach to visual perception.* Boston, MA: Houghton-Mifflin.

Gibson, J. J., & Gibson, E. J. (1955). Perceptual learning: Differentiation or enrichment? *Psychological Review, 62*, 32–41.

Girton, M. R. (1979). Infants' attention to intrastimulus motion. *Journal of Experimental Child Psychology, 28*, 416–423.

Gombrich, E. H. (1960). *Art and illusion.* Princeton, NJ: Princeton University Press.

Goodman, N. (1976). *Languages of art: An approach to a theory of symbols* (2nd ed.). Indianapolis, IN: Hackett.

Goren, C., Sarty, M., & Wu, P. (1975). Visual following and pattern discrimination of facelike stimuli by newborn infants. *Pediatrics, 56*, 544–549.

Greenberg, D. J. (1977). Visual attention in infancy: Processes, methods, and clinical applications. In I. C. Uzgiris & F. Weizmann (Eds.), *The structuring of experience.* New York: Plenum.

Gregory, R. L. (1972). Cognitive contours. *Nature (London), 238*, 51–52.

Haaf, R. A. (1974). Complexity and facial resemblance as determinants of response to facelike stimuli by 5- and 10-week-old infants. *Journal of Experimental Child Psychology, 18*, 480–487.

Haaf, R. A. (1977). Visual responses to complex facelike patterns by 15- and 20-week-old infants. *Developmental Psychology, 13*, 77–78.

Haaf, R. A. & Bell, R. Q. (1967). A facial dimension in visual discrimination by human infants. *Child Development, 38*, 893–899.

Haaf, R. A., & Brown, C. J. (1976). Infants' responses to facelike patterns: Developmental changes between 10 and 15 weeks of age. *Journal of Experimental Child Psychology,* *22,* 155–160.

Hagen, M. A. (1974). Picture perception: Toward a theoretical model. *Psychological Bulletin, 81,* 471–497.

Hainline, L. (1978). Developmental changes in visual scanning of face and nonface patterns by infants. *Journal of Experimental Child Psychology, 25,* 90–115.

Hainline, L. (1981). Eye movements and form perception in human infants. In D. Fisher, R. Monty, & J. Senders (Eds.), *Eye movements: Cognition and visual perception.* Hillsdale, NJ: Erlbaum.

Haith, M. M. (1978). Visual competence in early infancy. In R. Held, H. W. Leibowitz, & H.-L. Teuber (Eds.), *Handbook of sensory physiology: Vol. 8. Perception.* Berlin & New York: Springer Verlag.

Haith, M. M. (1980). *Rules that babies look by.* Hillsdale, NJ: Erlbaum.

Haith, M. M., Bergmann, T., & Moore, M. J. (1977). Eye contact and face scanning in early infancy. *Science, 198,* 853–855.

Harris, L. J., & Allen, T. W. (1974). Role of object constancy in the perception of object orientation: Some methodological considerations in studies of human infants. *Human Development, 17,* 187–200.

Hayes, L. A., & Watson, J. S. (1981). Neonatal imitation: Fact or artifact? *Developmental Psychology, 17,* 655–660.

Hebb, D. O. (1949). *The organization of behavior.* New York: Wiley.

Hettmansperger, T., & Thomas, H. (1973). Estimation of J scales for unidimensional unfolding. *Psychometrika, 38,* 269–284.

Hirsch, H. V. B., & Spinelli, D. N. (1970). Visual experience modifies distribution of horizontally and vertically oriented receptive fields in cats. *Science, 168,* 869–871.

Hoffman, R. F. (1978). Developmental changes in human infant visual-evoked potentials to patterned stimuli recorded at difference scalp locations. *Child Development, 49,* 110–118.

Hoffman, W. C. (1966). The Lie algebra of visual perception. *Journal of Mathematical Psychology, 3,* 65–98.

Hoffman, W. C. (1978). The Lie transformation group approach to visual neuropsychology. In E. L. J. Leeuwenberg & H. F. J. M. Buffart (Eds.), *Formal theories of visual perception.* New York: Wiley.

Howe, E. S. (1980). Effects of partial symmetry, exposure time and backward masking on judged goodness and reproduction of visual patterns. *Quarterly Journal of Experimental Psychology, 32,* 27–55.

Hubel, D. H., & Wiesel, T. N. (1962). Receptive fields, binocular interaction and functional architecture in the cat's visual cortex. *Journal of Physiology (London), 160,* 106–154.

Humphrey, G. K., & Humphrey, D. E. (1985). *Preference for symmetry in infants.* Poster presented at the Society for Research in Child Development, Toronto.

Humphrey, G. K., Humphrey, D. E., Muir, D. W., & Dodwell, P. C. (1986). Pattern perception in infants: Effects of structure and transformation. *Journal of Experimental Child Psychology, 41,* 128–148.

Humphrey, N. K. (1974). Vision in a monkey without striate cortex: A case study. *Perception, 3,* 241–255.

Jacobson, S. W. (1979). Matching behavior in the young infant. *Child Development, 50,* 425–430.

Jacobson, S. W., & Kagan, J. (1979). Interpreting "imitative" responses in early infancy. *Science, 205,* 215–217.

Jirari, C. (1970). Form perception, innate form preferences and visually mediated head-turning in human neonates. Unpublished doctoral dissertation, Committee on Human Development, University of Chicago.

Johansson, G. (1973). Visual perception of biological motion and a model for its analysis. *Perception and Psychophysics, 14*, 201–211.

Julesz, B., & Caelli, T. (1979). On the limits of Fourier decompositions in visual texture perception. *Perception, 8*, 69–73.

Kanizsa, G. (1955). Margina quasi-percettivi in campi con stimolazione omogenea. *Rivista di Psicologia, 49*, 7–30.

Karmel, B. Z., & Maisel, E. B. (1975). A neuronal activity model for infant visual attention. In L. B. Cohen & P. Salapatek (Eds.), *Infant perception: From sensation to cognition* (Vol. 1). New York: Academic Press.

Kaufmann, R., & Kaufmann, F. (1980). The face as schema in 3- and 4-month-old infants: The role of dynamic properties of the face. *Infant Behavior and Development, 3*, 331–339.

Kaufmann-Hayoz, R., Kaufmann, F., & Stucki, M. (1986). Kinetic contours in infants' visual perception. *Child Development, 57*, 292–299.

Kleiner, K. A., & Fagan, J. F. (1984). *Neonatal discrimination and imitation of facial expression: A failure to replicate.* Poster presented at the International Conference on Infant Studies, New York.

Koepke, J. E., Hamm, M., Legerstee, M., & Russell, M. (1983). Neonatal imitation: Two failures to replicate. *Infant Behavior and Development, 6*, 97–102.

Kellman, P. J. (1984). Perception of three-dimensional form by human infants. *Perception and Psychophysics, 36*, 353–358.

LaBarbera, V. S., Izard, C. E., Vietze, P., & Parisi, S. A. (1976). Four- and six-month-old infants' visual responses to joy, anger and neutral expressions. *Child Development, 47*, 535–538.

Lashley, K. S. (1942). The problem of cerebral organization in vision. *Biological Symposia, 7*, 301–322.

Lasky, R. E. (1979). Serial habituation or regression to the mean? *Child Development, 50*, 568–570.

Lennie, P. (1980). Parallel visual pathways: A review. *Vision Research, 20*, 561–594.

Lewkowicz, D. J., & Turkewitz, G. (1980). Cross-modal equivalence in early infancy: Auditory-visual intensity matching. *Developmental Psychology, 16*, 597–607.

Lorenz, K. (1965). *Evolution and the modification of behavior.* Chicago, IL: University of Chicago Press.

Luneberg, R. K. (1947). *Mathematical analysis of binocular vision.* Princeton, NJ: Princeton University Press.

Masters, J. C. (1979). Interpreting "imitative" responses in early infancy. *Science, 205*, 215.

Maurer, D. (1975). Infant visual perception: Methods of study. In L. B. Cohen & P. Salapatek (Eds.), *Infant perception: From sensation to cognition* (Vol. 1). New York: Academic Press, 1975.

Maurer, D., & Barrera, M. (1981). Infants' perception of natural and distorted arrangements of a schematic face. *Child Development, 52*, 196–202.

Maurer, D., & Lewis, T. L. (1979). A physiological explanation of infants' early visual development. *Canadian Journal of Psychology, 33*, 232–252.

Maurer, D., & Martello, M. (1980). The discrimination of orientation by young infants. *Vision Research, 3*, 201–204.

Maurer, D., & Salapatek, P. (1976). Developmental changes in the scanning of faces by young infants. *Child Development, 47*, 522–527.

Maurer, D., & Young, R. (1983). Newborns' following of natural and distorted arrangements of facial features. *Infant Behavior and Development, 6,* 127–131.

McDonnell, P. M., & Doyle, A. (1980). *Development of sensitivity to secondary depth cues.* Paper presented at the international Conference on Infant Studies, New Haven, CT.

McGurk, H. (1974). Visual perception in young infants. In B. Foss (Ed.), *New perspectives in child development.* Middlesex: Penguin.

McKenzie, B. E., & Day, R. H. (1972). Distance as a determinant of visual fixation in early infancy. *Science, 178,* 1108–1110.

McKenzie, B. E., & Over, R. (1983). Young infants fail to imitate facial and manual gestures. *Infant Behavior and Development, 6,* 85–95.

McKenzie, B. E., Tootell, H. E., & Day, R. H. (1980). The development of visual size constancy during the first year of human infancy. *Developmental Psychology, 16,* 163–174.

Meltzoff, A. N., & Borton, R. W. (1979). Intermodal matching by human neonates. *Nature (London), 282,* 403–404.

Meltzoff, A. N., & Moore, M. K. (1977). Imitation of facial and manual gestures by human neonates. *Science, 198,* 75–78.

Meltzoff, A. N., & Moore, M. K. (1979). Interpreting "imitative" responses in early infancy. *Science, 205,* 217–219.

Meltzoff, A. N., & Moore, M. K. (1983a). Methodological issues in studies of imitation: Comments on McKenzie & Over and Koepke et al. *Infant Development and Behavior, 6,* 103–108.

Meltzoff, A. N., & Moore, M. K. (1983b). Newborn infants imitate adult facial expressions. *Child Development, 54,* 702–709.

Meltzoff, A. N., & Moore, M. K. (1983c). The origins of imitation in infancy: Paradigm, phenomena and theories. In L. P. Lipsitt & C. Rovee-Collier (Eds.), *Advances in infancy research* (Vol. 2). Norwood, NJ: Ablex.

Mendelson, M. J., Haith, M. M., & Goldman, S. (1978). *Scanning of faces and responsiveness to social cues in infant rhesus monkeys.* Paper presented at the International Conference on Infant Studies, Providence, RI.

Milewski, A. E. (1976). Infants' discrimination of internal and external pattern elements. *Journal of Experimental Child Psychology, 22,* 229–246.

Milewski, A. E. (1979). Visual discrimination and detection of configurational invariance in 3-month infants. *Developmental Psychology, 15,* 357–363.

Miller, D. J. (1972). Visual habituation in the human infant. *Child Development, 43,* 481–493.

Mills, M., & Melhuish, E. (1974). Recognition of mother's voice in early infancy. *Nature (London), 252,* 123–124.

Muir, D., Abraham, W., Forbes, B., & Harris, L. (1979). The ontogenesis of an auditory localization response from birth to four months of age. *Canadian Journal of Psychology, 33,* 320–333.

Muir, D. W., Humphrey, G. K., Dodwell, P. C., & Humphrey, D. E. (in preparation). *The perception of vectorpatterns by 4-month-old infants.*

Nelson, C. A., & Horowitz, F. D. (1983). The perception of facial expressions and stimulus motion by two- and five-month-old infants using holographic stimuli. *Child Development, 54,* 868–877.

Noton, D., & Stark, L. (1971). Scanpaths in saccadic eye movements while viewing and recognizing patterns. *Vision Research, 11,* 929–942.

Olson, G. M., & Sherman, T. (1983). Attention, learning and memory in infants. In M. M. Haith & J. J. Campos (Eds.), *Handbook of child psychology* (Vol. 2). New York: Wiley.

Owsley, C. J. (1983). The role of motion in infants' perception of solid shape. *Perception, 12,* 707–717.

Palmer, S. E. (1982). Symmetry, transformation and the structure of perceptual systems. In J. Beck (Ed.), *Organization and representation in perception.* Hillsdale, NJ: Erlbaum.

Parmelee, A. H., & Sigman, M. (1976). Development of visual behavior and neurological organization in pre-term and full-term infants. In A. Pick (Ed.), *Minnesota symposia on child psychology* (Vol. 10). Minneapolis: University of Minnesota Press.

Pirenne, M. H. (1970). *Optics, painting, and photography.* London & New York: Cambridge University Press.

Pitts, W. H., & McCulloch, S. W. (1947). How we know universals: The perception of auditory and visual forms. *Bulletin of Mathematical Biophysics, 9,* 127–147.

Pollen, D. A., Lee, J. R., & Taylor, J. H. (1971). How does the striate cortex begin the reconstruction of the visual world? *Science, 173,* 74–77.

Postman, L. (1955). Association and perceptual learning. *Psychological Review, 62,* 438–446.

Robson, J. G. (1975). Receptive fields: Neural representation of the spatial and intensive attributes of the visual image. In E. C. Carterette & M. P. Friedman (Eds.), *Handbook of perception: Vol. 5. Seeing.* New York: Academic Press.

Robson, K. (1967). The role of eye-to-eye contact on maternal infant attachment. *Journal of Child Psychology and Psychiatry, 8,* 13–25.

Rose, G., & Lindsley, D. (1968). Development of visually evoked potentials in kittens: Specific and non-specific responses. *Journal of Neurophysiology, 31,* 607–623.

Rose, S. A. (1977). Infants' transfer of response between two-dimensional and three-dimensional stimuli. *Child Development, 48,* 1086–1091.

Royer, F. L. (1981). Detection of symmetry. *Journal of Experimental Psychology: Human Perception and Performance, 7,* 1186–1210.

Rudel, R. G., & Teuber, H.-L. (1964). Cross modal transfer of shape discrimination by children. *Neuropsychologia, 2,* 1–8.

Ruff, H. A. (1978). Infant recognition of the invariant form of objects. *Child Development, 49,* 293–306.

Ruff, H. A. (1980). The development of perception and recognition of objects. *Child Development, 51,* 981–992.

Ruff, H. A., Kohler, C. J., & Haupt, D. L. (1976). Infant recognition of two- and three-dimensional stimuli. *Developmental Psychology, 12,* 455–459.

Saayman, G., Ames, E. W., & Moffett, A. (1964). Response to novelty as an indicator of visual discrimination in the human infant. *Journal of Experimental Child Psychology, 1,* 189–198.

Salapatek, P. (1975). Pattern perception in early infancy. In L. B. Cohen & P. Salapatek (Eds.), *Infant perception: From sensation to cognition* (Vol. 1). New York: Academic Press.

Salapatek, P., & Kessen, W. (1966). Visual scanning of triangles by the human newborn. *Journal of Experimental Child Psychology, 3,* 155–167.

Schneider, G. E. (1969). Two visual systems. *Science, 163,* 895–902.

Schwartz, M., & Day, R. H. (1979). Visual shape perception in early infancy. *Monographs of the Society for Research in Child Development, 44,* (Serial No. 182).

Shapley, R., & So, Y. T. (1980). Is there an effect of monocular deprivation on the proportions of X and Y cells in the cat lateral geniculate nucleus? *Experimental Brain Research, 39,* 41–48.

Shepard, R. N. (1981). Psychophysical complementarity. In M. Kubovy & J. R. Pomerantz (Eds.), *Perceptual organization.* Hillsdale, NJ: Erlbaum.

Sherman, S. M., Hoffman, K. P., & Stone, J. (1972). Loss of a specific cell type from dorsal lateral geniculate nucleus in visually deprived cats. *Journal of Neurophysiology, 35,* 532–544.

Sherman, S. M., & Spear, P. D. (1982). Organization of visual pathways in normal and visually deprived cats. *Physiological Reviews, 62,* 738–855.

Sherrod, L. R. (1979). Social cognition in infants: Attention to the human face. *Infant Behavior and Development, 2,* 279–294.

Slater, A., & Sykes, M. (1977). Newborn infants' visual responses to square wave gratings. *Child Development, 48,* 545–554.

Sokolov, E. N. (1963). *Perception and the conditioned reflex.* New York: Macmillan.

Spelke, E., & Owsley, C. J. (1979). Intermodal exploration and knowledge in infancy. *Infant Behavior and Development, 2,* 13–27.

Spinelli, D. N., & Jensen, F. E. (1979). Plasticity: the mirror of experience. *Science, 203,* 75–78.

Spitz, E., & Wolf, K. (1946). The smiling response: A contribution to the ontogenesis of social relations. *Genetic Psychology Monographs, 34,* 57–125.

Stern, D. N. (1974). Mother and infant at play: The dyadic interaction involving facial, vocal and gaze behaviors. In M. Lewis & L. Rosenblum (Eds.), *The effect of the infant on its caregiver.* New York: Wiley.

Stone, J., Dreher, B., & Leventhal, A. (1979). Hierarchical and parallel mechanisms in the organization of visual cortex. *Brain Research Reviews, 1,* 345–394.

Strauss, N. M., & Curtiss, L. E. (1981). *Infant perception of patterns differing in goodness of form.* Paper presented at the Society for Research in Child Development, Boston, MA.

Stucki, M., & Kaufmann-Hayoz, R. (1984). *Infants' recognition of a face revealed through motion: Contribution of internal facial movements and head movements.* Poster presented at the International Conference on Infant Studies, New York.

Sutherland, N. S. (1957). Visual discrimination of orientation and shape by the octopus. *Nature (London), 179,* 11–13.

Tees, R. C. (1968). Effect of early restriction on later form discrimination in the rat. *Canadian Journal of Psychology, 22,* 294–301.

Teller, D. Y. (1979). A forced-choice preferential looking procedure: A psychophysical technique for use with human infants. *Infant Behavior and Development, 2,* 135–153.

Thomas, H. (1973). Unfolding the baby's mind: The infants selection of visual stimuli. *Psychological Review, 80,* 468–488.

Thomas, H., & Jones-Molfese, V. (1977). Infants and I scales: Inferring change from the ordinal stimulus selections of infants to configural stimuli. *Journal of Experimental Child Psychology, 23,* 329–339.

Treiber, F., & Wilcox, S. (1980). Perception of a "subjective" contour by infants. *Child Development, 51,* 915–917.

Ullman, S. (1979). *The interpretation of visual motion.* Cambridge, MA: M.I.T. Press.

Uttley, A. M. (1954). The classification of signals in the nervous system. *Electroencephalogry and Clinical Neurophysiology, 6,* 479–494.

Vine, I. (1973). The role of facial-visual signalling in early social development. In M. von Cranach & I. Vine (Eds.), *Social communications and movement: Studies of interaction and expression in man and chimpanzee.* London: Academic Press.

Volkman, F. C., & Dobson, M. V. (1976). Infant responses of ocular fixation to moving visual stimuli. *Journal of Experimental Child Psychology, 22,* 86–99.

von Noorden, G. K., & Maumenee, A. E. (1968). Clinical observations on stimulus deprivation amblyopia (amblyopia ex anopsia). *American Journal of Ophthalmology, 65,* 220–224.

Vurpillot, E., Ruel, J., & Castrec, A. (1977). L'organization perceptive chez le nourrisson: Résponse au tout au à ses éléments. *Bulletin de Psychologie, 327*, 396–405.

Weiskrantz, L. (1974). The interaction between occipital and temporal cortex in vision: An overview. In F. O. Schmitt (Ed.), *The neurosciences: Third study program.* Cambridge, MA: M.I.T. Press.

White, B., & Held, R. (1966). Plasticity of sensory-motor development in the human infant. In J. F. Rosenblith & W. Allinsmith (Eds.), *The causes of behavior* (2nd ed.). Boston, MA: Allyn & Bacon.

Wilkinson, F., & Dodwell, P. C. (1980). Young kittens can learn complex pattern discriminations. *Nature (London), 284*, 258–259.

Yarbus, A. L. (1967). *Eye movements and vision.* New York: Plenum.

Yonas, A., Pettersen, L., & Lockman, J. J. (1979). Young infants' sensitivity to optical information for collision. *Canadian Journal of Psychology, 33*, 268–276.

Younge-Browne, G., Rosenfeld, H. M., & Horowitz, F. D. (1977). Infant discrimination of facial expressions. *Child Development, 48*, 555–562.

Younger, B. A., & Cohen, L. B. (1983). Infant perception of correlations among attributes. *Child Development, 54*, 858–867.

Zusne, L. (1970). *Visual perception of form.* New York: Academic Press.

2

Development of Visual
Space Perception

ALBERT YONAS
Institute of Child Development
University of Minnesota
Minneapolis, Minnesota 55455

CYNTHIA OWSLEY
Department of Physiological Optics
School of Optometry/The Medical Center
University of Alabama in Birmingham
Birmingham, Alabama 35294

A traditional approach to writing a chapter on the development of space perception is to organize the discussion around what spatial properties the infant is capable of perceiving at certain ages. For example, sections might be devoted to the infant's perception of objects— their size, shape, relative and absolute distances; the infant's perception of events—such as changes in the environment that occur when an object alters position, or when its internal structure changes; or the infant's ability to plan a path of movement through an environment (E. J. Gibson & Spelke, 1983). Many experiments on infant space perception fall readily into these types of categories. We have chosen a different scheme of organization. Rather than organize the chapter in terms of object, event, or spatial property to be perceived, we will approach the development of space perception in terms of the *optical information* which specifies spatial properties to the infant. Borrowing some old perceptual terminology (see Koffka, 1935), our approach is in terms of the proximal stimulus rather than the distal object. Thus this chapter is divided according to three types of stimulus information for depth—binocular, static, and kinetic. In each section we

79

critically review experiments which have examined the effectiveness of depth information in human infancy.

I. SENSITIVITY TO BINOCULAR INFORMATION

Binocular depth perception is based on the fact that under normal circumstances, the two eyes receive slightly different retinal images as they fixate the same point in space. There are two related sources of binocular depth information: (1) the convergence angle of the eyes in bifoveal fixation, and (2) the horizontal disparity between the two retinal images. Although in the typical course of binocular depth perception, convergence and disparity are part of a single coordinated system for perceiving space, theoretically each could serve as depth information in isolation. Thus the developmental question concerns both the emergence of binocular depth perception as a unitary phenomenon and the effectiveness of each cue in isolation (see Aslin & Dumais, 1981, for a detailed consideration of infant binocular vision).

A. Convergence

Binocular convergence provides information about the absolute distance of objects up to about 2 m away from the mature perceiver (Gogel, 1961; von Hofsten, 1976). The convergence angle of the two eyes varies with target distance; smaller angles signify more distant objects. Convergence may be particularly salient information to the young infant; for him or her, near distances are the most accessible regions of the spatial layout. The young infant cannot, of its own volition, explore more distant locations in space because it cannot locomote independently. It thus seems that convergence, as a specifier of near space, could yield depth information which would be useful in the young infant's daily activities.

First, we must examine whether young infants are capable of binocular eye alignment, in order to assess the effectiveness of convergence as depth information in infancy. Early studies on binocular convergence in infancy suggested that neonates were unable to fixate a target binocularly or to move their eyes in a conjugate fashion (e.g., Gesell, Ilg, & Bullis, 1949; Peiper, 1963). These findings, however, are anecdotal and lack rigorous measurement of eye alignment. Hershenson (1964) used a corneal reflection method in which the experimenter determines the point on the display where the two visual axes intersect. He reported that neonates fixated targets binocularly and tended to exhibit conjugate eye movements. Wickelgren (1967, 1969), however, in similar experiments, found that although newborns used both eyes to fixate the same stimulus panel, each eye actually fixated a different region of the panel. Her results indicated that the neonate's eyes tend to diverge slightly: on most trials, the interpupillary distance was slightly larger than would be expected if the eyes were properly converged on the target.

Slater and Findlay (1975) have argued that findings indicating that the neonate's eyes diverge may be unjustified because they are based on the false assumption that the center of the pupil is on the line of sight. In the adult, the visual axis is actually displaced 5° from the optic axis; in the newborn, this displacement is larger, ranging from 8 to 10°. Infants in Wickelgren's studies may not have been fixating the stimulus judged to be in the center of their pupils. Slater and Findlay avoided this problem in their own study by correcting all measurements for the deviation between optic and visual axes in the neonate's eye. In addition, rather than measuring the point on the target where the two axes intersect, they measured the change in angle of convergence as a function of target distance. They found that neonates appropriately converged on stationary targets at 10 and 20 cm but failed to converge on targets at 5 cm. Thus, it appears that the neonate is capable of binocular fixation at certain distances, at least in the presence of stationary targets. Infants' ability to converge on moving targets, however, may not become accurate and reliable until 2 to 3 months. Aslin (1977) examined binocular fixation in infants at 1, 2, and 3 months by measuring the changing vergence angle as a target approached or receded between distances of about 12 and 57 cm from the infant. At 1 month of age, infants exhibited appropriate vergence movements but did so on an insignificant proportion of the trials. Only 2- and 3-month-olds reliably moved their eyes to an extent indicative of bifoveal fixation, a finding that agrees with Ling's earlier report (1942) based on a qualitative analysis of film records. The magnitude and speed of vergence movements increase over the first 3 months.

Together, these studies suggest that binocular fixation can be observed soon after birth and becomes a reliable response to moving targets by 2 months. The focus of the present discussion is the effectiveness of convergence as depth information in early infancy, as assessed through the observation of spatially appropriate behavior. Several studies have examined infants' reaching to an object when the object's position is defined by binocular information (Bower, Broughton, & Moore, 1970; Field, 1977; Gordon & Yonas, 1976). In each of these, both disparity and convergence information were available, so the effectiveness of either cue cannot be isolated. It could be argued that convergence was the predominant cue, since disparities were slight in these experiments (e.g., Yonas, 1979), but as we shall see later, infants are sensitive to disparities as small as 1 min of arc by 5 months. Thus, we cannot conclude that convergence is the predominant cue in these experiments. Nevertheless, these studies are informative and will be reviewed. Bower et al. (1970) reported that 1-week-olds reached out to a virtual object presented by a stereoscopic shadow caster. This finding is somewhat controversial. First, other investigators have not observed directed reaching in the neonate (DiFranco, Muir, & Dodwell, 1978; Ruff & Halton, 1978). Furthermore, it is unclear from their study the extent to which binocular information defined for these infants a specific location in space, or whether binocular cues merely elicited an arm movement toward a nonspecified location. If the latter is the case, then we should be guarded in concluding that binocular information specifies relative locations in a spatial layout. Gordon and Yonas (1976) also used a shadow-casting technique in their study of the reaching and postural behavior of 5-month-olds in the presence of a virtual object positioned within reach or out of reach. In general, the results indicated that the infants distinguished the objects' distances in at least a rudimentary fashion. The infants reached more frequently and engaged in more prehensile activity when viewing near objects; they also tended to move their heads forward when the object was in the far position. Using a similar setup, Bechtoldt and Hutz (1979) found that infants over 5 months of age reached readily to a binocularly specified object. They observed that reaching was qualitatively different in the virtual object versus no-depth trials: reaches to the virtual object involved hand-cupping, shaping, and swiping in front of the screen, whereas reaches in the no-depth trials involved pushing toward the screen with flattened hands or touching the screen. This differential reaching suggests that infants perceived a solid object in front of the screen in the virtual object condition and that they perceived a flat image on the screen in the no-depth condition.

Field (1977), in another virtual object study, used a Fresnel lens to present a binocularly specified object to infants of 3, 5, and 7 months of age. Not until 7 months did the infants exhibit reaching indicative of sensitivity to binocular depth information. Field's failure to find positive results in his 5-month-old group, in contrast to Gordon and Yonas' and Bechtoldt and Hutz's studies, is not readily understood but might be attributed to his use of the Fresnel lens, rather than a stereoscopic shadow caster, for creating the virtual object. A study by Yonas, Oberg, and Norcia (1978) provides additional support for the claim that 5-month-olds can use binocular information to perceive an object's location. Infants at this age responded to an approaching object specified by binocular information alone, whereas $3\frac{1}{2}$-month-old infants failed to do so. In view of these findings, it is reasonable to conclude that convergence, disparity, and/or some combination of the two are effective depth information by 5 months.

Von Hofsten (1977) evaluated infants' ability to use convergence information in locating the position of a target object. He modified the convergence angle necessary for the infant's binocular fixation of the object and observed whether reaches would be directed to the apparent location of the object. Infants aged from 4½ to 8 months wore 4-diopter displacing prisms which decreased binocular convergence, making the object look farther away than it actually was, or wore 10-diopter displacing prisms which increased convergence, making the object look closer than it actually was. Infants were tested under two lighting conditions: in full light, or in the dark with only the target object illuminated. Most reaches were directed to the location of the virtual object. Von Hofsten concluded that convergence is information for absolute depth by 4½ months. It could be argued, however, that the infants were using binocular disparity to localize the virtual object, utilizing the relative depth information provided by their hands and the virtual object. This hypothesis is strengthened by the fact that there was infrequent reaching when the infants were tested in the dark, a condition in which disparity cues relating the distance of hand and object were presumably absent. Convergence information may itself have been inadequate in specifying the virtual object's location. Therefore, von Hofsten's study has the same problem in interpretation as the virtual object studies previously discussed: due to the confounding of disparity and convergence, we cannot know whether either cue alone and/or their combination are effective depth information at 4 to 5 months.

Von Hofsten (1977) proposed that, throughout development, convergence can specify the absolute distance that an infant must extend his arm to reach an object. He combined data on changes in the interocular distance and in the length of the arm during the first 6 years (based on Davenport, 1940, 1944) to arrive at a function that shows that the convergence angle necessary to fixate a point at arm's length remains relatively constant throughout the first 6 years of life. In view of this relationship, he suggested that convergence could specify absolute distance from birth. Although convergence may be *potential* information for absolute distance from early on, it is an open question whether infants actually *use* this information. Some of the skills underlying a perceiver's sensitivity to convergence information, such as binocular eye alignment, are present from birth or at least by the second month, but the effectiveness of convergence as depth information during the first few months remains to be determined.

Before 4 months of age reaching may not be the most fruitful method for measuring depth perception. Because the reaching of young infants lacks the articulation and fine motor control of mature reaching (e.g., DiFranco et al., 1978), researchers may have difficulty making valid conclusions concerning young infants' ability to perceive depth. The impending collision paradigm—in which blinking, head withdrawal, and postural changes are measured—might prove to be more useful in evaluating young infants' sensitivity to convergence. This paradigm has been used to assess the effectiveness of other depth information during the first 4 months (see section on kinetic information in this chapter).

B. Disparity

The disparity between the two retinal images, when the eyes are converging on the same point in space, provides precise information about relative depth (see Kaufman, 1974, for a review). Research to date suggests that infants can detect stereoscopic disparities by 4 months, and perhaps by 2 months. A study by Appel and Campos (1977) used a recovery-from-habituation technique to examine 2-month-olds' ability to discriminate a display with disparity from one without disparity. The displays were created through a stereoscopic projection system with polarizing filters; the subjects wore polarizing goggles. The disparity display consisted of two slides of a toy rabbit, taken from slightly different perspectives. The nondisparity display consisted of the same slide presented to both eyes. The notable result was that there was a significant increment in heart rate for the group shifted from the nondisparity display to the disparity display (but not vice versa). The authors interpreted this result as indicating that 2-month-olds can discriminate between displays when disparity is the only difference. However, there is an alternative explanation of the data: the stimulus to one eye changed when the post-test was presented, thus allowing for the possibility that the discrimination was based on this monocular shape.

Atkinson and Braddick (1976) overcame this problem by using random dot stereograms to assess 2-month-olds' discrimination of disparity from nondisparity, eliminating the possibility that subjects could be making discriminations based on monocular cues. Both a fixation preference and a high-amplitude sucking procedure were used. Only four subjects were tested, two of whom discriminated a disparity from a nondisparity display. Although this study suggests that some infants at 2 months may make stereoscopic discriminations, positive findings with a larger sample of subjects would be more conclusive. Held, Birch, and Gwiazda (1980) have carried out a systematic investigation examining infants' sensitivity to a range of disparities. They used line stereograms in a visual preference procedure in which disparity and nondisparity displays were presented side by side. By 4 months of age, infants exhibited stereoacuity of 1°; by 5 months, they improved to a near-adult level (for this experiment) of 1 min of arc.

Stereoacuity may become quite refined by 4 to 5 months, but when in development does disparity serve as information for depth? Fox, Aslin, Shea, and Dumais (1980) examined this question both cross-sectionally and longitudinally with infants aged between $2\frac{1}{2}$ and 6 months. Using an anaglyph method, they presented infants with a dynamic, random-element form, which moved either to the left or right on a given trial. In the cross-sectional study, at $3\frac{1}{2}$ months, infants visually tracked the moving form at intermediate disparities (45 and 134 min of arc) but responded at chance level when viewing disparities so high that they exceeded adult fusional limits, as would be expected of adults under these circumstances. In the longitudinal study, this pattern of responding emerged between $3\frac{1}{2}$ and 6 months. Fox et al.'s conclusion is that infants were perceiving the form in depth, but another interpretation of these findings should be entertained. Tracking behavior can be used in a rather elegant way to indicate that infants can detect horizontal disparities in the visual field which change over time, but the tracking response does not necessarily imply that depth was perceived. It is possible that the detection of disparity is linked to a neural program for the control of eye movements and that the pickup of spatial information on the basis of stereoscopic cues develops later. The authors' interpretation could be strengthened by either (1) a "transfer" experiment in which a visual response (preference, habituation) is generalized from an object specified by one type of depth information to that object specified by another type of depth information (see Owsley, 1983; Yonas & Pick, 1975), or (2) an experiment measuring an adaptive, spatially meaningful behavior such as avoidance of an approaching object.

In summary, convergence may be an effective source of depth information by $4\frac{1}{2}$ to 5 months (Gordon & Yonas, 1976; von Hofsten, 1977; Yonas, Oberg, & Norcia, 1978), but studies to date have not successfully demonstrated the effectiveness of convergence in isolation from disparity. It does seem clear, however, that infants' eyes can converge accurately on targets perhaps as early as birth, and reliably by 2 months (Aslin, 1977; Slater & Findlay, 1975). As for infants' responsiveness to retinal disparity, stereoacuity reaches near-adult levels by 5 months (Held et al., 1980). Disparity appears to be effective depth information for infants by $3\frac{1}{2}$ months (Fox et al., 1980), although more research using the transfer paradigm or adaptive responses would strengthen this finding.

Reliable and accurate convergence of the eyes and responsiveness to small retinal disparities emerge at approximately the same time: 2 to 5 months, depending upon one's construal of the literature. This fact is not surprising when we recognize that binocular convergence and disparity detection are part of a coordinated system for perceiving depth. An issue that developmental research might fruitfully examine is how these abilities interact in development. For example, does detection of disparity depend upon the maturation of an accurate and reliable convergence system? Alternatively, does accurate binocular alignment require a fine-grained sensitivity to retinal disparity? Shea and Fox (1980) have begun to address these questions using the dynamic stereogram technique developed by Fox et al. (1980). They have reported that tracking a stereoscopically defined form was correlated with age, using subjects ranging in age from $2\frac{1}{2}$ to $4\frac{1}{2}$ months. Convergence on an approaching and receding target was also correlated with age, but the two skills—convergence and tracking the stereoscopic form—were not correlated with each other. Accommodation of the lens is also crucial to the successful functioning of binocular depth perception, and its role in relation to the other binocular functions should therefore be investigated. Aslin and Jackson (1979) have examined accommodative convergence in the young infant, reporting that this synergistic relationship is present by 2 months. Clearly, more research is needed concerning the interplay of these visual functions in development and how they relate to the infant's perception of a three-dimensional world.

II. SENSITIVITY TO STATIC MONOCULAR INFORMATION

If the reader were to look up from this page, the three-dimensional layout of the room would be immediately apparent. If the reader then closed one eye, binocular depth information would be eliminated, yet there would be very little loss of spatial definition, especially if the observer's head were in motion, making kinetic depth information available. If we take this scenario one step further, and remove kinetic information from the array, perhaps by asking the observer to minimize eye, head, and body movement and by preventing object movement, the observer would still perceive a world in three dimensions. The room would not appear as an arrangement of two-dimensional patches of color. Clearly, there must be a great deal of information for three-dimensional layout available to a single eye at a stationary point of observation when the optic array is static or frozen. This type of depth information is called static monocular information and is not dependent for its existence on continuous optical transition, or motion.

Static depth cues are often called "pictorial cues" because they are used by artists to create the impression of depth. In fact, it was the Renaissance artist Leonardo da Vinci who first described many of the depth cues that can be used by the painter. Examples of information in static arrays are relative size, shadows, interposition, linear perspective, texture gradients, and aerial perspective. Static monocular information is not limited to pictures, however, but is available in most real-world settings. This section will describe what is known about the early development of sensitivity to static monocular depth information.

One type of depth information available to the single eye may be based on accommodation of the lens. Accommodation is, at best, a weak cue to depth even at short distances (Heineman, Tulving, & Nachmias, 1959; see Hochberg, 1971, for review Künnapas, 1968;), so it will not be discussed in this section.

Although some early researchers (see Wilcox & Teightsoonian, 1971) believed that preschool-age children are insensitive to pictorial depth, it has been amply demonstrated in recent years that preschoolers respond to several types of pictorial information for three-dimensional layout. Yonas and Hagen (1973) found that when 3-year-olds were asked to point to the larger of two pictured objects, placed at different distances but identical in retinal size, their choice was influenced by the texture gradient information for the distance of the objects. Using a similar method, Benson and Yonas (1973) found that 3-year-olds also respond to linear perspective information when making size judgments.

Olson and Boswell (1976) and Olson, Cooper, and Yonas (1980) have pointed out that although the studies described above may provide evidence that 3-year-olds have some degree of size constancy based on static cues, these studies do not necessarily assess depth sensitivity per se. They point out that the judgment of a pictured object's size may be based on the amount of texture on which the object is resting (J. J. Gibson, 1950). To assess distance perception more directly, Olson and Boswell (1976) asked 2-year-old children to make relative depth judgments. They found that interposition and height in the picture plane were effective depth cues for these children.

Other important sources of static depth information are shadows, both attached shadows, as when an object has internal shading, and cast shadows. By 3 years of age, children can use the orientation of shading to distinguish convexities from concavities (Benson & Yonas, 1973; Yonas, Kuskowski, & Sternfels, 1979). Three-year-olds can also use the shape of the shadow cast by an object to judge correctly the object's shape and orientation (Yonas, Goldsmith, & Hallstrom, 1978). Furthermore, this study showed that they can determine an object's distance according to the location of the shadow the object casts and can judge whether the object is floating above or resting on a surface.

Given that by age 3, children are responsive to certain static cues, we will now explore the *onset* of sensitivity to static monocular information. Throughout our discussion, it will be apparent that one must be very careful in making inferences about infants' sensitivity to three-dimensional properties of the stimulus in situations when it may be equally, if not more appropriate, to conclude that they are responding only to two-dimensional pattern and not depth itself. Our discussion will center around three kinds of experiments: (1) experiments using pictures, (2) constancy experiments, and (3) analytic experiments on static information.

A. Experiments Using Pictures

An experiment by Hochberg and Brooks (1962) on picture perception in a 19-month-old boy illustrates our point about inference. Pictures were deliberately excluded from the child's environment, with reasonable success, until the child was 19 months old. Any pictured objects that he saw were not named. Nevertheless, on initial presentation of the pictures at 19 months, the child correctly named several pictured objects. He was able to transfer names learned with solid objects to both photographs and line drawings of the objects. It is evident from the child's transfer of words from the real object to the pictured object that he was not responding to the pictures simply as flat, two-dimensional surfaces that varied in the color and darkness of the pigment on the surface. It is possible, however, that the child based his identifications on the similarity between silhouettes of real objects and the two-dimensional patterns in the pictures. That is, the child need not have perceived any inherent tridimensionality in the pictures to have matched them with the appropriate real object. Whatever one's interpretation, however, the finding that a 19-month-old child regards an outline (as in the line drawings) as the edge of an object is quite remarkable in itself.

A great many studies of infant's responses to faces have used pictures of faces rather than real faces, partly for the convenience of the experimenter, thereby making these serendipitous experiments on pictorial information. In many of these studies, infants responded to the pictured face with the same behavior elicited by a real face. For example, infants at 4 months will smile when presented a picture face (e.g., Kagan, Henker, Hen-tou, & Lewis, 1966) and will look longer at a pictured face which is smiling than one that is not smiling (Le Barbera, Izard, Vietze, & Parisi, 1976). While these studies suggest that 4-month-olds treat a pictured face as if it represented a three-dimensional object, it is possible that it is not the three-dimensional properties of the face which produce the behavior, but rather, two-dimensional characteristics which are responsible. As the literature on smiling in infancy suggests, smiles can be elicited in young infants by a variety of stimuli, not only three-dimensional representations such as the human face (e.g., Ahrens, 1954; Watson, 1973).

Using a visual habituation–recovery procedure, Dirks and Gibson (1977) have found that 5-month-old infants detect some similarity between a real face and a full-sized color slide of a face. Infants who were first habituated to a live face showed no change in fixation time when presented with a photograph of the same face in a posttest. However, when the face and slide differed in gross features (such as hair color), they found an increase in the duration of fixation (dishabituation). The variations in luminance on the projected slide may be treated by the infant's visual system not simply as variations in colored light, but as information for the layout and reflectance of surfaces. We must also consider that the two-dimensional pattern of light on both the live face and the slide are probably quite similar and could thereby account for infants treating the live face and its two-dimensional representation as the same. Therefore, this study does not necessarily demonstrate that infants detect the three-dimensional shape of the pictured faces. Further, it is possible that the differentiation of three-dimensional shapes may play only a small part in the identification of an individual face. Perhaps a visual process involving the analysis of two-dimensional pattern alone is sufficient for this perceptual skill.

Cohen's (1977) study is another study that could be interpreted as an indication that pictorial depth sensitivity appears in the first year. Using a visual habituation–recovery procedure, he found evidence for a type of shape constancy with photographs of faces taken from different angles. Thirty-week-old infants were able to disregard a change in orientation in a dishabituation test; 18- and 24-week-olds could not. Cohen's results suggest that by 7 to 8 months, infants can abstract features from a pictured face that are invariant under a change in perspective. Whether infants detected the underlying three-dimensional configuration—the face—or whether they treated the different orientations the same on the basis of two-dimensional similarities is once again a moot point.

B. Constancy Experiments

Bower (1965) reported an elegant set of size constancy studies that contrasted the effectiveness of binocular, monocular, and pictorial depth information in a group of 5- to 8-week-old infants. Operant conditioning using a social reinforcer was employed to train infants to turn their heads when presented with a 30-cm cube at a distance of 1 m. Generalization of the head-turning response was assessed when the size and distance of the cube were varied. The transfer displays included the original cube presented at 3 m, a 30-cm cube at 1 m, and a 90-cm cube at 3 m. To evaluate pictorial sensitivity, slides of the displays taken from the infant's point of view were shown on a rear-projection screen.

During the 120-sec transfer test, in which real cubes were presented, infants generalized more to the original 30-cm cube at 3 m than to the 90-cm cube at 3 m, even though it projected a retinal image of the same size as the original training cube. The same result occurred with the infants who viewed the displays monocularly. Bower (1965) concluded that motion parallax provided the critical depth information for the perception of constant physical size (regardless of retinal size) and that binocular information was not necessary. We shall return to this condition in the section on kinetic information.

In contrast, no evidence of size constancy was found when slides were presented. Infants responded very frequently to the picture of the 90-cm cube presented at 3 m (an average of 96 responses were produced in 120 sec; the original training cube elicited 95 responses). Although this cube differed from the training cube in pictured size and distance, it was the same in size on the rear-projection screen. It was the size on the picture plane that controlled the infants' response rates.

This study was extraordinary in its systematic exploration of depth information, but firm conclusions from Bower's study must be tempered by findings of more recent research. In a study using a method similar to Bower's, Day and McKenzie (1977) examined the rate of acquisition of a size discrimination, as indexed by a socially reinforced head-turning response. They found that with all depth cues present, 6- and 12-week-old infants learned to discriminate objects that differed in retinal sizes with real size held constant as rapidly as they learned to discriminate objects that differed in real size with constant retinal size. They concluded that distance is a salient variable for young infants, but their study revealed no evidence of size constancy.

Given the importance of Bower's constancy studies, it is unfortunate that no studies have been published which used his conditioning and generalization method, other than that of Day and McKenzie (1977). One reason replication may be difficult is that there is no detailed description of the method that Bower used to produce the high response rates during training; we do not know how many sessions were involved or how many infants failed to reach the criterion. In regard to the response rate, Bower reported that 40- to 60-day-old infants made 75 responses per minute (a response every 800 msec) during the transfer period. Other investigators who have used social reinforcement to condition the head-turning response (e.g., McKenzie & Day, 1971; Watson & Ramey, 1972), have obtained response rates as low as 10 to 15 responses per minute. With such low response rates, assessment of generalization would be difficult. In a review of research on infant learning, Sameroff and Cavanaugh (1979) have even argued that infants in the age range studied by Bower cannot learn to associate an arbitrary stimulus with a response. They point out that studies purporting to show this type of learning are confounded by effects elicited by the reinforcer and by infants' labile states.

Shape constancy experiments by Day and McKenzie (1973) contrasted the effectiveness of pictorial and nonpictorial depth information in infants' perception of invariant shape. Infant subjects ranged from 6 to 16 weeks old. Habituation of visual fixation was assessed when infants were repeatedly presented with a small cube, either always in the same orientation or in a different orientation on each trial. The duration of fixation declined over the eight habituation trials for both conditions. In another condition, which presented photographs of the cube from different perspectives, infants did not habituate. Day and McKenzie argued that shape constancy was present for the three-dimensional cube shown at varying perspectives, in which kinetic cues were presumably available, but not for the photographs of the cube, in which static information alone was available. Their interpretation, however, must be questioned. Infants who viewed the real cube at different orientations may have habituated because of their failure to discriminate its orientations, rather than because they used the proximal changes over time to perceive an object of a particular shape. Another problem with Day and McKenzie's experiment is that infants' failure to habituate to photographs of the cube at different orientations does not necessarily imply that static information in the photographs ineffectively specified the cube's shape to them. It is possible that infants habituate more slowly to photographs than to real objects, although there have been reports that the converse is true (e.g., Fantz & Nevis, 1967). This possibility could have been tested by habituating infants to photographs of the object in a single orientation as a control. This experiment is not very informative about the roles of static and kinetic depth information in shape constancy.

Before concluding from Bower's (1965) and Day and McKenzie's (1973) work that infants in the first 4 months of life are insensitive to static monocular depth information, one must remember that kinetic, binocular, and perhaps texture information for the flat pictorial surface was present in both studies. Thus it is possible that infants' inability to demonstrate perception of the three-dimensional structure of the picture may be due to interference of this conflicting information with their sensitivity to pictorial depth.

C. Analytic Experiments on Static Information

Yonas, Cleaves, and Pettersen (1978) conducted a series of experiments on sensitivity to pictorial depth that reduced conflicting information for a flat surface. This was achieved in two ways. First, subjects wore an eye patch over one eye to eliminate binocular depth information; second, information for the pictorial surface itself was minimized. The display was a static, fronto-parallel, trapezoidal window (similar to those devised by Ames, 1951) created by photographing a rectangular window that was rotated 45°. The form was cut from the photograph so that the infant could look through the internal spaces of the display. The display provides several types of information for the virtual slant of the surface: linear perspective, shape perspective, and relative size. When viewed monocularly by adults, it elicits a clear experience of a rectangular window slanted so that one side is several inches closer than the other.

It was found in a preliminary experiment that 7-month-old infants reach toward the near rather than the far side of a real rectangular window when it is rotated so that only one side is within reach. Directional reaching in this situation was very consistent, even though each infant wore an eye patch that eliminated binocular depth information.

When the fronto-parallel trapezoidal window was presented to 16- to 30-week-old infants, they tended to reach for the larger (pictorially nearer) side of the window, albeit with less consistency than to the real window. To control for the possibility that infants simply prefer to reach for the larger side of the display, regardless of depth information, a size-control display was created in which one side was smaller than the other but which contained no information that the sides were at different distances from the viewer. The infants reached equally often to both sides of this display. A third display, which appeared to be one rectangle in front of another and which was identical in overall shape to the size-control display, was created to explore the effectiveness of interposition and relative size when perspective information was absent. The infants presented with the interposition display showed some preference to reach for the larger rectangle, but the effect was weak.

The finding of preferential reaching to the pictorially nearer side of the trapezoidal window was replicated in a study that contrasted responsiveness of infants wearing an eye patch to that of infants who viewed the display binocularly. Binocular presentation substantially reduced preferential reaching to the pictorially nearer side of the display, as compared with monocular presentation. Apparently, binocular information for the actual orientation of the display interfered with responsiveness to pictorial information. The study demonstrates that by 7 months of age, infants are sensitive to both pictorial and binocular information for depth.

In contrast, when $4\frac{1}{2}$- to 5-month-old infants were presented with the trapezoidal display, they did not exhibit preferential reaching. However, a second group of infants of the same age (also wearing eye patches) did reach consistently to the nearer side of an actual slanted, rectangular window.

To create a more sensitive measure of responsiveness to the trapezoidal window, Kaufmann, Maland, and Yonas (1981) slanted the trapezoidal window 45° from the fronto-parallel plane so that the smaller side of the window (the pictorially more distant side) was actually closer to the infant than the larger side. Twenty-week-old infants, viewing the display monocularly, were unaffected by the pictorial information and consistently reached to the actually closer side; 29- to 30-week-old infants tended to reach to the more distant side.

The finding that responsiveness to static information appears between the fifth and seventh months is also consistent with a study by Bertenthal, Campos, and Haith (1980). Using a habituation method, they found that at 7 months, infants discriminated between a display which for adults, created the impression of subjective contours defining a form, and a nonillusory display. Results from the 5-month-old group were not clear-cut. Although control conditions cast doubt on explanations that the bases of discrimination were pattern features such as symmetry, it is a large leap to conclude that the infants actually perceived an illusory form. If we grant the authors' conclusion, however, their experiment indicates that at 7 months infants are separating a form from a background plane based on pictorial cues.

Exploration is just beginning into the onset of infants' sensitivity to the various types of static monocular depth information. So far, the available data support the hypothesis that sensitivity to some types of static information appears between the fifth and seventh months. Although the trapezoidal window study indicates that infants become sensitive to certain static cues by 7 months, the display confounds the effects of relative size, linear perspective, and perhaps texture gradients; thus, it is unclear what particular depth information is detected. Yonas and his colleagues have conducted several studies to explore infants' sensitivity to various depth cues in isolation. The first of these studies examined the development of sensitivity to the cue of relative size.

1. Relative Size

When two objects that are equal in size are at different distances from an observer, the nearer object subtends a larger visual angle than the farther. If the two objects are taken to be approximately equal in distal size, the relationship between the objects' visual angles can be a source of information for the objects' relative distances. This depth cue is called relative size.

Although there is substantial evidence that adults can employ relative size information to perceive relative distance (e.g., Epstein & Baratz, 1964), no research on the development of this ability in infants has been carried out until recently. Yonas, Granrud, and Pettersen (1985) explored sensitivity to relative size in infants from 5 to 7 months of age. In these experiments, infants viewed two different-sized objects of various shapes (squares, circles, and triangles) presented side by side suspended in front of a dark vertical surface. The two objects were always at equal distances from the infant.

To establish the effectiveness of the illusion produced by the displays, they were first presented to adults both monocularly and binocularly. Pairs of triangles, squares, and diamonds were presented; the larger object was approximately twice the size of the smaller shape. When adults viewed the displays monocularly, the depth effect was striking. They reported that the larger object appeared closer than the smaller one on approximately 80% of the trials and that the objects appeared equidistant on 20% of the trials. When the displays were viewed with two eyes, the larger object was judged closer much less often—on only about 30% of the trials. However, some depth effect remained, since the smaller object was judged closer only 7% of the time (the objects were judged to be equidistant on the remaining trials). Furthermore, when the pair of objects differed in shape and in orientation of contours, adults viewing them monocularly perceived the larger one as closer just as frequently as they did when the objects did not differ in shape. Apparently, dissimilarity in shape does not diminish the relative size effect for adults.

In the relative size experiments with infants, reaching was used as an index of depth perception. Granrud, Yonas, and Pettersen (1984) found that infants as young as 5 months of age will reach for the nearer of two objects with great consistency if sufficient information for relative distance is available. The goal of this study was to determine whether relative size information for depth could influence reaching in the same way when binocular information for the objects' equal distance was eliminated. Seven-month-old infants were presented with pairs of disks and triangles both monocularly and binocularly. They showed a significantly greater tendency to reach for the larger object in the monocular condition than in the binocular condition.

This same pattern of reaching preferences was observed when a group of $5\frac{1}{2}$-month-olds (22 to 24 weeks) was presented with a pair of disks. They reached for the larger disk on 65% of the trials with monocular presentation, but on only 50% of the binocular trials. For the youngest infants studied (20- to 22-week-olds), behavior in the monocular and binocular conditions did not differ. In both conditions, they reached more frequently to the larger object.

The results indicate that for 7- and 5½-month-old infants the relationship between angular sizes of objects is an effective source of information for those objects' relative distances. Results from the binocular viewing conditions eliminate the possibility that infants preferred to reach for the larger objects without regard to their apparent distances. If this were the case, infants should have reached more frequently for the larger objects under both binocular and monocular viewing conditions, but no such preference was observed in these older infants. Thus, the most plausible explanation for the results is that infants perceived the larger objects as closer than the smaller objects in the monocular conditions and detected stereoscopic information which specified the objects as equidistant in the binocular conditions. In contrast, the 20- to 22-week-old infants did not provide evidence of sensitivity to relative size.

2. Familiar Size

Another source of distance information based on visual angle is familiar size. If the distal size of an object were known, its visual angle could be a source of information for the object's distance. Yonas, Pettersen, and Granrud (1982) studied infants' sensitivity to familiar size as information for distance. Again, a preliminary experiment tested adults in order to establish the effectiveness of the experimental displays. Adults judged the apparent distances of two sets of monocularly viewed photographs of faces (a familiar class of objects). One set was larger than life size, the other was smaller. Another group judged the distances of monocularly viewed checkerboard patterns (a class of objects with no familiar size) that were the same sizes as the faces.

Adults gave clear evidence that familiar size influenced perceived distance, corroborating earlier research on this topic (e.g., Ittleson, 1951). While the small face was judged to be more than twice as far from the viewer as the large face, distances judged for small and large checkerboards were not significantly different. Furthermore, adults judged the large faces to be at a distance within, and the small faces to be at a distance well beyond, reach for 5- to 7-month-old infants. Therefore, if infants viewing these displays monocularly perceive them as adults do, we would expect them to reach more often to the large than to the small faces. Moreover, from the adult data we would expect no differential reaching for the large and small checkerboards when viewed monocularly, or for the faces when viewed binocularly, since stereoscopic information would specify the large and small faces as equidistant. These hypotheses were tested with 5- and 7-month-old infants, using the same displays. Reaching was again used as a index of infants' spatial perception.

For the 7-month-olds under monocular viewing conditions, the large face elicited more seconds of reaching than the small face. This difference was significantly larger than the analogous differences observed in the binocularly viewed face condition or in the monocularly viewed checkerboard condition. For the 5-month-olds there were no significant differences in reaching duration among the three conditions.

The results indicate that in the monocular condition the 7-month-olds perceived the large faces as within reach and the small faces as out of reach. As in the relative size experiments, the control conditions rule out the possibility that the infants exhibited reaching preferences without regard to the displays' perceived distances. If the infants simply preferred to reach for large objects, we would also expect more reaching for the large checkerboard then for the small one, but no preference was observed. Furthermore, the infants were not simply showing a preference to reach for large faces, since binocular viewing eliminated the reaching preference observed in the monocular condition. Presumably, the infants detected binocular information which specified the faces as equidistant and therefore, they reached equally for the large and small faces.

We cannot draw firm conclusions from the 5-month-old's performance. The duration-of-reaching results were similar for both age groups, but the experimental effects for the 5-month-olds were smaller. While this suggests that 5-month-olds may use familiar size as distance information, the results are not clear. It is evident, however, that for infants as young as 7 months of age, the visual angle of an object, in conjunction with knowledge about the object's distal size, can be a source of information for the perception of distance. This finding may be theoretically important since it indicates that experience can influence spatial perception.

Another study completed by Granrud, Haake, and Yonas (1985) further investigated 7-month-olds' ability to use familiar size in distance perception, using objects with which the infants had only brief experience. Two pairs of objects (A and B) were constructed, the pairs differing in shape and color, and the members of each pair being identical except in size. During a familiarization period of 6 to 10 min, each infant played with one object from each pair—that is, with the large version of object A and a small object B, or vice versa. In the test, half of the infants monocularly viewed a simultaneous presentation of the large versions of objects A and B, suspended at equal distances from the infant. If the infant recalled that, for example, object B had previously been small relative to object A, one would expect more reaches for object B when it projected a retinal size equal to that of A, specifying that B was now the closer of the two. The other half of the infants viewed the same situation binocularly. The prediction was that with binocular depth cues available, reaches would be equally distributed between the objects, reflecting their actual equal distances from the infant.

The results confirmed predictions. In the monocular condition, a significantly greater proportion of infants' reaches were to the object which was small during familiarization; reaching was equal to the two objects for infants in the binocular condition. These results indicate that, in the absence of information to the contrary, 7-month-olds perceive the increased retinal size of the object as reflecting a decrease in distance and reach to what therefore appears to be the closer object. What is surprising is that familiar size information operates as a source of depth information after such brief experience with novel objects. This finding refutes the notion that the familiar size effect is, for adults, a result of cognitive strategy. It appears more likely that the effect, rather than reflecting a conscious decision, is an example of a powerful direct impact of memory on perception.

Unlike 7-month-olds, 5-month-olds in this study gave no evidence of sensitivity to familiar size. These infants reached equally for the two objects in the test phase of the experiment. We cannot conclude from this result that 5-month-olds are insensitive to familiar size. It is possible, of course, that future studies might reveal sensitivity in these infants. However, if 5-month-olds are insensitive to familiar size it is probably not due to an inability to encode and store information about objects in memory, since results from a number of studies suggest that 5-month-olds have impressive memory capabilities (e.g., Fagan, 1973). Rather, insensitivity to familiar size would most likely be due to an inability to use memory in perception. The findings of Granrud, Haake, and Yonas (1985) therefore, suggest the hypothesis that while 7-month-olds' perception is not completely determined by the information present in the visual input, insofar as memory can be used to perceive distance from visual angle, 5-month-olds' perception may be determined directly by the visual input. The ability to use memory in perception might first appear between 5 and 7 months of age.

3. Pictorially Specified Interposition

Research in computer vision exploring the information available in visual scenes has suggested that in two-dimensional images, line intersection features provide information for interposition and relative distance. Clowes (1971), Huffman (1971), and Waltz (1972) have made exhaustive studies of the ways edges of polyhedrons may intersect in two-dimensional images (for a review of this work, see Winston, 1977). They have found that given certain constraints (such as excluding special frozen viewpoints), when a "T" vertex occurs it is always true that the crossbar of the T is the edge of an occluding surface and that the stem of the T is the edge of an occluded surface. Thus, T-intersections at the edges of objects could provide a moving perceiver with invariant information for the spatial layout of objects. Intersection features could be ambiguous from certain frozen station points, as in some of Ames' well-known demonstrations (Ittleson, 1952). For a freely moving observer, the constraint against stationary viewpoints is unnecessary, since it is unlikely that, given the infinite number of possible viewpoints, one's eye would ever be located at the exact station point from which a T-intersection would be ambiguous. Moreover, even if one found this particular station point, any movement would eliminate the ambiguity. Finally, while a given retinal image at a fixed station point could be produced by an infinite number of distal layouts, a T-intersection which remains a T-intersection through a change in a moving observer's viewpoint can be produced by only one distal layout: interposition of surfaces. Therefore, for a moving observer, T-shaped intersections seem to be a source of specific information for distal interposition.

A study by Granrud and Yonas (1984) was conducted to test the hypothesis, based on the work by Clowes, Huffman, and Waltz, that the human visual system detects T-shaped intersections as specifying overlapping surfaces. The subjects were 5- and 7-month-old infants. Reaching was observed as an index of the perceived relative distances of sections of the test displays. In each experiment, infants viewed test displays monocularly to avoid attenuation of the effectiveness of pictorial interposition by binocular information. Figure 1 shows a schematic drawing of the test displays for the experiments. The outer contours were identical in the "T" and "Y" displays. These two displays differed only in their interior lines. The interior lines formed T-shaped intersections in one condition and formed Y-shaped intersections in the other condition. It was hypothesized that T-intersections should specify overlapping surfaces and that infants should reach more frequently for the apparently nearer surface. It was also predicted that Y-shaped intersections should specify no differential distance and, therefore, infants should show no reaching preference when viewing the Y-intersection display.

The 7-month-olds showed a significant preference to reach for the apparently nearer area in the "T" condition and showed no reaching preference in the "Y" condition. The reaching preference in the "T" condition suggests that the display was perceived as consisting of interposed surfaces. In the "Y" condition, the lack of a reaching preference suggests that no section of this display was seen as nearer than the others. The 5-month-olds showed no reaching preferences.

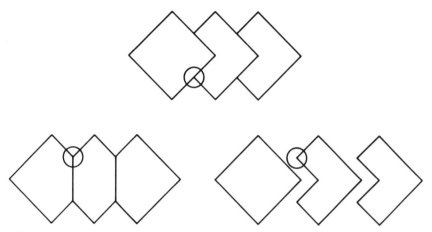

Figure 1. Schemata drawing of test displays used in interposition study. "T," "Y," and "L" shaped intersections are circled.

It could be argued that the 7-month-olds preferred to reach for the diamond-shaped region of the display rather than for the arrowhead-shaped sections, and that this preference, rather than the perception of differential distance, was responsible for the results in the "T" condition. A second experiment tested this hypothesis by separating the sections of the display. If infants preferred to reach for diamond-shaped section, we would expect to observe this preference even when information for overlap was removed from the display. Seven- and 5-month-olds were presented with the "T" and "L" displays pictured in Figure 1. Again the 7-month-olds preferred to reach for the side of the display that the T-intersections specify as nearer and showed no significant preference in the separation condition. Thus, it seems that the 7-month-olds were not simply reaching for the diamond-shaped area. This result supports the hypothesis that the 7-month-olds' reaching preference in the first experiment was a result of the perceived relative distances of the test displays' sections and was not due to a preference to reach for a particular shape. The 5-month-olds showed no significant reaching preference in either condition of the second experiment. Thus, we found no evidence that 5-month-olds perceive spatial layout on the basis of pictorial interposition.

Although these results demonstrate 7-month-olds' sensitivity to pictorially specified interposition, we cannot conclude with certainty that intersection features constitute the proximal stimulus variables responsible for perceived interposition. While infants' reaching preferences could be predicted from the displays' intersection features, they could also have been predicted on the basis of gestalt organization principles such as completeness or simplicity (Chapanis & McCleary, 1953; Dinnerstein &

Wertheimer, 1957; Hochberg, 1971). One could argue that three squares at different distances constitute a simpler or more complete precept than the alternative of one square and two equidistant interlocking arrowheads, since three squares might entail fewer lines and angles than the alternative (Hochberg & McAlister, 1953).

4. Shape from Shading

We have demonstrated infants' sensitivity to one final pictorial depth cue: shading. Shading provides information for the three-dimensional shapes of objects because of the lawful relationship that exists between the orientation of a surface and the luminance level in the retinal image projected by that surface. A surface that is oriented orthogonally to the source of illumination will be highly illuminated and will reflect a large amount of light. A surface that is oblique or parallel to the incident light will be less strongly illuminated and will reflect less light. As a result, for surfaces with uniform reflectance, smoothly varying gradients of luminance (i.e., shading) in the proximal stimulus correspond to changes in surface orientation relative to the source of illumination (when illumination is constant across a scene). This correspondence between distal surface orientation and shading in the proximal stimulus can provide a perceiver with information for the three-dimensional shapes of objects (J. J. Gibson, 1950, 1966). Figure 2 illustrates shading information for shape. Adults usually see this as a photograph of a surface containing a convexity (the region more brightly illuminated on top) and a concavity (the region more brightly illuminated on the bottom). When the photograph is inverted, the depth reverses. This demonstrates that shading is the only information for shape in the photograph. It also indicates that the visual system employs an "assumption," or constraint, that light comes from above.

In the first study of the development of sensitivity to shading, Benson and Yonas (1973) presented 3-year-olds with a surface containing a convexity and trained them to point to the convexity. They then showed the children a photograph of the surface containing only shading information for shape (see Figure 2). The children exhibited transfer of training to the photograph, pointing to the "convexity," the area which is brighter on top, on 85% of the trials. In a similar study, Granrud, Yonas, and Opland (1985) found that 7-month-olds perceive shape from shading. There were two conditions in the experiment. In one condition, 7-month-olds viewed a surface containing a convexity and a concavity. In the other, they viewed an enlargement of the photograph in Figure 2. With monocular vision, the infants reached preferentially for the convexity when viewing both the actual surface and the photograph. With binocular vision, the

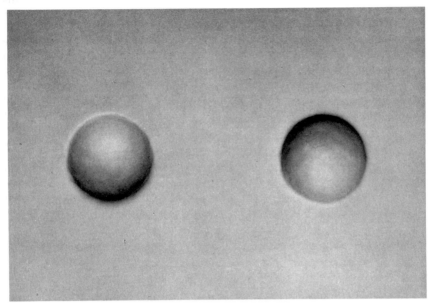

Figure 2.   Displays used in shape from shading study.

infants reached preferentially for the convexity in the actual surface but reached equally for the two areas in the photograph.

The results from the real surface condition indicated that 7-month-olds reach preferentially for convexities. The infants' preference to reach for the "convexity" in the monocularly viewed photograph indicated that they perceived this region to be an actual convexity. This result demonstrated these infants' perception of shape from shading. This conclusion is supported by the finding of no reaching preference when the infants viewed the photograph binocularly, which indicated that the infants' reaching was based on perceived depth and not on nonspatial proximal stimulus variables, such as a preference to reach for the region in the photograph that was more highly illuminated on top. Five-month-olds, in contrast, showed no significant reaching preference when viewing the photograph monocularly; thus, they showed no evidence of depth perception from shading.

Infants' perception of shape from shading is particularly interesting because it illustrates the sorts of constraints, or "decoding principles" (Johansson, 1970), that might operate in the visual system. Information for an object's shape is confounded in retinal image luminance since a given luminance value could result from an infinite number of combinations of three variables: surface orientation, surface reflectance, and illumination intensity. In order to recover information for shape from luminance gradients (i.e., shading), the visual system apparently constrains the possible interpretations of the proximal stimulus through a process analogous to making assumptions about the scene that is being perceived. If there is no evidence to the contrary, the visual system seems to operate on the "assumptions," or constraints, that illumination comes from above, that illumination is uniform across the scene, and that reflectance is uniform across a surface (Barrow & Tenenbaum, 1978; Horn, 1975). Without these constraints, shading would be ambiguous and there would be no basis for perceiving a convexity and a concavity in Figure 2. That infants perceive a convexity and a concavity when viewing this photograph suggests that the visual system incorporates these constraints very early in life.

A consistent trend has emerged from the results of these studies on pictorial depth information. In each study (trapezoidal window, relative size, familiar size, interposition, and shading), 7-month-olds have shown sensitivity to pictorial information, while 5-month-olds have not. In addition, in the relative size study, 5½-month-olds were found to be sensitive to pictorial information. Thus, it seems that sensitivity to pictorial depth information first appears at some time after 20 to 22 weeks and before 30 weeks. This hypothesis is consistent with results from Bertenthal et al. (1980) and Kellman and Spelke (1983) which suggest that infants under 5 months of age are not sensitive to configurational information such as subjective contours or the gestalt principles of similarity and good continuation.

III. SENSITIVITY TO KINETIC INFORMATION

Kinetic information for depth is produced by continuously changing structure in the retinal array ("optical motion"), which can be either observer-induced, as when the observer moves his eyes, head, and/or body, or environmentally induced, as when a viewed object moves. Examples of kinetic information are motion parallax, optical expansion, and accretion–deletion of texture and perspective transformation (see J. J. Gibson, 1950, 1966, for an overview).

Kinetic variables are a readily available source of depth information throughout development. The perceptual process is active; the observer at any age is capable of engaging in exploratory movements which produce optical motion. Furthermore, unlike binocular depth cues, kinetic information does not depend on precise and reliable interocular coordination, which is uncommon in the very young infant (see Section I on binocular information). Although kinetic information is available to the infant perceiver, only empirical work can determine whether he uses information produced by a moving array. Yet many experiments on infant visual perception utilize two-dimensional stationary stimuli; a tacit assumption in much of this work is that a moving display is somehow more difficult for the infant to process and thus is a hindrance to his effort to perceive the world. This notion deserves to be rejected for at least two reasons. First, several experiments discussed in this section indicate that infants are adept at extracting information about spatial properties from moving displays. Not only does empirical work suggest that infants are sensitive to kinetic information, but it also implies that in the first few months of infancy, kinetic information may be the *only* effective type of depth cue. Second, a great deal of psychophysical work with adults has implicated the existence of visual mechanisms specially tuned to motion (see Sekuler, 1975, for review). In this framework, motion is not more complex for the perceiver than is static pattern. Each is a different type of stimulus property; motion can be characterized as a temporal property, while static pattern can be characterized as a spatial property. Neither property of visual stimulation—temporal or spatial—is *a priori* simpler in a psychological sense, for what would simpler mean? Nor can we assume that in development infants are sensitive to one type of property before the other. This is an empirical question, and the development of temporal and spatial mechanisms certainly deserves more attention (e.g., Regal, 1981; Salapatek & Banks, 1977; Volkmann & Dobson, 1976).

This section is organized around five types of experiments concerning the role of kinetic information in infants' perception of space: (1) the perception of impending collision, (2) the role of accretion and deletion of texture, (3) the perception of object shape and size, (4) the perception of rigidity and elasticity, and (5) visually controlled postural stability.

A. Perceiving Impending Collision

When an object or surface approaches a perceiver, it projects a centrifugal flow pattern which serves as information for the impending collision of perceiver and object (J. J. Gibson, 1958; Schiff, 1965). A symmetrical contraction of texture is information for a withdrawing object. At what point in development does the optical flow projected by these events become effective depth information? Bower et al. (1970) studied perception of impending collision in infants less than 3 weeks old. Infants reacted to the approach of a real object with a response consisting of three components: rotating the head upward, bringing the hands between object and face, and widening the eyes. Violent upset was also reported. Bower et al. interpreted these responses as avoidance behavior. In another experiment reported in the same paper, the authors attempted to disentangle the roles of optical and air pressure factors in eliciting the avoidance behavior. An optical display was produced by a shadow-caster apparatus similar to one used by Schiff (1965). An approaching or withdrawing object was projected on a screen. The optical result was an expanding or contracting closed form, corresponding to the approach and withdrawal, respectively, of an object. In this situation the only information available for impending collision would be optical expansion of a closed form. The results were described in a qualitative fashion: "No full-scale avoidance response occurred to the reduced visual presentation, although the components were discernable" (Bower et al., 1970, p. 195). While there appears to be some suggestion that infants were sensitive to the optical information for collision, it is difficult to interpret the results since the data were not presented in a detailed fashion.

Ball and Tronick (1971) also found avoidancelike behaviors to optical displays specifying an approaching object. That is, their 1-month-old subjects moved their heads back and brought their hands between face and object when the object approached, whether it was real or simulated by the shadow-caster. Furthermore, infants distinguished between "hit" and "miss" courses, responding with avoidance behavior only to the former. Together, the Ball and Tronick and Bower et al. (1970) studies imply that infants can use information based on closed-form magnification.

These two experiments used displays with no texture variation; the only information for impending collision was the expansion of a closed contour. Textural flow without a closed contour also specifies approach of a surface, at least for adults. Ball and Vurpillot (1976) compared the effectiveness of texture flow and of closed-form magnification in 2-month-olds' perception of impending collision. Displays were created using a movie camera with a zoom lens. The texture-flow display was an 800-dot pattern that filled the entire screen. During approach and withdrawal of the apparent surface, there were two kinds of changes in the flow field—in the density of elements and in the size of elements. Approach and withdrawal trials differed in the direction of flow. Two other displays were also used: a one-element and a three-element pattern. The elements in both of these displays were comparable to the sizes of closed contour stimuli in previous experiments; that is, they were larger than the elements in the 800-dot display. The crucial difference between the two types of display was that the one- and three-element displays contained no texture flow, whereas the 800-dot display did.

The results were that avoidance behavior occurred only in the approach trials of the 800-dot condition. There were no approach–withdrawal dif-

ferences for the one- and three-element displays. What is especially interesting in this study is that optical flow elicited avoidance in a situation
where closed-form expansion did not. The magnifying contour is theoretically equivocal in its specification of a unique environmental event in that
it corresponds to both an approaching object and an approaching surface
with an aperture in it (J. J. Gibson, 1979). Textural flow, on the other
hand, may be less ambiguous and may in fact be unequivocal in its relationship to a distal property. Because of this, it may be more reliable
information for the inexperienced perceiver.

These experiments suggest that infants as young as 1 to 2 months can
use optical expansion patterns as information for impending collision. Yet
the interpretation of these studies has been challenged by Yonas et al.
(1977). They suggest that the so-called avoidance behavior reported by
previous researchers may be an artifact of the experimental situation.
Most important, the upward head rotation that was consistently reported
by Bower et al. and by Ball and Tronick, and in the Yonas et al. (1977)
replication as well, may be due to tracking of the rising contour of the
expanding pattern. Yonas et al. (1977) found that upward head rotations
occurred in the presence of both an expanding closed form specifying
collision and a rising contour of a nonexpanding form which did not
specify collision. In fact, there was more head movement in response to
the latter. A second experiment by Yonas et al. (1977) presented a collision and a noncollision display. In these displays, when the closed form
expanded, the top contour did not rise. There were no differences in head
movement to the two types of display. Yonas et al.'s work (1977) suggests
that head rotation may be a poor indicator for young infants of a tendency
to avoid impending collision.

The contour-tracking hypothesis has similarly been applied to Ball and
Vurpillot's results with their texture-flow display (Yonas, 1981). Recall
that Ball and Vurpillot observed backward head movement only with the
textured display and not with the closed-contour displays. Yonas (1981)
points out that in the textured display, the moving dots fill the upper half
of the visual field, whereas in the other displays upward motion fills a
smaller area. Therefore, on the basis of Yonas' contour-tracking hypothesis, one would expect a higher frequency of backward head movement in
the texture-flow display.

The role of textural changes in infants' perception of events was also
examined by Carroll and Gibson (1981). They were interested in whether
3-month-olds could distinguish between an approaching object and an
approaching aperture, as when one approaches a doorway. In both cases
there is a symmetrically expanding pattern. Adults have no problem in
visually differentiating the two, so there must be information that speci-

fies each event, other than the magnifying form. J. J. Gibson (1979) suggests that this information is texture change in optical flow, specifically the unique way in which texture is deleted and accreted in each case. Carroll and Gibson used pressure against a headrest as a measure of avoidance and found that there was significantly more backward head movement to the approaching object than to the aperture. The implication is that 3-month-olds can use the different patterns of texture flow to distinguish between the consequences of the two events. Analysis of the video records supported this interpretation. Bower (1977b) reports that he and Dunkeld obtained similar findings. Since there is upward-moving texture in both the object and aperture displays, the contour-tracking hypothesis does not readily account for the results. In fact, it could be argued that in the aperture display, upward flow fills more of the field than in the object display, leading to a prediction opposite to the obtained results.

Two further comments about the Carroll and Gibson study are relevant. First, binocular information may also have been effective in specifying the relative distances of surfaces. Subjects were around 3 months old, the age at which stereopsis has been reported to emerge (Fox et al., 1980). While infants' behavior may have been based on kinetic information such as texture accretion and deletion, Carroll and Gibson's experiment does not unequivocally demonstrate this. Second, from an optical standpoint, the approach of an aperture toward an observer is not the same as the approach of the observer towards an aperture. In both conditions the texture within the aperture undergoes accretion. In addition, in the observer-approach condition there is textural expansion inside the aperture; this is not the case for the aperture-approach condition. Although this point may seem trivial if one's purpose is to demonstrate infants' differentiation of two kinds of flow patterns, it is not trivial from the standpoint of ecological optics (see J. J. Gibson, 1961).

In a reply to Yonas et al.'s article (1977), Bower (1977a) describes data from a study by Dunkeld and himself which cannot be accounted for by the contour-tracking hypothesis. Infants were presented with a polar-projected display of an object either falling forward or rising upward. The former appeared to be on a collision course with the perceiver, while the latter did not. Head movement was recorded by means of a pressure transducer. Parallel projections of the two displays were used as control. If Yonas et al. (1977) are correct, both polar- and parallel-projected objects that rise upward (presenting a rising contour in the visual field) should have elicited backwards head rotation; if the distal event is perceived, however, head movement should only have occurred when the infant viewed the polar projection of the falling object. The data were in line with the latter prediction, supporting Bower's claim that infants visually perceive impending collision during the first month. They apparently did so on the basis of a source of information other than optical expansion. The object rotated downward or upward in this study, producing a continuous perspective transformation.

To complicate the story even further, Yonas, Pettersen, and Lockman (1979) failed to replicate Bower's "object-falling-forward" study. They, too, used pressure changes on the back of the infants' chair as the major dependent measure. Their experiment yielded results opposite to Bower's. There was upward head rotation when the object rotated upward, and downward head rotation when the object fell forward on an apparent collision course with the infant's head. These data are consistent with the contour-tracking hypothesis.

The inconsistency between findings from the Yonas and the Bower laboratories points to the need for evidence concerning infants' perception of impending collision using a dependent measure other than head movement. Pettersen, Yonas, and Fisch (1980) found that blinking may be a suitable dependent measure. Although the probability of a blink to an approaching object is low during the first month (16%), it differs significantly from the probability of a blink to object withdrawal. The probability of a blink to approach increases during early development from 16% at 6 weeks, to 45% at 8 weeks, to 75% at 10 weeks.

The question arises as to what optical stimulus parameters control the blinking response of the very young infant. Blinking is considered to be a rather primitive, reflexive behavior, and as Yonas (1981) has pointed out, the blinking may be "activated by a perceptual process so primitive that it would be unwarranted to infer that spatial information is being picked up." Therefore, it would be desirable to know whether the blink is elicited by virtually any kind of optical expansion or whether it is controlled by fairly specific spatial information. This issue was examined by Yonas, Pettersen, Lockman, and Eisenberg (1980), with subjects between 3 and 4 months of age. Responsiveness (blinking and head movement) to several kinds of optical displays was assessed: (1) closed-form magnification which accelerated geometrically, corresponding to an object approaching at a constant rate (an important characteristic of this display was that the expansion pattern expanded "explosively" in the last few seconds before impact); (2) closed-form magnification in which acceleration was linear, corresponding to an object slowing as it approaches; (3) a rapid change in luminance, as when an object fills the visual field just before collision.

The stimulus event that elicited avoidance behavior at 3 months of age was fairly specific. Significant blinking and backward head movement occurred only when there was an explosion in the expansion pattern, the condition which corresponds to a pattern approaching at a constant rate. Younger infants (1 month old) were also tested, and it was found that they blink with equal frequency to both explosive and nonexplosive expansion. Younger infants seem to be at a more general level of perceptual specificity (see E. J. Gibson, 1969) in perceiving impending collision than are infants at 3 to 4 months.

In summary, Yonas and collaborators argue that when blinking is used as the dependent measure, there is evidence that infants perceive impending collision by 3 months. They also found that 1-month-olds will blink to magnifying contours which specify approach but do so whether the explosive property is present or not. Bower and Ball propose that there is evidence that infants perceive impending collision during the first month when defensive and avoidance behaviors were used as the dependent measures, but Yonas' contour-tracking hypothesis also gives a feasible interpretation of the data, one that suggests that backward head movement may not be the best dependent measure.

It is difficult to draw a line marking the age of onset of sensitivity to object approach, but this is probably a misguided enterprise anyway. Developmental research, instead of centering around the age at which a perceptual skill emerges, should address the course of development, for instance, how the effective depth information changes with age, or whether the depth information eliciting a behavior becomes more specific with age. Experiments like that of Yonas et al. (1980), which looked at the role of explosive magnification, and that of Carroll and Gibson (1981), which looked at the role of textural change, illustrate this approach. These experiments, and others like them (e.g., Fox et al., 1980; Owsley, 1983), have as their goal the discovery of the optical variables which specify depth to the young infant, rather than the mere demonstration that the infant at some age is capable of a given spatial behavior.

B. Accretion and Deletion of Texture

In addition to producing expansion patterns in the optic array, movement by the observer or by objects in the environment results in disruption of the pattern of visible texture projected to the observer's eyes. Since terrestrial environments are filled with opaque objects and surfaces, the visual world is divided into visible and occluded surfaces at each possible observation point. When the observer moves through the environment, or when an object moves relative to an observer, some surfaces are occluded and others are revealed (J. J. Gibson, 1966). At the level of the proximal stimulus, movement produces accretion and deletion of visible texture. For example, when a single object moves through a cluttered environment, its leading edge deletes texture from the proximal stimulus while texture is added at its trailing edge. J. J. Gibson (1966, 1979) has argued that since this change in the proximal stimulus is lawfully determined by the spatial layout of objects and surfaces in the environment, accretion and deletion of texture in the proximal stimulus unambiguously specify an edge and one surface in front of another at that edge. Gibson's hypothesis has been supported by Kaplan (1969), who found that for adults, accretion and deletion of texture provide effective information for depth at an edge.

In a more recent study, Granrud, Yonas, Smith, et al. (1984) found that 7-month-old infants can also use this information to perceive the spatial layout of surfaces. Seven-month-old infants (26–30 weeks) viewed computer-generated random-dot displays in which accretion and deletion of texture provided the only information for contours or for depth at an edge (see Figure 3). When the display was in motion, accretion and deletion specified a foreground surface moving in front of and occluding a moving background surface. When the display was motionless, it appeared to be a flat array of dots; the foreground and background were indistinguishable.

The infants reached significantly more often for the "foreground" than for the "background." A number of studies have shown that infants reach preferentially for the nearer of two surfaces when sufficient information for relative distance is available (Granrud, Yonas, & Pettersen, 1984; Yonas, Sorknes, & Smith, 1983). As no other information was available to distinguish the two regions, the reaching preference indicated that 7-month-olds are sensitive to accretion and deletion of texture as information for the spatial layout of surfaces.

Attempts to find evidence of 5-month-olds' sensitivity to accretion and deletion of texture were hampered initially by the low frequency of younger infants' reaching for the random-dot display used with 7-month-olds. C. E. Granrud and C. von Hofsten (unpublished), therefore, tested 5-

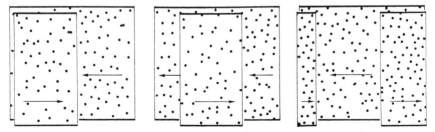

Figure 3. Schematic drawing of random-dot displays used in study of sensitivity to accretion and deletion of texture. Note that only dots were visible and the vertical lines in the display indicate subjective contours. From Granrud, Yonas, Smith, et al. (1984).

month-olds for sensitivity to accretion and deletion of texture produced either by a real object moving against a textured background or by an equally large aperture moving relative to the background. Less than 1 mm of differential depth separated the background from the object or aperture. Significantly more reaches were observed to the object than to the aperture. This was not the case in control conditions in which either the entire display was stationary or in which the object or aperture moved with the background, resulting in no accretion and deletion of texture. These results support the hypothesis that accretion and deletion of texture specify spatial layout for infants as young as 5 months of age.

Granrud, Yonas, Smith, et al. (1984) subsequently corroborated this finding. They presented 5-month-olds with a computer-generated random-dot display, in which accretion and deletion of texture again provided the only information for contours or for depth and specified two partially overlapping surfaces at different distances. The 5-month-olds showed a significant preference to reach for the apparently nearer region of the display. Again, since accretion and deletion was the only information that distinguished the two regions, this result indicated that 5-month-olds are sensitive to accretion and deletion of texture as information for the relative distances of two surfaces.

C. Perceiving Object Shape and Size

Several experiments suggest that by 4 months infants can perceive both object size (e.g., Bower, 1964, 1965, 1972; Bruner & Koslowski, 1972; Day & McKenzie, 1977; McKenzie, Tootel, & Day, 1980) and object shape (e.g., Bower, 1966a; Caron, Caron, & Carison, 1979; Cook, Field, & Griffiths, 1978; Day & McKenzie, 1973). Discussion of this literature will be limited to those studies in which the depth information present in the displays was manipulated and controlled.

Bower (1965, 1966b) carried out two experiments on "size constancy" in infants about 2 months old which suggest that kinetic information may play a crucial role in their ability to perceive invariant size. The details of the procedure, as well as methodological comments, were described in the section on static monocular information and so will not be presented again. To summarize, infants were conditioned to turn their heads when presented a stationary 30-cm cube at a distance of 1 m. Generalization was tested as the size and distance of the cube were varied. Combining Bower's two experiments, there were four viewing conditions: binocular viewing of a real cube, monocular viewing of a real cube, viewing of a stereoscopically defined cube for which disparity was the only depth information available, and viewing of a slide projection of a cube, in which only static depth cues were available. Only when infants viewed the real object were results consistent with size constancy. When only static depth information was available, as in the slide projection condition, or when only binocular disparity was available, as in the stereoscopic condition, infants did not exhibit behaviors consistent with size constancy. Bower concluded that the availability of kinetic information, specifically motion parallax, in the real object display was responsible for infants' perception of size and distance. If this was the case, since objects were stationary, infants in this experiment presumably moved their heads to produce optical motion.

The implication of Bower's experiments is that infants at 2 months can use kinetic variables in perceiving the constant sizes of objects. Furthermore, kinetic information may be the sole specifier of invariant size at this age, since neither binocular disparity nor static cues presented alone led to infants responding in a manner consistent with a size constancy interpretation. Other experiments have demonstrated size constancy in early infancy, but all three types of depth information were available in these studies, making it impossible to dissociate the roles of kinetic, static, and binocular cues. For example, McKenzie et al. (1980), using a visual habituation–recovery procedure, found that infants exhibit size constancy by 6 months. The results for their 4-month-old group were mixed; some infants provided evidence for constancy and some did not. Bower's work suggests that kinetic variables may be necessary for the perception of constant size during the earliest months of infancy. By 6 to 8 months infants have reliable stereopsis (Fox et al., 1980) and have an emerging sensitivity to static depth information (Yonas, Cleaves, & Pettersen, 1978). Thus the 6- and 8-month-old groups in the McKenzie et al. study may be relying on several depth cues. The 4-month-olds, however, may be forced to rely on kinetic cues alone, which could only be available in their experiment if infants induced optical motion themselves through body movement. The hypothesis should be examined that with moving displays, in which kinetic depth variables are readily available, 4-month-olds will perceive constant size.

A few experiments have demonstrated that infants can perceive the three-dimensional ("solid") shape of objects. Bower (1966a), using a conditioning paradigm similar to that used in his size constancy experiments, found that at 1 to 2 months, infants exhibit shape constancy. More recently Caron et al. (1979), using a visual habituation–recovery paradigm, reported that their 3-month-old subjects provided evidence of shape constancy. Cook et al. (1978) report findings consistent with those of Caron et al. Yet these experiments tell us little about what optical information is effective in young infants' perception of shape, since all three types of information—kinetic, static, and binocular—were presumably present in the stimulus displays.

The objects presented in the experiments mentioned above were stationary. E. J. Gibson, Owsley, Walker, and Megaw-Nyce (1979) have demonstrated that infants at 3 months can extract information about object shape from a moving array. Three-month-olds were visually habituated to an object that underwent two different rigid motions on consecutive trials. A posthabituation test revealed that during habituation infants perceived the object's shape while it was moving. Subjects remained habituated in a no-change control condition but dishabituated dramatically when a moving object with a different shape was presented. This pattern of results was obtained even when the objects were stationary in the posttest.

This experiment indicates that a continuously changing array should not be considered a hindrance to the infant perceiver's detection of object shape. The static stimulus need not be considered simpler for the infant than the kinetic stimulus. Although kinetic information was available in the E. J. Gibson et al. (1979) study, it cannot be determined from these data whether infants actually used this information to perceive object shape. Other types of depth information—static and binocular—were presumably available.

Owsley (1983) was interested in the type of depth information young infants found useful in their perception of solid shape. Four-month-olds were habituated monocularly to either a stationary wedge-shaped object or to the same object rotating about its vertical axis. Adults who viewed the stationary wedge monocularly reported that they perceived a cube. Since kinetic and binocular depth cues were absent, adults' perception was presumably based on static depth information. Adults who viewed the moving wedge monocularly perceived the wedge's shape correctly. The changing optic array must have contained effective information about the object's shape. The question of interest was whether infants could extract information about the object's shape from the moving array. Also of interest was whether infants would perceive the wedge as a cube during habituation, as do adults, demonstrating their ability to use static depth information. Three posthabituation tests presented in both conditions were designed to address these questions; stimuli consisted of the wedge in a familiar pose, the wedge in a novel pose, and a real cube. All posttest objects were stationary. Viewing was binocular. It was predicted that if 4-month-olds are sensitive to depth information presented in a moving array, then they should correctly perceive the shape of the moving wedge. They would recognize the wedge as a familiar object (remaining habituated), while perceiving the cube as novel (dishabituation). If 4-month-olds are insensitive to static depth information, as previous research has indicated (Yonas, Cleaves, & Pettersen, 1978), then infants viewing the stationary wedge would fail to perceive a cube during habituation, as static cues would be the only information available. They would therefore exhibit the same fixation level in all three posttests.

The predictions were confirmed in both conditions. Four-month-olds are apparently capable of extracting information about object shape from a continuously changing array even when binocular depth information is absent. Furthermore, there was no evidence that they are sensitive to static information provided by a single orientation of an object. The question remained unanswered, however, as to what optical variable specified the object's shape for infants viewing the moving wedge. One possibility is that kinetic variables contained in the continuous transitions of the array specified the object's shape. Alternatively, infants may have based their perception of the wedge on a series of static cues available as the object rotated. In a further experiment, 4-month-olds were habituated to the wedge in several stationary orientations. Since viewing was monocular, only static depth information was present. The same posttests followed habituation. There was no evidence that infants perceived the wedge's shape when exposed to the series of stationary views. This finding agrees with earlier work by Yonas, Cleaves, & Pettersen (1978) that static information is not effective until 6 to 7 months.

In a similar study, Kellman (1984) habituated 4-month-old infants to a videotape display of a continuously rotating three-dimensional solid object or to series of static views of the same rotating object. Infants who were habituated to the continuously rotating object showed recovery from habituation when presented with a novel-shaped object, while infants habituated to successive static views showed no recovery from habituation. These findings, like Owsley's, suggest that 4-month-olds can perceive three-dimensional shape when kinetic information is present but cannot perceive an object's shape from a series of stationary views.

Because infants were capable of perceiving the object's shape from kinetic information but not from static cues, it appears that kinetic information is crucial in their perception of object shape. It could be that kinetic information is the earliest specifier of depth for the infant, that is, it is effective earlier in development than are binocular and static cues. Static cues do not appear to be effective before 6 months or so; binocular information is not available until 3 to 4 months. Yet infants do perceive depth before this age. A hypothesis which deserves further investigation is that kinetic information mediates these earlier experiences of depth.

D. Perceiving Rigidity and Elasticity

The type of optical motion an object produces when it moves reveals whether the object is made of a rigid substance or an elastic, yielding substance. When a rigid object moves, any alignment of texture elements in the projected array remains throughout its movement. In contrast, when a nonrigid or elastic object moves, there is destruction, rather than preservation, of the alignment of texture elements. These kinetic properties could be the basis for the perceiver's differentiation of rigid and elastic objects. E. J. Gibson and colleagues were interested in determining whether young infants can differentiate rigid and nonrigid objects. If they can, they may be doing so on the basis of information carried by these distinctive optical motions.

In the first study, E. J. Gibson, Owsley, and Johnston (1978) investigated the ability of 5-month-olds to perceive the rigidity of a substance as specified by various motions of a rigid object. Infants were habituated to an object undergoing three different rigid motions on consecutive trials. In a posthabituation test, they were presented with the object undergoing a fourth rigid motion, not seen during habituation, and with the same object undergoing a deforming motion. Subjects remained habituated to the fourth rigid motion, despite the fact that they had not been previously habituated to it. They dishabituated to the deforming motion. The results implied that infants at 5 months are capable of extracting information from a changing array which specified a distal property—in this case the rigidity of a substance.

In a second series of experiments (E. J. Gibson et al., 1979), this result was replicated with 3-month-olds, using a slightly different procedure. Apparently the ability to extract information from a moving array is present very early. The inverse of the experimental design was also carried out by Walker, Owsley, Megaw-Nyce, Gibson, and Bahrick (1980). Would infants perceive the elasticity of a substance as specified by various motions of a nonrigid object? Three-month-olds were habituated to an object in two deforming motions. Following habituation, the infants were tested with either a third (novel) deforming motion or a rigid motion, and a control group was tested with the same motions viewed during habituation. The control group and the new deforming motion group performed similarly, remaining habituated, whereas the rigid motion group significantly dishabituated. The results indicated that infants were sensitive to information specifying elasticity present in a moving array. It is debatable whether infants in these experiments actually perceived the "meaning" of the object—rigidity or elasticity *per se,* or whether they were responding to the optical stimulation devoid of meaning. Only further research can resolve this issue.

E. Visual Control of Postural Stability

An experiment by Lee and Aronson (1974) suggests that infants who have begun to stand alone use information produced by optical flow patterns to control their posture. Infants about 1 year old stood in an experimental room with three walls and a ceiling and faced the closed end of the room. The floor was stationary, but the walls and ceiling could be moved. Movement of the room forward (away from the infant) produced an optical flow pattern similar to the flow produced when a perceiver sways or falls backward. Movement of the room backward (toward the infant) produced optical flow similar to flow produced by forward sway of the body. When infants stood in this room as it moved, they swayed or fell in the direction opposite to its movement, as if adjusting their posture on the basis of information in the optical flow which specified that they were falling forward or backward. Butterworth and Hicks (1977) extended this finding in a similar experiment in which they found that 11-month-old infants who can sit up independently but are not yet capable of standing use information in the optical flow to adjust their seated posture. The implication is that infants capable of upright posture, whether seated or standing, can use information in the optical flow to perceive the relationship of their bodies to the environment.

IV. CONCLUDING COMMENTS

We would like to close this chapter by discussing a few issues which we feel are important in the study of the development of visual space perception. First, demonstrations that the infant can discriminate two-dimensional patterns which specify depth (at least to the adult) do not imply that the infant actually perceives the three-dimensional relationships specified by the stimulus. As is apparent from our review, this is an error which is still occasionally made. This point has been raised on several occasions by others (e.g., Yonas & Pick, 1975), but it is worth reiterating. There are alternatives to discrimination methods: experiments using adaptive responses (e.g., reaching, blinking, crawling) and those using the transfer paradigm reviewed earlier (see also Owsley, 1983; Yonas & Pick, 1975). Spatially meaningful behavior is difficult to observe in the very young infant; for this reason the transfer paradigm might prove useful at early ages when visual fixation can be used as the dependent measure.

Since previous work has been designed to establish that infants are sensitive to the *general* types of depth information (binocular, static, kinetic), what is needed now are more analytic studies which examine what *specific* properties of the three types of stimulation are informative to the infant. For example, what aspects of optical flow specify three-dimensional relationships to the infant? What specific pictorial cues are effective in infancy? Furthermore, research should be devoted to the roles of maturation, learning, and their interaction; there are only a few studies which have investigated the epigenesis of space perception (Pettersen et al., 1980; Rader, Bausano, & Richards, 1980).

In defining our research problems, we should consider the constraints that the infant's visual system may place on his ability to respond to depth information. For example, if infants of a given age have poor stereoacuity or cannot reliably converge their eyes, their ability to use stereoscopic depth information may be impaired relative to that of a visually mature observer. Similarly, infants' visual sensitivity to motion and pattern may set limits on the aspects of kinetic and static arrays that they can find informative. To make this link between basic visual capacities and depth perception, it is necessary to know more about infants' temporal and spatial sensitivities. Much of the necessary methodology has already been established by those researchers who study the development of acuity. We are not arguing that the leap from basic visual capacity to spatial perception is simple and straightforward, only that psychophysical research on the temporal and spatial sensitivities of infants might be helpful to our understanding of their depth sensitivity.

Our review indicates that kinetic information may be the earliest specifier of space for the young infant. Binocular depth information does not appear to be effective until around 3 months, and static information may not be effective until 6 to 7 months. Yet the infant does appear to perceive some spatial properties during the first 3 months of life. By the process of elimination, we can conjecture that the effective information in early infancy may be kinetic stimulus variables; research discussed in Section III on kinetic information supports this idea. This notion deserves further attention, as only a few experiments have directly examined it.

Finally, the study of infant space perception would benefit from research which manipulates the depth information available in stimulus displays. This approach would supplement work designed to determine what environmental properties the infant can perceive by describing the stimulus information which makes those perceptual capacities possible.

ACKNOWLEDGMENTS

A. Yonas' participation in preparing this chapter was made possible in part by grants HD-05027, HD-01136, and HD-16924 from the National Institute of Child Health and Human Development. C. Owsley's participation was made possible by NIH grant AG-EY 01251 to

Northwestern University and by NIH CORE grant EY-03039 to the University of Alabama in Birmingham. The authors thank Carl Granrud for his contribution to the chapter and Isabel Smith for editorial assistance.

REFERENCES

Ahrens, R. (1954). Beiträge zur Entwicklung des Physiognomie und Mimikerkennes. *Zeitschrift fur Experimentelle und Angewandte Psychologie, 2,* 412–454, 599–633.

Ames, A., Jr. (1951). Visual perception and the rotating trapezoidal window. *Psychological Monographs, 65* (Whole No. 324).

Appel, M. A., & Campos, J. J. (1977). Binocular disparity as a discriminable stimulus parameter for young infants. *Journal of Experimental Child Psychology, 23,* 47–65.

Aslin, R. N. (1977). Development of binocular fixation in human infants. *Journal of Experimental Child Psychology, 23,* 133–150.

Aslin, R., & Dumais, S. (1981). Binocular vision in infants: A review and theoretical framework. In H. W. Reese & L. P. Lipsitt (Eds.), *Advances in child development and behavior* (Vol. 15). New York: Academic Press.

Aslin, R. N., & Jackson, R. W. (1979). Accommodative convergence in young infants: Development of a synergistic sensory-motor system. *Canadian Journal of Psychology, 33,* 222–231.

Atkinson, J., & Braddick, O. (1976). Stereoscopic discrimination in infants. *Perception, 5,* 29–38.

Ball, W., & Tronick, E. (1971). Infant responses to impending collision: Optical and real. *Science, 171,* 818–820.

Ball, W., & Vurpillot, E. (1976). Perception of movement in depth in infancy. *Annee Psychologique, 76,* 383–399.

Barrow, H. G., & Tenenbaum, J. M. (1978). Recovering intrinsic scene characteristics from images. In A. R. Hanson & E. M. Riseman (Eds.), *Computer vision systems.* New York: Academic Press.

Bechtoldt, H. P., & Hutz, C. S. (1979). Stereopsis in young infants and stereopsis in an infant with congenital esotropia. *Journal of Pediatric Ophthalmology and Strabismus, 16,* 49–54.

Benson, C., & Yonas, A. (1973). Development of sensitivity to static pictorial depth information. *Perception and Psychophysics, 13,* 361–366.

Bertenthal, B. I., Campos, J. J., & Haith, M. M. (1980). Development of visual organization: The perception of subjective contours. *Child Development, 51,* 1072–1080.

Bower, T. G. R. (1964). Discrimination of depth in premotor infants. *Psychonomic Science, 1,* 368.

Bower, T. G. R. (1965). Stimulus variables determining space perception in infants. *Science, 149,* 88–89.

Bower, T. G. R. (1966a). Slant perception and shape constancy in infants. *Science, 151,* 832–834.

Bower, T. G. R. (1966b). The visual world of infants. *Scientific American, 215,* 80–92.

Bower, T. G. R. (1972). Object perception in infants. *Perception, 1,* 15–30.

Bower, T. G. R. (1977a). Comment on Yonas et al. Development of sensitivity to information for impending collision. *Perception and Psychophysics, 21,* 281–282.

Bower, T. G. R. (1977b). *The perceptual world of the child.* Cambridge, MA: Harvard University Press.

Bower, T. G. R. (1979). *Human development*. San Francisco, CA: Freeman.

Bower, T. G. R., Broughton, J. M., & Moore, M. K. (1970). Infant responses to approaching objects: An indicator of response to distal variables. *Perception and Psychophysics, 9*, 193–196.

Bruner, J. S., & Koslowski, B. (1972). Visually preadapted constituents of manipulating action. *Perception, 1*, 3–14.

Butterworth, G., & Hicks, L. (1977). Visual proprioception and postural stability in infancy: A developmental study. *Perception, 6*, 255–262.

Caron, A. J., Caron, R. F., & Carlson, V. R. (1979). Infant perception of the invariant shape of objects varying in slant. *Child Development, 50*, 716–721.

Carroll, J. J., & Gibson, E. J. (1981). *Infants' differentiation of an aperture and an obstacle*. Paper presented at the meeting of the Society for Research in Child Development, Boston, MA.

Chapanis, A., & McCleary, R. A. (1953). Interposition as a cue for the perception of relative distance. *Journal of General Psychology, 48*, 113–132.

Clowes, M. B. (1971). On seeing things. *Artificial Intelligence, 2*(1), 79–112.

Cohen, L. B. (1977). *Concept acquisition in the human infant*. Paper presented at the meeting of the Society for Research in Child Development, New Orleans, LA.

Cook, M., Field, J., & Griffiths, K. (1978). The perception of solid forms in early infancy. *Child Development, 49*, 866–869.

Davenport, C. B. (1940). Post-natal development of the head. *Proceedings of the American Philosophical Society, 83*, 1–216.

Davenport, C. B. (1944). Post-natal development of the human extremities. *Proceedings of the American Philosophical Society, 88*, 375–456.

Day, R. H., & McKenzie, B. E. (1973). Perceptual shape constancy in early infancy. *Perception, 2*, 315–320.

Day, R. H., & McKenzie, B. E. (1977). Constancies in the perceptual world of the infant. In W. Epstein (Ed.) *Stability and constancy in visual perception: Mechanisms and processes*. New York: Wiley.

DiFranco, D., Muir, D. W., & Dodwell, D. C. (1978). Reaching in young infants. *Perception, 7*, 385–392.

Dinnerstein, A., & Wertheimer, M. (1957). Some determinants of phenomenal overlapping. *American Journal of Psychology, 70*, 21–37.

Dirks, J., & Gibson, E. (1977). Infants' perception of similarity between live people and their photographs. *Child Development, 48*, 124–130.

Epstein, W., & Baratz, S. S. (1964). Relative size in isolation as a stimulus for relative perceived distance. *Journal of Experimental Psychology, 67*, 507–513.

Fagan, J. F., III. (1973). Infants' delayed recognition memory and forgetting. *Journal of Experimental Child Psychology, 16*, 424–450.

Fantz, R. H., & Nevis, S. (1967). pattern preferences and perceptual-cognitive development in early infancy. *Merrill-Palmer Quarterly, 13*, 77–108.

Field, J. (1977). Coordination of vision and prehension in young infants. *Child Development, 48*, 97–103.

Fox, R., Aslin, R. N., Shea, S. L., & Dumais, S. T. (1980). Stereopsis in human infants. *Science, 207*, 323–324.

Gesell, A., Ilg, F., & Bullis, G. (1949). *Vision: Its development in infant and child*. New York: Hafner.

Gibson, E. J. (1969). *Principles of perceptual learning and development*. New York: Appleton-Century-Crofts.

Gibson, E. J., Owsley, C., & Johnston, J. (1978). Perception of invariants by five-month-old infants: Differentiation of two types of motion. *Developmental Psychology, 14,* 407–415.

Gibson, E. J., Owsley, C., Walker, A., & Megaw-Nyce, J. (1979). Development of the perception of invariants: Substance and shape. *Perception, 8,* 609–619.

Gibson, E. J., & Spelke, E. (1983). The development of perception. In J. H. Flavell & E. Markman (Eds.), *Handbook of child psychology* (Vol. 3). New York: Wiley.

Gibson, J. J. (1950). *Perception of the visual world.* Boston, MA: Houghton-Mifflin.

Gibson, J. J. (1958). Visually controlled locomotion and visual orientation in animals. *British Journal of Psychology, 49,* 182–194.

Gibson, J. J. (1961). Ecological optics. *Vision Research, 1,* 253–262.

Gibson, J. J. (1966). *The senses considered as perceptual system.* Boston, MA: Houghton-Mifflin.

Gibson, J. J. (1979). *The ecological approach to visual perception.* Boston, MA: Houghton-Mifflin.

Gogel, W. C. (1961). Convergence as cue for absolute depth. *Journal of Psychology, 52,* 287–301.

Gordon, F. R., & Yonas, A. (1976). Sensitivity to binocular depth information in infants. *Journal of Experimental Child Psychology, 22,* 413–422.

Granrud, C. E., Haake, R., & Yonas, A. (1985). Infants' sensitivity to familiar size: The effect of memory on spatial perception. *Perception and Psychophysics, 37,* 457–466.

Granrud, C. E., & Yonas, A. (1984). Infants' perception of pictorially specified interposition. *Journal of Experimental Child Psychology, 37,* 500–511.

Granrud, C. E., Yonas, A., & Opland, E. A. (1985). Infants' sensitivity to depth cue of shading. *Perception and Psychophysics, 37,* 415–419.

Granrud, C. E., Yonas, A., & Pettersen, L. (1984). A comparison of responsiveness to monocular and binocular depth information in 5- and 7-month-old infants. *Journal of Experimental Child Psychology, 38,* 19–32.

Granrud, C. E., Yonas, A., Smith, I. M., Arterberry, M. E., Glicksman, M. L., & Sorknes, A. C. (1984). Infants' sensitivity to accretion and deletion of texture as information for depth at an edge. *Child Development, 55,* 1630–1636.

Heineman, E. G., Tulving, E., & Nachmias, J. (1959). The effect of oculomotor adjustments on apparent size. *American Journal of Psychology, 72,* 32–45.

Held, R., Birch, E., & Gwiazda, J. (1980). Stereoacuity in human infants. *Proceedings of the National Academy of Sciences of the U.S.A., 77,* 5572–5574.

Hershenson, M. (1964). Visual discrimination in the newborn. *Journal of Comparative and Physiological Psychology, 58,* 270–276.

Hochberg, J. (1971). Perception: Space and movement. In J. W. Kling & L. A. Riggs (Eds.), *Woodworth and Schlosberg's experimental psychology.* New York: Holt, Rinehart & Winston.

Hochberg, J., & Brooks, V. (1962). Pictorial recognition as an unlearned ability: A study of one child's performance. *American Journal of Psychology, 75,* 624–628.

Hochberg, J., & McAlister, E. (1953). A quantitative approach to figural "goodness." *Journal of Experimental Psychology, 46,* 361–364.

Horn, B. K. P. (1975). Obtaining shape from shading information. In P. H. Winston (Ed.), *The psychology of computer vision.* New York: McGraw-Hill.

Huffman, D. A. (1971). Impossible objects as nonsense sentences. In R. Maltzer & D. Michie (Eds.), *Machine intelligence* (Vol. 6). Edinburgh: Edinburgh University Press.

Ittleson, W. H. (1951). Size as a cue to distance: Static localization. *American Journal of Psychology, 64,* 54–67.

Ittleson, W. H. (1952). *The Ames demonstrations in perception.* New York: Hafner.

Johansson, G. (1970). On theories for visual space perception. *Scandinavian Journal of Psychology, 11,* 67–74.

Kagan, J., Henker, B. A., Hen-tou, A., & Lewis, M. (1966). Infants' differential reactions to familiar and distorted faces. *Child Development, 37,* 519–532.

Kaplan, G. A. (1969). Kinetic disruption of optical texture: The perception of depth at an edge. *Perception and Psychophysics, 6,* 193–198.

Kaufman, L. (1974). *Sight and mind.* London & New York: Oxford University Press.

Kaufmann, R., Maland, J., & Yonas, A. (1981). Sensitivity of 5- and 7-month-old infants to pictorial depth information. *Journal of Experimental Child Psychology, 32,* 162–168.

Kellman, P. J. (1984). Perception of three-dimensional form by human infants. *Perception and Psychophysics, 36,* 353–358.

Kellman, P. J., & Spelke, E. S. (1983). Perception of partly occluded objects in infancy. *Cognitive Psychology, 15,* 483–524.

Koffka, K. (1935). *Principles of Gestalt psychology.* New York: Harcourt-Brace.

Künnapas, T. (1968). Distance perception as a function of available visual cues. *Journal of Experimental Psychology, 77,* 523–579.

Le Barbera, J. D., Izard, C. E., Vietze, P., & Parisi, S. A. (1976). Four- and six-month-old infants' visual responses to joy, anger, and neutral expressions. *Child Development, 47,* 535–538.

Lee, D. N., & Aronson, E. (1974). Visual proprioceptive control of standing in infants. *Perception and Psychophysics, 15,* 529–532.

Ling, B. C. (1942). A genetic study of sustained visual fixation and associated behavior in the human infant from birth to six months. *Journal of Genetic Psychology, 61,* 227–277.

McKenzie, B. E., & Day, R. H. (1971). Operant learning of visual pattern discrimination in young infants. *Journal of Experimental Child Psychology, 11,* 45–53.

McKenzie, B. E., Tootel, H., & Day, R. H. (1980). Development of visual size constancy during the first year of human infancy. *Developmental Psychology, 16,* 163–174.

Olson, R. K., & Boswell, S. (1976). Pictorial depth sensitivity in two-year-old children. *Child Development, 47,* 1175–1178.

Olson, R. K., Cooper, R., & Yonas, A. (1980). Pictorial perception in children. In M. Hagen (Ed.), *The perception of pictures: Vol. 2. Durer's devices: Beyond the projective model of pictures.* New York: Academic Press.

Owsley, C. (1983). The role of motion in infants' perception of solid shape. *Perception, 12,* 707–717.

Peiper, A. (1963). *Cerebral function in infancy and childhood.* New York: Consultants Bureau.

Pettersen, L., Yonas, A., & Fisch, R. O. (1980). The development of blinking in response to impending collision in preterm, full term, and postterm infants. *Infant Behavior and Development, 3,* 155–165.

Rader, N., Bausano, M., & Richards, J. E. (1980). On the nature of the visual-cliff-avoidance response in human infants. *Child Development, 51,* 61–68.

Regal, D. M. (1981). Development of critical flicker frequency in human infants. *Vision Research, 21,* 549–555.

Ruff, H., & Halton, A. (1978). Is there directed reaching in the human neonate? *Developmental Psychology, 14,* 425–426.

Salapatek, P., & Banks, M. S. (1977). Infant sensory assessment: Vision. In F. D. Minifie & L. L. Lloyd (Eds.), *Communicative and cognitive abilities—Early behavioral assessment.* Baltimore, MD: University Park Press.

Sameroff, A., & Cavanaugh, P. J. (1979). Learning in infancy: A developmental perspective. In J. D. Osofsky (Ed.), *Handbook of infant development*. New York: Wiley.

Schiff, W. (1965). Perception of impending collision: A study of visually directed avoidant behavior. *Psychological Monographs, 79* (Whole No. 604).

Sekuler, R. (1975). Visual motion perception. In E. C. Carterette, & M. P. Friedman (Eds.), *Handbook of perception: Vol. 5. Seeing*. New York: Academic Press.

Shea, S., & Fox, R. (1980). *Development of stereopsis in human infants*. Paper presented at the International Conference on Infant Studies, New Haven, CT.

Slater, A. M., & Findlay, J. M. (1975). Binocular fixation in the newborn baby. *Journal of Experimental Child Psychology, 20,* 248–273.

Volkmann, F. C., & Dobson, M. V. (1976). Infant responses of ocular fixation to moving stimuli. *Journal of Experimental Child Psychology, 21,* 86–99.

von Hofsten, C. (1976). The role of convergence in visual space perception. *Vision Research, 16,* 193–198.

von Hofsten, C. (1977). Binocular convergence as a determinant of reaching behavior in infancy. *Perception, 6,* 139–144.

Walker, A., Owsley, C. J., Megaw-Nyce, J., Gibson, E. J., & Bahrick, L. B. (1980). Detection of elasticity as an invariant property of objects by young infants. *Perception, 9,* 713–718.

Waltz, D. L. (1972, November). *Generating semantic descriptions from drawings of scenes with shadows* (Tech. Rep. AI-TR-271). Cambridge, MA: Artificial Intelligence Laboratory, Massachusetts Institute of Technology.

Watson, J. S. (1973). Smiling, cooing, and "The Game". In F. Rebelsky & L. Dorman (Eds.), *Child development and behavior* (2nd ed.). New York: Alfred A. Knopf.

Watson, J. S., & Ramey, C. T. (1972). Reactions to response-contingent stimulation in early infancy. *Merrill-Palmer Quarterly, 18,* 219–227.

Wickelgren, L. (1967). Convergence in the human newborn. *Journal of Experimental Child Psychology, 5,* 74–85.

Wickelgren, L. (1969). The ocular response of human newborns to intermittent movement. *Journal of Experimental Child Psychology, 8,* 469–482.

Wilcox, B. L., & Teghtsoonian, M. (1971). The control of relative size by pictorial depth cues in children and adults. *Journal of Experimental Child Psychology, 11,* 413–429.

Winston, P. H. (1977). *Artificial intelligence*. Reading, MA: Addison-Wesley.

Yonas, A. (1979). Studies of spatial perception in infancy. In A. D. Pick (ed.), *Perception and its development: A tribute to Eleanor J. Gibson*. Hillsdale, NJ: Erlbaum.

Yonas, A. (1981). Infants' responses to optical information for collision. In R. N. Aslin, J. R. Alberts, & M. R. Pettersen (Eds.), *The Development of perception: Psychobiological perspectives: Vol. 2. The visual system*. New York: Academic Press.

Yonas, A., Bechtold, A. G., Frankel, D., Gordon, F. R., McRoberts, G., Norcia, A., & Sternfels, S. (1977). Development of sensitivity to information for impending collision. *Perception and Psychophysics, 21,* 97–104.

Yonas, A., Cleaves, W., & Pettersen, L. (1978). Development of sensitivity to pictorial depth. *Science, 200,* 77–79.

Yonas, A., Goldsmith, L. T., & Hallstrom, J. L. (1978). The development of sensitivity to information from cast shadows in pictures. *Perception, 7,* 333–342.

Yonas, A., Granrud, C. E., & Pettersen, L. (1985). Infants' sensitivity to relative size as information for distance. *Developmental Psychology, 21,* 161–167.

Yonas, A., Granrud, C. E., & Smith, I. M. (1982). *Infants perceive accretion/deletion information for depth*. Paper presented at the meeting of the Association for Research in Vision and Ophthalmology, Sarasota, FL. (Abstract published in *Investigative Ophthalmology & Visual Science, 1982, 22,* 124)

Yonas, A., & Hagen, M. (1973). Effects of static and motion parallax information on perception of size in children and adults. *Journal of Experimental Child Psychology, 15,* 254–266.

Yonas, A., Kuskowski, M. A., & Sternfels, S. (1979). The role of frames of reference in the development of responsiveness to shading information. *Child Development, 50,* 495–500.

Yonas, A., Oberg, C., & Norcia, A. (1978). Development of sensitivity to binocular information for the approach of an object. *Developmental Psychology, 14,* 147–152.

Yonas, A., Pettersen, L., & Granrud, C. E. (1982). Infants' sensitivity to familiar size as information for distance. *Child Development, 53,* 1285–1290.

Yonas, A., Pettersen, L., & Lockman, J. (1979). Young infants' sensitivity to optical information for collision. *Canadian Journal of Psychology, 33,* 268–276.

Yonas, A., Pettersen, L., Lockman, J., & Eisenberg, P. (1980). *The perception of impending collision in 3-month-old infants.* Paper presented at the International Conference on Infant Studies, New Haven, CT.

Yonas, A., & Pick, H. L., Jr. (1975). An approach to the study of infant space perception. In L. B. Cohen & P. Salapatek (Eds.), *Infant perception: From sensation to cognition* (Vol. 2). New York: Academic Press.

Yonas, A., Sorknes, A. C., & Smith, I. M. (1983). *Infants' sensitivity to variation in target distance and availability of depth cues.* Paper presented at the Society for Research in Child Development, Detroit, MI.

3

Visual Motion Perception in Infancy: A Review and Synthesis

CHARLES A. NELSON
Institute of Child Development
University of Minnesota
Minneapolis, Minnesota 55455

FRANCES DEGEN HOROWITZ
Department of Human Development
University of Kansas
Lawrence, Kansas 66045

I. INTRODUCTION

There has been a significant increase in our understanding of the young infant's visual abilities over the past two decades. Even a cursory review of the literature reveals that considerable attention has been directed toward the study of early sensory processes, the perception of simple forms and patterns, faces, depth, and color (for comprehensive reviews of these and other areas, see Banks & Salapatek, 1983; E. J. Gibson & Spelke, 1983; Haith, 1978; Maurer, 1985). Noticeably lacking from this literature is a systematic treatment of the infant's perception of motion. This is particularly surprising when one considers the fact that motion is pervasive in the infant's natural environment, and that numerous investigators have incorporated motion into experiments that were designed to examine some other ability (e.g., object permanence), seemingly taking for granted the infant's ability to perceive motion.

Given the prevalence of motion in the infant's environment, and the obvious but unexamined importance of this ability in infant development, it will be useful to establish a framework for the systematic consideration of motion as a significant variable in the infant's visual world.

The relative importance of motion perception in development can be

HANDBOOK OF INFANT
PERCEPTION, VOLUME 2

illustrated indirectly in two ways. First, it has long been known that when brain injuries to adults cause temporary loss of all visual functions, motion perception is often the first to recover (Riddoch, 1917). Second, although the development of a number of visual functions in many newborn mammals depends upon environmental stimulation, sensitivity to the *direction* of motion is present at birth, requiring minimal priming (Barlow & Pettigrew, 1971; Blakemore, 1974). The mammalian brain (including man's) thus appears to a certain extent to be "prewired" to perceive motion. Indeed, Sekuler (1975) has gone so far as to suggest that such biological preparedness may be adaptive for the young human: responding to a moving object may be more important than knowing what exactly has moved. Motion perception thus appears to be a fundamental ability of our species' young.

We begin our chapter by briefly describing the eye movements involved in motion perception, paying particularly close attention to the literature on smooth pursuit. This will be followed by a more general review of what, for lack of a better term, will be referred to as the visual tracking literature. In this section we will concentrate on the role of the eyes and head in motion perception and discuss some of the stimulus parameters impinging upon this ability (e.g., velocity). We will also discuss some of the recent work in which reaching has been used as an index of visual pursuit. In the next two sections we grapple with the motion preference literature (i.e., do infants attend more to moving versus nonmoving stimuli?), and then with recent work on infants' sensitivity to the information contained in motion. Finally, we attempt to integrate the evidence to date, discuss the implications such findings have for our understanding of subsequent perceptual development, and, finally, outline some directions for future research.[1]

---

[1] It should be noted that excluded from this review will be discussion of studies that have simply used moving stimuli to examine other abilities such as object permanence (e.g., Bower, Broughton, & Moore, 1971), gestalt principles (e.g., Kellman, Spelke, & Short, 1981), cross-modal integration (e.g., Spelke, Born, & Chu, 1981), stimulus complexity (e.g., Haith, Kessen, & Collins, 1969), the determination of the effective visual field (e.g., Finlay, Quinn, & Ivinskis, 1982; Finlay & Ivinskis, 1984); depth perception (e.g., Granrud, Yonas, Smith, Arterberry, Glicksman, & Sorkness, 1984; Owsley, 1983); and imitation (e.g., Vinter, 1986). The rationale for excluding such topics from discussion was based on the observation that because motion did not serve as an independent variable, it was frequently confounded with some other variable (e.g., occluding an object behind a screen), therefore making any interpretation of the results difficult at best. In terms of the topics that *were* chosen for discussion, the decision was made to include any study that had as its express purpose motion perception. Despite this qualification, it was frequently difficult to decide how to organize the studies into topic areas. Thus, when it was not perfectly apparent under which heading (e.g., "visual tracking") to review a given study, the authors debated between themselves until a consensus was reached. It is hoped that such agreement extends to the reader.

II. STUDIES OF SMOOTH PURSUIT

The ability to detect and track moving stimuli with the eyes has been studied in infants using a variety of procedures and stimuli. Studies of optokinetic nystagmus (OKN), for example, have most frequently relied on stimuli that encompass most if not all of the visual field, as these are the ones most likely to elicit the response. Such stimuli might be composed of a series of vertical stripes moving horizontally across the visual field, or a large single stimulus moving against a stationary or moving background. In either case, because the stimuli are full-field, such motion is more apparent than real and thus may not accurately describe tracking behavior *per se*. This is in contrast to studies in which a stimulus taking up only part of the visual field is used, while simultaneously recording the infant's eye movements. Such eye movements are generally recorded using electrooculography (EOG), or more recently, corneal photography. It is only in this latter case that the perception of real motion can be said to have been studied. Despite the attendant problems of using full-field stimuli, it was decided to review such studies so as to describe more broadly the infant's ability to perceive motion using eye movements only.

In the first study to examine infants' tracking behavior to moving stimuli, McGinnis (1930) filmed infants' eye movements as they fixated a black vertically oriented bar moving laterally against a white background. McGinnis reported that tracking movements were saccadic until approximately 6 weeks.

As Aslin (1981) has noted, nearly 30 years passed before the subject of infants' eye movements to moving stimuli again received attention. In an attempt to reexamine McGinnis's original findings, Dayton and Jones (1964), and Dayton, Jones, Steele, and Rose (1964) used electrooculography to record infants' tracking responses (as indexed by the OKN) to a single 15° diameter black dot moving across a white background at 16°/sec. As McGinnis (1930) had originally reported, tracking movements were saccadic until 6 to 8 weeks, after which smooth pursuit movements emerged, interspersed with saccadic movements. The finding that young infants' eye movements to single moving targets are entirely saccadic has been replicated by other investigators (e.g., Aslin, 1981; Barten, Birns, & Ronch, 1971; Brazelton, Scholl, & Robey, 1966; Gorman, Cogan, & Gellis, 1957).

Kremenitzer, Vaughn, Kurtzberg, and Dowling (1979) compared saccadic and smooth pursuit eye movements in 1- to 3-day-old infants, also using electrooculography. The EOG was recorded as infants tracked a 12° black circle mounted on a white background moving at six different speeds (9, 14, 19, 25, 32, and 40°/sec), while the OKN was elicited by a black-and-white striped field moving at the same six speeds. During the single-target tracking task, the authors reported that only 15% of the total viewing time was occupied by smooth pursuit movements. These movements were of an average duration of only 300–400 msec before they regressed to saccadic movements. Additionally, no smooth pursuit was present at all above 32°/sec. In contrast to the single-target tracking task, the OKN was observed at all velocities except 40°/sec. The presence of brief, smooth eye movements during the OKN task replicated previous reports by other investigators (Dayton, Jones, Aiu, et al. 1964; Doris & Cooper, 1966; Fantz, Ordy, & Udelf, 1962; Gorman et al., 1957; McGinnis, 1930; Tauber & Koffler, 1966). Unfortunately, it may not be valid to compare such findings to those obtained in the single-target tracking task, as the size of the stimulus differed in the two tasks and the tasks may have been assessing different abilities. Thus, the results of the single-target tracking task should probably be considered the more valid of the two.

In an attempt to avoid some of the problems inherent in EOG studies of smooth pursuit (e.g, calibration; DC drift; irritation due to electrode placement; head movement artifact), Aslin (1981) carried out what is perhaps the most ambitious study to date of smooth pursuit eye movements. Using infrared corneal photography, Aslin reported data on 32 infants who were tested weekly from roughly 5 to 12 weeks postnatally. Each sesssion consisted of a number of trials during which a 2° wide × 8° high black bar on a white background moved through a 20° sinusoidal oscillation in the horizontal meridian. Infants were tested at 10, 13.3, 20, 26.7, and 40°/sec velocities. Aslin reported that tracking responses were totally saccadic for 5- to 6-week-old infants. There was some evidence of smooth pursuit by 8 weeks to slow to moderately slow velocities (e.g., 20°/sec), with tracking becoming much more proficient at 10 and 12 weeks (although the accuracy of tracking again fell off at the higher velocities). Interestingly, Aslin also reported evidence of predictive tracking in several of the 10-week-olds.

Summary of Eye Movement Studies

The literature on smooth pursuit eye movements can be summarized as follows. There is the suggestion from the OKN data that the ability to detect motion with the eyes alone may be present in the first few days of life, although it must be noted that in such studies the entire visual field moved and thus the motion perceived may have been more apparent than real. Restricting our discussion to single-target tracking tasks using partial-field stimuli, we can conclude that eye movements to such stimuli seem largely saccadic until at least 6 weeks, after which some smooth movements may occur to slow-moving stimuli. The accuracy of smooth pursuit improves significantly through 10 to 12 weeks, although it is presently not clear at what age such movements become adultlike. We do not know what mechanisms underlie smooth pursuit. Is smooth pursuit an outgrowth of the saccadic system, as Aslin (1981) and others have suggested, or is it a separate system entirely? We also do not understand why smooth pursuit movements are largely absent until the second month of life.

The detailed examination of smooth pursuit eye movement in infants viewing moving stimuli has provided indirect evidence that the detection of motion is possible very early in life, and direct evidence that the smooth pursuit of motion only becomes relatively sophisticated in the second to third month of life. Motion perception typically involves the coordination of the eyes and head, not one or the other in isolation. Unfortunately, there has not yet been a thorough examination of how the eyes and the head work together in the perception of motion. This may be due to the difficulty in calibrating such movements, or in measuring eye movements when the head is free to move (e.g., do the eyes lead the head or vice versa? Are early head movements ballistic, as are early eye movements? What is the nature of compensatory eye movements when the head is moving?) Instead, investigators have focused principally upon the infant's ability simply to track and/or attend to a moving stimulus with both the eyes and the head. This literature will be reviewed next.

III. STUDIES OF VISUAL TRACKING

The visual tracking literature involves several studies on general visual following and a number on the effects of different stimulus parameters (size, sound, relative motion, and velocity) on such following. There have also been studies of motion discrimination and preferences for moving versus stationary stimuli, and there are a few investigations on the role of motion in attracting and maintaining infant attention.

A. Visual Following and the Effects of Size and Sound

Two studies expressly designed to examine general visual following have been reported by Ruff and her colleagues. In one (Ruff, Lawson, Kurtzberg, McCarton-Daum, & Vaughan 1982), the 1- and 2-month-old pre- and full-term infant's ability to track a variety of objects along the horizontal meridian was studied. Infants were presented with large (27°) and small (10°) three-dimensional objects that moved along a 1.68 m track at different rates (5°/sec, 2° 30 min/sec). During all trials the object was initially positioned at the midline and then moved continuously first to one side, then back to midline, and then to the other side. Duration of fixation served as the dependent measure. The authors reported several findings. Younger infants were found to look less than older infants; infants at both ages tended to follow the objects more in the midsections than in the periphery, although this was more true for the younger infants; the effect of type of object had little effect on following, but the higher-contrast objects did seem to elicit somewhat more following; finally, while there were essentially no differences between the pre- and full-term infants, when the pre-terms were divided into groups of normal or "deviant," the latter tended to follow less than the former.

In a related study, Lawson and Ruff (1984) conducted four experiments to examine the effects of size and sound on the following behavior of 1- and 2-month-old infants. (Both pre- and full-term infants served as subjects, but the data were pooled because the groups did not differ from one another.) In the first experiment infants were presented with a large (29.8°) and small (15.2°) three-dimensional object accompanied by either a loud (72–76 db) or soft (67–72 db) recording of a female speaking in child-directed speech (e.g., "Hi, baby, look at me," etc.). The same procedure used by Ruff et al. (1982) was employed, with the exception that only one rate of motion was used (5°/sec), and that each object was presented for only one trial. The authors reported that infants followed more at 2 months than at 1 month, that the large object was followed more than the small object, and that more following was evident in the "soft sound" condition than in the "loud sound" condition.

In the second experiment 1- and 2-month-old infants were tested again using a similar procedure, a variety of objects, and no sound. The authors reported that 2-month-olds looked longer than 1-month-olds, large objects were looked at longer than small objects, and the effect of object size was genearlly limited to the 1-month-olds.

In the third experiment only 2-month-olds were tested. A variety of 19° three-dimensional targets were used. These objects were variably accompanied by two periodic sounds and two continuous sounds. Some trials contained sound while others did not. The authors reported that sounding objects were looked at more than nonsounding objects and that there were no differences between types of sound.

In the fourth and final experiment 2-month-old infants were again tested, using the same stimuli as in Experiment 3, except that sound was present on all trials. However, this sound could either be spatially conjoint with the object, as was the case in the earlier experiments, or spatially displaced. The authors reported that infants' following was unaffected by type of sound. When viewed in context with the other experiments, the authors concluded that at 2 months of age sound apparently influences tracking behavior more through alterations in arousal than through facilitation of localization.

B. Effects of Relative Motion

The earliest studies of relative motion cues on infant visual tracking behavior were conducted by Harris, Cassel, and Bamborough (1974). The authors presented 10- and 16-week-old infants with a 9° striped cylinder that moved against a stationary background at 9°/sec or moved with the background at the same speed. They found that for both groups, tracking was impaired when the object did not move in relation to the background. In a second experiment, three groups of infants (14, 21, and 27 weeks old) were each presented with the same conditions as in the first experiment, as well as with a condition in which the object and the screen moved at the same speed in opposite directions. In this experiment, tracking was also found to be supported by the displacement of an object relative to the background, whether or not the background was stationary or moving. Relative displacement served to maintain tracking, rather than to elicit capture. In both experiments there were no age effects, although there was some evidence that the younger subjects may have been more sensitive to the difference between the stationary-and-background condition and the background-and-object together condition.

Using a different paradigm, Lasky and Gogol (1978) also explored the importance of relative motion cues on visual attention, although pursuit or tracking was not the dependent variable. The authors presented 5-month-old infants with two 1.9-cm dots that moved horizontally back and forth in a parallel fashion and a third dot that traveled vertically up and down between the other two (at approximately 2.6 cycles/sec). Adult subjects typically perceive the path of the third dot to be slanted counterclockwise from vertical when the dot moves up (and the horizontal dots move right), and clockwise from vertical when the dot moves down (and the horizontal dot moves left). The authors reported that infants perceive the display as do adults and hence concluded that infants were sensitive to the relative motion cues.

C. Stimulus Velocity

An important physical parameter thought to affect visual tracking is stimulus velocity. This has been studied in two contexts. The first has been concerned with velocity discrimination, while the second has been concerned with the influence of velocity on infant attention.

1. Discrimination

Silfen and Ames (1964) presented groups of 7-, 16-, and 24-week-old infants with simultaneous presentations of a moving and nonmoving checkerboard, with the velocity of the moving target varying between 1° 47 min/sec to 13°/sec. The authors reported that 7-week-old infants manifested no preferences for the moving versus nonmoving stimuli. In contrast, 16-week-old infants showed a peak preference for a fairly slow-moving stimulus (i.e., an angular speed of 1° 12/min sec), and less preference for faster speeds. Finally, the oldest group showed a steady increase in preference for faster speeds over the entire range used. Unfortunately, the failure to discriminate cannot, as the authors believed, be inferred from a failure to prefer one stimulus over another. Thus, few conclusions can be drawn from this study.

Using a somewhat more rigorous procedure, Volkman and Dobson (1976) presented 1-, 2-, and 3-month-old infants with two rear-projected, simultaneous displays of identical checkerboards, one of which was stationary while the other moved. The moving stimulus varied in eight steps, beeween 3.5 and 120 cycles per minute (CPM) (the actual speed was not specified). During control trials neither stimulus moved. Observers rated the infant's behavior on each of 18 trials with respect to three factors: (a) the stimulus to which the first fixation occurred, (b) where the infant was judged to be looking at the end of a 5-sec interval during a trial (left, right, neither), and (c) a report at the end of the trial indicating which stimulus was judged to be the moving one. The authors reported that by at least 1 month, infants behaved differently when presented with moving and stationary stimuli, and that this differential behavior provided reliable cues for the observer to judge which was the moving stimulus. These cues were more discernable as the rate of motion increased up to 90 CPM, after which they became less discernable. Finally, the cues provided by all three age groups led to essentially the same judgments, but the cues provided by the 3-month-olds were somewhat stronger than those provided at 1 or 2 months. It is not clear how small a change in velocity could be discriminated, allowing us to conclude only that infants as young as 1 or 2 months are capable of discriminating stimuli that vary over a *range* of velocities, and that older infants are perhaps more sensitive to changes in velocity.

Also using a preferential looking method, Kaufmann, Stucki, & Kaufmann-Hayoz (1985) examined 1- and 3-month-old infants' sensitivity to slow and rapid motions. Infants were presented with pairs of rotating dot circles. In the slow motion condition, infants saw one dot circle remain in a stationary position, while the other dot circle rotated in place on each trial at one of five predetermined velocities. In the rapid motion condition, one dot circle rotated at a velocity high enough to produce, in adults, stimulus fusion, while the other dot circle rotated at one of four predetermined (prefusion) velocities. The velocity at which 50% of the infants showed a clear visual preference of 60% or more of the total fixation time was taken as threshold. The authors reported that in the slow motion condition, the minimal velocity at which the moving stimulus was fixated significantly longer than the stationary stimulus was 84 min/sec for the 1-month-olds and 56 min/sec for the 3-month-olds. The minimal velocity at which more than 50% of the infants showed a visual preference was 126 min/sec for the 1-month-olds and 104 min/sec for the 3-month-olds. In general, then, the younger infants were less sensitive to the slow motions than were the older infants (although this conclusion was based on a lack of preference for faster velocities, and must thus be considered speculative).

In the rapid motion condition, the maximal velocity at which the slow-moving stimulus was fixated significantly longer than the fast stimulus for both age groups was 118°/second. The maximal velocity at which more than 50% of the infants showed a visual preference was also 118°/second. Collectively, these findings suggest that (1) infants are more sensitive to rapid motion than to slow motion and (2) the ability to respond to rapid motion develops little from 1 to 3 months, while the ability to respond to slow motion develops considerably.

Byrne and Horowitz (1984) examined the 3-month-old infant's ability to discriminate geometric forms moving at two different velocities, using an habituation paradigm. Infants were presented with a variety of achromatic geometric figures moving along a 120° trajectory at either 34.8 or 103.3°/sec (i.e., infants were habituated to a target moving at one velocity and tested on the same target moving at the other velocity). The authors reported that infants could discriminate between the same shape moving at both velocities, and that during the habituation phase infants spent the same amount of time looking at both the slow- and fast-moving shapes.

2. Effects of Motion on Attention

Girton (1979) asked if 5-week-old infants' attention to a schematic face would increase as the velocity of oscillating eye dots increased, using a sucking response as the dependent measure. Infants watched either a *face* perimeter condition, in which the eyes in a schematic face oscillated at 1, 4, or 7 cm/sec, or watched the eye dots alone, with no surrounding face (*no face* condition). Infants were given 36 16-sec stimulus presentations, 18 of the face condition and 18 of the no face condition. Within each condition, infants saw the eyes move for three trials at three different speeds, and for three trials with no motion. Girton reported that infants sucked less (i.e., attended more) during the trials in which the eye dots oscillated at 4 or 7 cm/sec than at 1 cm/second. This pattern of preferring the faster-moving eyes occurred regardless of whether or not the face was present.

Ivinskis and Finlay (1980) recorded both heart rate and visual fixation in 4-month-old infants viewing a 7-cm black square that moved in the horizontal meridian at either 3.6, 31.0, or 41.0 cm/second. The authors reported that there was significantly more heart-rate deceleration (an orienting response) to the fastest velocity relative to the slow and medium velocities. In addition, infants initially looked longer at the stimulus in the fast condition versus the slow and medium conditions, although these effects disappeared with repeated presentations.

Burnham and Dickinson (1981) presented 11- and 17-week-old infants with a variety of colored geometric forms (e.g., red circle) that moved in a 53° arc at 4 and at 10°/sec. Infants' eye movements were recorded on still film at a high sampling rate (e.g., .52 frames/sec). The authors reported that the probability of detecting and foveating the stimulus improved signficantly with age, although the speed of the stimulus did not affect capture. Interestingly, there were no age effects in pursuing the stimulus once captured, although pursuit was signficantly better (i.e., more accurate) at faster speeds.

D. Summary of Visual Tracking Studies

It is difficult to draw any firm conclusions from the studies reviewed above, as each differed on a number of important dimensions (e.g., rate of motion; type of motion; dependent variable; age of subject). Nevertheless, some tenable conclusions seem to have emerged from the studies as a whole.

First, it appears that soon after birth infants are capable of detecting and localizing motion in the peripheral field (see Finlay, Quinn, & Ivinskis, 1982, and Finlay & Ivinskis, 1984). Unlike smooth pursuit movements that do not become proficient until nearly the third month, tracking with the head and eyes seems quite developed by 1 to 2 months (e.g., Lawson & Ruff, 1984; Ruff et al., 1982). One caveat is that such tracking seems to be facilitated by the use of larger targets, and perhaps by the use of higher contrast targets. One might therefore propose that visual tracking is reasonably proficient in young infants so long as the limits of the visual system are not greatly exceeded (e.g., acuity, contrast sensitivity).

In addition to target size and possibly contrast, it seems that sound and relative motion cues also aid tracking. The former appears to do so by general arousal, while the latter may actually compensate for poor visual resolution (e.g., relative motion may provide additional contrast and make the moving object stand out from the background).

Infants seem to be able to discriminate changes in velocity over a rather broad range of velocities, although their specific aptitude in discriminating discrete changes is not yet clear. Infants tend to "prefer" fast- to relatively slow-moving stimuli, though the "fast" speed in one study may be the slow speed in another study. Both sensory and cognitive explanations of these findings exist. In terms of the former, Kaufmann, Stucki & Kaufmann-Hayoz (1985) reported that infants' sensitivity to slow-moving stimuli was still undergoing development over the first few months, while sensitivity to fast-moving stimuli seemed largely developed by 1 month. Thus, it may be that the limits of an infant's visual system preclude mainfesting a preference for slow-moving stimuli. However, the lack of a standard for what is "fast" and what is "slow" raises difficulties in comparing results of different studies.

There is also a cognitive explanation of the above findings. Given that object size and perhaps object contrast influence tracking, it may be that relatively slow-moving stimuli place more of a demand on an infant's rather limited cognitive resources because such stimuli facilitate not only detection and tracking, but also identification. In contrast, fast-moving stimuli are often not easily identified, as they cannot be fixated for long, and hence can only be tracked. In this case the demands of the task are less than in the former case. Both the present and foregoing explanations for the evidence that infants "prefer" fast- to slow-moving stimuli are reasonable but await empirical validation and better standardization of stimulus categories.

Overall, based on the evidence reported to date, the most parsimonious conclusions that can be drawn from the visual tracking literature are that (1) by the first month infants are able to detect and track moving stimuli with their eyes and heads, (2) such tracking can be facilitated by using larger objects, sounding objects, perhaps objects with higher contrast, and by providing relative motion cues, and (3) infants generally tend to prefer the faster of two moving stimuli, so long as such stimuli do not exceed the limits of the infant's perceptual–motor systems (i.e., eye and head.)

IV. REACHING AS AN INDEX OF TRACKING

Von Hofsten has adopted a considerably different approach to studying visual pursuit in which the criterion behavior has been the infant's reaching for stimuli moving in the horizontal meridian (von Hofsten, 1979, 1980; von Hofsten & Lindhagen, 1979). This behavior requires that the infant take note of both the spatial and temporal characteristics of the stimulus. In addition, the hand must be coordinated with the object's motion and in fact, must somehow predict the future location of the object if the object is to be accurately apprehended. The limitation of this technique, of course, is that directed reaching is not clearly in the infant's behavioral repertoire much before 12 weeks of age. Further, although it is not problematic for von Hofsten's purposes (who was primarily interested in describing reaching behavior), it is difficult to interpret instances in which reaching does not occur. That is, can one infer that an infant *cannot* track a stimulus if he/she fails to reach for it?

Von Hofsten and Lindhagen (1979) recorded the reaching behavior of 11 12- to 24-week-old infants at 3-week intervals until 30 weeks, and then again at 36 weeks. Infants sat in a semi-reclining seat and watched (at a distance of 11 or 16 cm) a brightly colored object (at a distance of 11 or 16 cm) move in a 115-cm horizontal path at 3.4, 15, or 30 cm/second. All the infants were successful in visually capturing the stimulus, although the 12-week-olds fixated less than the 24-week-olds. Analysis of the reaching records indicated that the slowest speed (3.4 cm/sec) elicited the largest number of reaching attempts at all ages. As the speed increased, however, the number of reaching attempts decreased with age; fewer younger versus older infants reached in the 30 cm/sec condition. Finally, while viewing distance had no bearing on the results, gender did: girls were more likely than boys to reach, although this effect too decreased with age.

Von Hofsten (1979) subsequently reanalyzed the data from five of the infants in the original study in an attempt to measure the specific spatio-temporal characteristics of the approach phase of infant reaching. A microanalysis of these data revealed that reaching skill, in general, improved considerably from 15 to 36 weeks. The reaching behavior of the younger infants was characterized most by ataxiclike movements (which von Hofsten referred to as "overdamping"), and a high instability in the arm transport. Such ballistic and awkward movements also coincided with immature grasping. It was also reported that, over time, reaching became less ataxic and the movements smoother, as well as the grasping more mature. A surprising finding was that approach to the object in all age groups tended to be most efficient in the fastest (30 cm/sec) condition.

In yet another reanalysis of the original data set, von Hofsten (1980) focused on the relationship of the grasp itself to object motion. Five infants from the original study (von Hofsten & Lindhagen, 1979) who had reached for the object in the fastest condition beginning at 18 weeks provided data for the reanalysis. The focus here was on how individual reaching was aimed relative to the moving object. Von Hofsten reported that a great majority of reaching behavior appeared to predict object location (i.e., was ahead of the moving object), and there was apparently no improvement of this skill over time. Nevertheless, while reaching was predictive, it still appeared somewhat inefficient (*vis-a-vis* transporting the arm through space), although as reported earlier (von Hofsten, 1979) this improved with age.

It is difficult to compare directly Von Hofsten's work on visual pursuit with the literature reviewed earlier, primarily because of the difference in response systems evaluated (i.e., visual fixation versus reaching) and the a priori goals of the studies (i.e., visual pursuit versus reaching behavior). In addition, one must interpret von Hofsten's later studies (1979, 1980) with some caution; in each of these studies the data from only five subjects were used, and these five were highly selected from the original already small sample of 11. Thus, to what extent these findings would generalize to a larger, more randomly selected sample of infants is not clear. Nevertheless, several aspects of Von Hofsten's findings merit serious consideration.

First, von Hofsten and Lindhagen (1979) reported that even 12-week-old infants were successful in visually capturing a moving target, although somewhat less so than the 24-week-olds. Such age trends roughly parallel the development of smooth pursuit abilities reported by Aslin (1981). That is, the ability to detect and visually capture a moving stimulus precedes the ability to track the stimulus smoothly through space. In addition, these findings essentially replicate those of Burnham and Dickinson (1981), who reported improvement in the ability to detect and foveate a moving stimulus from 11 to 17 weeks. Interestingly, von Hofsten and Lindhagen (1979) reported a decrease in reaching with increasing speed. However, Burnham and Dickinson (1981) reported that there were no age effects in pursuing the stimulus once captured and that pursuit improved with faster speeds. The fastest speed in the Burnham and Dickinson (1981) study was 10°/sec, which was considerably slower than that used by von Hofsten and Lindhagen (1979). Thus, the infants in the Burnham and Dickinson (1981) study might have also pursued less efficiently if the speed had been increased. Similarly, although infants in the study by von Hofsten and Lindhagen (1979) reached less at faster speeds, no mention was made as to whether they pursued less or were less efficient in their pursuit. Indeed, the increased attention to faster speeds reported by other investigators (e.g., Ivinskis & Finaly, 1980) may have inhibited reaching while increasing visual attention. This, of course, remains to be tested.

Also of interest to emerge from the von Hofsten work is the evidence for predictive reaching in the infants older than 18 weeks. Aslin (1981) reported anticipatory eye movements in several 10-week-olds. From these findings, then, there is the suggestion that predictive reaching and/ or tracking presuppose some, albeit primitive, notion of identity constancy. That is, to anticipate a change in an object's spatial location is tantamount to believing in the existence of the object despite a permutation in one of the object's defining features (i.e., a change in location). (For a more complete summary of identity constancy and object permanence skills, see Harris, 1983.)

Perhaps the most intriguing finding of von Hofsten's was that reaching was most efficient in the fastest (30 cm/sec) condition, even though infants tended to reach less in this condition than in the slower conditions. One may recall the speculation raised earlier, that relatively fast stimuli are more effective at recruiting and maintaining attention than slow-moving stimuli, perhaps because the former place fewer demands on the infant's sensory and/or cognitive capabilities. On the basis of von Hofsten's findings, it is possible to suggest further that less motor control is required, both of the eye–head movement system and of the reaching system, in apprehending fast-moving objects than slow-moving objects. Whether infants' reaching for fast versus slow-moving stimuli is better because less motor control is required or because fast-moving stimuli promote more attention is not clear and awaits direct examination (as does an exact determination of what constitutes "fast" versus "slow" movement). Nevertheless, the parallel between the visual following and reaching findings is intriguing.

V. PREFERENCE-FOR-MOTION STUDIES

We have commented that motion is considered a very salient stimulus parameter in the infant's visual world. What additional evidence is there for such a proposition?

Wilcox and Clayton (1968) presented 5-month-old infants with a silent, color motion picture of a woman's face that varied on two dimensions; motion (still or not) and facial expression (smiling, frowning, and neutral). Based on looking times, a strong visual preference was found for the moving versus stationary face, although there was little evidence that infants differentially fixated the different facial expressions.

Carpenter (1974) also explored the infant's perception of moving versus stationary faces. From 2 to 7 weeks of age infants were presented with the mother's face, a Caucasian manikin head, and a black manikin head as stimuli, with each infant seeing the stimuli in both stationary and moving conditions. In the movement condition, the stimulus moved 8.25 cm in the horizontal plane at a range of one excursion across and back per 2 sec (angular velocity was not specified). Carpenter reported that attention increased linearly with age (from 2 to 7 weeks) in both the moving and stationary conditions, and that faces received more attention when moving than when stationary. Interestingly, manikin faces attracted more attention than the infant's mother's face, but there was no differential attention to the two manikin faces.

In three more recent studies the infant's perception of moving versus stationary faces has been further explored. Using a paired comparison procedure, Sherrod (1979) presented 1-, 3-, and 5-month-old infants with a set of photographic stimuli consisting of the infant's mother's face (M), a stranger's face (S), a manikin face (Mn), a schematic face (Sch), and a geometric stimulus (G). All infants "ranked" the stimuli in order of S-M-Mn-Sch-G, with most attention directed to the animated as compared to the still faces. In a related study, R. Kaufmann and Kaufmann (1980) presented 3- and 4-month-old infants with a videotape of an immobile and moving human face. The authors reported that infants at both ages looked longer at the moving face. In addition, the 4-month-olds smiled more to the moving face, although the 3-month-olds did not. Finally, Nelson and Horowitz (1983) presented 5-month-old infants with a hologram of a face that either moved or remained stationary. Based on a number of response measures across two different experiments (e.g., total fixation time, trials to habituation criterion), there was no evidence that infants preferred the moving face over the stationary face. We will return to this discrepant finding.

Using nonface stimuli, McKenzie and Day (1976) recorded the fixation durations of 2- and 4-month-old infants as they watched stationary and moving patterned cylinders presented at distances of 30, 50, 70, and 90 cm object–observer distances. The authors reported that younger infants looked longer than older infants at all distances in both movement conditions and that moving objects were fixated longer than stationary objects. In addition, the fixation durations of stationary objects decreased with increasing distances, while the fixation durations for moving objects were unaffected by object–observer distance.

The simplest and most parsimonious conclusion to be drawn from the motion-preference literature is that infants as young as 2 weeks prefer to look at moving versus stationary two-dimensional stimuli, even when these stimuli are identical on all other dimensions. One qualifier to this conclusion, however, is that Nelson and Horowitz (1983) failed to find a preference among 5-month-olds for a moving three-dimensional (hologram) of a face. One possible explanation for this discrepancy may be that for infants old enough to be sensitive to binocular and monocular depth cues (see Fox, Aslin, Shea, & Dumais, 1980; Granrud, 1984), the information present in a three-dimensional stimulus (e.g., perspective transformations brought about by head movements) may be as or more compelling than the motion of the stimulus *per se*. [This explanation would also account for the difference between the 5-month-old infants tested in the Nelson & Horowitz (1983) study, and the 2- to 7-week-old infants tested in the Carpenter (1974) study, as the latter would be relatively insensitive to the depth information.] Leaving aside this speculation, however, it does appear that at the very least motion plays a significant role in influencing infant attention.

VI. STUDIES OF INFORMATION CONTAINED IN MOTION

Two of the important issues in relation to motion perception are whether there is information in moving stimuli to which infants are particularly sensitive, and whether motion does more than merely recruit and sustain infant looking. The notion that there is "information" contained in motion to which the organism is sensitive has been most forceably argued by J. J. Gibson (1966, 1979). For example, J. J. Gibson (1966) has proposed that the state of motion of an object, as well as its form, can be detected by attending to optical transformations and to the distinctive features mapped onto the optic array. Thus, when a three-dimensional object moves, there is a progressive occlusion and disocculsion of the object's surface features. These continuous changes in perspective essentially provide the observer with a constant flux of information about the object proper. Illustrative of this would be a moving versus stationary face: If a static observer viewed a static face, the face would be seen from but one perspective (a frontal view, for example). However, if the same face were suddenly to begin to move back and forth on its axis, the observer would now witness the same face from a variety of perspectives (e.g., from frontal view to three-quarter pose to full profile and back). Thus, these changes in perspective brought about by motion provide information about the object (e.g., seeing a person from different points of view) that would not be provided had the object (and observer) not moved. Whether young infants are sensitive to such information has been the topic of several investigations.

E. J. Gibson, Owsley, and Johnston (1978), using an habituation paradigm, presented 5-month-old infants with successive random presentations of three types of rigid motion until an habituation criterion was obtained. Following habituation, half the infants received a fourth type of rigid motion, while the other half saw a deformation. The authors reported that infants habituated at different rates to different types of motion (i.e., fastest to looming motion, second to rotation around the vertical axis, and slowest to rotation in the frontal plane and around a horizontal axis). Furthermore, subjects dishabituated to the deformation but not to the fourth type of rigid motion, suggesting that infants detected the invariant property of rigidity and differentiated it from the deformation.

E. J. Gibson, Owsley, Walker, and Megaw-Nyce (1979) conducted three experiments with 3-month-old infants in an attempt to replicate and extend their earlier findings. In the first experiment, infants were presented with a rigid motion with alternating shapes (circles, squares, and triangles) until an habituation criterion was met. Following habituation, the infants were presented with the objects undergoing a different rigid motion, a deforming motion, or the same rigid motion. Habituation was maintained to the new rigid motion, indicating that the two rigid motions were perceived as sharing an invariant property. In contrast, dishabituation was found when a deforming motion followed a rigid motion. In the second experiment, infants were habituated to one shape undergoing two different rigid motions. Following habituation, the shape was changed but the two motions continued. Dishabituation occurred in response to the new shape but did not occur in the no-shape control condition. Shape thus appeared to be distinguished as an invariant property over two rigid motions. In the final experiment, habituation to a shape undergoing two rigid motions was followed by a new shape presented motionless or by the same shape presented motionless. It was found that there was no recovery when the shape stayed the same and the motion stopped, but there was recovery when the shape changed. The authors concluded that infants were able to detect the invariant information present in both shape and rigid motion.

Ball (1980) conducted two experiments with $3\frac{1}{2}$ and $4\frac{1}{2}$-month-old infants to determine if they could extract information about the features and the configuration of elements moving in a circular path. The first experiment employed three main sets of stimuli: one set consisted of cutouts of a scrambled and regular face, while the remaining two sets consisted of geometric patterns. Infants were presented with three blocks of four trials each, each trial lasting 15 sec with an intertrial interval of 10 sec. During a given trial block, infants were presented with a pair of stimuli from a given set, first in a stationary position and then moving in a rotating fashion (4 revolutions/min) or the reverse. Each subsequent trial block preserved the same order of moving to still or the reverse. The author reported that infants preferred the regular face over the scrambled face independent of whether or not the face was moving or still. In terms of the other two pairs of stimuli, infants tended in both cases to prefer the moving to the stationary stimuli, although this was more true for one pair than the other. In a second experiment, comparably aged infants were presented with three new sets of stimuli (all geometric patterns), using the same procedure as before, except that now the stimuli turned constantly on all trials. The only significant result was that infants preferred one stimulus set over another (i.e., the rounded cross over the square). Overall, Ball concluded that the extraction of figural information does not seem to depend upon seeing the object in a static orientation. As is the case with all studies examining visual preferences, however, it is difficult to interpret findings based on a lack of a preference.

Ruff (1982) conducted three experiments using a paired-comparison procedure and 6-month-old infants. In the first experiment infants were familiarized to two types of motion. In one case the orientation of the object changed from trial to trial (orientation condition), while in the second the object changed location without rotation, so that perspective but not orientation changes were seen (translation condition). Infants were tested after the third and sixth trials with a novel object paired with the familiar object (both objects were stationary and appeared in the same orientation). Only infants who had seen the objects translating discriminated the novel from familiar objects. In a second experiment, infants were again divided into two groups. In one, infants were familiarized to an object that only rotated and did not translate. In another, infants were familiarized to an object that only changed its orientation once during a trial (versus the continuous changes in the first experiment). The design was essentially the same as in Experiment 1. It was found that both groups successfully discriminated the novel from familiar objects, but only on the second test. These results were extended in a final experiment that departed in some ways from the first two. More discriminable objects were employed, and the degree of change from familiarization to test was kept constant by having the objects move in the same way during the test trials as during the familiarization trials. Additionally, only one test was given that followed a long (1.5 min) familiarization period, and, more important, an attempt was made to equate the looking times in the translation and rotation conditions by displacing the rotating object against the background as it was rotated (promoting more attention). In all other respects Experiment 3 was identical to Experiment 1. Infants again evidenced reliable discrimination only in the translation condition. However, when a second group of infants who were given additional familiarization time was tested with the rotation condition, discrimination obtained. Ruff concluded, on the basis of all three experiments, that infants demonstrate better differentiation between novel and familiar objects after prior exposure to a translating object than after exposure to the same object rotating. Moreover, it appears that 6-month-old infants require more time to recognize the structure of a rotating object than a translating one.[2]

In a series of studies, Day and colleagues (Burnham & Day, 1979; Day & Burnham, 1981) also examined the infant's sensitivity to the information contained in moving objects. In a first study, Burnham and Day (1979) asked if 8- and 20-week-old infants could detect the color of stationary and moving objects and maintain this discrimination over changes in velocity. Infants were familiarized during the habituation trials to either a stationary or a revolving patterned cylinder (Experiment 1), or the same object when it was revolving at one of two angular velocities (42° and 84°/sec) and at two different distances (90 and 100 cm, respectively, for Experiments 2 and 3). In the postfamiliarization trials, angular velocity was changed, with the color of the pattern either the same as or different from that in the familiarization trials. It was found in Experiment 1 that infants at both ages looked longer to the moving versus stationary cylinder, with the younger infants looking longer than the older infants. Furthermore, the duration of fixation to patterns of a familiar color decreased from the pre- to the postfamiliarization stage, while the duration for those of a novel color remained the same, indicating that infants could detect a pattern of a familiar color even when it changed from stationary to moving or vice versa. In Experiments 2 and 3 subjects tended to look longer at fast versus slow-moving patterns in both pre- and postfamiliarization trials, and novel colors were looked at longer than familiar colors in the postfamiliarization stage after exposure to a familiar color. This was more true of the older than of the younger subjects but did occur for both ages. The authors concluded that 8- to 20-week-old infants are sensitive to the movement of a revolving pattern and to at least one other feature (color) and respond to this feature when the pattern changes from movement to stationary and vice versa, and from slow to fast and vice versa.

Day and Burnham (1981) subsequently followed up their earlier study, asking essentially the same question, "Can 8- to 20-week-old infants perceive and later recognize features of laterally moving objects in both moving and stationary conditions?" Five experiments were conducted, all of which used four separate objects (red and green circles and triangles). In the first two experiments infants were habituated to one of the above objects moving at 4°/sec and tested on a novel object moving at the same speed or not moving at all. It was found that infants could discriminate the shapes of objects and could generalize this discrimination from

[2] Ruff (1985) published a study in which more detailed knowledge of object motion was studied in 3½- and 5-month old infants. For more information on this topic, the reader is encouraged to consult this study.

the moving to stationary condition, although this result failed to obtain for color. In the third experiment, infants were habituated to one of the above objects in a stationary position and tested with a novel object moving at 4°/second. Infants' looking recovered equally during all test trials, prohibiting any conclusions from being drawn regarding the discrimination of shape and color but suggesting that infants were responding instead to the motion component alone. The fourth experiment was a replication of the first experiment, except that the speed was increased to 10°/sec. No recovery was obtained, suggesting that infants could not discriminate shape or color at the faster speed. In the final experiment, infants were again familiarized to one of the objects moving at 10°/sec but were tested with the novel object in a stationary position. Unlike the results of Experiment 2, there was no evidence that infants could discriminate and generalize their discrimination of shape from moving to stationary conditions. The authors concluded that 8- to 20-week-old infants are capable of discriminating shape (but not color) at the slower (4°/sec) but not faster (10°/sec) speeds, and of generalizing this discrimination from the moving to stationary but not stationary to moving conditions. These results are contradicted by Byrne and Horowitz (1984), who did find shape discrimination in 3-month-old infants at both 34.8 and 103.3°/sec, speeds considerably faster than those used by Day and Burnham. It is not clear how to interpret these rather disparate sets of findings, given that the age of the younger infants was similar across studies, as were the stimuli and the paradigm used.

Two final sets of studies dealing with infants' perception of the information contained in motion will now be considered. Both employed somewhat unorthodox stimulus media, the first involving the perception of "biological motion" and the second with motion present in holograms.

Fox and McDaniel (1982) tested 2-, 4-, and 6-month-old infants on their sensitivity to "biological motion," a term used by Johannsson (e.g., 1978) to refer to the observation that one can infer the pattern of human activity (e.g., walking) from the motion of luminous dots attached to the torso and limbs of a moving human. As the authors point out, such perceptions have been taken as evidence that the visual system is sensitive to invariant higher-order stimulus information imbedded in the pattern. In addition, Johannsson (1978), among others, has hypothesized this sensitivity to be an innate capacity of the visual system rather than one acquired through experience. To test these claims, the authors conducted three experiments. In the first experiment, infants were presented with a biological motion pattern of a human running in place paired with a pattern comprising the same number of dots but moving in random directions. An observer judged to which side of the screen the infant attended during each trial (minimum of 10 15-sec trials). It was found that the two oldest groups preferred the biological motion pattern. A second experiment was designed in which the biological motion pattern and a random dot pattern were more similar (i.e., in the first experiment the latter pattern differed from the former in the rate and magnitude of the motion). The biological motion pattern in this experiment was the same as in Experiment 1, while the dot pattern was identical but inverted 180°. Only 4- and 6-month-old infants were tested and both groups once again preferred the biological motion pattern. To extend these findings to yet another biological motion pattern, a third experiment was conducted. Here the pattern consisted of a pair of hands that appeared to come together to clasp an invisible glass and then withdraw. The control pattern was comprised of dots put on the same pair of hands but in off-joint locations. Two-, 4-, and 6-month-olds were tested as before, and this time only the older age group preferred the biological motion pattern. Overall, the authors concluded that between the ages of 4 and 6 months infants become sensitive to biological motion. Similar conclusions have been drawn by Bertenthal, Proffitt, and Cutting (1984).[3]

Nelson and Horowitz (1983, Experiment 3) tested 5-month-old infants under two conditions, using a holographic stereogram of a woman's face that, when moved horizontally, changed expression from happy to neutral and back again. In one condition infants were habituated to one "scene" in the face (e.g., the woman with a neutral expression) presented in a static position and were then presented with the same stimulus with motion added (resulting in the woman repeatedly changing her expression and orientation: i.e., full-face to three-quarter profile). Infants in a second condition saw the reverse (moving to stationary). If infants are able to abstract higher-order invariant information from a moving display and generalize this to a stationary display (as demonstrated by Day & Burnham, 1981), then during the test phase infants in the moving to stationary condition should recognize the woman's face as "same" and their looking should not recover. On the other hand, since such information is not present in a static three-dimensional display with a relatively immobile observer (as was the case here), then infants in the stationary to moving condition *should* increase their looking when the face begins to move, as the face they see should appear in a multitude of orientations and appear to be changing expression. These were the findings reported by the authors, leading them to conclude that infants were able to detect

---

[3] Bertenthal and colleagues (e.g., Bertenthal & Proffitt, 1984; Bertenthal, Proffitt, Spetner, & Thomas, 1985) have conducted an extensive series of studies on "biomechanical motion." The reader is encouraged to consult this work for excellent coverage of this topic.

the invariant information in the moving face and generalize this to the stationary face. Although this conclusion seems tenable, one must entertain the notion that infants in the stationary to moving condition dishabituated not because they saw the face as new, but simply because the addition of motion attracted their attention. If this explanation is correct, however, why then did the *cessation* of motion in the moving to stationary condition result in generalized habituation? (The question here, of course, is whether it is motion *per se* that recruits attention, or motion contrasts.)

Summary of Information-Contained-in-Motion Studies

There are now in the literature a relatively large number of studies designed to examine infants' sensitivity to the information contained in moving stimuli. At first glance, it appears that J. J. Gibson (1966, 1979) was correct in assuming that infants are sensitive to such information. The consensus seems to indicate that infants are able to detect invariant information in moving stimuli (information that is not present in stationary stimuli) and generalize this information to a different type of motion or to a nonmoving stimulus. Such information ranges from how rigid or elastic an object is to biological motion patterns to changes in the perspective of a face. In all cases such information seems to be brought about by the onset of motion: that is, should the same object suddenly stop moving this information fails to exist, as long as the observer is also relatively stationary. If we assume that the information "picked up" by an infant is the same regardless of whether or not the object moves and the observer remains still, or the observer moves and the object remains still, one could make the argument that motion-induced information is an inherent part of the stimulus itself, available under either conditions of object or observer motion. One might be thus tempted to claim that detecting and perceiving motion is critical to the infant's coding of information about the real world, as motion parameters impart higher-order information not available from any other source. The critical test of this assumption is not easy, as motion is ubiquitous in the infant's experience from birth onward. However, specially constructed stimuli presented in creative experimental paradigms could be devised to explore the issues involved.

VII.   GENERAL DISCUSSION

It would appear that human infants, presumably along with the infants of many other animal species, come into the world specially adapted to perceive motion. Though infants are unable to track a moving target smoothly with the eyes alone until about 3 months of age, tracking with the head and eyes occurs much earlier, and detection of motion is apparent shortly after birth. When comparisons are made between moving and static stimuli in the laboratory, preference is shown for the moving stimulus; when stimuli are presented moving at two different speeds, preference is shown for the faster of the two speeds, though the calibration of speed of movement is not standard for fast–slow comparisons. More comparative analyses are needed before anything definitive can be said about the absolute speed of motion in relation to attention or preference. At about 3–4 months of age, and perhaps earlier, infants begin to resonate to the information contained in moving stimuli, information that appears to be lacking if the same stimulus is presented motionless and the infant is not moving.

We know much more about the role of motion when movement is associated with the stimulus than when the infant's own movements reveal information about the stimulus.[4] Although a reasonable starting assumption is that there is not a significant difference between the two, there is no evidence that bears directly upon this at the present time. However, given the pervasiveness of infant movement in relation to objects in the natural environment, it is likely that this is a very important source of information for the young infant. Our current knowledge about the details of the role of motion in facilitating the infant's perceptual and cognitive development is clearly fragmentary, but we know both from informal observations in the natural environment and from the experimental evidence we do have that motion and movement cues are critical components of the infant's experience.

A variety of theoretical implications and a number of issues related to empirical questions can be generated from this chapter. In his discussion of newborn scanning of visual stimuli, Haith (1980) proposed a set of "rules" that appear to govern newborn visual scanning. Although enough is not yet known about motion perception in infants to propose a comparable set of rules, several observations about infants' knowledge of moving objects can be made. One observation is that infants typically pay attention to all objects moving in the visual field, and indeed, tend to prefer such objects over stationary objects. A second observation is that once such objects are detected, infants tend to move their eyes and/or eyes and head (perhaps depending on the age and motoric intactness of the infant) in the direction of the moving target, and to track the target.

---

[4] See Bertenthal, Campos, and Barrett (1984) for a discussion of the effects of self-produced locomotion on nonperceptual abilities.

The likelihood of tracking seems to depend on four factors: the infant's age, the size of the object, perhaps the contrast of the object, and whether the object is moving relative to a stationary background or perhaps a moving background. With moving stimuli, age, size, and contrast are interdependent and must also relate to factors of contour density and spatial frequency. Older infants, more tolerant of smaller objects containing less contrast, may track independent of size and contrast so long as both aspects are within certain limits. Younger infants, on the other hand, are less likely to track for long or at all if the object is too small to be detected or resolved, or the contrast is beyond an infant's contrast sensitivity function. One intriguing question that arises here is whether we could ultimately fit and extend the age-related data from the tracking literature to the data from the static stimulus–visual perception literature. This might permit us to enhance our understanding of early perceptual and cognitive development and to enable us to move toward an ecologically valid picture of the developmental course as it integrates across moving and static stimuli.

Yet another observation of infant motion perception is that infants typically maintain attention to fast-moving objects (a definition of which is still lacking) vis-a-vis prolonged tracking, but they generally make little attempt to identify the moving object. On the other hand, such identification is generally more successful when the objects move slowly. Because of the increased demand the latter situation may place on the infant's somewhat limited cognitive resources, relatively slow-moving stimuli will be attended to for shorter periods of time than faster-moving stimuli, and indeed, if a choice exists, infants often choose to track the "fast" rather than the "slow" stimulus.

The preceding observations are, of course, first approximations to what may be involved in the prominent role played by motion parameters of stimuli in the infant's perceptual world. It would be naive to assume that it is *because* moving stimuli contain information not contained in stationary stimuli that infants resonate most to the former. However appealing such a functional explanation appears, there are presently no data to support this claim directly. Nevertheless, as indicated in this chapter, motion does seem to play a special role in the infant's world. While it appears not to be until 3 months of age that infants become more sensitive to the information contained in moving objects (e.g., Fox & McDaniel, 1982; E. J. Gibson et al., 1979), it may be that the importance of motion perception prior to this age is that it provides a period of training for what is to come. An adequate understanding of the role of motion will, however, undoubtedly require a much more elaborate description than is presently possible. Both Gibson and Piaget referred to the infant's "active" role in seeking out information from the environment. J. J. Gibson (1979) particularly singles out active pursuit of information from the "ambient optic array," but it is not clear whether such activity requires locomotor skills. Obviously, in the very earliest months locomotor skills are limited. However, Piaget's analogous characterization of the infant's active concourse with the environment initially requires only eye movements and then the development of directed reaching, both of which probably interact with elements of movement inherent in stimuli in the environment and in the infant's own movement. Though, as we have noted, there is almost no experimental evidence that deals with the role of movement on the part of the infant as it affects perceptual and cognitive functioning (but see Bertenthal, Campos, & Barrett, 1984), at a theoretical level much of what Piaget talks about in terms of the child "acting" on the environment may functionally involve self-produced movement, resulting in repeated exposure to stimulus information about objects and people from the vantage point of different positions. One is reminded of Hebb's (1949) notion of the formation of cell assemblies as the result of repeated exposure to the same stimulus or stimulus set from various vantage points—many of which are "self-produced" by infant motion in relation to stimulus objects. In fact, since the infant controls movement speed more directly in infant-produced movement than when stimuli in the environment move independently of the infant, such variety of information as results from the self-produced movement cues may be more effective stimulants to perceptual and cognitive development than the information cues detected as the result of independent object movement. There may be more "temporal regularity" in self-produced movement cues, and this temporal regularity may be an important source for handling information about the world. Anderson (1972) has noted that temporal regularity may have a role in information transfer that is analogous to spatial regularity. Temporal regularity has been increasingly implicated as important in the auditory domain for affecting infant responsivity (Miller & Byrne, 1983). It is exciting to think that temporal cues, coded in movement for visual stimuli, and in signal intervals in auditory stimuli, might provide the basis for the theoretical integration of the laws that govern visual and auditory perception. Any attempt to do so now is obviously premature.

Observers of episodes of mothers and infants in interaction have long noted that positive interactions seem to be characterized by "synchrony" and negative ones by "asynchrony" (e.g., Condon & Sander, 1974). Movement cues appear to play an important role in these different kinds of interactions, though quantification and even qualitative descriptors have not been easy accomplishments. However, both the smoothness of movement and the speed of movement involved in synchronous and asynchronous interactions would appear to be important dimensions of these episodes. Indeed, interactions with premature infants are often noted as disconcerting to parents because the movement cues of the premature infant are often jerky and precipitous and it is more difficult to establish synchronous interactions.

Though our discussion has taken us considerably beyond the data base on the role of motion in infant perception, the ubiquity of motion in the natural environment cannot be ignored in trying to think how it affects early infant perceptual and cognitive development.

For example, it is interesting to consider that there may be nothing special about moving objects *per se*. The information contained in such objects can be thought of as merely elicited when the objects begin to undergo some transformation, such as rotation or translation. Infants may not be specially equipped to attend to such information. Rather, initially they may simply be prepared to attend to anything that moves. Such as assertion, however, can be deceptive. Being "primed" to perceive motion could be thought of as a significant adaptive advantage. This advantage serves a basic sensory purpose during the first few months of life, providing the infant, for example, with practice in smooth pursuit. Once some of the basic motion perception skills have been sufficiently sharpened (e.g., motion detection), the infant is now in a position to reap the fruits of his/her labor, namely, to pick up the higher-order information (presumably) inherent in such stimuli. Had the infant not been prepared to do so by the previous months of experience (natural training?), a critical aspect of the infant's perceptual development would be lacking.

The skills of motion perception are more advanced at birth than other perceptual skills. This "head start" could be thought of as having adaptive significance of two sorts. First, in terms of survival value it is important to attend more to moving objects than to stationary objects, as stationary objects do not ordinarily threaten survival. Second, if infants are eventually to take advantage of the information that is inherent in moving objects, then they must practice perceiving such objects. It is only after such skills are sufficiently developed that such information becomes available and it is only at this time that a whole new aspect of the visual world is opened up to the infant. Whether the result is a growing bank of cell assemblies, or S–R and S–S associations, or the coding of stimulus information, or the facilitation of information processing strategies—or all of the above—remains to be understood. Some of the empirical and theoretical advances will come from programmatic research involving the experimental manipulation of the variables involved in motion, perhaps aided by the increased experimental control of stimulus dimensions possible in specially constructed holographic stimuli. However, it is probably also important to analyze, through observations of naturally occurring environmental events, the ecologically effective aspects of motion. For example, codifying the movement speeds involved in mother–infant interactions of both infant and mother, expecially during episodes judged to involve "synchrony" and to facilitate positive affect interchanges, may provide us with important clues with respect to the movement speeds that might most fruitfully be investigated in the laboratory. Techniques that build upon the eye-movement camera strategies employed to study reading behavior may yield useful information about the self-produced stimulus information that the infant generates by his or her own movement in relation to both static and moving stimuli.

In writing this chapter our goal was to summarize the existing literature related to motion perception, to identify the kinds of questions that need to be asked, and to consider what we believe are the important contributions that systematic research on these questions will make to our understanding of early infant development. Ultimately, we hope that this chapter will stimulate the kinds of research that will result in broadening the empirical data base on motion perception and provide for promising theoretical advances.

ACKNOWLEDGMENTS

The writing of this paper was made possible by the following sources of support: NICHD (HD 1R32 07173, 1F32 HD 06231, HD5R01 1608); the BEH through the Institute for Early Childhood Research at the University of Kansas (USDE 300-33-0308); and by the Center for Study in the Behavioral Sciences, where Frances Degen Horowitz was a Fellow (1983-84) supported by the John D. and Kathleen T. MacArthur Foundation. The authors are indebted to Herbert Pick, Jr., for his careful reading of the manuscript and his many helpful suggestions.

REFERENCES

Anderson, P. N. (1972). More is different. *Science, 177,* 393–396.
Aslin, R. N. (1981). Development of smooth pursuit in human infants. In D. F. Fisher, R. A. Monty, & E. J. Senders (Eds.), *Eye movements: Cognition and visual perception* (pp. 33–51). Hillsdale, NJ: Erlbaum.
Ball, W. A. (1980). Infants' perception of structure of form across changing orientations. *International Journal of Behavioral Development, 3,* 147–157.
Banks, M. S., & Salapatek, P. (1983). Infant visual perception. In M. Haith & J. Campos (Eds.), *Handbook of child psychology: Vol. 2. Infancy and developmental psychobiology* (pp. 435–571). New York: Wiley.
Barlow, H. B., & Pettigrew, J. O. (1971). Lack of specificity of neurones in the visual cortex of young kittens. *Journal of Physiology, (London), 218,* 98–100.
Barten, S., Birns, B., & Ronch, J. (1971). Individual differences in the visual pursuit behavior of neonates. *Child Development, 42,* 313–319.

Bertenthal, B. I., Campos, J. J., & Barrett, K. C. (1984). Self-produced locomotion: An organizer of emotional, cognitive, and social development in infancy. In R. N. Emde & R. J. Harmon (Eds.), *Continuities and discontinuities in development* (pp. 175–210). New York: Plenum.

Bertenthal, B. I., & Proffitt, D. R. (1984). Infants' encoding of kinetic displays varying in figural coherence. *Infant Behavior and Development, 7,* 34.

Bertenthal, B. I., Proffitt, D. R., & Cutting, J. E. (1984). Infant sensitivity to figural coherence in biomechanical motions. *Journal of Experimental Child Psychology, 37,* 213–230.

Bertenthal, B. I., Proffitt, D. R., Spetner, N. B., & Thomas, M. A. (1985). The development of infant sensitivity to biomechanical motions. *Child Development, 56,* 531–543.

Blakemore, C. (1974). Developmental factors in the formation of feature extracting neurons. In F. O. Schmitt & F. G. Worden (Eds.), *The neurosciences: Third study program.* Cambridge, MA: M.I.T. Press.

Bower, T. G. R., Broughton, J., & Moore, M. K. (1971). Development of the object concept as manifested in changes in the tracking behavior of infants between 7 and 20 weeks of age. *Journal of Experimental Child Psychology, 11,* 182–193.

Brazelton, T. B., Scholl, M. L., & Robey, J. S. (1966). Visual responses in the newborn. *Pediatrics, 37,* 284–290.

Burnham, D. K., & Day, R. H. (1979). Detection of color in rotating objects by infants and its generalization over changes in velocity. *Journal of Experimental Child Psychology, 28,* 191–204.

Burnham, D. K., & Dickinson, R. G. (1981). The determinants of visual capture and visual pursuit in infancy. *Infant Behavior and Development, 4,* 359–372.

Byrne, J. M., & Horowitz, F. D. (1984). The perception of stimulus shape: The influence of velocity of stimulus movement. *Child Development, 55,* 1625–1629.

Carpenter, G. (1974). Visual regard of moving and stationary faces in early infancy. *Merrill-Palmer Quarterly, 20,* 181–194.

Condon, W. S., & Sander, L. W. (1974). Synchrony demonstrated between movements of the neonate and adult speech. *Child Development, 45,* 456–462.

Day, R. H., & Burnham, D. K. (1981). Infants' perception of shape and color in laterally moving patterns. *Infant Behavior and Development, 4,* 341–357.

Dayton, G. O., & Jones, M. H. (1964). Analysis of characteristics of fixation reflex in infants by use of direct electrooculography. *Neurology, 14,* 1152-1156.

Dayton, G. O., Jones, M. H., Aiu, P., Rawson, R. A., Steele, B., & Rose, M. (1964). Developmental study of coordinated eye movements in the human infant. I. Visual acuity in the newborn human: A study based on induced optokinetic nystagmus recorded by electrooculography. *Archives of Ophthalmology, 71,* 865–870.

Dayton, G. O., Jones, M. H., Steele, B., & Rose, M. (1964). Developmental study of coordinated eye movements in the human infant. II. An electrooculographic study of the fixation reflex in the newborn. *Archives of Ophthalmology, 71,* 871–875.

Doris, J., & Cooper, L. (1966). Brightness discrimination in infancy. *Journal of Experimental Child Psychology, 3,* 31–39.

Fantz, R. L., Ordy, J. M., & Udelf, M. S. (1962). Maturation of pattern vision in infants during the first six months. *Journal of Comparative and Physiological Psychology, 55,* 907–917.

Finlay, D., & Ivinskis, A. (1984). Cardiac and visual responses to moving stimuli presented either successively or simultaneously to the central and peripheral visual fields in 4-month-old infants. *Developmental Psychology, 20,* 29–36.

Finlay, D., Quinn, K., & Ivinskis, A. (1982). Detection of moving stimuli in the binocular and nasal visual fields by infants three and four months old. *Perception, 11,* 685–690.

Fox, R., Aslin, R. N., Shea, S. L., & Dumais, S. T. (1980). Stereopsis in human infants. *Science, 207,* 323–324.

Fox, R., & McDaniel, C. (1982). The perception of biological motion by human infants. *Science, 218,* 486–487.

Gibson, E. J., Owsley, C. J., & Johnston, J. (1978). Perception of invariants by five-month-old infants: Differentiation of two types of motion. *Developmental Psychology, 14,* 407–415.

Gibson, E. J., Owsley, C. J., Walker, A., & Megaw-Nyce, J. (1979). Development of the perception of invariants: Substance and shape. *Perception, 8,* 609–619.

Gibson, E. J., & Spelke, E. S. (1983). The development of perception. In J. H. Flavell & E. M. Markman (Eds.), *Handbook of child psychology: Vol. 3. Cognitive development* (pp. 1–76). New York: Wiley.

Gibson, J. J. (1966). *The senses considered as perceptual systems.* Boston, MA: Houghton-Mifflin.

Gibson, J. J. (1979). *The ecological approach to visual perception.* Boston, MA: Houghton-Mifflin.

Girton, M. R. (1979). Infants' attention to intrastimulus motion. *Journal of Experimental Child Psychology, 28,* 416–423.

Gorman, J. J., Cogan, D. G., & Gellis, S. S. (1957). An apparatus for grading the visual acuity of infants on the basis of optiokinetic nystagmus. *Pediatrics, 19,* 1088–1092.

Granrud, C. E. (1984). Infants' perception of pictorially specified interposition. *Journal of Experimental Child Psychology, 37,* 500–511.

Granrud, C. E., Yonas, A., Smith, I. M., Anterberry, M. E., Glicksman, M. L., & Sorkness, A. C. (1984). Infants' sensitivity to accretion and deletion of texture as information for depth at an edge. *Child Development, 55,* 1630–1636.

Haith, M. M. (1978). Visual competence in early infancy. In R. Held, H. Leibowitz, & H. L. Teuber (Eds.), *Handbook of sensory physiology,* (Vol. 8. pp. 311–356). Berlin & New York: Springer-Verlag.

Haith, M. M. (1980). *Rules that babies look by.* Hillsdale, NJ: Erlbaum.

Haith, M. M., Kessen, W., & Collins, D. (1969). Response of the human infant to level of complexity of intermittent visual movement. *Journal of Experimental Child Psychology, 7,* 52–69.

Harris, P. L. (1983). Infant cognition. In M. Haith & J. Campos (Eds.), *Handbook of child psychology: Vol 2. Infancy and developmental psychobiology* (pp. 689–782.) New York: Wiley.

Harris, P. L., Cassel, T. Z., & Bamborough, P. (1974). Tracking by young infants. *British Journal of Psychology, 65,* 345–349.

Hebb, D. O. (1949). *The organization of behavior.* New York: Wiley.

Ivinskis, A., & Finlay, D. C. (April, 1980). *Cardiac responses in four-month-old infants to stimuli moving at three different velocities.* Paper presented at the International Conference on Infant Studies, New Haven, CT.

Johannsson, G. (1978). Visual event-perception. In R. Held, H. W. Leibowitz, & H. L. Teuber (Eds.), *Handbook of sensory physiology: Vol. 8. Perception* (pp. 675–711). Berlin & New York: Springer-Verlag.

Kaufmann, F., Stucki, M., & Kaufman-Hayoz, R. (1985). Development of sensitivity for slow and rapid motions. *Infant Behavior and Development, 8,* 89–98.

Kaufmann, R., & Kaufmann, F. (1980). The face schema in 3- and 4-month-old infants: The role of dynamic properties of the face. *Infant Behavior and Development, 3,* 331–339.

Kellman, P. J., Spelke, E. S., & Shontt, K. R. (1986). Infants' perception of object unity from translatory motion in depth and vertical translation. *Child Development, 57,* 72–86.

Kremenitzer, J. P., Vaughn, H. G., Kurtzberg, D., & Dowling, K. (1979). Smooth-pursuit eye movements in the newborn infant. *Child Development, 50,* 442–448.

Lasky, R. E., & Gogol, W. C. (1978). The perception of relative motion by young infants. *Perception, 7,* 617–623.

Lawson, K. R., & Ruff, H. A. (1984). Infants' visual following: Effects of size and sound. *Developmental Psychology, 20,* 427–434.

McGinnis, J. M. (1930). Eye movements and optic nystagmus in early infancy. *Genetic Psychology Monographs, 8,* 321–430.

McKenzie, B. E., & Day, R. H. (1977). Infants' attention to stationary and moving objects at different distances. *Australian Journal of Psychology, 28,* 45–51.

Maurer, D. (1985). Infants' perception of faces. In T. M. Field & N. A. Fox (Eds.), *Social perception in infants* (pp. 73–100). New Jersey: Ablex.

Miller, C. L., & Byrne, J. M. (1983). Psychophysiological and behavioral responses to auditory stimuli in the newborn. *Infant Behavior and Development, 6,* 369–389.

Miller, N. E. (1959). Liberalization of basic S-R concepts: Extensions to conflict behavior, motivation and social learning. In S. Koch (Ed.), *Psychology, a study of a science* (Vol. 2). New York: McGraw-Hill.

Nelson, C. A., & Horowitz, F. D. (1983). The perception of facial expressions and stimulus motion by 2- and 5-month-old infants using holographic stimuli. *Child Development, 54,* 868–877.

Owsley, C. (1983). The role of motion in infants' perception of solid shape. *Perception, 12,* 707–717.

Riddoch, G. (1917). Dissociation of visual perceptions due to occipital injuries with special reference to appreciation of movement. *Brain, 40,* 15–57.

Ruff, H. A. (1982). Effect of object movement on infants' detection of object structure. *Developmental Psychology, 18,* 462–472.

Ruff, H. A. (1985). Detection of information specifying the motion of objects by 3- and 5-month-old infants. *Developmental Psychology, 21,* 295–305.

Ruff, H. A., Lawson, K. R., Kurtzburg, D., McCarton-Daum, C., & Vaughan, H. G. (1982). Visual following of moving objects by full-term and preterm infants. *Journal of Pediatric Psychology, 7,* 375–386.

Sekuler, R. (1975). Visual motion perception. In E. C. Careterette & M. P. Friedman (Eds.), *Handbook of perception: Vol. 5. Seeing.* (pp. 387–430). New York: Academic Press.

Sherrod, L. R. (1979). Social cognition in infants: Attention to the human face. *Infant Behavior and Development, 2,* 279–294.

Silfen, C. K., & Ames, E. W. (1964, April). *Visual movement preference in the human infant.* Paper presented at the meetings of the Eastern Psychological Association, Philadelphia, PA.

Skinner, B. F. (1974). *About Behaviorism. New York: Knopf.*

Spelke, E., Born, W. S., & Chu, F. (April, 1981). *Auditory-visual perception of moving objects in infancy. Paper presented at the Society for Research in Child Development, Boston, MA.*

Tauber, E. S., & Koffler, S. (1966). Optomotor response in human infants to apparent motion: Evidence of innateness. *Science, 152,* 382.

Volkman, F. C., & Dobson, M. V. (1976). Infant responses of ocular fixation to moving visual stimuli. *Journal of Experimental Child Psychology, 22,* 86–99.

von Hofsten, C. (1979). Development of visually directed reaching: The approach phase. *Journal of Human Movement Studies, 5,* 160–178.

von Hofsten, C. (1980). Predictive reaching for moving objects by human infants. *Journal of Experimental Child Psychology, 30,* 369–382.

von Hofsten, C., & Lindhagen, K. (1979). Observations on the development of reaching for moving objects. *Journal of Experimental Child Psychology, 28, 158–173.*

Wilcox, B. M., & Clayton, F. L. (1968). Infant visual fixation on motion pictures of the human face. *Journal of Experimental Child Psychology, 6, 22–32.*

Vinter, A. (1986). The role of movement in eliciting early imitations. *Child Development, 59, 66–71.*

4

The Development of Search

P. L. HARRIS
Department of Experimental Psychology
University of Oxford
Oxford, England

I. INTRODUCTION

An object can be subected to various kinds of perceptual transformation: it can be rotated, moved toward or away from an observer or made to disappear. Despite the changes in perceptual appearance which result from such transformations, the object retains its shape and identity. Piaget (1954) argued that infants only gradually appreciate the invariance of an object across such perceptual changes. In particular, he argued that the infant only gradually appreciates the continued existence or permanence of an object which is moved to a new location or hiding place. Piaget devised a set of search tasks in order to diagnose the infant's developing appreciation of object permanence and the development of search has since become one of the few areas of research on infants which has been guided by a coherent theoretical framework. In the pages that follow, I shall refer to search behavior as a set of observations which require explanation. In contrast, I shall refer to object permanence as a theoretical construct which may or may not offer a convincing explanation for the development of search behavior.

In the last decade, there has been a considerable effort to check Piaget's original observations on the development of search. Extensive reviews of the evidence (Brainerd, 1978a; Gratch, 1975, 1976; Harris, 1975) have concluded that the bulk of the evidence fits the theory. Nevertheless, I shall argue that there is a small set of discordant findings. These

155

might be explained by a judicious selection from among Piaget's fulsome theoretical proposals, but a simpler theoretical statement which offered a direct explanation would be more satisfactory.

The format of the chapter is as follows. First, I shall briefly review replication studies of the developmental sequence observed by Piaget. Second, Piaget's interpretation of the sequence will be described. Third, the more detailed experimental studies which have tested Piaget's interpretation will be examined; in the course of this latter section the difficulties facing Piagetian theory will emerge. Fourth, I shall evaluate current alternatives to Piaget's theory, concluding with an account of the interpretation that I favor myself.

A. The Developmental Sequence and its Replication

Piaget described six stages in the development of search. In the first stage the infant exhibits no systematic search for an object which disappears from sight. By the age of 18 months, when the infant has typically reached the sixth stage, the infant can find an object even if it has gone through a complicated series of hidden movements. For example, if the experimenter clasps the object in her hand, then moves it under several hiding places in turn, the infant will check through the hiding places until the object is found. The fundamental issue in understanding the development of search is to figure out exactly what skills or insights the infant is acquiring as more and more elaborate search tasks are solved. Before tackling this issue, we need a more detailed description of Piaget's sequence of stages.

B. Task Sequence

Stage 1 and 2: 0–4 months. No active search is exhibited. Infants simply look in the same direction as they did before the object moved or disappeared.

Stage 3: 4–8 months. Infants now begin to adjust their actions towards the object in acknowledgement of its disappearance or displacement. For example, if the object is moving, they look toward its anticipated future position. If the object is tugged out of their hand, they grope in the same direction. If the object is half-hidden under a cloth, they pull it out, at least toward the end of this stage.

Stage 4: 8–12 months. Infants now search for an object completely hidden, as opposed to only half-hidden, by a cloth. However, frequently when the object is subsequently hidden under a second cloth, infants search incorrectly back at the first one.

Stage 5: 12–18 months. Infants no longer make the perseverative errors found in Stage 4 but still have difficulty if they cannot see the object as it is moved to its hiding place. For example, if the experimenter conceals the object in her hand and then moves the object to a hiding place, infants will search incorrectly in the experimenter's hand.

Stage 6: Approximately 18 months onward. The movement of invisible objects that disrupted search at Stage 5 can now be taken into account.

Replication studies have asked simply: can the sequence observed by Piaget on his own three infants be found if a wider sample is tested? A more precise question is frequently embedded within such large-scale replications. Can children who solve the tasks associated with stage N also solve the tasks associated with $N - 1$ ($N - 2$) etc.? A child who cannot do this—for example, who can manage a Stage 4 task, but not a Stage 3 task—violates Piaget's theoretical assumption that task 3 has to be understood before task 4 can be mastered.

Brainerd (1978a) has provided a clear review of the various large-scale replication studies. He concludes that they provide rather strong support for Piaget's claim that children solve the object permanence tasks in the sequence proposed by Piaget. Whether the tasks are presented in order of supposed difficulty (Corman & Escalona, 1969; Uzgiris & Hunt, 1975) or whether they are administered in a random order (Kramer, Hill, & Cohen, 1975) the same order of difficulty is found.

Only one exception to this straightforward picture needs to be noted. Miller, Cohen, and Hill (1970) found that they could not arrange their items in a clear order of difficulty as predicted by Piaget, and, moreover, various Stage 6 tasks appeared to be easier to solve than a Stage 5 task. However, these results did not hold up in a later study, cited above (Kramer et al., (1975).

Despite the almost unanimous support for Piaget's observations obtained in such large-scale replication studies, the theoretical importance of the sequence in itself has been questioned (Brainerd, 1978b): tasks which characterize the later stages often presuppose solution of tasks characterizing an earlier stage. For example, an infant who can search for an object placed under a single cloth (Stage 4) must necessarily be able to track a moving object to a temporary resting place (Stage 3). An infant who can search under cloth A and then under cloth B (Stage 5) must necessarily be able to search under cloth A (Stage 4). Logic, rather than psychological processes, ensures that such developmental sequences will be universal (Brainerd, 1978b; Cornell, 1979b). Nevertheless, even where such necessary sequences do exist—and they cannot be said to characterize the entire six-stage sequence reported by Piaget—their analysis remains worthwhile, because the infant's difficulties at any point are not transparent. For example, if an infant can search accurately at a first hiding place A, but errs at a second, B, experimental analysis is needed to indicate why. More generally we may say that when a task involving X is solved before a task involving X + Y, only an analysis of Y can show why that component, or a subcomponent of Y, increases the original difficulty of task X.

For Piaget, the development of search indexes the infant's growing appreciation of the concept of object permanence, a concept which in its turn is one facet of the infant's growing appreciation of the stability and constancy of the object despite changes in its appearance. Below, the concept of object permanence is explained in more detail.

C. Piaget's Interpretation of the Sequence

Distillations of Piagetian ideas are always risky, since Piaget himself avoids concise formulations of his theory, and commentators do not always agree on the most acceptable distillation. Nevertheless, in order to render the theory testable, we must formulate it in explicit terms even if those terms go beyond what Piaget himself may have been prepared to state. In my view, Piaget stressed two interrelated problems for the infant which are resolved as he or she moves through the sequence of stages. First, the infant does not acknowledge that objects continue to exist when they are invisible. An important corollary of this failure to believe in permanence is that the young infant regards the reappearance of an object either as the re-creation of that object or as the creation of some similar-looking object. Thus the infant lives in a world where objects are continually made and unmade. The infant's second problem is that of egocentricity: the infant regards such a creation or re-creation as being contingent on his or her actions at the time of or just prior to reappearance. Thus, the infant believes that staring or groping does not bring about perceptual contact with an independently existing object. Rather, the existence of the object depends upon the infant's activities.

The gradual acknowledgement of permanence together with the waning of egocentricity form part of two more pervasive trends during infancy according to Piaget. First, the infant becomes more objective, not just about object permanence, but about size and shape constancy and indeed about other basic concepts such as time and causality. Second, the decline of egocentricity reflects the fact that the external world is understood in a less piecemeal and local fashion given the intercoordination of the various schemes, such as looking, grasping, and sucking.

It is also worth noting at this point that the problem of permanence and the problem of egocentricity are potentially separable. More precisely, an infant might lack permanence without thinking that his or her actions lead to an object's re-creation. Equally, the infant might suffer from egocentricity but believe that the object's position rather than its very existence was contingent on looking or grasping at a particular place. In short, the infant's two difficulties—the lack of a belief in permanence and the tendency toward egocentricity—are related but potentially separable difficulties. In consequence, evidence for the infant's lack of a belief in permanence does not necessarily constitute evidence for egocentricity and vice versa.

The gradual subordination of these two difficulties serves fairly well as an explanation for the development of search. In Stages 1 and 2, the infant has no concept of permanence and has yet to discover the potential efficacy of actions such as tracking and grasping in restoring the object. [The very young infant can learn to suck in order to bring about visual stimulation (Siqueland & DeLucia, 1969), but such artificial conditions are not met outside the laboratory.] By Stage 3, a limited appreciation of the efficacy of such actions has emerged: the infant searches visually and gropes manually for a missing object. In Stage 4, progress has been made to the point where the infant is over-confident of the efficacy of action. Having successfully found the object in one place, search is again directed at that place even when the object has been seen to disappear elsewhere. By Stage 5, the infant acknowledges the permanence of a stationary, invisible object and its relative independence from prior actions; accordingly, search is accurately directed at both a new and an old hiding place. Finally, the infant at Stage 6 acknowledges the permanence of a moving invisible object and can conceive of the movement of the object independent of seeing it or touching it. This last stage—the full admission of permanence together with the complete suppression of infantile egocentricity—involves, according to Piaget, the capacity to represent or imagine the hidden object, a capacity which emerges in Stage 6 at the end of the sensory–motor period.

Armed with this distillation of Piaget's position, we can now indicate in a prospective fashion where the difficulties will lie for the theory: they will be linked to Piaget's twin postulates. The permanence postulate implies that the infant will encounter difficulties in retrieving an object when it disappears from sight. As will be discussed later, Piaget himself noted that errors occasionally occur even when the object remains visible but he devoted little attention to such errors. Nevertheless, recent research indicates that they are quite prevalent and must be systematically incorporated into an account of search development rather than mentioned in passing. Second, I shall emphasize studies which show that although the infant does often err by returning to a location previously occupied by the object, the pattern of such errors does not appear to vary with the previous efficacy of the infant's actions at that location, thereby calling into question Piaget's claim that perseverative error reflects the infant's egocentricity.

In order to review this evidence in an orderly way, it will be useful to review the relevant experimental studies in their approximate sequence with respect to the stages of search. Throughout the review, one caveat should be borne in mind. In the short history of research on infants, various experimental results have not proved replicable. This lack of replicability exists not only when investigators try to replicate results from other laboratories, but also when they try to replicate their own earlier results. An example of this latter problem was mentioned above in connection with the studies of Miller et al. (1970) and Kramer et al. (1975). For this reason, more weight will be given to those results which have been obtained in more than one study and in different laboratories. Relatively little weight will be given to single-shot studies, however dramatic their results.

II. REVIEW OF EXPERIMENTAL STUDIES

A. Stages 1 and 2: No Active Search

In the first 2 months of life, Piaget argues, the infant exhibits virtually no search for an object which disappears. Current evidence indicates that Piaget's conclusion is probably a sound one. This is, in part, surprising because in other areas, research has suggested that Piaget may have gravely underestimated the capacity of the neonate. [For example, there are indications (Meltzoff & Moore, 1977; Zazzo, 1957), albeit controversial (Jacobson, 1979), that neonates can imitate facial movements.] The only evidence which might suggest a modification of Piaget's position has been offered by Bower (1967). He found that an infant of approximately 2 months was capable of detecting the visual event of gradual occlusion and distinguishing it from other types of visual disappearance such as a sudden and instantaneous disappearance. In addition, there was some indication that infants could retain a memory of the occluded object and anticipate its re-emergence; when an object was gradually occluded infants briefly suppressed their spontaneous sucking and started sucking again when the object reappeared. Bower inferred that infants expected the object to reappear because when it was made to disappear more quickly, or the time of reappearance was delayed, sucking was slow to recover, suggesting that the reappearance had not been expected.

However, even if the replicability of these results is taken for granted—and no replication has yet been published—they do not threaten Piaget's claim that the infant has no belief in permanence. Provided we assume that the infant does not invest the object with any substantial existence during its period of invisibility, Piaget's claim is left more or less intact. For example, the infant might learn to expect that an object will reappear in the visual field some time after its disappearance, and even show some signs of recognizing it, without realizing that the object continued to exist throughout its period of invisibility.

B.   Stage 3: The Beginning of Search

As noted above, Stage 3 comprises a variety of behaviors. I shall concentrate on two: anticipatory tracking of the future positions of a moving object and search for an object with the hand.

1.   Visual Tracking

A survey of the evidence on visual tracking fails to challenge Piaget's claim that although the infant can turn toward the future position of a moving object, such search behavior is not based on any appreciation of the permanence of the object throughout such displacements.

First, we may ask whether infants beyond 3 months can, as Piaget suggested, show some rudimentary appreciation of the future positions of a moving object. The simplest way to examine this question is to observe whether infants who can track a moving object will anticipate its re-emergence from behind a screen by looking toward the exit point. Several studies have examined this issue. One of the most systematic studies was carried out by Nelson (1971), who tested two age groups, a younger group aged 14–26 weeks and an older group aged 27–38 weeks. Infants watched a train moving around a rectangular track, part of which was occluded by a tunnel that hid the train for 1 to 4 sec approximately, depending on the speed of the train. When the train disappeared for the first time into the tunnel, infants in both age groups tended to concentrate on the point of entry rather than the far end of the tunnel where the train might be expected to reappear. Several trials later, infants behaved somewhat differently. Both age groups looked further along the tunnel, but anticipation of the train's reappearance by looking at the exit point prior to the moment of reappearance was still the exception rather than the rule.

Meicler and Gratch (1980) carried out another detailed study on the infant's ability to keep track of a moving object which enters a tunnel. Infants of 5 and 9 months watched an object move along a horizontal track, which was sometimes occluded by a screen. On such occlusion trials, when the object disappeared into the tunnel, younger infants tended to look at the entry-point or to look away from the tunnel altogether. Nine-month-old infants were more likely to look at the place where the object would reappear but also looked back and forth between entry and exit points.

Putting these two studies together, we may conclude that over a series of trials infants come to learn to orient toward a place where an object will re-emerge. However, even at 9 months, infants can only sometimes succeed in looking at the exit prior to the actual reappearance of the object.

Once an infant has become accustomed to the disappearance and reappearance of a moving object, several transformations may be introduced. First, we may ask how the infant will react if a different object emerges in place of the one that disappeared. Goldberg (1976) found that for infants of 5 months neither heart rate nor fixation varied with a change in object identity during the occlusion period. Meicler and Gratch (1980) and Gratch (1982) looked at the reactions of infants ranging from 5 to 16 months to various types of object change, including a change from mother to stranger. Infants did exhibit somewhat more puzzled frowning when a new object or person re-emerged, particularly at 16 months, but insufficient controls were included to decide whether this was a reaction to the visual novelty of the emerging object or its lack of correspondence with the object which had disappeared. Certainly, the change in identity had no detectable effect on tracking. Thus, infants did not look back for the missing object. Similarly, Muller and Aslin (1978) found no disruption of tracking among infants of 2, 4, and 6 months, whether the object's shape of color was altered in the tunnel.

Thus in four experiments, infants from 2 to 16 months continue to track an emerging object whether or not it corresponds to the object they saw disappear. Searching back for the object which disappeared but has failed to re-emerge is rare or nonexistent. The only reaction to a new object appears to be a slight frowning, but this could be a reactionto the visual novelty of the object, not its discrepancy from the one which disappeared.

These conclusions contrast quite sharply with those reached by Moore, Borton, and Darby (1978) and by von Hofsten and Lindhagen (1982). When the features of the object changed during its occlusion, Moore et al. (1978) observed more looking back or looking away in infants of 5 and 9 months; von Hofsten and Lindhagen (1982) observed more heart rate deceleration in infants of $4\frac{1}{2}$ months, though they could discern no disruption of tracking comparable to that observed by Moore et al. (1978).

Why should these two studies have produced evidence suggesting that young infants do notice a change of identity when the other studies, reported above, failed to do so? Von Hofsten and Lindhagen (1982) stress the fact that in their study, the occlusion of the object was brief (less than 1 sec). However, variation in occlusion times does not offer a full explanation of the discrepant findings. Muller and Aslin (1978) varied occlusion time from 1 to 4 sec and observed no increase in the disruption of tracking when identity was switched during occlusion but Moore et al. (1978), using an occlusion time of 4 sec, did observe such an increase. For the moment then, the bulk of the evidence suggests that young infants turn toward a place of reappearance with no precise expectations about the identity of the object that may appear. Two experiments, however, have suggested that young infants do possess such expectations since when they are violated either heart rate deceleration or disruption of tracking ensues. The reason for this discrepancy remains unclear.

Having watched an object move regularly along a trajectory, infants might form expectancies about the temporal parameters of that trajectory. For example, the object might be expected to move at a given rate, or if it stops, to stop for a fixed period. Meicler and Gratch (1980) looked at this question in the study mentioned earlier. They introduced occasional stop trials in which the object came to a halt behind the screen for 10 sec rather than moving continuously. Younger infants either looked away or looked briefly at the screen, while older infants were more likely to look at the screen and its edges in a prolonged fashion.

Muller and Aslin (1978) also looked at stop trials, but in their experiments the object stopped on its way toward the screen, so that it remained fully visible. Not surprisingly, infants simply stopped tracking. Earlier experiments, however, undertaken by Bower and his colleagues (Bower, Broughton, & Moore, 1971; Bower & Paterson, 1973), had suggested that following such a sudden stop in an otherwise regular trajectory, 2–5-month-old infants exhibit "false anticipations:" they turn toward the place at which the object would normally have reappeared. Given that infants of 9 months do not systematically anticipate the reapperance of an occluded train, as we noted earlier, it seems unlikely that infants of 5 months or less possess expectations, either valid or false, about where an object can be seen. Since Bower and his colleagues observed the infant's direction of gaze for 6 sec after the arrest of the object, and since they treated any continuation of tracking as evidence for "false anticipations," it may be that they were simply observing a shift of gaze away from the stationary object, rather than genuinely perseverative behavior. Thus, when a moving object comes to a halt either visibly or behind a screen, there is no consistent evidence that infants have any persistent or precise expectation about the place that the object will eventually move to.

In a third type of experiment, the spatial features of the object's trajectory have been altered, as opposed to the temporal features. Nelson's (1971) data on the infant's progressive accommodation to a temporarily hidden moving object were outlined earlier. After infants reached criterion on this task by turning toward (without necessarily looking at) the train's exit point, they were presented with a reversal of direction, so that the train entered by the previous exit point. The ensuing trials were intended to discover whether the infant had learned a very local rule specific to one direction of travel, or a more general rule, valid despite a change of direction. In fact, infants seemed to have acquired a local rule only. On the initial two reversal trials, infants looked at the entry point, took approximately 1.0 sec to locate the train after it had re-emerged, and very rarely looked at the exit point prior to the train's re-emergence. Indeed, behavior was very similar to that shown on the first two trials of the initial series. In the course of the succeeding reversal trials, infants again gradually learned to look toward but not necessarily at the place where the train would reappear. Surprisingly, however, there was some indication that younger infants exhibited more improvement during the series of reversal trials than older infants. Whereas older infants spotted the train on its re-emergence no faster at the end of the reversal series than at the beginning, younger infants did get quicker, thereby suggesting that older infants may have acquired habits during the initial series which interfered with their adaptation to the change in direction.

In summary, the experiments on visual tracking indicate that infants of 5 and even 9 months old do not reliably and spontaneously turn to the likely future position of a moving object. It is true that they can learn to turn toward a place where an object regularly reappears, but such a response appears to be executed on the basis of experience with a regularly repeated sequence of events in a particular situation, rather than any insight into object displacement in general. Thus when a regular trajectory is altered so as to deviate from the standard type of object displacement, for example by surreptitiously switching objects, most investigators report that infants show no search for the original object although some have reported behaviors indicating surprise. When a regular trajectory is altered but remains in conformity with the standard type of object displacement, for example by reversing the direction of travel, infants do not spontaneously alter their direction of search to suit this new situation, but only gradually adapt to it with repeated experience.

To what extent do these findings on visual tracking conform to Piaget's own observations and interpretation? Piaget argues that at the third stage the infant only rediscovers a vanished object by extending some action pattern set in motion by the earlier presence of the object. Thus, the permanence attributed to the object is tied to the infant's own action. It is clear that recent findings fit quite well into this formulation; the results of Nelson (1971), in particular, illustrate how the tracking movement elicited by the train is gradually extended so as to facilitate rediscovery of the train upon its reappearance further along the track. Indeed, if anything, the recent findings suggest that even at 9 months the infant's knowledge may be more restricted than Piaget supposed: he implies that toward the end of the third stage, infants spontaneously extend their tracking irrespective of the direction of travel (Piaget, 1954; observation 12), but Nelson's (1971) results cast doubt on this conclusion.

2. The Emergence of Manual Retrieval

Although the infant of 4 to 5 months is capable of reaching out and grasping a free-standing object (White, Castle, & Held, 1964) retrieval can be disrupted if the object is moved or hidden in various ways. I shall consider three such situations: first, the object can be made to disappear; second, the object can be presented on a support rather than free-standing; third, the object can be moved from one place to another, albeit remaining visible. In all these cases, Piaget would expect the infant of the third stage to do little more than extend movements of accommodation to the object.

Considering first an object which is made to disappear, infants of 4 to 5 months will not withdraw an object that they are already grasping from underneath a cloth (Gratch, 1972; Gratch & Landers, 1971). This ability emerges only at around $6\frac{1}{2}$–$7\frac{1}{2}$ months but is still restricted. An object which is not being grasped by the infant when it is covered by a cloth will not be withdrawn. By 8 months this latter restriction is overcome, provided the object was touched immediately prior to its being covered (Harris, 1971). Finally, by 12 months even this restriction is overcome, and the infant will search under a cloth whether or not the object has been touched prior to its disappearance (Harris, 1971). This developmental progression fits quite neatly into Piaget's theorizing in so far as the act of manual retrieval is at first only executed as an extension of the act of grasping the object, but later in development, retrieval is initiated on the basis of stored tactual information and eventually on the basis of visual information alone.

To what extent does successful manual retrieval depend upon the nature of the barrier occluding the object? Piaget (1954) does not discuss this issue in any detail by Bower (1974) has argued that infants retrieve an object more readily from behind a two-dimensional screen than from under a three-dimensional box. However, there is no consistent evidence that one type of hiding is easier than the other (Dunst, Brooks, & Doxsey,

1982; Lucas & Uzgiris, 1977). The former authors did obtain some data in an initial study suggesting that two-dimensional screens were easier than three-dimensional screens but this effect did not emerge in a later study. Several other findings do not fit easily into the straightforward Piagetian story. First, the infant of 4 to 5 months will not withdraw a clasped object from underneath a cloth, but an infant of the same age will carry an object placed into its hand outside the field of view to the midline for visual inspection (Bower, Broughton, & Moore, 1970; Piaget, 1952; White et al., 1964). Why should the infant succeed in making an object outside of the visual field available for inspection but fail to withdraw a clasped object from underneath a cloth? It may be that although both situations concern the ability to make an invisible object visible, the young infant has had more experience in bringing objects into the visual field than in making objects reappear when they have been occluded within that field. In addition, retrieval from under a cloth is more complex motorically than carrying an object to the midline. Whatever the explanation for the young infant's success in carrying a clasped object to the midline, it does not seem to involve anything radically different from an extension of the movements of accommodation triggered by the placement of the object in the infant's hand.

A second embarrassment to Piagetian theory was reported by Bower and Wishart (1972). They observed that infants of 5 months, presented with a free-standing object, would reach out for that object even if the room were plunged into darkness before they could grasp it. When the object is hidden by a cloth, however, the infant will retrieve it only at 12 months when it has not been touched prior to its disappearance (Harris, 1971). However, there are two difficulties in interpreting the results of Bower and Wishart (1972). First, Haith and Campos (1977) point out that the infant may have already initiated the act of reaching when the light went out. Bower and Wishart (1972) had suggested that this was not so, but as yet we have no clear criterion for deciding when a reach is being initiated. Second, random flailing in the dark may have produced chance rather than deliberate contact with the object. Bower and Wishart (1972) failed to include the appropriate control to rule out this possibility, namely, the introduction of an object just after as well as just before the room was plunged into darkness.

Finally, Rader, Spiro, and Firestone (1979) report that infants as young as 5 to 6 months will search for an object that is taken out of their hand, placed in a well, and covered with a small manipulable card. Much less success was observed when a large washcloth was used as a cover. One possible explanation of these findings is that Rader et al. (1979) gave their subjects pretraining trials in which an object was placed in the same well but not covered. Any repetition of the simple act of reaching to the well on subsequent hiding trials may have been sufficient to displace the small cover but not the large washcloth.

Turning to the second type of manual retrieval—the retrieval of an object from a support—Bower (1979) has concluded that the infant's difficulty in recovering objects in Stage 3 is not restricted to invisible objects. He makes the bold claim that an object becomes "functionally invisible" even when it is placed in full view on a support. "Something is an object to be looked at or picked up only when it has no boundaries in common with any other object" (Bower, 1979, p. 149). An evaluation of this claim has been made by Bresson, Maury, Pieraut-le Bonniec, and de Schönen (1977). They point out that mature reaching tends to be visually guided rather than ballistic. Hence, as infants reach for the object they may be disrupted by a distracting reference point which their hand necessarily also approaches, namely, the support itself. Evidence for this interpretation came from the fact that reaching was least disrupted when the object was placed on a support whose boundaries did not extend beyond those of the object being reached for (e.g., the tips of the fingers). If this argument is accepted, we can scarcely talk of an object on a platform as being "functionally invisible;" we may simply talk of an object whose recovery requires more than an extension of the standard movements of accomodation elicited by a free-standing object.

Finally, we may consider object movement from one location to another. Willatts (1979) presented an object several times on one side of an infant and then shifted it to the other side. Infants of 4 months tended to approach and look at the visible object both in its new position and the position it had formerly occupied even though this latter position was visibly empty. This perseverative behavior disappeared at 5 months. Such behavior is similar in several respects to that observed in Stage 4 when the object is fully hidden at first one and then a second location. Accordingly, discussion of the implications of this finding will be deferred until the next section.

Reviewing the main findings on manual retrieval, we obtain a picture which is fairly consistent with Piaget's claims. Although infants of 4 to 5 months can retrieve a visible object, they are disrupted by occlusion of the object. Even if they are holding the object when it disappears, they only gradually learn to withdraw it from under the cloth. Solution of occlusion problems seems to emerge at approximately the same time for disappearance under a box and behind a screen. There are two studies which have claimed that infants will recover an invisible object, even at 4 to 5 months (Bower & Wishart, 1972; Rader et al., 1979) but both are open to alternative interpretations. Finally, having become accustomed to approaching an object at one place, infants of 4 to 5 months will return to that place despite a visible movement of the object elsewhere.

C. Stage 4: The AB̄ Error

1. Frequency of the Error and the Role of Delay
   and Invisibility

Piaget observed a simple error among infants at Stage 4. Having found an object under a cloth A, they continue to search there even when the object is visibly moved to a new cloth B and hidden there. This phenomenon is central to both of the Piagetian postulates described earlier. It provides support for the claim that a belief in permanence develops only slowly: many of the infant's earlier difficulties in search, be it in tracking a moving object or in recovering an object from under a cloth, could conceivably be attributed to motor difficulties. The failure to search at B, on the other hand, is obviously not a motor problem, since the infant has already demonstrated an ability to make a response of equal motoric complexity, namely, to search at A. Perseveration to A also supports Piaget's claim that the infant is egocentric: the infant acts as if the object remains at the disposal of previously successful actions, even in the face of fairly simple perceptual evidence to the contrary, namely, the object's displacement to B.

Recent evidence has uncovered at least three qualifications on the claim initially proposed by Piaget. First, Piaget argues that there is a period of 2 to 4 weeks during which the infant systematically returns to place A or returns to A much more often than approaching B. Recent research provides only equivocal support for such a period. In a longitudinal study, Gratch and Landers (1971) did observe a short period in which the AB̄ pattern predominated. The typical error rate in cross-sectional studies, however, is 50% or less (Butterworth, 1974, 1975, 1977). However, these studies do not provide a strict replication of Piaget (1954), since the additional factor of a delay was introduced.

Indeed, the second qualification is that error is eliminated almost entirely if subjects are permitted to search at B as soon as the object has disappeared there. Error rates significantly above zero only emerge when the infant is forced to wait for one or more seconds after the disappearance of the object at B (Gratch, Appel, Evans, LeCompte, & Wright, 1974; Harris, 1973). Piaget might explain these findings by arguing that when there is no delay the infant will have already begun reaching for the object at B before it is covered up, so that search need be no more than an extension of the act of reaching, a pattern which characterizes the third stage. Indeed, Piaget attributes some of Laurent's deviations from the typical reaction of the fourth stage to such extensions of reaching (Piaget, 1954; obs. 45, p. 60). However, Gratch et al. (1974) studied infants who were restrained until the object was completely recovered and only then permitted to initiate a reach. Again, almost none of the infants erred. Of course, it is still possible to claim that some less obvious "place-orient-ing" process is initiated, despite such restraints, and indeed Gratch and his associates have made such an argument (Gratch, 1975; Gratch et al., 1974), but such an argument certainly amounts to a qualification on Piaget's more straightforward claim that the typical reaction is persever-ation.

The third problematic finding is that when delay is present, even the visibility of the object (e.g., by means of a transparent cover at B) does not eliminate error (Butterworth, 1977; Harris, 1974). Thus the disappear-ance of the object at B is not a precondition for error. Some commenta-tors have attempted to defend Piaget in this connection by pointing out that he too observed perseverative errors despite the visibility of the object (Piaget, 1954, obs. 39, p. 55 and obs. 51, p. 64). The hidden assump-tion behind this defense is that Piaget would scarcely cite evidence that did not fit his theory. Yet Piaget himself would be the first to admit that all observations are assimilated to a theoretical structure, and their occa-sional violation of that structure will not always be perceived. Accord-ingly, in characterizing a set of observations which includes observation 39, mentioned above, Piaget writes: "The general fact common to all these observations is that the child, after seeing an object disappear under a screen B, goes to look for it under screen A." This is manifestly an inaccurate summary. Indeed, Piaget goes on to imply that were the object to remain visible no difficulty would be encountered: "Surely, if he saw the object uninterruptedly, nothing would be easier for him than to . . ." search accurately at B. (Piaget, 1954, p. 67). Thus, although it is con-ceivable that Piaget's own account could be extended to error in the face of a visible object, he was attempting to account for error following disap-pearance at B.

Taking the second and third qualifications discussed above, and consid-ering them simultaneously, we have the very paradixocal conclusion that the infant searches without error for a completely hidden object, provided there is no delay. On the other hand, the infant makes errors in searching for a completely visible object, if there is a delay. Thus, the presence or absence of a delay has a stronger impact on error rates than the visibility of an object. This conclusion is certainly not one which follows naturally from Piaget's theory and hitherto no satisfactory explanation has been offered.

2. Increasing the Number of Hiding Places

As noted above, Piaget claimed that for a short period at least, search was predominantly directed toward A. Recent research, on the other hand, suggests that the typical error rate is 50% on B trials. This raises a thorny methodological issue. If infants do not perseverate to A more than half the number of B trials, their tendency to approach A may simply be due to random error. Suppose, for example, the infant becomes muddled as soon as the object has been hidden at more than one hiding place and simply guesses. This strategy would produce a 50% error rate to A but it is not necessarily perseverative.

Three studies have used more than two hiding places. This permits an assessment of the extent to which errors are directed at A or at some hiding place other than either A or B. Cummings and Bjork (1977) tested 9-month-old infants with five hiding places and found that although errors did occur on B trials, they tended to be directed not toward A but toward hiding places near the B location. Subsequently, Cummings and Bjork (1981) obtained similar results when they tested 12- to 14-month-old infants on an invisible displacement task in which the object was carried in a container to A or B, rather than carried visibly in the experimenter's hand. Again, errors did occur on B trials but were predominantly directed at hiding places near the B location.

Cummings and Bjork (1981) interpret these results as showing that errors occur because of inaccuracies in memory for the exact hiding place rather than because of any conceptual difficulty. Such mnemonic errors also occur in the standard two-choice task but because there is only one alternative to the correct hiding-place, namely, A, they appear to be perseverative. In an attempted replication of Cummings and Bjork (1981) however, Schubert and Gratch (1981) failed to obtain the same results. On the first B trial, all of the eight infants tested made an error, five at the original A location.

Sophian and Wellman (1983) tested infants of 9 and 16 months with three hiding places, A, B, and C, on the standard visible displacement task. The object was hidden in various ways at A and then hidden at B. The results indicated that 9-month-old infants who made an error on B trials were just as likely to approach A or C. The 16-month-old infants, on the other hand, tended to return to A if they made an error, rather than approach C. In addition, most 16-month-olds chose the correct hiding place, B, if they were given a second opportunity to search after a perseverative error, while 9-month-old infants did not. These results confirm earlier findings obtained by Webb, Massar, and Nadolny (1972). They too found that 16-month-old infants tended to make perseverative errors to A rather than C and usually chose the correct B location after an error.

Overall, then the picture is inconsistent. Some investigators report that errors are clustered near B, while others claim that they are divided between A and C, or directed toward A, particularly among older infants. Further work is needed to explain these inconsistencies. For the moment, one general comment is in order. Piaget tested his infants under naturalistic conditions and employed a variety of distinctive covers: hats, quilts, cloths, and so forth. The majority of recent studies have used a bare table top with two or more identical covers. In all of these studies, investigators have found that on B trials errors consist either in returning to the cover at A, or in returning to a cover that looks identical to the one at A, even though it is actually located at C or D or E. In short, virtually all of the evidence is consistent with the claim that the baby quickly learns to associate the object with a particular type of cover and makes errors by returning to that type of cover. There are no reports of infants searching at a type of cover where the object has never been hidden: infants do not search under the table or in the experimenter's pocket. In this broad sense then, infants can be said to make perseverative errors. This issue is explored in more detail below.

3. Perseveration of a Motor Response or Perseveration
   to a Cover?

If and when the infant perseverates by returning to cover A, the error involves both the repetition of a response and a return to a cover that was previously correct. Has the infant come to associate a particular motor response or a particular cover with finding the object again? To answer this question, investigators have attempted to vary either the association between making the motor response and finding the object or, alternatively, the association between the cover and the object. Evans (1973) and Landers (1971) failed to find any consistent evidence that infants were more likely to perseverate to A if their own motor response (rather than the experimenter's) had made the object reappear more frequently.

The association between object and cloth has been varied in three ways, with more effect upon perseveration. First, the presence or absence of a cover or landmark may be varied. Thus, Lucas and Uzgiris (1977) placed an object on the table during A trials either with or without an adjacent landmark. Butterworth (1975) placed an object at A, either with or without a transparent cover. Both of these manipulations produced clear effects: perseveration to A was reduced if the cover or landmark was eliminated. In a second type of manipulation, Lucas and Uzgiris (1977) varied the distance between an object and an adjacent landmark. Again, perseverative responding was reduced when the object could be dissociated (i.e., was further) from the landmark.

A third type of manipulation, introduced by Freeman, Lloyd, and Sinha (1980), requires more detailed comment. These investigators used either a pair of upright cups or a pair of inverted cups with which to hide the object, the object being hidden in, under, or behind one of the two cups. A series of experiments showed that perseveration to A on B trials was greater when both cups were inverted rather than upright.

Moreover, this effect was obtained irrespective of the type of hiding (i.e., in, under, or behind) and irrespective of whether the object was directly moved to the B cup, as in the standard AB̄ task, or alternatively, the object was hidden in the original A cup and the position of the two cups transposed. One plausible interpretation of these findings is that accurate search is facilitated to the extent that the infant can encode the identity of the cup concealing the object on test trials. Such encoding should be easier if the cup is in a familiar orientation, rendering it easily recognizable. This interpretation receives some support from a later experiment carried out by Lloyd, Sinha, and Freeman (1981). In this study, it was found that the infant could keep better track of a baited moving cup if it was upright rather than inverted. Conversely, an empty moving cup proved less of a distractor from accurate search if it was inverted rather than upright.

To summarize the findings presented so far, we have seen that the association between the hiding place and the object hidden is a more potent determinant of perseveration than the frequency with which a given motor response has caused the object to reappear. The association between the object and the hiding place can either help or hinder accurate search. If there is a cover or landmark with which the object can be readily associated during A trials, perseveration is increased. Conversely, if the object can be linked with an easily identifiable landmark on B trials, perseveration to A is reduced.

If the infant is capable of using landmarks to guide search, we might expect to see similar developments when tasks other than standard object permanence items are used. Research on spatial learning provides strong support for this expectation. Thus, Cornell and Heth (1979) taught infants of 4, 8, and 12 months to turn in an anticipatory fashion in the direction that novel stimulation would appear. On transfer trials, infants were rotated 180°, so that a new response was required if the infant was to look in the direction that stimulation would appear. Whereas 4-month-old infants tended to perseverate with the same response, 8- and 12-month-old infants were more likely to look toward the appropriate part of the room despite their new position. The implication is that older infants were guided by one or more of the landmarks in the room.

More direct evidence for the influence of a landmark comes from a study by Acredolo (1978). Subjects were 24 infants tested longitudinally at 6, 11, and 16 months. Again infants learned to turn in a particular direction for visual stimulation. For half the infants, this direction was marked by a colored star. For the remaining infants, no landmark was present. On test trials, in which a rotation of 180° was introduced, 6-month-old infants tended to perseverate with the same response whether or not a landmark was present; 11-month-old infants also frequently exhibited response perseveration but when a landmark was present, accurate responding increased; finally, 16-month-old infants were accurate whether or not a landmark was present. Direct evidence for the use of a landmark was also obtained by Presson and Ihrig (1982). They tested 9-month-old infants on a visual learning task similar to that employed by Acredolo, save that when infants were rotated, their mother either remained stationary or moved along with them. Responses were more often directed to the correct window if the mother had remained stationary.

Acredolo and Evans (1980) asked whether the presence of a more salient landmark would help even 6-month-old infants. Four landmark conditions were investigated. In the No Landmark condition, response perseveration predominated at 6, 9, and 11 months. In the Direct Landmark condition, in which the target window was marked by lights and stripes, response perseveration decreased at all ages, to be replaced by accurate responding among the 9- and 11-month-old infants and an uncertain glance at both windows among the 6-month-olds. In two other conditions with less salient landmarks, response perseveration was reduced in the 11-month-olds, and to a lesser extent in the 9-month-olds, but remained frequent in the 6-month-olds. In a similar study, Rieser (1979) also found that accurate responding could be increased among 6-month-olds by the introduction of a salient landmark, but such responding remained inconsistent compared to that obtained with older infants.

Taken together these experiments suggest that between 6 and 12 months, the infant increasingly guides spatial responses in terms of distinctive landmarks if they are available. At first, this is achieved only hesitantly among 6-month-olds when a salient landmark is introduced, and among older infants, it is achieved more consistently, even when a less obvious landmark is present. When all landmarks are removed, infants of 6 to 12 months tend to repeat the response that they have learned rather than adjusting the direction of that response. Finally, Acredolo (1978) found evidence which suggested that infants of 16 months can compensate for their changes of position, irrespective of the presence or absence of landmarks. Rieser and Heiman (1982) report further evidence in support of this conclusion. They first trained infants of 18 months to approach one of eight test windows, which, when touched, opened up to reveal a toy. After training, infants were turned away so as to face another window. Since the testing environment was an otherwise featureless chamber, subjects could not keep track of the target window by means of landmarks. Nevertheless, subjects typically attempted to return to the target window by reversing the direction of turn, and by turning back further if they had been rotated 180° rather than 135°. In a second experiment, infants of 14 and 18 months were turned through either 135° or 315°. In the latter case, a return to the target window was most efficiently achieved by continuing to turn in the same direction rather than backtracking. Both age groups tended to backtrack or continue, whichever was appropriate, although as in the first experiment, they did not usually turn far enough.

In summary, whether we examine the standard object permanence paradigm or studies in which the infant is trained to seek visual stimulation in a particular part of the room, there is strong evidence that between 6 and 12 months the infant increasingly guides search in terms of salient landmarks, such as a cloth or distinctive window. By 14 to 18 months, the infant can compensate for a change of position even in the absence of such landmarks.

4.   Identifying the Cover

Accepting that the infant guides his search in terms of suitable landmarks such as the cover concealing the object, how does the infant identify the cover itself? Broadly speaking, we may distinguish between two types of spatial coding. First, the infant might identify the cover in terms of its position relative to his own body. For example, the infant might note that the cover is "to my left" or "straight ahead." Such self-referent codings are particularly useful if the infant is faced with two or more identical covers or is searching within a relatively featureless environment.

The cover may, however, be identified in terms of a second type of spatial code. It can be located in terms of its distinctive features such as color or shape (where those are present) or it can be located in terms of its proximity to some additional landmark such as door or window. Research indicates that infants makes use of both self-referent and distinctive feature codes (Pick, Yonas, & Rieser, 1979). Research on spatial coding in manual search has adopted two different procedures. First, after several A trials and prior to any B trial, the spatial relationship between the covers and infant has been altered. Second, the object has been hidden and before the infant is permitted to retrieve it, the spatial relationship between covers and infant is altered. Since the latter procedure involves an invisible displacement of the object relative to the infant (or of the infant relative to the object), I shall postpone its discussion until behavior at Stages 5 and 6 is discussed.

If infants make use of a self-referent code, one would expect responding on B trials to be more accurate to certain bodily positions than others. Butterworth (1976) and Lloyd et al. (1981) found that search was more accurate on B trials if it was directed towards a cover at the midline rather than the periphery.

Bremner and Bryant (1977) and Bremner (1978b) provide evidence that the infant is guided by distinctive features of the cloth or surrounding framework, as well as approaching particular locations relative to his or her own body (Figure 1). They altered the position of the infant relative to

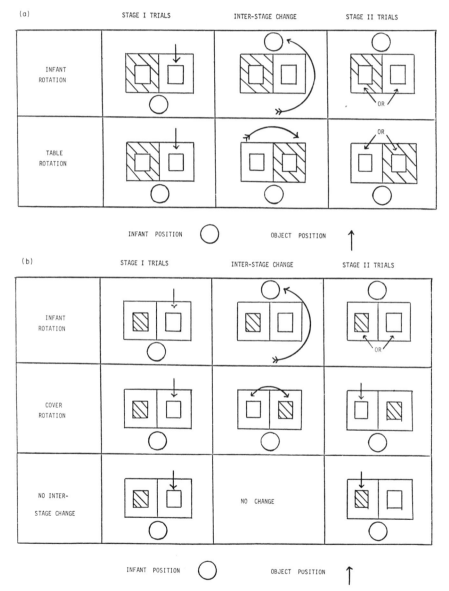

Figure 1. (a) Illustration of experimental setup in Bremner and Bryant (1977). (b) Illustration of experimental setup in Bremner (1978b).

two covers between A and B trials, either by rotating the infant or by rotating the two covers relative to the two distinctly colored sides of the table top.

The initial experiment (Bremner & Bryant, 1977) suggested that infants were returning to a particular location relative to their own bodies (or simply repeating the same motor response) rather than being guided by a distinctive side of the table. However, Bremner (1978b) concluded that infants can use distinctive landmarks. Provided the A cover was clearly distinct from the B cover, infants tended to go back to A even if it occupied a new location relative to their body, so that a new motor response was required. This dominance of cover cue over a particular bodily direction was not very potent: it emerged only if the infant had been moved relative to the covers, rather than the covers being moved relative to the infant. On the other hand, Butterworth, Jarrett, and Hicks (1982) observed a similar use of distinctive landmarks even when the infant remained stationary. The color of the cloth, and/or its surround, and/or its absolute location in space was altered between A and B trials. When the absolute location of the hidden object was changed, thereby necessitating a new motor response, errors were minimal provided the object was hidden under the same distinctive cover with the same distinctive surround as before. When, as in the conventional $A\bar{B}$ task, these distinctive features were eliminated, a change of absolute location led to the usual error rate of 50%.

A final study by Cornell (1981) offers an opportunity to look at the use of distinctive features across a fairly wide age range. Infants of 9 and 16 months were tested on a standard two-choice manual search task. Either the covers varied in distinctiveness, thereby varying the availability of a distinctive landmark code, or alternatively, the spatial separation of the covers as they were moved within reach of the infant was varied, thereby varying the availability of distinctive responses and/or directions relative to the self. Both groups proved to be more accurate not only when the containers were more widely separated but also when they were different. Gaze maintenance on the correct container, which tended to be predictive of accurate search, was also influenced by these two variables. Both groups were better able to keep their eye on the correct container if the containers were spatially separated, and the older group was also aided by differences between the containers.

In summary, the displacement of the infant or the covers between A and B trials suggests that infants of 9 months approximately identify the correct cover by means of two codes. If the cover and/or its surround is distinctive, infants tend to be guided by those distinctive features even if this requires a change of motor response. If, on the other hand, the covers are identical, infants tend to return to a given position relative to the self: they do not change their motor response. Accuracy across a series of trials is aided by the availability of both distinctive containers and distinctive positions relative to the self.

5. Overview of Research on the AB̄ Error

Piaget's description of the typical reaction of the fourth stage runs as follows. "Suppose an object is hidden at point A: the child searches for it and finds it. Next the object is placed in B and is covered before the child's eyes; although the child has continued to watch the object and has seen it disappear in B, he nevertheless immediately tries to find it in A!" (Piaget, 1954, p. 54). Recent research has indicated that this description needs qualification in several ways. First, this reaction is not representative of the fourth stage in that it emerges only at the very beginning of that stage. Thereafter, the infant tends to return to A on some but not all B trials. Second, if the infant can search immediately, the so-called typical reaction rarely occurs at all; instead, the infant searches at B, and this occurs even when the infant is restrained during the actual hiding at B. Third, in line with Piaget's own observations, but contrary to his summary of the facts, the error can also be observed when the object remains visible at B rather than disappearing at B. Fourth, the infant appears to associate the object with a particular cover rather than a particular action. The cover serves as a landmark for the location of the object and is identified either by its distinctive features or by its position relative to the infant.

Finally, it is worth underlining that the perseverative tendencies discussed in this section can be observed well past the initial stage of manual search. Piaget (1954) also noted such errors, referring to them as residual reactions. Thus Harris (1974) observed perseveration at 12 months if the object was visible at B, but behind a locked screen. Webb et al. (1972) observed that with delays ranging from 5 to 15 sec, 16-month-old infants frequently perseverated on B trials. Infants were allowed to make a second choice after an error and revealed that they had at least registered the new location, since they chose to approach it on their second choice rather than the empty third hiding place. In addition, their data hinted at the possibility that younger and older infants perform comparably, if the length of delay is increased for older infants. Diamond (1983) has demonstrated this effect more systematically. Using a titration procedure, she has shown that although older infants will avoid error at short delay intervals they are prone to perseveration if delay length is increased.

Sophian and Wellman (1983) used three hiding places and a 3-sec delay. Like Webb et al. (1972), they found that although 16-month-old infants did make perseverative errors, given a second choice after an error they would typically return to the correct location. Finally, DeLoache and Brown (1983) observed infants of 21 and 27 months searching for an object hidden in one of several locations in their home. When subjects made an error, they typically searched at a hiding place from a previous trial, especially the immediately preceding one. These five studies all indicate that perseveration to a previously correct location is observed well beyond 9 months, even when infants exhibit clear signs of having encoded the new hiding place and remembered its location. The tendency toward perseveration is increased by longer delays and by obstacles preventing immediate retrieval of the object at a new hiding place.

6.   The Infant's Conception of the Hidden Object during
      Manual Search

In discussing the infant's ability to track a moving object, various tasks were considered in which the object re-emerged after its disappearance with changed features. Goldberg (1976) pointed out that unless the relevant controls are included, a surprise reaction to the change of object identity is hard to interpret: it might either indicate a response to perceptual novelty as such, or it might indicate surprise at the violation of an expectation to the effect that what momentarily disappears will usually reappear unaltered. The same issue and the same interpretive problems arise in connection with manual search.

LeCompte and Gratch (1972) had infants of 9, 12, and 18 months find a toy three times in succession at one place. On the fourth trial the same object was hidden, but it was surreptitiously altered after its disappearance so that the infant found a grossly different object. The 18-month-olds were likely to both look puzzled and to search for the missing toy. The 9-month-old infants tended to examine the novel toy with curiosity or hesitation. The 12-month-old group fell in between these two types of reaction. If we attempt to interpret these results, we are on safe ground with the older group. Their search for the missing toy appears to be triggered by an understanding of the fact that a toy hidden in one place tends to remain the same. On the other hand, the behavior of the 9-month-olds infants is ambiguous. It might be interpreted as the type of cautious exploratory behavior that an infant of 9 months will exhibit to a visually unfamiliar object (Schaffer & Parry, 1970). Alternatively, 9-month-old infants might be puzzled about the whereabouts of the missing toy but, unlike the 18-month-old infants, have no idea where to look for it once they have tried the most obvious place, namely, the cover where it disappeared. In short, these results lend support to Piaget's claim that the 18-month-old infant can represent a hidden object and indeed distinguish it from substitutes in the same hiding place, but they do not throw any further light on the conceptualization of the 9-month-old infant.

Evans and Gratch (1972) took up the same problem but related it the AB̄ error discussed in the previous section. They reasoned that the infant who makes such an error might not be muddled about the whereabouts of a particular object but lured into believing, after success at A, that any object whatever can be found there. An infant who believes that objects in general are to be found at A should return to A even if a quite different object is hidden at B. An infant who believes that object X is hidden at A should return to A only if object X or one like it is hidden at B. In line with their expectations, Evans and Gratch (1972) found that perseveration was equally likely whether the same toy or a new toy was hidden at B. If we accept the interpretation offered by Evans and Gratch (1972), it implies that the infants should direct their search for any object whatever to one or at best a few places, a misconception of the universe that is so odd that one would have expected it to be reported by Piaget or subsequent investigators. In any case, Schubert, Werner, and Lipsitt (1978) failed to replicate the results obtained by Evans and Gratch (1972). Instead, they found that perseveration was more frequent if the same toy was hidden at B rather than a different toy (11 out of 12 versus four out of 12 infants respectively). Why exactly the two studies should have produced different results is not clear.

To summarize this section, we have come to a conclusion which is similar to that we reached with respect to visual tracking: when an infant searches manually for an object, be it in the correct or the wrong place, there is no firm evidence indicating what particular object the young infant expects to find. Only at 18 months is there unambiguous evidence that infants expect to find the particular object that they saw disappear.

D. Stages 5 and 6: Search despite Invisible Displacements

The hallmark of stage 5 is that the infant can search correctly if the object is visibly moved and hidden at a new hiding place, but not if it is invisibly moved (e.g., in a container). During stage 6, the difficulty with invisible displacements is overcome.

The invisible displacement task involves a rather complicated sequence of events and it is not clear which component of these events creates difficulties for the infant. The task involves both the invisible movement of an object inside a container and its invisible transfer from a container to a hiding place. Some investigations have now been carried out in which only an invisible movement is present with no invisible transfer. To be precise, two different types of movement have been carried out: a rotation of the infant relative to the two containers and a rotation of the containers relative to the infant. One of the most extensive studies of such intratrial shifts was carried out by Wishart and Bower (1982). They tested three different groups of infants: one cross-sectional from 12 to 24 months, one longitudinal from 12 to 24 months, and an accelerated group from 8 to 20 months (the accelerated group had been given training on a tracking task prior to 8 months). The clearest results emerged from a task involving three containers, which permitted an assessment of whether infants responded to the correct container, the container that would have been in the appropriate direction had no movement occurred, or the third container. Correct responding increased with age, the improvement being particularly smooth and steady for the two groups tested on a longitudinal basis. By around 18 months, choices were virtually errorless for the two longitudinal groups; their errors in progressing to that point were more or less evenly divided between the two empty containers. The pattern of development was somewhat different for the cross-sectional group. Performance even at 24 months was only about 70% correct, and errors throughout development chiefly consisted in reaching for the container that would have been in the correct location had no movement occurred. These results, then, suggest that repeated testing instructs the infant to pay attention to the consequences of movement, be it the infant's own movement or that of the containers, and to suppress the response that would have been correct had no movement intervened.

Sophian (1984) provides further data in support of these general conclusions. She tested infants of 20, 30, and 40 months on a task which involved transposing two of three containers. Although the absolute level of performance was a good deal worse than that reported by Wishart and Bower (1982) for their cross-sectional group, Sophian confirmed their finding that the major source of error was reaching for the container at the location that would have been correct had no transposition occurred.

To what extent can infants cope with invisible movements before 18 months? Several studies have been carried out with infants of approximately 9 months but the typical finding is that performance is at chance level, or indeed at worse than chance level. Nevertheless, under certain conditions performance does rise above chance. Goldfield and Dickerson (1981) and Cornell (1979a) found that if the object was hidden for several trials in one of two distinctive containers, infants of approximately 9 months could search fairly accurately despite transposition of the two containers. Performance approximated chance, however, if the containers were identical (Goldfield & Dickerson, 1981) or if the object was not hidden consistently in one of the distinctive containers across trials (Cornell, 1979a). A similar effect of cover distinctiveness was obtained by

Bremner (1978a, Experiment 2). The containers were rotated 180° on the first test trial, immediately after four partial-hiding, warmup trials. Infants who were tested with covers that differed in color made fewer errors than infants who were given identical covers, each located on a distinctive background. This latter result is particularly interesting since it suggests that for this age group, at any rate, only those distinctive features which occlude the object are used to keep track of its movement. Of course, this strategy makes sense since objects usually move with their containers but not necessarily with landmarks adjacent to those containers.

Indirect evidence for the importance of a distinct container is also provided by Sophian and Sage (1983). They contrasted two types of invisible displacement: either the standard Piagetian procedure was used in which the experimenter carried the object in her hand and transferred it to one of three identical containers, or alternatively, the object was visibly moved to one of the three containers, hidden there, and then that container was transposed with another. Infants of 13 and 21 months made fewer errors on the first task despite the fact that it included an invisible transfer. One plausible source of facilitation was the fact that the object was moved in a single distinctive container (i.e., the experimenter's hand), whereas in the transposition task two identical containers were simultaneously displaced such that the appearance and arrangement of the containers was identical before and after transposition.

Somerville and Haake (1983) looked at infants' ability to realize that when an object is moved inside a distinctive container such as the experimenter's hand and transferred at some point to another hiding place, the hidden object must lie between two points: the point at which the container was last seen with the object inside it and the point at which the container was first seen to be empty. They showed that by 15 months and even more clearly at 18 months, infants grasp the import of being given information about either of these two points. They confine their search to hiding places beyond the point where the object was last seen in the moving container but prior to the point where the container was first seen to be empty.

Turning to movements of the infant rather than the containers, Bremner (1978a) found better than chance performance in 9-month-old infants, provided the covers were distinctive. Performance was less accurate for the same age group, however, in two other investigations (Acredolo, 1979; Goldfield & Dickerson, 1981). Several factors could account for this variation. Acredolo (1979) found that selection of the wrong cover was frequent if infants were moved in an unfamiliar room rather than in their own homes. Goldfield and Dickerson (1981) found that accuracy was reduced if identical rather than distinctive covers were used, at least for infants of 9½ months. Finally, in a spatial learning task, Presson and Ihrig (1982) found that accurate responding was reduced after the infant was moved if the mother was not available as a stationary landmark. Bremner (1978a) obtained above-chance responding when all three of these facilitating factors were present: infants were tested with distinctive covers, in the home, and the mother remained stationary throughout testing. The common thread to all of these factors is that some distinctive feature of the spatial environment, the cover, the mother, or some familiar landmark in the home appears to be helping the infant. Presumably, such landmarks help the infant because no matter where he or she moves, the landmarks maintain a constant relationship with the hidden object.

Tentatively, putting together the studies on infant movement and container movement, we arrive at the following conclusions: in coping with container movement, infants are helped by the presence of landmarks that occlude and move along with the hidden object: more distant cues such as the table cloth do not provide any help. In contrast, stable landmarks that lie at some distance from the hidden object as well as those that occlude it appear to help infants keep track of the consequences of their own movements. This conclusion should be treated with caution since it rests on comparisons across several studies. However, it makes ecological sense. The mobile infant must eventually learn that relationships between an object and other landmarks, however remote, will remain constant despite his or her movement. On the other hand, if the container moves, its contents remain stable with respect to only its most immediate landmark, namely, the container itself; its relationship to all other landmarks must be updated. Certainly, the prediction that distinctive landmarks at varying distances can help an infant cope with his or her own movement, while only distinctive containers can help the infant cope with container movement, is one that can be readily tested.

Provided the object is moved inside a distinctive container, infants of 15 and 18 months can cope with an invisible transfer. They correctly infer that they should look for the object beyond the point at which it was last seen being carried in the moving container but prior to the point at which the container was first seen to be empty.

In conclusion, it should be clear that the Piagetian notion of invisible displacements is too global to illuminate the pattern of success and error described above. At least three different variables would appear to require systematic investigation: whether or not the object is invisibly transferred from one container to another; whether the invisible movement is brought about by moving the infant or the container; and whether or not distinctive landmarks are available both occluding the object and at some distance from the object.

E. Overview of the Difficulties with Piaget's Interpretation

A considerable number of experimental findings have been examined in the previous section. Accordingly, it will be helpful in considering alternative accounts to have a summary of the major findings that such alternatives should explain. First, the infant does exhibit difficulties in tracking, in recovering a hidden object, and in keeping track of more than one hiding place. These findings can be readily explained in Piagetian terms. Nevertheless, perseverative errors in manual search also occur in the face of a visible object and are almost entirely eliminated if there is no enforced delay period. Neither of these findings can be readily explained by the claim that infants do not attribute permanence to invisible objects.

The concept of egocentricity has also been called into question. In making the AB error, the infant does not appear to be repeating a particular action. Instead, the infant appears to be returning to a particular place, namely, the cover hiding the object. The location of the cover is coded sometimes in relation to the self and sometimes in relation to its distinctive features or landmarks in the wider spatial framework. This evidence suggests that the infant is muddled about where to search for the object rather than incapable of dissociating its location from some prior search activity.

Finally, the later developments in search are not explained with precision by Piagetian theory. The Stage 6 task involves a complex sequence of invisible transfer and invisible movement. Simplification of the procedure so as to involve only invisible movement permits accurate search, at least under some conditions. Yet Piaget saw invisible movement as the critical factor involved in the transition from Stage 5 to Stage 6.

III. ALTERNATIVE THEORIES

In this section, we shall examine various attempts to reinterpret Piaget's observations on the development of search. Having established some of the difficulties facing Piaget's theory in the previous section, we shall be especially concerned to see how well the various alternatives can handle those same difficulties.

A. Bower's Theory

The primary thrust of Bower's theory is an attempt to shift the focus of attention away from the problem of object permanence toward the problem of object position. Bower asserts that the infant is puzzled not about whether the object exists but where it is located.

Bower (1974, 1977, 1979) makes three claims which contrast with those of Piaget: first that the infant, even at 2 to 3 months, possesses a concept of permanence; second, that the infant is unable to unite the various loci of an object until around 5 months; third, that the infant has difficulties not with invisibility *per se* but with the spatial relations that can temporarily exist between a desired object and some reference object, spatial relations such as occlusion or support. With respect to a fourth claim, that the infant has difficulty with the invisible displacement of the object, Bower scarcely differs from Piaget. Accordingly, I examine the first three claims only below.

1. An Early Concept of Permanence

Bower (1974, 1977, 1979) cites two major pieces of evidence in support of the claim that infants have a concept of permanence from an early age: first, the finding that, even at 2 to 3 months, the infant is surprised if an object which has been occluded by a screen is not there when the screen is removed (Bower, 1967) and second, the finding that infants of 5 months will reach out in the dark for a previously visible object (Bower & Wishart, 1972). Of these two pieces of evidence, the second is probably stronger than the first, because even when the ambiguities surrounding indices of surprise are put aside, it is not clear whether the infant is exhibiting anything except an expectancy about the reappearance of an object which has disappeared, an expectancy which does not entail a belief in its continued existence while invisible. Search in the dark, on the other hand, would appear to index a belief in permanence in a much less ambiguous fashion. For this reason this important result deserves replication in order to show that it is a reliable phenomenon that cannot be explained away either as movements of accommodation initiated just prior to the room's being plunged into darkness or as random arm flailing that produces contact with the object on a fortuitous basis.

2. The Coordination of Place and Movement

In interpreting the various tracking errors uncovered by Bower et al. (1971) and Bower and Paterson (1973), Bower (1974, 1977, 1979) suggests that the infant does not realize that a stationary object remains the same object once it starts to move, nor that a moving object remains the same object when it stops. As a result, the infant ignores a stationary visible object and searches along a prior trajectory or ignores a new trajectory and searches back at a previous place.

A variety of experiments have been carried out on visual tracking and an earlier review of the evidence (Harris, 1975) suggested that perseverative errors in visual tracking were a reliable phenomenon. This conclusion turns out to be premature. Investigations by Muller and Aslin (1978) have failed to uncover any perseverative tendencies or "false anticipations" among infants of 2 to 5 months. Indeed, recent research on visual tracking suggests that the expectations that an infant does formulate at this age regarding the future locations of a moving object are so diffuse that it is unlikely that the visible violation of those expectations by the object would be overridden by any perseverative tendency. Nevertheless, in defence of the original observations by Bower and his colleagues, it may be noted that infants in the earlier experiments were observed for a longer period after the violation of the previously established trajectory. It may be that Muller and Aslin (1978) did not allow sufficient time for the perseverative tendencies to emerge. As they rightly point out, however, a long period of observation is likely to include a change in the direction of the infant's gaze and such a change of direction might give the false impression that the infant was perseverating.

3. Spatial Relationships between a Desired Object and a
    Reference Object

Bower (1977) argues that infants between 5 and 12 months exhibit difficulties in understanding the spatial relations that can exist between two objects. If a desired object is placed on, in, behind, or in front of another object, the infant usually exhibits a two-stage development. In an initial period of complete incomprehension, the desired object is ignored when it is placed in relation to the reference object; in a second period, the spatial relation is partially understood since the object can be retrieved but is not fully understood since when the desired object is now placed in relation to a second reference object, the infant turns back to the first. The infant's difficulties with such spatial relationships are all attributed to a single common problem—the fact that the desired object loses or shares one or more of its boundaries with those of the reference object. In support of this claim, Bower et al. (1971) suggest that when the boundary loss is minimized, for example, by placing a curved object such as a ball (rather than a flat object) on a platform, or by placing the desired object in front of or behind a screen but at some distance from it, the retrieval problems are reduced.

Subsequently, Bower (1979) has offered a more elaborate account, which comes close to that of Piaget (1954) in stressing that the infant does not attribute a fully independent existence to the object on the support. Bower (1979) notes that an adult is usually aware of the fact that an object on a platform is a separate object because the adult remembers its previous free-standing state when all its boundaries were visible, before it was placed on the platform. If, however, the infant cannot link the object on the platform with the object which was seen just previously moving toward the platform (i.e., in line with the hypothesis discussed in the previous section), then the shared boundary with the platform may be seen as a permanent rather than a temporary state, and the object will be regarded as "functionally invisible."

Several interpretive problems arise regarding these various hypotheses. First, as has been noted earlier, it is not clear that the infant ever reacts toward an object on a platform as if it were functionally invisible. Rather, the infant has difficulty in executing the terminal adjustments to a reach that must be made if an object is on a support rather than completely free-standing (Bresson et al., 1977). Second, the difficulties with the platform, the screen, and the container are overcome at different ages. In the case of the screen and the container, they are overcome well past 5 months. Yet Bower (1979) attributes the infant's difficulties with boundary loss to an inability to coordinate movement and place, a problem which is resolved at approximately 5 months. These age variations might be explicable in terms of varying degrees of boundary loss but Bower (1979) makes no systematic attempt to do so. In any case, Bower and Wishart (1972) have themselves proposed that infants of 5 months can retrieve an object despite its loss of all boundaries by being plunged into darkness. Finally, Bower's account of the perseverative errors that persist even when infants can search behind screens or under cloths is *ad hoc*. In particular, it takes no account of the fact that an absence of delay eliminates perseverative error entirely. The explanation is couched exclusively in terms of the spatial relations which exist between the desired object and the reference object and it is not clear how such understanding could be improved by the elimination of delay.

In summary, Bower offers a radical alternative to Piaget, particularly in asserting the early emergence of permanence. His emphasis on the infant's later difficulties with the spatial relations that can temporarily exist between one object and another has something in common with the theory advanced by Piaget to explain both the development of the object concept and the elaboration of groups of spatial displacements. Nevertheless, whereas Piaget stresses the infant's difficulty in dissociating the object from actions upon it, Bower claims instead that the infant cannot grasp the link between two perceived states of the object: motion and rest. Bower's account is clear and provocative. However, close examination indicates that it contains certain internal inconsistencies and also runs counter to data obtained in other laboratories.

B. Identity Theory

Moore (1975) and Moore and Meltzoff (1978) have offered an alternative to both Piaget and Bower. They argue that the neonate has much richer sensory–motor coordinations than Piaget has allowed, but unlike

Bower they are not prepared to attribute a belief in permanence to infants below 9 months. They agree with Piaget in claiming that the infant only gradually comes to understand transformations such as movement and disappearance, but they argue that this development is the reflection of an increasingly complex rule system, rather than the increasingly sophisticated coordination of sensory–motor schemas.

The rules are conceived as rules for understanding the enduring identity of an object. This stress on identity can be understood by means of an analogy. Suppose we watch a conjuror make a dove disappear in one box only to find it a few seconds later in another box, the dove having mysteriously "flown" from one box to the other. If we cannot understand how exactly the bird has managed to get from one box to another, we might be tempted to shrug our shoulders and say that there were really two doves involved, one in the first box and a different dove (admittedly with the same appearance) in the second box. Moore (1975) and Moore and Meltzoff (1978) argue that young infants are forced to shrug their shoulders in this fashion very often, simply because, like the adult faced with the tricks performed by a conjuror, they do not understand the perfectly routine spatial transformations that a single object may undergo. The attraction of this theory is that it shifts attention away from the issue of permanence to the ultimately more encompassing notion of the enduring identity of a single object. To be fair to Piaget, he does discuss the problem of permanence in relation to the problem of identity (Piaget, 1954, p. 69), yet Piaget does not appear to see the problem of identity as either logically prior to, or more encompassing than, the problem of permanence. In contrast, Moore and Meltzoff (1978) argue that the realization that an object which reappears from a hiding place is the same object as the one which disappeared is logically prior to any insight into its permanence during that disappearance.

In attempting to shift the focus of theorizing away from the problem of permanence, the approach of Moore and Meltzoff (1978) is similar to that of Bower (1979). All three authors are dissatisfied with the narrow emphasis on the problem of disappearance and wish to recognize the infant's difficulties with visible as well as invisible objects. However, Moore and his colleagues (1978; Moore & Meltzoff, 1978) do not assume, as does Bower (1979), that the young infant has a belief in the permanence of a visible object. They argue instead that this belief is a product of coordinating, not only a stationary object with one which moves, but also an object which disappears with one which reappears. Thus whereas Bower (1979) emphasizes that infants are puzzled about where to look for an object, Moore and his colleagues emphasize that they may not realize that the object they saw disappear corresponds to the one that reappears, even if they themselves have caused it to reappear.

Moore and Meltzoff (1978) postulate three successive levels in the infant's acquisition of rules for identity. In the first 4 months of life, the infant only acknowledges that identity is maintained for either an object which remains stationary or an object which remains in motion (on a given trajectory). Between 5 and 8 months these two types of identity are linked, so that the infant acknowledges the continued identity of a stationary object that starts to move, or a moving object that comes to rest. Finally, between 9 and 18 months the infant elaborates rules for objects which disappear.

As this brief sketch indicates, identity theory, like the theory proposed by Bower (1979), is more detailed in its characterization of the first stages of search—up until 9 months—than in its characterization of the later stages. Indeed, Moore and Meltzoff (1978) describe a series of seven tasks which fall within the Level 3 period (i.e. from 9 to 18 months), but no explanation is offered for the ordering of these tasks. To take one example, task 3.2, which involves the movement of a screen to cover a stationary object, is solved before task 3.4 which involves the movement of an object so that it ends up behind or under a screen. If such a difference in difficulty does exist, it is an intriguing difference but Moore and Meltzoff (1978) do not address this issue.

The proposals put forward by Moore and Meltzoff (1978) also suffer from the same insularity as those made by Bower (1979). No explanation is offered for the fact that difficulties with visible objects can be found well after 9 months, and the well-established effects of delay on search are not discussed. Thus, although identity theory offers us a fresh way of thinking about the development of search, it appears, at least for the present, to be offering a way of thinking rather than a detailed theory. Obviously, this may change in the future, particularly given the fact that Moore and his colleagues claim to have established a task sequence with more detail than that of Piaget.

C. Cornell

Cornell (1978) does not put forward an entire theory of object permanence but suggests a radically different approach to the interpretation of search data. He makes the traditional Skinnerian point that what we observe is an infant's search, be it correct or incorrect, rather than the infant's knowledge. We can take note of this point in two ways. On the one hand, we can simply admit that behavior is always a fallible guide to the infant's knowledge, sometimes luring us to infer knowledge that the infant actually lacks or alternatively to deny knowledge that the infant actually possesses. This is certainly the position taken within the mainstream of research on cognitive development (e.g., Flavell, 1977). However, one may take a different approach—as Skinner does—and assert that it is more theoretically fruitful to talk about the infant's development as if it were nothing more than the detection of certain contingencies between a response in a particular situation and a particular outcome.

Cornell (1978) adopts this second approach in analyzing the perseverative errors that characterize the infant's search at various points in development. In discussing the AB̄ error, Cornell points out that the A and B locations differ from one another in their association with the reappearance of the object, which is contingent upon search: this reappearance has occured in the infant's previous experience at A but not at B. Hence, the infant returns to A.

Two cautionary remarks may be made about this approach. First, it is not as radically different from Piaget's analysis as it might at first appear. At some point, the AB̄ error is not committed. In order to explain this more sophisticated search behavior, Cornell suggests that infants respond to more and more complex cues regarding the current location of the object, cues which depend upon an encoding of movement and which distinguish the most recent location from previous locations (Cornell, 1979a). Piaget, however, argues that the infant comes to appreciate that an object's reappearance is contingent upon search only to the extent that search is guided by the independent movements of the object rather than the infant's previous success. Thus, both approaches stress the increasing attention of the infant to objective indices of the object's whereabouts. Nevertheless, it is possible that Cornell's emphasis on the analytic techniques of learning theory may encourage a more precise specification of the exact nature of those contingencies and their mode of acquisition.

A second criticism of Cornell's approach pertains to the infant's success on A trials. If the infant's search is guided by the discovery of a local contingency, namely, that the object's reappearance will follow search at A, why does the infant search on the first trial at A? After all, the object has never appeared there before, so that search cannot be guided on an initial trial by specific local contingencies. Cornell (1978, 1979a) suggests that the infant's initial search is guided by more general contingencies, such as the fact that most objects in the world do not move. However, why are such general contingencies not extended to the B location when the object is seen to disappear there? An adequate explanation of the AB̄ error, then, requires something more subtle than a hypothesis of response perseveration. It must explain exactly why the general contingencies which guide search accurately for the initial A trial are overridden by local contingencies on the first B trial.

In summary, Cornell's approach is to offer a dose of skepticism in place of the more dramatic claims of Bower, Moore, and his colleagues. More-over, he has suggested that we pay close attention to the actual contingencies which the infant must detect in the environment. At present, however, this approach does not offer a full explanation of the pattern of error and success that is observed in the course of development.

D. Butterworth

Butterworth (1976), like Moore and his colleagues (Moore & Meltzoff, 1976; Moore, 1975), stresses the problem of object identity. However, he offers a different account of how the infant actually resolves this problem. His starting point is an idea, initially proposed by Bryant (1969, 1974), that young children compare successively presented visual stimuli by means of a third term—the visual framework. For example, a child might be shown a vertical line and note that it lies in the same orientation as (the long axis of) a door visible near the line. Subsequently, the child might be shown a second line and note that it too lies parallel to the door. Putting these two pieces of information together, the child can deduce that the second line is in the same orientation as the first, even if there is no opportunity to see them side-by-side. Thus the door serves as a middle term by which two successive pieces of information can be compared. Analogously, Butterworth points out that "the infant requires some means to connect up the momentary positions occupied by the object to one another." He goes on to suggest that successive positions may be compared to one another in the same indirect fashion as line orientations—via a framework. However, Butterworth departs from Bryant's (1974) analysis in emphasizing the importance of an egocentric or self-related framework, rather than an external visual framework. The egocentric framework may be particularly useful in linking up the successive positions of a stationary object. For example, the infant might note the object's position relative to himself at a given moment (e.g., "to my left, within reaching distance"). If a similar-looking object occupies the same position relative to himself a moment later, the infant can conclude that the object's position has remained invariant. This seems to be a plausible hypothesis. However, Butterworth goes on to suggest that "the identity of the object can then be deduced from the fact that it has occupied a stable position over time." Such a deduction surely does not follow. From the fact that an object of a given appearance is in the same position relative to oneself on two successive occasions, nothing appears to follow about identity as opposed to position. Either the same object may have remained in the same position, or an identical object may have replaced the first. The deduction about identity does not follow any more than would an equivalent deduction about the identity of two successively presented lines in the setup described by Bryant (1969, 1974). Thus it is not at all clear how the rather complex apparatus introduced by Butterworth—the use of an egocentric framework as a middle term—actually helps the infant, unless we are prepared to credit the infant with deductions which are illogical. One possibility is that the infant makes a probabilistic inference rather than a deduction. After all, it may indeed by true, particularly for short intervals, that an identical-looking object seen successfully in the same self-related position is, in fact, the same object. However, this suggestion is at best ad hoc.

Butterworth considers next the problem of the moving object. This arises when "the object that occupies position p_1 at time t_1 now occupies position p_2 at time t_2. The infant has somehow to decide whether this is a single object that has moved or a qualitative replica at a new position." According to Butterworth, the infant can use the visual framework, rather than the egocentric framework, as a third term to solve this problem. However, it is again unclear whether the framework might help, for two reasons. First, an object which moves is likely to change its position relative to various landmarks in the visual field—to be, for example, "on the table" at one moment and "on the floor" the next. In such cases, it is not clear how a third term is available to link up the object's successive positions, simply because the table and the floor are different landmarks. It might be possible for the infant to use a very loose framework coding, such as "within this room." An object could then move but retain at each successive moment its invariant relationship to the room. This solution does appear to provide a third term but it takes us back immediately to the difficulty raised in relation to the egocentric framework: two successive sightings of an object having a particular appearance "within this room" may or may not be sightings of the same object.

Turning finally to the errors in manual search, Butterworth (1977) makes the following points. First, an object which disappears and reappears at A is coded as the same object because it has remained in the same place relative to the self. Second, when the object moves from A to B, the infant abandons the use of an egocentric code, because it is inadequate for coping with moving objects. Instead, the infant plots movement relative to the external visual framework or relative to some salient component of it such as the table edge or a nearby door. This results in a conflict between the two codes, the outdated egocentric code specifying position A and the correctly updated visual framework specifying position B.

There appear to be several difficulties with this formulation, even if we ignore the arguments presented earlier against the egocentric or the external framework as a third term. First, we may note that at the beginning of most experiments on the A̅B̅ error, the object does not start at A but is moved by the experimenter to A from some other visible location. For example, the object is lifted from the tabletop or is taken from the infant's hands by the experimenter and is placed at A. However, according to Butterworth, the infant cannot update his initial egocentric specification of the object's location. Hence the infant would continue to encode the object's location as being on the table or in the hand, rather than under a cloth. In short, the infant should perseverate to the location of the object before it was shifted to A. If it is acknowledged that the egocentric code can be updated, however, why cannot it be updated to cope with the switch from A to B?

A second problem with Butterworth's formulation is that there is evidence that the infant does not always perseverate to a location which is specified in terms of an egocentric code. Distinctive covers can also elicit perseveration under certain conditions (Bremner, 1978b). Indeed, Butterworth (1977) noted that infants rarely perseverate to a previous location if there was no cover there as opposed to a transparent or opaque cover. Such a finding strongly suggests that the infant's return to A is not simply a question of reverting to a prior egocentric specification, since such a code would presumably yield the same specification whether or not the object were covered.

Finally, Butterworth's formulation provides no clear explanation of the fact that the A̅B̅ error is eliminated with zero delay. The conflict between spatial codes, described by Butterworth (1977), should be present as soon as the object begins to move from A toward B, rather than manifesting itself a second or more after the object has come to rest at B and disappeared there.

Although Butterworth has introduced a set of clear and provocative postulates, when their consequences are examined in detail there appear to be various logical and empirical difficulties. Nevertheless, Butterworth has played an important role in drawing attention to the fact that we cannot leave the notion of position unanalyzed. If the infant searches in the wrong place, it is important to analyze the way in which the infant codes position. In addition, the hypothesis that there may be a conflict between the two ways of specifying an object's position is very useful because it allows us to explain why a group of infants typically divides their searches between an old and a new hiding place and indeed may sometimes search at both locations (Harris, 1974). As we shall see below, Bremner (1980) takes up the idea of spatial codes and places them in a functional context.

E. Bremner

Bremner (1980) points out that infants below approximately 9 months cannot change the position of their whole body. This means that they depend upon their caretakers or parents for placing them in various positions such as in a cot or highchair. As they lie or sit in these familiar positions, they will come to notice that various objects occupy a roughly constant position. Thus a mobile might always be visible above the cot, a tray in front of the highchair and so forth. These positions can be specified as constant self-related positions (e.g., "above me, just out of reaching distance") because infants have little possibility of altering their position in any particular context. As a result, suggests Bremner, they may come to rely on such self-related positions as fairly reliable specifications of an objects's position in a given context. Applying this idea to the AB̄ error, it can be argued that infants tend to return to the same self-related position, even though the object has been seen to move elsewhere. Gradually, however, particularly as a result of learning to crawl, infants experience the fact that objects can occupy a series of positions relative to their own body. Hence they abandon their belief in the stability of such self-related specifications. As an alternative, they can begin to code objects in relation to distinctive spatial landmarks, for example, "above the cot" or "under the white cloth." In support of this claim Bremner (1978b) reports that 9-month-old infants tend to return to a distinctive cloth where they have seen an object hidden before, even if they are moved relative to that cloth, thereby necessitating a change in the actual motor response needed to retrieve the object.

This account of the AB̄ error has several attractive features. First, it is fairly clear and straightforward; second, it places the search errors exhibited by the infant in a functional context: the spatial codes suggested by Bremner for the precrawling and crawling infant make functional sense. However, there are certain difficulties which remain. First, Bremner's account makes better sense for objects which are out of sight. Infants lying in their cot might learn to reach out in a certain direction to retrieve an object that they are not directly looking at. In the same way, we, as adults, reach out in the dark for a familiar light switch. In this fashion, a stored self-related coding can come to substitute for the actual visual specification of the object's position. Less plausible is the notion that such stored specifications will function not only in the absence of a visual specification but will also override some new visual specification which the infant has definitely seen. Yet as we saw in earlier sections of this chapter, perseverative errors to A to occur even when the new location has been registered and the object remains visible there. Second, although

Bremner (1980) offers a plausible explanation for the increased tendency to use a framework code, namely, that the infant who crawls constantly renders an egocentric specification out of date, he does not explain why perseveration should persist after crawling has been acquired and despite the adoption of a framework code. Finally, Bremner does not attempt to offer an explanation for the fact that the AB̄ error is eliminated with zero delay. There is no obvious reason to suppose that a prior self-related specification should be especially potent after a delay. Indeed, given the fact that by 9 months infants can alter their posture, Bremner's account would suggest that the delay, by being associated with self-initiated movement, would suppress reliance on a previously valid but now out-dated self-related position.

F. Alternatives to Piaget: Overview

This review of alternatives to Piaget has indicated that although investigators have offered detailed accounts of particular stages of search development, their accounts have not usually had the full sweep of Piaget's initial proposals. Investigators have been concerned to offer an explanation which is sufficient for the phenomena they have uncovered and have ignored the wide range of data that is currently available. Nevertheless, it is clear that these alternative interpretations have either introduced new concepts of considerable power or have emphasized concepts which Piaget mentions but does not elaborate. Thus, the stress which Moore and Meltzoff (1978) have placed on the problem of identity suggests that the problem of permanence is part of a much wider problem concerning the way in which the infant reidentifies an object as the same object through time, whether or not the object has disappeared.

Piaget (1954) recognized the link between the concept of permanence and the wider issue of identity. For example, Piaget writes of the infant at Stage 4: "But, without being truly conceived as having several copies, the object may manifest itself to the child as assuming a limited number of distinct forms of a nature intermediate between unity and plurality . . ." However, his discussion of the object concept returns time and again to the child's lack of a belief in permanence, whereas references to potential confusion about the identity of the object, as in the above quotation, are made in passing. Thus, Piaget appears to regard problems of identity as a by-product of the infant's lack of a belief in permanence. As I shall attempt to argue, however, it may be more fruitful to regard the infant as lacking criteria for reidentifying an object and therefore unable to infer that an invisible object continues to exist during its period of invisibility.

Bower (1979), Butterworth (1978), and Bremner (1980) have also drawn attention to the infant's difficulties with the coding of position. In particular, Butterworth (1978), Bremner (1980), and Cornell and Heth (1979) have drawn attention to the important distinction between two types of spatial code: the self-related or egocentric coding of position and the allocentric or framework coding of position. Again, this distinction is one which Piaget (1954) makes, but recent data permit a more systematic deployment of the distinction in accounting for the development of search. In the next section, I shall take up the concept of identity and spatial coding in order to offer an account of search development which, although not radically different from Piaget's account, tries to address recent findings in a more systematic way.

IV. CATEGORIZING AND LOCATING OBJECTS

In previous discussions of the development of object permanence, I have sketched two somewhat different accounts of search development (Harris, 1975, 1976, 1977, 1979). On the one hand, I have suggested that the infant may only gradually acquire a rule stating that an object can occupy one place at any given time (Harris, 1975). On the other hand, I have also stressed that the infant gradually comes to make use of two different codes for the spatial position of an object: a self-related code and a framework code (Harris, 1976, 1977, 1979). Both of these approaches have something to offer and I believe a reasonably satisfying interpretation of the development of search can be achieved by their integration.

The successive appearances of a single object are connected in a continuous causal chain in two senses. First, the current position or trajectory of the object can be used to predict where it will be in the future. Second, the current position or trajectory of the object can be used to provide information about where it will no longer be. The first major hypothesis is that young infants only gradually come to understand these reciprocal relationships between earlier and later positions of a single object. Thus, they only gradually appreciate that the present location can be used to predict future locations and that the present location can be used to delete and update information about past locations.

The exact reason for this difficulty in coordinating earlier and later positions is unclear but two likely candidates deserve discussion, one candidate pertaining to the complexity of the environment facing the infant, the other pertaining to limits on information processing by the infant. The environment confronts the infant with two sets of spatio–temporal relations: those that apply to the displacements of a single object and those that apply to the displacements of different members of a class of objects. Consider, for a moment, the average domestic environment. It contains duplicates of many objects—spoons, chairs, and so forth. Moreover, infants, even in the first 6 months of life are capable of detecting similarities across repeated presentations of the same object, presentations of distinct but similar objects from the same class, and presentations of the same object in different orientations (Cohen & Strauss, 1979; Fagan, 1976; Harris, 1983; McGurk, 1972). Thus, infants will certainly be capable of seeing a similarity between, say, two spoons at different locations on the table. Accordingly, infants will be constantly confronted with violations of the rules that apply to a single object. Although the successive appearances of a single object are contingent upon one another in a predictable and general fashion, the spatial relations that hold between two instances of a class of objects are merely local and arbitrary. Thus, the current position of one instance cannot be used to predict the location of another instance. Nor does any current position of one instance require deletion or updating of information about the location of other instances. Indeed, in complete violation of the rules pertaining to a single object, instances of the same class may be located in different places at the same time. Accordingly, the discovery of the highly consistent but local regularities which exist for the successive appearances of a single object may be hampered by the way in which different instances of a class of objects appear to violate those regularities.

The second possibility is that the infant finds it difficult to discover the regularity that exists, not because of apparent violations of that regularity but because of limitations in information processing. The discovery of the regularity depends critically on the ability to assign a temporal order to memories or perceptions. Suppose that the infant sees and remembers several successive positions of an object but cannot encode the temporal order of those positions or can retain the temporal order for only a very brief period. The various positions of the object would take on the same degree of arbitrariness as was described above for instances of a class of objects. In the absence or information about which was the most recent position, the infant would neither be able to predict the object's future position nor be able to select past positions for deletion as possible loci for the object.

In summary, the first hypothesis is that infants only gradually discover the contingencies that exist between earlier and later positions of an object: the discovery of such contingencies may be hampered either by their apparent violation when two instances of a class of objects are encountered or by their opacity when information about the temporal order of successive positions is lost.

The second hypothesis is that the infant gradually comes to deploy two spatial codes in keeping track of object position. The self-referent code permits spatially adjusted action in the face of visible objects. Thus, it specifies where an object is in relation to the infant so that appropriate eye movements, reaching movements, crawling movements, etc. may be executed. The framework code permits spatially adjusted action to objects by encoding their relationship to salient landmarks in the environment. The framework code has one major advantage over the self-referent code: the position of objects relative to landmarks remains valid despite movement of the infant. In addition, an object remains inside a given cover even when the cover is moved. One might therefore expect the infant increasingly to adopt a framework code in addition to the self-related code in order to cope with movement, be it of self or cover.

Combining the two hypotheses above, we can predict that the infant will initially be confused by the displacements of a single visible object whose position is encoded simply in terms of the self-referent code. Such confusion will be revealed by inappropriate tracking movements and reaching movements. More specifically, the infant will lack any general rule for using the current position or trajectory of an object to predict its future position and will not necessarily delete past positions of an object in the light of its current position. With the emergence of a framework code, these problems will be repeated: in particular, movement to a new landmark will not be sufficient to delete a past landmark as a possible location for the object.

This hypothesis differs from that of Piaget in three major respects. First, it argues that displacements of all kinds, both visible and invisible, will be a source of potential difficulty for the infant. Piaget, as noted earlier, stresses the infant's difficulties with invisible objects. Second, the present account makes use of recent evidence in explicitly crediting the infant with two spatial codes. Third, the present account does not at any point attribute the infant's difficulties to egocentricity. Instead, two other possible sources of difficulty are identified: the arbitrary relations of distinct but similar objects, and the need to retain information about temporal order.

Finally, the two accounts differ in the problem that they suppose the infant is trying to solve. Piaget asserts that the infant comes to resolve the question of whether or not objects continue to exist when they are hidden. I would argue instead that the infant comes to resolve the question of where to search for an object when it has moved or disappeared, or when he or she has moved relative to the object. In fact, the child may never gain a belief in object permanence in the Piagetian sense. That is to say, the child may never come to answer the question of whether or not objects exist when they are invisible. Children do, however, acquire a set of rules for searching for objects that are accurate enough to ensure success on most occasions. Thus, conjurors fascinate children not because they violate their belief in object permanence but because they violate their generally accurate expectations about where an object is to be found.

While this difference between the two accounts may sound inconsequential, it does have a role to play in thinking about how development occurs. Piaget characterizes the infant as attempting to resolve a nonempirical question: by definition, there is no perceptual information which can resolve the question of whether hidden objects continue to exist. In contrast, the question of where an object is to be found is readily answerable: perceptual feedback is available to tell the infant whether or not search has been directed at the correct location and to teach the infant the regularities that exist between earlier and later positions.

A. Tracking Behavior Revisited

The tracking behavior of the infant between approximately 3 and 9 months, as outlined earlier, can be understood in the light of the hypothesized inability to relate earlier and later positions of a moving object. Such tracking exhibits the following characteristics. First, when an object moves and disappears in a given direction, infants do not spontaneously turn along the trajectory to the likely point of reappearance. Instead, they stare at the point of entry, learn on an empirical basis only to turn toward the point of reappearance, and rarely look at that point prior to the actual re-emergence of the moving object (Meicler & Gratch, 1980; Nelson, 1971). Second, infants have no precise expectations about the identity of the object that will reappear: the majority of studies report little or no disruption of tracking or puzzlement when one object disappears and a second, different object reappears (Goldberg, 1976; Meicler & Gratch, 1980; Muller & Aslin, 1978). Third, if an object reverses direction, infants do not spontaneously reverse the direction of their visual search: they again look at the point of disappearance and are forced to relearn where the object will reappear (Nelson, 1971).

These three findings can be explained by the hypothesis that the infant does not regard the successive positions of a single object as a set of mutually exclusive positions but regards them as a set of independent and coexisting positions where objects of a similar description can be seen. Given that the infant does not see the disappearing and reappearing object as one and the same object, he or she can only learn to turn on an empirical basis from one to the other; nor will the infant search back for the object which disappeared should a new object emerge, and nor will the infant spontaneously adapt to a change in the direction of travel. Finally, the present hypothesis would not be embarrassed by the finding that the infant sometimes turns away from the present position of a visible object to look at its past position as if in expectation of finding the object there too (Bower et al., 1971; Bower & Paterson, 1973). However, there is at present only inconsistent evidence that such perseverative errors occur.

B. The Coordination of Vision and Touch Revisited

The infant's search for an object under a cloth develops slowly. At $6\frac{1}{2}$ to $7\frac{1}{2}$ months, the infant will withdraw a clasped object from under a cloth (Gratch, 1972; Gratch & Landers, 1971). At 8 months, the infant will withdraw the object if it was grasped just prior to its disappearance under the cloth (Harris, 1971). Finally, at 12 months, withdrawal is possible after mere visual inspection (Harris, 1971).

This developmental progression becomes interpretable if we extend the above hypothesis as follows: just as the infant treats the successive visible locations of a moving object as belonging to similar and independent objects rather than to a single object, so the infant also regards the visual and tactual aspects of an object as belonging to similar but independent objects rather than to a single object. Since the positions of these "similar" objects are regarded as independent rather than coextensive, a movement of the "tactual object" will not be expected to produce a restoration of the "visual object." We may further suppose that, as for visual tracking, the infant discovers empirical procedures for producing visual stimulation given tactual input; first, such procedures may be applied when tactual input is currently available (at $6\frac{1}{2}$ to $7\frac{1}{2}$ months); next, when it has just been available (8 months); and third, when it is potentially available (12 months).

C. The AB̄ Error Revisited

The AB̄ error exhibits the following characteristics. First, with the exception of a brief initial period (Gratch & Landers, 1971) the typical error rate, at least when two hiding places are employed, is 50% (Butterworth, 1977). Second, error can be eliminated if immediate search at B is possible (Gratch et al., 1974; Harris, 1973) but it is only reduced rather than eliminated if the object remains visible at B (Butterworth, 1977; Harris, 1973). Third, the infant appears to be returning to a cover rather than repeating a particular motor response: the extent to which the object has been associated with a cover or landmark at A has a stronger effect on error rates (Butterworth, 1977; Lucas & Uzgiris, 1977) than the number of times the infant has found the object at A (Evans, 1973; Landers, 1971). Such a landmark-based code has been independently established in studies of spatial learning (Acredolo, 1978; Acredolo & Evans, 1980; Cornell & Heth, 1979; Rieser, 1979). Its emergence is correlated with the increasing mobility of the infant, although current research has not yet established any causal connection. Discrimination of the A cover from the B cover appears to be based either on distinctive features of the A cover when available or, alternatively, on its position relative to the infant. Finally, the AB̄ error is quite persistent. It has been observed at 16 months, even when the pattern of the infant's second choice indicates that the new hiding place has been encoded. Among older infants, it seems like that longer delays continue to precipitate the error (Diamond, 1983; Webb et al., 1972).

This pattern of errors can be explained by reference to the two hypotheses advanced earlier: the infant begins to code the successive positions of the object in relation to landmarks such as cloths or covers but does not regard these successive landmark positions as a set of mutually exclusive positions for a single object. Instead, they are regarded as a set of independent and coexisting positions where objects of a similiar description can be seen.

This formulation predicts that infants should divide their search between A and B not in terms of their temporal order as positions for the object but simply in terms of their relative salience. Thus, if the infant is looking at B, as is typically the case in a 0-sec delay task, search should be directed at B. If the object is visible at B, this should encourage but not ensure fixation at B and hence search at B should be probable but not inevitable. With delay, the infant should be as likely to fixate A as B, and therefore search should be divided between A and B. Finally, the extent to which an object has been associated with a landmark, such as a cover at A, should be a stronger determinant of error than the frequency with which the infant (as opposed to the experimenter) has made the object reappear at A.

There is one outstanding difficulty. Why should perseverative errors persist well into the second year of life, at least when longer delay intervals are introduced? If the infant comes to appreciate that movement to a new location eliminates a prior landmark as a useful guide to the whereabouts of the object, why is this insight not applied equally at short and long delays? One possible answer to this puzzle is that although infants do gradually come to understand the priority that should be given to the object's last position, they have only a very brief memory for temporal order information, although the duration of this memory increases with age. Thus, for any given age group, it would be possible to produce search divided between A and B, by exceeding the infant's memory span for temporal order information. As noted earlier, a limit on retention of temporal order information is in any case a plausible hypothesis on more general grounds: it offers an explanation of why infants have such difficulties in elaborating the rules for the displacements of a single object.

D. Invisible Displacements Revisited

In reviewing research on invisible displacements, it was noted that Piaget's notion may be too global to permit an analysis of the exact pattern of success and error. First, it is possible to carry out an invisible movement without introducing an invisible transfer. Second, invisible movements can involve rotation of the containers relative to the infant, or rotation of the infant relative to the containers.

A review of the evidence suggested that the ability to solve invisible movements when no invisible transfer is involved appears under certain conditions at around 9 months: distinctive landmarks both covering the object and at some distance from it help the infant search accurately despite his or her movement after the disappearance of the object. Second, distinctive cues marking the container that conceals the object help the infant search accurately despite movement of the container. When an invisible displacement occurs, the predominant source of error is to search at the container location that would have been correct had no movement occured. By 15 to 18 months infants begin to infer that when an object is moved inside a container and transferred to another hiding place, they should look for the object beyond the point at which it was last seen being carried in the moving container but prior to the point at which the container was first seen to be empty.

These findings are compatible with the hypothesis that the 9-month-old infant can encode the position of the object in relation to landmarks but often fails to update such an encoding in the light of an invisible displacement. If distinctive landmarks are available, the updating process is facilitated. Landmarks both close to and more distant from the object help infants cope with their own movements, since the infant's movement in no way alters the relation of the object to those landmarks. Distinctive cues marking the container itself help the infant to cope with movements of the container, since the object remains in the same place relative to those cues even when it is moved inside the container.

Finally, the infant's increasing ability to confine search to appropriate points along a container's movement is compatible with the notion that the infant is gradually coming to see the successive locations of a single object as contingent upon one another in a predictable fashion. The infant uses the last point of appearance in the container to delete prior locations as candidates for finding the object and also uses the point of disappearance from the container to delete subsequent locations of the container as candidate locations for finding the object.

V. SUMMARY

In the beginning of this chapter, Piaget's account of the development of object permanence was distilled into two postulates. First, infants only gradually acknowledge the permanence of the invisible object. Second, the errors made by infants are attributable to their egocentric assumption that the object's reappearance is brought about by their own actions. In reviewing, the evidence pertaining to Piaget's theory, two broad conclusions emerged. First, broad-scale replication studies and also many of the more detailed experimental studies support Piaget's claims regarding the developmental sequence to be observed. This does not, however, mean that Piaget's interpretation of that sequence must be accepted. In fact, a fairly exhaustive review of the many experimental studies uncovered a good deal of evidence which, while not necessarily contradicting Piagetian theory, does highlight its imprecision or lack of theoretical parsimony. A review of the various theoretical alternatives to Piaget indicated, however, that investigators have concentrated on a small sample of the avaialable findings. Rarely do these alternative proposals compete with Piaget's account in terms of their range of explanation. Finally, an attempt was made to interpret the development of search in terms of the infant's difficulties in uniting the successive locations of an object into a single object, difficulties which Piaget also recognized but regarded as symptomatic of the infant' egocentricity and lack of a belief in permanence. It was argued that the infant, hampered either by the apparently arbitrary relations between similar-looking objects or by difficulty in retaining temporal order information, only gradually discovers that the earlier and later appearances of an object are connected in a regular and predictable fashion. Until this discovery is made, both with respect to free-standing objects and eventually with respect to objects located in relation to containers or landmarks, the infant will fail to treat the successive positions as related to one another in a mutually exclusive fashion.

ACKNOWLEDGMENT

Several people looked at draft versions of this manuscript and provided helpful comments. I should like to thank Gavin Bremner, George Butterworth, Ed Cornell, Gerald Gratch, Andrew Meltzoff, and Peter Willatts.

REFERENCES

Acredolo, L. P. (1978). Development of spatial orientation in infancy. *Developmental Psychology, 14*, 224–234.

Acredolo, L. P. (1979). Laboratory versus home: The effect of environment on the 9-month-old infant's choice of spatial reference system. *Developmental Psychology, 15*, 666–667.

Acredolo, L. P. & Evans, D. (1980). Developmental changes in the effects of landmarks on infant spatial behaviour. *Developmental Psychology, 16*, 312–318.

Bower, T. G. R. (1967). The development of object-permanence: Some studies of existence constancy. *Perception and Psychophysics, 2*, 411–418.

Bower, T. G. R. (1974). *Development in infancy*. San Francisco, CA: Freeman.

Bower, T. G. R. (1977). *A primer of infant development*. San Francisco, CA: Freeman.

Bower, T. G. R. (1979). *Human development*. San Francisco, CA: Freeman.

Bower, T. G. R., Broughton, J. M., & Moore, M. K. (1970). The coordination of visual and tactual input in infants. *Perception and Psychophysics, 8*, 51–53.

Bower, T. G. R., Broughton, J. M., & Moore, M. K. (1971). Development of the object concept as manifested in the tracking behavior of infants between 7 and 20 weeks of age. *Journal of Experimental Child Psychology, 11*, 182–193.

Bower, T. G. R., & Paterson, J. G. (1973). The separation of place, movement, and object in the world of the infant. *Journal of Experimental Child Psychology, 15*, 161–168.

Bower, T. G. R., & Wishart, J. G. (1972). The effects of motor skill on object permanence. *Cognition, 1*, 165–172.

Brainerd, C. J. (1978a). *Piaget's theory of intelligence*. Englewood Cliffs, NJ: Prentice-Hall.

Brainerd, C. J. (1978b). The stage question in cognitive-developmental theory. *Behavioral and Brain Sciences, 1*, 173–213.

Bremner, J. G. (1978a). Egocentric versus allocentric spatial coding in nine-month old infants: Factors influencing the choice of code. *Developmental Psychology, 14*, 346–355.

Bremner, J. G. (1978b). Spatial errors made by infants: Inadequate spatial cues or evidence of egocentrism? *British Journal of Psychology, 69*, 77–84.

Bremner, J. G. (1980). The infant's understanding of space. In M. V. Cox (Ed.), *Are young children egocentric?* London: Batsford.

Bremner, J. G., & Bryant, P. E. (1977). Place versus response as the basis of spatial errors made by young infants. *Journal of Experimental Child Psychology, 23*, 162–171.

Bresson, F., Maury, L., Pieraut-le Bonniec, G., & de Schönen, S. (1977). Organisation and lateralisation of reaching in infants: An instance of asymmetric function in hand collaboration. *Neuropsychologica, 15*, 311–320.

Bryant, P. E. (1969). Perception and memory of the orientation of visually presented lines by children. *Nature, (London), 224*, 1331–1332.

Bryant, P. E. (1974). *Perception and understanding in young children*. London: Methuen.

Butterworth, G. (1974). *The development of the object concept in human infants*. Unpublished doctoral thesis, University of Oxford.

Butterworth, G. (1975). Object identity in infancy: The interaction of spatial location codes in determining search errors. *Child Development, 46*, 866–870.

Butterworth, G. (1976). Asymmetrical search errors in infancy. *Child Development, 47*, 864–867.

Butterworth, G. (1977). Object disappearance and error in Piaget's stage IV task. *Journal of Experimental Child Psychology, 23*, 391–401.

Butterworth, G. (1978). Thought and things: Piaget's theory. In A. Burton & J. Radford (Eds.), *Perspectives on thinking*. London: Methuen.

Butterworth, G., Jarrett, N., & Hicks, L. (1982). Spatiotemporal identity in infancy: Perceptual competence or conceptual deficit. *Developmental Psychology, 18*, 435–449.

Cohen, L. B., & Strauss, M. (1979). Concept acquisition in the human infant. *Child Development, 50*, 419–424.

Corman, H. H., & Escalona, S. K. (1969). Stages of sensorimotor development: A replication study. *Merrill-Palmer Quarterly, 15*, 351–361.

Cornell, E. H., (1978). Learning to find things: A reinterpretation of object permanence studies. In L. Siegel & C. Brainerd (Eds.), *Alternatives to Piaget: Critical essays on the theory.* New York: Academic Press.

Cornell, E. H. (1979a). The effects of cue reliability on infant's manual search. *Journal of Experimental Child Psychology, 28*, 81–91.

Cornell, E. H. (1979b). The stage heuristic in the sudy of sensorimotor intelligence. *Behavioral and Brain Sciences, 2*, 140–141.

Cornell, E. H. (1981). The effects of cue distinctiveness on infants' manual search. *Journal of Experimental Child Psychology, 32*, 330–342.

Cornell, E. H., & Heth, C. D. (1979). Response versus place learning by human infants. *Journal of Experimental Psychology: Human Learning and Memory, 5*, 188–196.

Cummings, E. M., and Bjork, E. L. (1977, April). *Piaget's stage IV object concept error: Evidence of perceptual confusion, state change, or failure to assimilate?* Paper presented at the meeting of the Western Psychological Association, Seattle, WA.

Cummings, E. M., & Bjork, E. L. (1981). The search behavior of 12 to 14 month-old infants on a five-choice invisible displacement task. *Infant Behavior and Development, 4*, 47–60.

DeLoache, J. S., & Brown, A. L. (1983). Very young children's memory for the location of objects in a large scale environment. *Child Development, 54*, 888–897.

Diamond, A. (1983). *The development of recall memory from 7 to 12 months.* Paper given at Society for Research in Child Development meeting, Detroit, MI.

Dunst, C. J., Brooks, P. H., & Doxsey, P. A. (1982). Characteristics of hiding places and the transition to Stage IV performance in object permanence tasks. *Developmental Psychology, 18*, 671–681.

Evans, W. F. (1973). The Stage IV error in Piaget's theory of object concept development: An investigation of the role of activity. Unpublished dissertation proposal, University of Houston, Houston, TX.

Evans, W. F., & Gratch, G. (1972). The Stage IV error in Piaget's theory of object concept development: Difficulties in object conceptualization or spatial localization? *Child Development, 43*, 682–688.

Fagan, J. F., III (1976). Infants' recognition of invariant features of faces. *Child Development, 47*, 627–638.

Flavell, J. H. (1977). *Cognitive development.* Englewood Cliffs, NJ: Prentice-Hall.

Freeman, N., Lloyd, S., & Sinha, C. G. (1980). Infant search tasks reveal early concepts of containment and canonical usage of objects. *Cognition, 8*, 243–262.

Goldberg, S. (1976). Visual tracking and existence constancy in 5-month-old infants. *Journal of Experimental Child Psychology, 22*, 478–491.

Goldfield, E. C., & Dickerson, D. J. (1981). Keeping track of locations during movement in 8 to 10-month old infants. *Journal of Experimental Child Psychology, 32*, 48–64.

Gratch, G. (1972). A study of the relative dominance of vision and touch in six-month-old infants. *Child Development, 43*, 615–623.

Gratch, G. (1975). Recent studies based on Piaget's view of object concept development. In L. B. Cohen & P. Salapatek (Eds.), *Infant perception: From sensation to cognition* (Vol. 2, pp. 51–99). New York: Academic Press.

Gratch, G. (1976). Review of Piaget infancy research: Object concept development. In W. F.

Overton & J. M. Gallagher (Eds.) *Knowledge and development: Advances in research and theory* (Vol. 1). New York: Plenum.

Gratch, G. (1982). Responses to hidden persons and things by 5-, 9-, and 16-month-old infants in a visual tracking situation. *Developmental Psychology, 18,* 232–237.

Gratch, G., Appel, K. J., Evans, W. F., LeCompte, G. K., & Wright, N. A. (1974). Piaget's Stage IV object concept error: Evidence of forgetting or object conception? *Child Development, 45,* 71–77.

Gratch, G., & Landers, W. F. (1971). Stage IV of Piaget's theory of infants' object concepts: A longitudinal study. *Child Development, 42,* 359–372.

Haith, M. M., & Campos, J. J. (1977). Human infancy. *Annual review of Psychology, 28,* 251–293.

Harris, P. L. (1971). Examination and search in infants. *British Journal of Psychology, 62,* 469–473.

Harris, P. L. (1973). Perseverative errors in search by young infants. *Child Development, 44,* 28–33.

Harris, P. L. (1974). Perseverative search at a visibly empty place by young infants. *Journal of Experimental Child Psychology, 18,* 535–542.

Harris, P. L. (1975). Development of search and object permanence during infancy. *Psychological Bulletin, 82,* 332–344.

Harris, P. L. (1976). Subject, object and framework: A theory of spatial development Unpublished manuscript, University of Lancaster, Department of Psychology, U.K.

Harris, P. L. (1977). The child's representation of space. In G. Butterworth (Ed.), *The child's representation of the world.* New York: Plenum.

Harris, P. L. (1979). Perception and cognition in infancy. In K. Connolly (Ed.), *Psychology Survey No. 2.* London: Allen & Unwin.

Harris, P. L. (1983). Infant cognition. In M. M. Haith & J. J. Campos (Eds.), *Mussen's handbook of child psychology* (Vol. 2). New York: Wiley.

Jacobson, S. W. (1979). Matching behavior in the young infant. *Child Development, 50,* 425–430.

Kramer, J., Hill, K., & Cohen, L. (1975). Infant's development of object permanence: A refined methodology and new evidence of Piaget's hypothesized ordinality. *Child Development, 46,* 149–155.

Landers, W. F. (1971). The effect of differential experience on infants' performance in a Piagetian Stage IV object-concept task. *Developmental Psychology, 5,* 48–54.

LeCompte, G. K., & Gratch, G. (1972). Violation of a rule as a method of diagnosing infants' levels of object concept. *Child Development, 43,* 385–396.

Lloyd, S., Sinha, C. G., & Freeman, N. H. (1981). Spatial reference systems and the canonicality effect in infant search. *Journal of Experimental Child Psychology, 32,* 1–10.

Lucas, T. C. & Utzgiris, I. C. (1977). Spatial factors in the development of the object concept. *Developmental Psychology, 13,* 492–500.

McGurk, H. (1972). Infant discrimination of orientation. *Journal of Experimental Child Psychology, 14,* 151–164.

Meicler, M., & Gratch, G. (1980). Do 5-month olds show object conception in Piaget's sense? *Infant Behavior and Development, 3,* 265–282.

Meltzoff, A. N., & Moore, M. K. (1977). Imitation of facial and manual gestures by human neonates. *Science, 1977, 198,* 75–8.

Miller, D., Cohen, L., & Hill, K. (1970). A methodological investigation of Piaget's theory of object concept development in the sensory-motor period. *Journal of Experimental Child Psychology, 1970, 9,* 59–85.

Moore, M. K. (1975, April). *Object permanence and object identity: A stage developmental model*. Paper presented at the meeting of the Society for Research in Child Development, Denver, CO.

Moore, M. K., Borton, R., & Darby, B. L. (1978). Visual tracking in young infants: Evidence for object identity or object permanence? *Journal of Experimental Child Psychology, 25,* 183–198.

Moore, M. K., & Meltzoff, A. N. (1978). Imitation, object permanence and language development in infancy: Toward a neo-Piagetian perspective on communicative and cognitive development. In F. D. Minifie & L. L. Lloyd (Eds.), *Communicative and cognitive abilities—Early behavioral assessment*. Baltimore, MD: University Park Press.

Muller, A. A., & Aslin, R. N. (1978). Visual tracking as an index of the object concept. *Infant Behavior and Development, 1,* 309–319.

Nelson, K. E. (1971). Accommodation of visual-tracking patterns in human infants to object movement patterns. *Journal of Experimental Child Psychology, 12,* 182–196.

Piaget, J. (1952). *The origins of intelligence in children*. New York: International Universities Press.

Piaget, J. (1954). *The construction of reality in the child*. New York: Basic Books.

Pick, H. L., Yonas, A., & Rieser, J. (1979). Spatial reference systems in perceptual development. In M. Bornstein & W. Kessen (Eds.), *Psychological development from infancy: Image to intention*. Hillsdale, NJ: Erlbaum.

Presson, C. C., & Ihrig, L. H. (1982). Using mother as a spatial landmark: Evidence against egocentric coding in infancy. *Developmental Psychology, 18,* 699–703.

Rader, N., Spiro, D. J., & Firestone, P. B. (1979). Performance on a stage IV object permanence task with standard and nonstandard covers. *Child Development, 50,* 908–910.

Rieser, J. (1979). Spatial orientation of six-month-old infants. *Child Development, 50,* 1078–1087.

Rieser, J. J., & Heiman, M. L. (1982). Spatial self-reference systems and shortest-route behavior in toddlers. *Child Development, 53,* 524–533.

Schaffer, H. R., & Parry, M. H. (1970). The effects of short-term familiarization on infants' perceptual-motor coordination in a simultaneous discrimination situation. *British Journal of Psychology, 61,* 559–569.

Schubert, R. E., and Gratch, G. (1981). Search on a five-choice invisible displacement hiding task: A reply to Cummings and Bjork. *Infant Behavior and Development, 4,* 61–64.

Schubert, R. E., Werner, J. S., & Lipsitt, L. P. (1978). The stage IV error in Piaget's theory of object concept development: A reconsideration of the spatial localization hypothesis. *Child Development, 49,* 744-748.

Siqueland, E., & DeLucia, C. (1969). Visual reinforcement of nonnutritive sucking in human infants. *Science, 165,* 1144–1146.

Somerville, S. C., & Haake, R. J. (1983). *Selective search skills of infants and young children*. Paper given at the Society for Research in Child Development meeting, Detroit, MI.

Sophian, C. (1984). Spatial transpositions and the early development of search. *Developmental Psychology, 35,* 369–390.

Sophian, C., & Sage, S. (1983). Developments in infants' search for displaced objects. *Journal of Experimental Child Psychology, 35,* 143–160.

Sophian, C., & Wellman, H. (1983). Selective information use and perseveration in the search behavior of infants and young children. *Journal of Experimental Child Psychology, 35,* 369–390.

Uzgiris, I. C., & Hunt, J. M. (1975). *Assessment in Infancy: Ordinal Scales of Infant Development.* Urbana, ILL: University of Illinois Press.

von Hofsten, C., & Lindhagen, K. (1982). Perception of visual occlusion in $4\frac{1}{2}$-month-old infants. *Infant Behavior and Development, 5,* 215–226.

Webb, R. A., Massar, D., & Nadolny, T. (1982). Information and strategy in the young child's search for hidden objects. *Child Development, 43,* 91–104.

White, B. L., Castle, P., and Held, R. (1964). Observations on the development of visually directed reaching. *Child Development, 35,* 349–364.

Willatts, P. (1979). Adjustment of reaching to change in object position by young infants. *Child Development, 50,* 911–913.

Wishart, J. G., and Bower, T. G. R. (1982). The development of spatial understanding in infancy. *Journal of Experimental Child Psychology, 33,* 363–385.

Zazzo, P. (1957). La problème de l'imitation chez le nouveau-né. *Enfance, 2,* 135–142.

5

Event Encoding in Infancy

JANELLEN HUTTENLOCHER
THERESA SMYTH-BURKE
Departments of Behavioral Sciences and Education
University of Chicago
Chicago, Illinois 60637

I. INTRODUCTION

This chapter concerns the encoding of events by children in the first two years of life. By events here, as in ordinary usage, we mean movements and other changes in objects, both animate and inanimate, occurring through time. An event may end in a state of affairs different from that which preceded it—a change in the state of an object or in the spatial relations among objects—or it may involve only a temporary change and end in a state of affairs indistinguishable from that which preceded it (as when an object moves about in place). Most events in the child's environment involve the behavior of animate creatures, chiefly persons. These events consist of bodily movemetns, often in relation to objects and to other persons. People's behavior, like other kinds of events, may cause changes in the states of objects (things may be eaten, broken, etc.), or in the spatial relations among objects (things may be given, taken, etc.); or their behavior may cause no net change in the state of affairs (people may jump up and down, bounce balls, etc.).

We have seen in earlier chapters that infants form equivalence classes involving different stimuli among which they can discriminate. The equivalence classes discussed in these other chapters can be described as perceptual categories in that they are based on the perceptual similarity of

209

the instances. For these, information relevant to the category is available from each instance of the category, and their formation simply requires the ability to encode individual instances and to relate successive instances to one another on the basis of perceptual similarity. Perceptual categories include categories of objects (e.g., apple or tree) and of absolute properties (e.g., red or square). Certain event categories also would seem to be based on the perceptual similarity of the instances. These would include, for example, the coming into view or disappearance of objects and directed movements of objects, such as rising or falling.

There are many event categories, notably those involving the behavior of persons, which are not based on perceptual similarities among all the category instances. For example, the act of running is very different to an observer than to a person performing it. Yet as adults we have a single category of running which includes acts we experience from both perspectives. To classify them together we need to make inferences about how the actions in which we participate must look to this outside observer, or about how the actions we observe must be experienced by the participants.

Because the adult knows that action he observes are accompanied by feelings of effort and are based on intentions like those which underlie his or her own behavior, he or she can categorize those actions in terms of the intentions and goals that motivate them. Thus he may categorize together observed behaviors which are perceptually very different from one another but which have a common goal. For example, the adult who sees one person stirring flour into a mixing bowl and another pouring batter into a pan may describe each as "baking a cake." The goals and plans which guide the behavior of adults, and which adults infer in categorizing the actions of others, sometimes involve lenthly sequences of behavior in the service of a single goal, for example, "cleaning the house." Indeed, in adults, the chunks of behavior which are categorized together into equivalence classes on the basis of a common goal can be analyzed into subsidiary acts reflecting subgoals. These acts may bear various relations to each other: inclusion (e.g., "cleaning the house" includes dusting and vacuuming) temporal succession (e.g., dusting the living room, then dusting the dining room), or causation (e.g., removing the lint from the rug by moving the vacuum cleaner).

In short, the encoding of events by adults involves complex knowledge of the physical and social world—of the nature and functions of objects, of physical causation, and of other people's characteristics, most notably the fact that they possess internal states, including intentions and goals. Indeed, the goals in terms of which adults categorize behavior are often socially defined, involving people's roles in society (e.g., doctor, fireman), family (e.g., father), etc. It seems clear that not all of this knowledge is accessible to the infant under 2 years of age. Our aim here is to gather together the existing evidence about how they *do* encode the events they observe.

The first issue we will discuss is the infant's developing notions of objects, since object encoding is crucial to the encoding of events. In order to encode events which involve changes in object location, the infant must first be able to encode the objects as permanent entities bearing particular spatial relations to one another and to discriminate one spatial arrangement from another as these succeed each other in time. Otherwise the configuration of objects existing at one point in time and the differing configuration that preceded or followed it would not be perceived as a change of object loaction at all. Likewise, in order to encode events which involve changes of object state, the infant must be able to encode the enduring characteristics of objects which define them across time (being red or green, round or square, etc.) as well as those which identify them as being in particular states (being open or closed, clean or dirty, etc.). Further, he must recognize that changes in state do not change the identity of an object—that an object's identity is defined by those charateristics which endure across transformations of state.

The next issue we will discuss is the development of event encoding *per se*. We examine the evidence that infants encode various aspects of the movements of a single entity, either an object or a person (such as that the person jumped or the object fell), as well as the evidence that they encode events that involve more than one entity (such as that a person touched an object). We will also examine the infant's encoding of events in which a person's movements bring about a change in the position or state of an object (such as that a person has put down or broken an object), and his developing ability to encode the causal relations in these events. Finally, we consider the encoding of events as goal-directed actions. To infer that observed actions are goal-directed, one must necessarily encode other persons not just as material objects, but also as creatures with internal states parallel to one's own. We will review the evidence concerning the infant's encoding of other persons and consider what this evidence implies about how the infant encodes actions.

II. OBJECT ENCODING

A. Objects within a Spatio-Temporal Framework

Piaget (1954) has argued that children only gradually acquire the notion that objects are permanent: that the same objects continue to exist in particular places even when one turns away from them, that they can only appear in a new place by moving continuously from their earlier location, etc. In a series of well-known studies, Piaget examined this development by covering an object in the infant's presence and then observing his efforts to find it. The infants searched for the object from the same vantage point from which they had watched the hiding. Piaget found that if an object is covered over, even partially, children below 6 months will act as though it simply ceased to exist; they will not search for it. By 8 months children will retrieve a partially covered object; by 10 months, they will search for a vanished object, but only in its original location; and by about 12 months, they will search in the last location at which an object was visibly displaced. After about 16 months, children will search for an object even after invisible displacements. The order of this sequence has been confirmed by later investigators (e.g., Kramer, Hill, & Cohen, 1975).

The studies of object permanence require the child to encode and retain the location of the object. To locate an object at all means to locate it *with respect to* something else. In Piaget's studies, there are several potential landmarks—the cover which hides the object, the larger spatial framework of the room with its permanent features such as the furniture, and the infant himself, since he remains stationary while he watches an object disappear and searches for it. Piaget's studies date the start of spatial associations between objects and landmarks at about 10 months of age. However, Lucas and Uzgiris (1977) report that even younger infants have at least an undifferentiated notion of objects' proximity to landmarks; that is, 7- and 8-month-olds associate objects to landmarks, although they fail to encode correctly the precise spatial relation between them. If a toy is initially located in front of a distinctive landmark, and then is whisked away behind a cloth while the landmark remains, infants under 9 months will seek that toy behind the landmark. Lucas and Uzgiris conclude that these infants had not encoded the toy as being "in front of" but simply as being "near" the landmark (topological proximtiy).

If the infant can change his own position relative to a hidden object and still find that object when he approaches it from a different side, this provides evidence that he has actually associated the object to some outside spatial framework independent of himself, either the local landmark of the cover in an object permanence study, or the larger framework of the room. Piaget, Inhelder, and Szeminska (1960) report anecdotal evidence that by the middle of the second year of life, the infant begins to note that the positions of objects relative to external landmarks remain fixed even as he himself moves within the environment. Recent studies show that if landmarks are salient or familiar enough, infants can change position and still locate objects in a spatial framework even at 9 months. Insofar as the spatial framework and the cover which hides an object serve as landmarks, they are stimuli to which target objects are associated. Findings with other types of paired associates (e.g., Goss & Nodine, 1965) would lead one to expect that the characteristics of these landmarks would affect the ease of forming the association, and this is indeed the case.

Bremner and Bryant (1977) tested 9-month-olds by hiding an object under one of two covers and then moving the infant to the opposite side of the display before allowing him to search. If the covers were similar, the infant first approached the wrong cover, even when there were distinctive cues within the larger spatial framework (Bremner, 1978a; Bremner & Bryant, 1977). If the covers were distinctive, however, correct searches were above chance (Bremner, 1978a, 1978b). In these studies, only local landmarks such as covers were effective, not features of the larger background. However, when the large-scale space within which objects are located is thoroughly familiar, it does provide a source of effective landmarks for the infant. Acredolo (1979) found that 9-month-olds who failed a task like Bremner's in an unfamiliar room searched correctly when they were given the same task in their own homes.

Acredolo (1978; Acredolo & Evans, 1980) studied infants' ability to locate events as well as stationary objects in relation to landmarks. Infants were trained to expect an interesting event at one of two laterally located windows in an experimental room and then were turned 180° to an opposite orientation. Even when windows were marked with a large yellow star, infants under 1 year subsequently turned to the wrong window, whereas those of 16 months turned toward the true location. However, with an even more salient landmark, 9-month-olds consistently turned toward the true location and only 6-month-olds responded inconsistently. Thus regardless of whether the infant looks for an object or for an event, if there are extremely salient environmental features to which he can associate it, he does so at 9 months. One might conclude that since the infant can locate an event within a spatiotemporal framework, he must have encoded the event itself. This is not the case, since the "interesting event" in Acredolo's task involved unique objects, and hence the infant had only to look in the place where those objects had appeared. But although Acredolo's findings do not give us information about event encoding *per se,* they do provide additional evidence that 9-month-olds can encode an object's relation to very salient landmarks.

B. The Characteristics of Objects

In the search studies we have discussed so far, no evidence was obtained as to whether children retain information about the particular enduring characteristics of objects. LeCompte and Gratch (1972) used a variation of the Piagetian techniques to investigate this issue. Testing children from 9 to 18 months, they surreptitiously substituted a different toy on some trials of the hiding task; one toy was big and colorful, the other small and drab. Nine-month-olds typically responded by staring longer at the toy on substitution trials than on control trials; 12-month-olds typically reacted with a slight frown or baffled look; strong, persistent frowns and momentary "freezing" followed by persistent search for the original toy were typical of 18-month-olds. In a similar study, Ramsay and Campos (1975) found that 8-, 12-, and 17-month-olds all looked longer after uncovering a different toy than after uncovering the same toy that had been hidden; frequency of persistent search increased with age. These studies indicate that by 8 or 9 months, infants encode obvious properties of objects and notice differences among them. Yet they are less likely than older infants to search for the original toy in these tasks, probably because they have no strong conviction that objects are permanent and hence little motivation to search when one subject disappears and another takes its place. In support of this view, Ramsay and Campos (1978) found that the likelihood of search by 10- to 16-month-olds in this task is related to their performance on object permanence tasks.

Evidence about the formation of equivalence classes becomes available as infants acquire words; that is, when the same word is used across a set of instances form a category. Infants acquire object names (e.g., "ball," "bottle," "dog") starting at 10 to 15 months of age. This would suggest that they form categories of objects by early in their second year. However, various investigators have argued that early words do *not* represent true object categories, but rather are associated with the situation in general, including not just objects, but also ongoing events, particular viewing perspectives, etc. (e.g., Guillaume, 1927/1973; Piaget, 1951). The claim is not that these early words represent pure event categories (which, as we shall see, emerge a few months later with words like "up" and "bye-bye"), but rather that the year-old infant in some way encodes events along with objects.

The empirical basis for this claim is that early words are "overextended" in production. Thus Guillaume (1927/1973) cites the use of "breast" at 12 months to name a red button and a bare elbow as well as the breast, and also to request food. Piaget (1951) cites the use of "bowwow" for small animals, moving vehicles, and also to name anything seen from the same balcony where the infant had once observed a dog. These investigators argue that early words are used overgenerally because the infant does not possess object categories. However, the fact that infants overextend some words is not convincing evidence for such a claim. Rather, one would have to show that they lack any words which *do* encode object categories, and this would require a systematic examination of the child's entire lexicon. Further, one would expect that if infants encoded events along with objects, names should be overgeneralized to objects with similar movement or function. However, as Bowerman (1976, 1978a, 1978b) has pointed out, overgeneralization tends instead to be to objects which are similar in appearance.

There are more recent claims, too, that early words are action-based, but, again, the evidence is not convincing. Bloom (1973) has reported that her daughter used function words (e.g., "more") in situations involving "salient and recurring behaviors" more frequently and persistently than object words (e.g., "chair") in the period before development of object permanence. However, other investigators report that "more" emerges late, after many object words are acquired (e.g., Carter, 1975; Corrigan, 1978; Greenfield & Smith, 1976), and Corrigan (1978) found many substantives before object permanence was fully attained by her three longitudinal subjects. Nelson (1974) has argued that the child encodes objects in their action contexts (e.g., ball rolling under couch, ball being thrown by person), only later abstracting out the notion of the object from its various action contexts. Her evidence was drawn from an earlier study in which she obtained mothers' diaries of their children's first 50 words (Nelson, 1973). She observed that early object words usually named objects on which the child can act (e.g., "shoe," "keys"), or which move themselves (e.g., "dog," "car"). It should be noted that this would not necessarily mean that actions were encoded. Action or movement might simply make these objects more salient. Nelson also found that certain early words occurred only in particular action contexts, for example, "door" to ask to go out. Griffiths and Atkinson (1978) also using mothers' diaries, claimed that four of their subjects used "door" as a request for opening, removing, or inserting objects, not as an object name, until 21 months.

Leaving aside the problem of accuracy of mother reports, the fact that a child produces a given word only in a selected context does not provide conclusive evidence about word meaning. The child who uses "door" only when a particular action is desired may actually be referring to the object but have no reason to refer to it in other contexts. While spontaneous speech can sometimes provide strong evidence as to the presence of particular categories, it does not provide good evidence about the absence of categories. To test meaning in cases of ambiguity one must use comprehension tests or attempt to elicit production in other contexts; for example, one may point at the door when the child has no desire to leave and ask, "What is that?"

Huttenlocher and Smiley (1986) have provided evidence that children do indeed categorize objects on the basis of their enduring perceptual characteristics, not their actions, at the time when they begin to use object names. Systematic examination of the lexicons in a group of infants between 12 and 16 months indicates that they possess at least some words which categorize objects *per se* (e.g., dog, flower). First, the infants were given comprehension tests which indicated that they could consistently choose particular objects on the basis of their names even when they were presented in an array, out of their usual contexts. Second, systematic recording of the contexts in which words were produced indicated that certain words were used to name particular types of objects, regardless of the event contexts in which those objects occurred. Frequently (although by no means always), the children were acting on these objects when they named them. However, the same acts tended to occur for all the objects named (e.g., getting or showing objects).

Another sort of evidence that the infant groups objects into equivalence classes is the development of appropriate differential use of objects with different perceptual characteristics, such as using a broom to sweep and knife to cut. In the first year of life, objects are all treated similarly: babies mouth, grasp, clutch, turn, and transfer objects from hand to hand and touch and bump them against one another (Hutt, 1967; Fenson, Kagan, Kearsley, & Zelazo, 1976). Between 12 and 18 months, however, actions become more specific and appropriate to the object; for example, children will "drink" from a cup and use a comb on their hair (Fenson et al., 1976; Lowe, 1975). (Such behavior not only shows that the child possesses equivalence class of objects to which he makes a common response but also shows that the infant has encoded the events in which those objects are habitually involved, a point we will take up later in this chapter.) Thus, starting at about 1 year, infants categorize particular objects as having particular functions.

C. Summary

In summary, starting at 8 or 9 months, and certainly by about 1 year of age, the infant encodes some of the obvious perceptual characteristics of different types of objects, as well as their relations to salient landmarks. Starting at about 1 year, he also begins to associate words with objects, words which are object-specific and not context-specific. Finally, at this same age, the child begins to use particular types of objects in distinctive appropriate ways, demomonstrating familiarity with the habitual functions of those objects in actions. Both of these categorization skills, productive language and differential object use, presuppose encoding of particular properties of objects. Thus early in the second year of life the infant encodes certain aspects of his surroundings critical for encoding events: he has a notion of objects with particular enduring properties which are located within a spatiotemporal framework.

III. EVENT ENCODING

A. Object Movement

There is evidence that even young infants encode particular kinds of movements. Some of this evidence comes from dishabituation studies where infants are shown multiple instances of one type of event until they become habituated to it and then are presented with an instance of a different type of event; heart deceleration or longer visual fixation relative to the last response to the habituated event is taken as evidence that the infants noticed the change. Gibson and her collaborators (Gibson, Owsley, & Johnston, 1978; Gibson, Owsley, Walker, & Megaw-Nyce, 1979) used this technique to show that even 3- to 5-month-old infants distinguish between a rigid motion of an object and a deformation of its surface. The infants were habituated to various continuous, cyclical movements of a disk that left its surface intact. They showed much greater dishabituation effects when the surface of the disk (which was actually foam rubber) was rippled than when a new type of rigid motion was presented (Gibson et al., 1978, 1979). Similarly, 3- and 4-month-olds who habituated to various deforming motions dishabituated more to a rigid motion of the object than to a new type of deforming motion (Walker et al., 1980).

Dishabituation studies also show that, only a little later, infants encode the direction of motion of an object. Robertson (1975) found dishabituation to change in the direction of motion (left to right or vice versa) in some 5-month-olds. Infants' reaching behavior confirms that they encode direction of movement by 5 months and shows they encode information about velocity as well. Von Hofsten (1980) analyzed infants' reaches for moving objects and found predictive reaching as early as 18 weeks. That is, when infants begin their reaches, they aim not at the object's current position but at a point farther along its trajectory. The faster the object is moving, the farther ahead of it the infants aim their reach.

While these studies show that infants encode movements of objects across their visual field and deformations of object shape, they do not provide evidence as to whether they encode differences in the movements of body parts. Observation of the infant's imitative behavior does provide such evidence, although it only allows us to evaluate the encoding of those aspects of people's movement that are within the infant's own behavioral repertoire, and this at a time when his motor abilities are not well developed. Still, successful imitation of observed behavior demonstrates that the child has encoded the movements of a model and/or the effects of those movements on objects. Further, accurate imitation of a new bodily movement indicates that the child relates the movements he observes to parallel movements of his own; indeed, this may be true even when only familiar acts are imitated.

The reproduction of particular movements in response to the movements of a model—as opposed to the spontaneous production of movements which coincidentally resemble those of nearby adults—first appears at about the fifth or sixth month (Guilluame, 1926/1971; Piaget, 1951). Early imitation involves acts which are already in the infant's repertoire as spontaneous acts and which he can see himself perform. Even a complex act with these characteristics will be imitated by 5 to 8 months, but it is an "unanalyzed unit"; if only part of it is modeled, the child will not imitate it unless it has already appeared alone in her spontaneous activity (Piaget, 1951). Indeed, the earliest imitations occur in cases where the child's spontaneous movements are imitated by the caretaker and then are repeated by the infant. Sometimes such imitative interactions continue through several cycles in which the model's response both reinforces the infant's making a particular movement and also provides a discriminative stimulus for producing the movement.

Imitations of this sort show clearly that the infant encodes enough information about the model's movements to discriminate among different sorts of movements, for he responds to them differentially. The question of whether he encodes the model's movements as resembling his own is more debatable. One might argue that the infant could carry on such "mutual imitation" cycles without noting the resemblance, just as he might produce a particular movement in response to any sort of signal, including other people's movements that are quite different from his own. Later on, a model's movements will elicit parallel "unanalyzed" movements even when the infant was not just previously making those movements. If the same movements have figured in earlier "mutual imitation" cycles like those described above, however, it could still be argued that the infant need not notice the resemblance; he could simply be responding to a well-learned discriminative stimulus.

On the other hand, to hypothesize that the 6-month-old does note the resemblance of his own movements to the model's seems to yield a more straightforward interpretation of the evidence. Since he imitates in precisely those cases where both his own movements and those of the model are fully within his visual field, the simplest account is that he sees the modeled action as perceptually similar to an event he has often brought about himself. Both Guillaume (1926/1971) and Piaget (1951) suggest that the infant has watched the movements of his own limbs while performing the same actions previously and perceives the movements of the model's limbs as being of the same type. When the infant starts to imitate familiar actions which he cannot see himself perform (both Guilluame and Piaget date this at around 8 or 9 months), he probably begins by noticing an auditory resemblance. Piaget (1951) reports that the first imitations of facial gestures are mediated by sounds; for example, an infant may first imitate a familiar mouth movement when it produces a sound and, since he also watches the model's mouth, it can later be imitated when the model introduces the same movement without sound.

In any case, the infant must encode resemblances between the model's movements and his own when he begins to imitate novel movements, which occurs at about 1 year (Guillaume, 1926/1971; Piaget, 1951). At this point, his imitation can no longer be explained in terms of the retrieval of familiar behavior schemas in response to associated cues. Both Guillaume and Piaget observed that year-old infants "separate" familiar movements into components (movement-type, location, direction, etc.) and recombine them to produce imitations of novel and complex movements. At first, the new actions the infant can imitate differ only slightly from others he has previously performed. He tries out familiar movements singly and then in combination, until convergence with the model is achieved. For example, Piaget (1951) reports the case of an infant who first responded to leg raising by waving goodbye (a similar movement with a different body part), then by moving his feet slightly (focusing on the correct body part), and finally imitated correctly. Piaget notes that during the first half of the second year, the ability to focus on and combine component aspects of novel movements comes to be applied systematically and efficiently to a wide range of new models. He reports that, by 16 to 18 months, when the infant sees a new movement by a model, he can immediately select the nearest familiar movement and match it on the first overt attempt, for both visible and nonvisible movements. Uzgiris and Hunt (1975) provide norms for elicited imitation on a large sample of children, and these replicate the general chronology reported by Piaget: infants imitate familiar visible movements by about 7 months and reproduce novel visible movements through gradual approximations by 9 months and immediately by 11 months. Novel facial expressions are not readily imitated until 20 months.

While the 1-year-old can imitate novel movements of a model, there is nevertheless evidence that he does not clearly differentiate the movements of inanimate objects from the movements of persons. Piaget (1954) reports that children imitate movements of inanimate objects by making corresponding movements of their own bodies; for example, a 12-month-old responded to repeated openings and closings of a box by opening and closing his hand, and later his mouth. Consistent with such observations, Golinkoff (1975; Golinkoff & Kerr, 1978) has obtained evidence which suggests that while infants encode the initiator of movement, they do not encode whether that initiator is animate. Infants were habituated to a film of a man pushing an object, or a film of a man pushing a woman. Dishabituation films involved changes in the direction of motion, the positions of the participants, or the identities of the initiator and recipient. For man–object films, the latter change results in an anomalous situation of a table or chair pushing a man. Infants of 14 to 18 months showed some dishabituation to changes in initiator versus recipient roles—more than for reversals of position or of direction of movement. However, they showed no more surprise at shifts where an inanimate object became the initiator than at role reversals between two persons.

The findings on imitation show when the infant can encode observed movements and relate these to his own movements, but not when he forms equivalence classes for events of various kinds. Evidence for such categorizations is found when words become associated with events. Such associations first occur between 14 and 18 months. Initially, these equivalence classes of actions involve only instances where the infant himself is the actor, not observed actions. This has been shown in studies of both productive and receptive language (Huttenlocher & Charney, in preparation; Huttenlocher & Kane, in preparation). Besides examining the contexts in which infants produce words to encode actions (e.g., "up"), the researchers used two sorts of comprehension tasks, which, respectively, test for categorization of the child's own actions and of actions he observes. One task involved carrying out actions on command (the infant was asked to "get" an object, "walk," etc.), while the other involved choosing between two films of contrasting actions (the infant was required to distinguish observed acts of "getting" from pushing an object, "walking" from running, etc., by pointing in response to a verb). Infants both comprehend commands to act and describe their own actions earlier than they either comprehend verbs in relation to observed actions or describe observed actions.

Before 2 years of age, children do associate verbs with observed movements involving a single entity (e.g., run and walk), although not with observed relational actions (e.g., get and push). Thus the infant forms some equivalence classes that involve two different sorts of instances— that is, categories that include movements he observes as well as the corresponding movements he experiences as an actor—within several months from the time he first forms any equivalence classes of events. We believe that the infant's categorization of observed movements, and indeed of observed actions generally, involves the extension to others of the child's categorizations of his own actions. That is, we would argue that adult movement categories emerge only after the child relates not just the particular movements of others to his own movements, but also categories of his own movements to categories of observed movements.

B.   Relational Actions and Causal Relations

We next consider evidence about the development of the infant's ability to encode relational actions, in which initiators move in particular ways in relation to objects or other people. As we noted earlier, the year-old infant encodes some information about the actions in which certain objects are habitually involved; he will put a cup to his lips, use a comb or hairbrush on his hair, etc. (Fenson *et al.*, 1976; Lowe, 1975). While these artifacts are used correctly in relation to the self from about 12 months on, they are often used inappropriately in relation to other persons or things (e.g., brushing a doll's face or a book with a hairbrush) until about 18 months (Lezine, 1973). Thus the 12-month-old need not have encoded these relational actions from the observer's perspective; he has probably learned the function of a comb, for example, through repeated experiences of having his own hair combed by someone else. After 18 months, when the child begins to carry out these same acts on dolls or other people, we have more convincing evidence that he has encoded not only the experience of being fed, having one's hair combed, etc. but also the appearance of these events when they do not involve him.

All of these are highly familiar events. When the child sees a novel relational act and immediately imitates it, we know that she can encode such actions on the spot, taking in at once the relation among actor, act, and object. Both Guillaume (1926/1971) and Piaget (1951) noted that infants imitate the effects people produce on objects by 1 year of age, a finding which has been confirmed with elicited imitation (Abravanel, Levan-Goldschmidt, & Stevenson, 1976). At first glance, this suggests that infants encode people's movements in relation to objects as producing particular effects on those objects. However, Guillaume argues that such imitation actually involves noticing only the effects, not the model's movements, since the infant attempts to duplicate the results without using the same bodily movements. If the infant did encode the effects as being caused by the model's movements, Guillaume argues, one would expect him to attempt to duplicate those movements. After repeated efforts, the infant's movements sometimes do approximate those of the model, but one cannot then determine whether he noted those movements or simply discovered the most efficient way to create the particular effect.

Findings with elicited imitation support Guillaume's interpretation. Abravanel *et al.* (1976) found that 12-month-olds reliably imitate such object-centered actions as scribbling on paper or squeezing a toy duck but did not evaluate the precision with which the infants matched the models' actual body movements. When McCall, Parke, and Kavanaugh (1977) systematically examined the child's ability to imitate a model's exact movements as well as the resultant state, they found that acts which produced effects on objects were not successfully imitated most of the time until 2 years. At 1 year, children typically manipulated the objects in ways unrelated to the model; by $1\frac{1}{2}$ years, they typically approximated the model's movements but not precisely, and by 2 years, they were usually successful. The same course of development appeared whether or not the relational action produced a change in that object.

By Piaget's account (1954), the development of the infant's notion of causality proceeds from a sense of the causal force of his own acts to inferences that such causal relations exist among events he observes as well. He believes that there is evidence for such inferences by about 18 months. At a much earlier age, 7–8 months, the infant gives evidence that, on seeing one event, he expects another event which has frequently followed it in his experience. Sometimes these expectant behaviors create the impression that the infant infers causal relations, as when he hears a familiar sound and then watches for the appearance of the person who caused it. Piaget (1954) argues that these are only simple signal relations; the infant has learned an association between two familiar events without understanding the causal relations between them at all. The notion of causality involves recognizing not merely that one event succeeds another, but also that the first provides the force which brings about the second.

According to Piaget (1954), the infant's sense of his own efficacy in relation to events begins as he watches intently the movements of his own hands and feet, between 3 and 8 months, with an apparent interest in his power to bring these movements about. Also, he will make a particular movement repeatedly to prolong an interesting event which coincided with it in time; he may arch his body or shake his head at the cessation of an interesting sound or movement in an apparent attempt to make it recommence. Such movements may be used repeatedly despite failures to produce the desired effect. The child also uses these "magical" gestures to prolong other people's movements on objects, suggesting that he attributes causal efficacy to his own gestures rather than to the other person.

Such gestures may be imitative; for example, after a swinging object stops, the child may swing his arm while looking at the object but without trying to touch it. The child pays no attention to the spatial connections between causes and effects. Thus if he pulls a blanket toward himself and gets a desired object that rests on it, then if that same object is later placed beside rather than on the blanket, he will pull it nevertheless.

Between 8 and 11 months, Piaget notes, infants act on other people's body parts in an attempt to bring about events, such as moving an adult's hand into contact with an object when they want an act performed, or pressing an adult's lips when they want him to resume making sounds. It is as if they expect that their own efforts, rather than any independent effort by the adult, will bring about the desired change. Starting at about 1 year, they no longer push people's body parts to bring about desired actions. Rather, they seem to regard the entire person as a unit which can bring about various effects which they seek. They may simply place themselves in an appropriate position and wait expectantly for an adult to continue blowing their hair, etc. When they want an adult to act on an object, for example, to get a box opened, they will simply give it to him. When adult intervention is required, for example, reaching a high object, they may call out or point to the object.

At the same time that infants begin to treat persons as the origins of effects they seek, Piaget argues that they also treat inanimate objects as if they too might be capable of spontaneous movement and have causal efficacy. Thus children may position inanimate objects in an apparent attempt to get them to move, as in gently pushing an object which is near the edge of a surface. They may set an object on a flat surface and watch it as if expecting it to move by itself, then change its location repeatedly, each time releasing it and waiting. On seeing one object set another into motion (e.g., a chair pushed by an unseen foot, bumps an open door), children will investigate the first object and touch it to the second, apparently trying to reproduce the phenomenon.

After about 16 months, children begin to seek causes for the movements of inanimate objects; if an object is moved by a hidden adult, the child may search for the adult. Similarly, children may search for the unseen cause of an obstruction, for example, walking around a garden gate that was blocked by a chair and removing the chair. Even as late as 18 months, however, children still occasionally use particular gestures that previously brought about desired effects without regard for the absence of the spatial connections that mediated the original successes (e.g., after bumping an open door with a chair, the child may shake another chair across the room while watching the door as if expecting it to move).

We noted above that the infant's language provides evidence that he forms equivalence classes involving his own goal-directed actions before 2 years, within a short time after he develops the notion of cause. Huttenlocher, Smiley, and Charney (1983) found that, by age two, infants describe their own actions which cause effects on objects (e.g., "eat cookie," "get ball"), and Huttenlocher and Smiley (1986) found that they follow instructions with such verbs even earlier. However, these equivalence classes, which grouped the child's goal-directed actions, did not include observed actions by 2 years. That is, 2-year-olds did not describe other people's relational actions nor did they select correctly when shown movies of contrasting actions (e.g., "get the toy" versus "put down the toy"). Causal actions (getting, opening, etc.) bring about changes, and those changes are caused intentionally by people whose behavior is goal-directed. Infants' failure to extend categorizations of their own causal actions to encompass observed actions may reflect a difficulty with one or both of these concepts; they may fail to categorize events as involving people causing change or as involving people *intentionally* causing the change.

C. Events as the Intentional Actions of Persons

Of the events the infant witnesses, people's actions are probably the most numerous and the most salient; people do many things to and for the infant that have important consequences for his confort and well-being. People are material objects and have some important similarities to inanimate objects; they can be seen to move about, to undergo spatial displacements, and to contact other objects, often bringing about effects on the objects around them. Because people also have internal experiences, however, their actions are not like the movements of inanimate objects; actions are based on intentions to achieve certain goals and are accompanied by feelings of effort and kinesthetic sensations. To encode events as the goal-directed actions of people rather than as the mere movements of objects in relation to other objects, one must infer these inner experiences. Some writers have claimed that the concept of persons as subjects of experience is an innate idea (e.g., Strawson, 1959, or even that infants at first perceive *all* objects as subjects of experience (e.g., Hamlyn, 1974). However, the more commonly held view is that the notion that others have inner experiences develops out of interaction with other people during infancy.

Sarbin (1952) claims that as the infant starts to move around independently by about 1 year of age, he comes to perceive the acts of others as being "the same" as his own acts. There are, however, various types of analogy between one's own acts and those of others, and the evidence indicates that the infant does not encode all of these at 1 year of age. As we have seen, infants by 1 year of age *do* encode observed movements as being similar to movements they themselves can make. However, the analogy will ultimately involve parallels with respect to causal role and goal-directed intentions as well. As we have seen, it is not until at least 16 months that the infant clearly invests other people with a causal force that sets them apart from inanimate objects. The evidence suggests that awareness that other people possess intentions or other internal states is an even later development. That is, the infant can encode others as causing change without attributing to them the *intention* to cause change.

It has been argued that after the infant becomes aware of his own goals, he attributes goals to other persons by analogy (e.g., Secord & Peevers, 1974). While Secord and Peevers do not specify the age when this development takes place, several other investigators attribute a notion of intentionality to infants under 2 years. In Piaget's (1954) discussion of causality he does not explicitly separate out the notion that people have causal powers from the notion that their acts are goal-directed and intentional. However, he seems to assume that the development of the realization that others have causal powers also involves the realization that they have internal states; he asserts, for example, that the infant "understands, from a smile or an expression of displeasure, the intentions of another person" (p. 406).

Since the infant's categorization of events will differ according to whether he attributes intentions to the people he observes—that is, whether he perceives people as *agents* whose movements are directed toward internally determined goals—let us consider what evidence there is as to when such inferences emerge. Several investigators have noted that, beginning at about 1 year of age, children start to initiate social interchanges with other people. They begin to show and to give objects to other people (e.g., Bates, Camioni, & Volterra, 1975; Escalona, 1973) and to point at objects while looking at a person. Such behavior might be taken as indicating that the infant realizes that other people have internal states, and he realizes that others want objects and see objects as he does. Some investigators believe that this is the case, but we will argue that what evidence there is suggests that it is only much later that the child infers that other people have intentions.

Bruner (1975) argues that inferences about other people's intentions arise even before age one and postulates that this ability grows out of recurrent interaction patterns during the later part of the first year of life. He observed that after several repetitions of simple interaction sequences, the 9- to 11-month-old shows evidence of anticipating his partner's actions (e.g., reaching for an object as the caretaker moves it toward him) and carries out actions reciprocal to those in which he has been a passive participant (e.g., moving an object toward his partner after it has been moved toward him). Bruner regards this behavior as evidence that the infant infers his partner's intentions. However, he presents no convincing argument as to why such interaction requires inferences about the intentions of one's partner. Clearly, one can anticipate the recurring movements of an inanimate object (e.g., the swing of a pendulum) and even imitate it without attributing intentionality to it. There is no compelling reason to suppose that the infants Bruner observed did not regard their partners in just this way, as predictably moving objects.

Greenfield and Smith (1976) argue that the infant's early single-word utterances, which appear early in the second year of life, provide evidence of a notion of "agency." They claim that infants insert their single words into a framework of nonverbal elements in which these utterances encode complex messages that refer to agents, actions, and objects. As evidence that the infant possesses the notion of agency, they cite the fact that infants name people who are acting earlier than they name people who are recipients of actions. If movement catches the child's attention, however, he will be more likely to name a moving entity because it is more salient than a stationary one, without necessarily encoding its movement at all. Furthermore, when people act, the infant who names them may be encoding them as moving objects without necessarily encoding intentional agency. The one-word utterance provides us very little information; it is impossible to determine how much of the contextual framework the infant actually takes into account.

Many investigators have claimed that early multiword utterances, which often appear before 2 years, encode agent–action and agent–object relations (e.g., Bowerman, 1973a, 1973b; Brown, 1973; Schlesinger, 1971). If children consistently produced people's names followed by action verbs in conjunction with people carrying out those actions, one could conclude that the child must have encoded them as initiators of those actions. Of course, they might still be encoding movements without intentionality. Examination of infants' speech, as we have said, indicates that they produce very few spontaneous utterances which describe observed actions at all, and when they do, they describe movements of a single object (e.g., "car go"), not goal-directed actions (e.g., "get cookie") (Huttenlocher & Charney, in preparation). Children under 2 years use verbs like "get" or "open" to announce their own impending actions or, less frequently, to request others to act in their behalf. In either case it is only the child's own goal or intention that is encoded. Another indication that the child encodes only his own goals is that although the internal state verbs "want" and "need" are used frequently by the end of the second year, they too are used exclusively in relation to self. Thus although infants do encode their own intentions and other internal states, we have no evidence from language that they encode anyone else's.

One possible explanation for the infant's failure to describe other people's goal-directed actions is purely pragmatic: the infant might actually be able to encode notions of agency in her speech but lack communicative reasons to do so. This explanation, however, is effectively ruled out by the results of comprehension tasks (Huttenlocher, Smiley, and Charney, 1983). In these tasks, infants could select between movies of other people's movements (jumping versus kicking, etc.). However, they could not select between movies of other people's relational actions (getting versus giving, etc.), which are identified primarily on the basis of a common goal rather than any distinctive movement pattern. Thus infants do not encode these goal-directed actions in language, even when asked to do so, if the actions are performed by other people. Given that infants do have verbs that encompass other people's distinctive movement patterns as well as their own and yet restrict their verbs for goal-directed actions to encode only their own goals, it appears that the child's awareness of the parallel between other persons and himself begins with the recognition that others move in a manner parallel to his own movements; only later, in the period beyond infancy, does he realize that these movements of others are accompanied by inner experiences like those that he feels when carrying out the same movements.

Evidence from infants' play with dolls and other objects also suggests that they may not view other people as intentional actors until about $2\frac{1}{2}$ years. As noted above, infants make appropriate differential use of objects early in the second year. Before 18 months, however, these object-appropriate acts are primarily self-related; the infant will use objects to act on himself but not on other people or dolls. There is a transition to more doll-related activities, around 18–21 months (Lezine, 1973; Lowe, 1975). For example, given a miniature hairbrush, infants of this age will brush the doll's hair; younger children will brush their own hair. By 21 months, infants also "feed" dolls with toy dishes and put them to bed. Even at this stage the doll is typically placed in a passive role; the infant does not move the doll's arm to make it brush its own hair or feed itself. Only after $2\frac{1}{2}$ years do children reliably make dolls active agents by making the doll "hold" its fork, "walk" to its bed, etc. (Lowe, 1975). Watson and Fischer (1977) claim that infants under 2 years do make dolls active agents after watching demonstrations of such play; when an infant has watched a model acting on a doll, however, he can perform the same actions imitatively without thinking of the doll as an agent.

The fact that dolls are not spontaneously made the agents of goal-directed actions like walking to bed until after age $2\frac{1}{2}$ suggests that the notion of other people as intentional agents may first emerge at about this age. One might object that infants could have this concept without incorporating it into their doll play; perhaps until age $2\frac{1}{2}$ the child lacks the necessary motor skills to manipulate dolls as agents. Compared with placing the doll in a passive role, manipulating it as though it were an agent may require more motor coordination. It is unlikely, however, that motor development alone accounts for the findings, since the evidence from language also points to the absence of any notion of agency in infants.

D. Summary

In summary, by the middle of the first year infants encode the direction and relative velocity of motion, and its rigidity or elasticity. They also encode simple motions of others when these resemble movements they can make themselves. At least by the end of the first year, there is clear evidence that they notice the resemblance between other people's movements and their own. This seen in their ability to imitate even movements which are quite new to them. That is, the 1-year-old can integrate the component features of movements he knows how to make (direction, location, motion type) in order to imitate even a highly novel combination of features. The categorization of observed movements also seems to involve relating these to parallel movements of his own. By the middle of the second year of life, infants categorize their own movements of particular kinds (e.g., walk, sit), and before 2 years, they also categorize observed movements, thus forming equivalence classes which include both the experience of moving and the appearance of others moving.

The 1-year-old will reproduce the effects other people produce on objects, but this does not warrant the conclusion that he simultaneously takes account of the object's movement and the movement of the person bringing it about. Instead, it seems that he attends only to the movements of a single entity, and in casual actions he focuses on the object. It is not until about 2 years that imitative behavior reflects a coordinated perception of the person's movements and the movements of the objects he acts upon. In the first year the infant develops expectancies that certain of his own actions will be followed by particular events, but not notions of physical causality *per se*. During the second year of life, infants begin to note how they themselves may cause changes, and late in the second year their naming indicates that they categorize various goal-directed causal actions which they themselves carry out. By the middle of the second year they also discover that only animate creatures engage in self-propelled movements, and they seek some outside cause when changes in inanimate objects occur.

The 2-year-old does not yet encode events as involving other people as intentional agents. Claims that infants begin life with the notion that other persons are subjects of experience, or that such a notion is well developed in infancy, are not supported by empirical evidence. Rather, the evidence from both language and play suggests that although the infant comes to perceive a parallel between other persons and himself in some respects, this parallel is not at all like the adult concept of person as an entity that has both observable physical properties and covert internal experiences. The infant notices that others' bodies and body parts move about in ways that correspond to his own movements and, later, that these movements of others can bring about effects on other objects as his own movements do, but it is in the period beyond infancy that the child first extends the analogy to infer that others also have intentions and goals like his own.

REFERENCES

Abranavel, E., Levan-Goldschmidt, E., & Stevenson, M. B. (1976). Action imitation: The early phase of infancy. *Child Development, 47*(4), 1932–1044.

Acredolo, L. P. (1978). Development of spatial orientation in infancy. *Developmental Psychology, 14*, 224–234.

Acredolo, L. P. (1979). Laboratory versus home: The effect of environment on the 9-month-old infant's choice of spatial reference system. *Developmental Psychology, 15*(6), 666–667.

Acredolo, L. P., & Evans, D. (1980). Developmental changes in the effects of landmarks on infant spatial behavior. *Developmental Psychology, 16*, 312–318.

Bates, E., Camaioni, L., & Voltera, V. (1975). The acquisition of performatives prior to speech. *Merrill-Palmer Quarterly, 21*, 205–226.

Bloom, J. M. (1973). *One word at a time.* The Hague: Mouton.

Bowerman, M. (1973a). *Early syntactic development: A cross-linguistic study with special reference to Finnish.* London & New York: Cambridge University Press.

Bowerman, M. (1973b). Structural relationships in children's utterances: Syntactic or semantic? In T. E. Moore (Ed.), *Cognitive development and the acquisition of language* (pp. 197–213). New York: Academic Press.

Bowerman, M. (1976). Semantic factors in the acquisition of rules for word use and sentence construction. In D. Morehead & A. Morehead (Eds.), *Directions in normal and deficient child language* (pp. 99–179). Baltimore, MD: University Park Press.

Bowerman, M. (1978a). Semantic and syntactic development: A review of what, when, and how in language acquisition. In R. L. Schiefelbusch (Ed.), *The bases of language intervention* (pp. 98–189). Baltimore, MD: University Park Press.

Bowerman, M. (1978b). The acquisition of word meaning: An investigation of some current conflicts. In N. Waterson & C. Snow (Eds.), *Development of communication: Social and pragmatic factors in language acquisition.* New York: Wiley.

Bremner, J. G. (1978a). Egocentric versus allocentric spatial coding in nine-month-old infants: Factors influencing the choice of code. *Developmental Psychology, 14*, 346–355.

Bremner, J. G. (1978b). Spatial errors made by infants: Inadequate spatial cues or evidence of egocentrism? *British Journal of Psychology, 69*(1), 77–84.

Bremner, J. G., & Bryant, P. E. (1977). Place versus response as the basis of spatial errors made by young infants. *Journal of Experimental Child Psychology, 23,* 162–171.

Brown, R. (1973). *A first language: The early stages.* Cambridge, MA: Harvard University Press.

Bruner, J. S. (1975). The ontogenesis of speech acts. *Journal of Child Language, 2,* 19.

Carter, A. L. (1975). The transformation of sensorimotor morphemes into words: A case study of the development of "more" and "mine." *Journal of Child Language, 2,* 233–250.

Corrigan, R. (1978). Language development as related to stage 6 object permanence development. *Journal of Child Language, 5,* 173–189.

Escalona, S. (1973). Basic modes of social interaction: Their emergence and patterning during the first two years of life. *Merrill-Palmer Quarterly, 19,* 205–232.

Fenson, L., Kagan, J., Kearsley, R. B., & Zelazo, P. R. (1976). The developmental progression of manipulative play in the first two years. *Child Development, 47,* 232–236.

Gibson, E. J., Owsley, C. J., & Johnston, J. (1978). Perception of invariants by five-month-old infants: Differentiation of two types of motion. *Developmental Psychology, 14,* 407–415.

Gibson, E. J., Owsley, C. J., Walker, A., & Megaw-Nyce, J. (1979). Development of the perception of invariants: Substance and shape. *Perception, 8,* 609–619.

Golinkoff, R. M. (1975). Semantic development in infants: The concepts of agent and recipient. *Merrill-Palmer Quarterly, 21,* 181–193.

Golinkoff, R. M., & Kerr, J. L. (1978). Infants' perception of semantically defined action role changes in filmed events. *Merrill-Palmer Quarterly, 24,* 53–61.

Goss, A. E., & Nodine, C. F. (1965). *Paired associate learning: The role of meaningfulness, similarity and familiarization.* New York: Academic Press.

Greenfield, P. M., & Smith, J. H. (1976). *The structure of communication in early language development.* New York: Academic Press.

Griffiths, P., & Atkinson, M. (1978). A "door" to verbs. In N. Waterson and C. Snow (Eds.), *The development of communication* (pp. 311–319). New York: Wiley.

Guillaume, P. (1971). *Imitation in children.* Chicago, IL: University of Chicago Press. (Original work published 1926)

Guillaume, P. (1927). Les débuts de la phrase dans le language de l'enfant. [First stages of sentence formation in children's speech.] *Journal de Psychologie, 24,* 1–25. [English translation appeared in C. A. Ferguson & D. I. Slobin (Eds.), *Studies of child language development* (pp. 522–541). New York: Holt, 1973]

Hamlyn, D. W. (1974). Person perception and our understanding of others. In T. Mischel (Ed.), *Understanding other persons* (pp. 1–36). Totowa, NJ: Rowman & Littlefield.

Hutt, C. (1967). Effects of stimulus novelty on manipulatory exploration in an infant. *Journal of Child Psychology and Psychiatry, 8,* 241–247.

Huttenlocher, J., & Smiley, P. (1986). Early word meanings: The case of object names. *Cognitive Psychology* (in press).

Huttenlocher, J., Smiley, P., & Charney, R. (1983). Emergence of action categories in the child: Evidence from verb meanings. *Psychological Review, 90,* 72–93.

Kramer, J. A., Hill, K. T., & Cohen, L. B. (1975). Infants' development of object permanence: A refined methodology and new evidence for Piaget's hypothesized ordinality. *Child Development, 46,* 149–155.

LeCompte, G., & Gratch, G. (1972). Violation of a rule as a method of diagnosing infants' levels of object concept. *Child Development, 43,* 385–396.

Lezine, I. (1973). The transition from sensorimotor to earliest symbolic function in early development. In J. I. Nurnberger (Ed.), *Biological and environmental determinants of early development*. Baltimore, MD: Williams & Wilkins.

Lowe, M. (1975). Trends in the development of representational play in infants from one to three years: An observational study. *Child Psychology and Psychiatry, 16*, 33–47.

Lucas, T. C., and Uzgiris, I. C. (1977). Spatial factors in the development of the object concept. *Developmental Psychology, 13*(5), 492–500.

McCall, R. B., Parke, R. D., and Kavanaugh, P. D. (1977). Imitation of live and televised models by children one to three years of age. *Monographs of the Society for Research in Child Development, 42*(5, Serial No. 173).

Nelson, K. (1973). Structure and strategy in learning to talk. *Monographs of the Society for Research in Child Development, 38*(1–2, Serial No. 149).

Nelson, K. (1974). Concept, word, and sentence: Interrelations in acquisition and development. *Psychological Review, 81*, 267–285.

Piaget, J. (1951). *Play, dreams and imitation in childhood*. New York: Norton.

Piaget, J. (1954). *The construction of reality in the child*. New York: Basic Books.

Piaget, J., Inhelder, B., & Szeminska, A. (1960). *The child's conception of geometry*. New York: Basic Books.

Ramsay, D., & Campos, J. (1975). Memory by the infant in an object notion task. *Developmental Psychology, 11*, 411–412.

Ramsay, D., & Campos, J. (1978). The onset of representation and entry into stage 6 of object permanence development. *Developmental Psychology, 14*, 79–86.

Robertson, S. S. (1975). *The cognitive organization of action events: A developmental perspective*. Paper presented at the 83rd annual meeting of the American Psychological Association, Chicago, IL.

Sarbin, T. R. (1952). A preface to a psychological analysis of the self. *Psychological Review, 59*, 11–22.

Schlesinger, I. M. (1971). Production of utterances and language acquisition. In D. I. Slobin (Ed.), *The ontogenesis of grammar* (pp. 63–101). New York: Academic Press.

Secord, P. F., & Peevers, B. H. (1974). The development and attribution of person concepts. In T. Mischel (Ed.), *Understanding other persons* (pp. 117–142). Totowa, NJ: Rowman & Littlefield.

Strawson, P. F. (1959). *Individuals*. London: Methuen.

Uzgiris, I. D., & Hunt, J. McV. (1975). *Assessment in infancy: Ordinal scales of psychological development*. Urbana: University of Illinois Press.

von Hofsten, C. (1980). *Predictive reaching for moving objects by human infants*. Unpublished manuscript, University of Uppsala, Sweden.

Walker, A. S., Owsley, C. J., Megaw-Nyce, J., Gibson, E. J., & Bahrick, L. E. (1980). *Detection of elasticity as an invariant property of objects by young infants*. *Perception, 9*, 713–718.

Watson, M. W., & Fischer, K. W. (1977). A developmental sequence of agent use in late infancy. *Child Development, 48*, 828–836.

6

The Development of Intermodal Perception*

ELIZABETH S. SPELKE

Department of Psychology
University of Pennsylvania
Philadelphia, Pennsylvania 19174

I. INTRODUCTION

As people make their way around the world, they encounter objects and events by looking, listening, and touching. Adults perceive a single layout through these actions. When we look and listen to a singing bird, or see and feel the surface of a table, we are aware of unitary objects, not separate streams of sensation. This experience is possible, in part, because we are able to detect relationships among the sight, sound, and feel of an object. If a person can detect such relationships and thereby perceive a world of unitary objects and events, she will be said to be capable of "intermodal perception."

This chapter is concerned with the origins and development of the capacity for intermodal perception. It will discuss the primitive structures which might serve as the foundation for this ability, and the mechanisms of learning and development that might guide its growth. The discussion is organized around three theoretical perspectives on perceptual development, which I will call the "sensation-centered," the "action-centered," and the "perception-centered" perspectives. These perspectives were

---

* This chapter was originally conceived in 1979. To the author's regret, it treats only briefly the work of newer investigators of infant perception.

HANDBOOK OF INFANT
PERCEPTION, VOLUME 2

chosen because each roots the capacity for intermodal perception in a different kind of primitive structure, and each postulates different principles and mechanisms of development. After these perspectives have been described, the chapter turns to selected research on intermodal perception in human infancy. It closes with an evaluation of the perspectives and with some suggestions about further research.

II. THREE PERSPECTIVES ON THE DEVELOPMENT OF INTERMODAL PERCEPTION

All theories of the development of intermodal perception agree on two points. First, the capacity for intermodal perception is influenced by learning. Relationships between sounds, feelings, and visible objects can be quite arbitrary: the sound of a certain kind of siren signals the approach of a fire engine, for example, only because of the conventions of our culture. As adults, we increase our ability to detect intermodal relationships by learning about the arbitrary connections between visible, audible, and tangible events. To account for this and other kinds of learning, each theory provides means by which the capacity for intermodal perception can grow as perceivers gain experience.

The second point of agreement is more subtle. All theories of intermodal perception acknowledge that humans have some unlearned ability to detect relationships among that which they see, hear, and feel. Logic demands that perceivers be sensitive innately to some intermodal relationships: if the eye, ear, and hand gave rise to fully separate streams of sensation on no common base, children could never have experiences through which to learn, on their own, that certain visible episodes belong with certain auditory or tactile episodes. In order to learn that fire engines make siren sounds, for example, children must experience some relation between the visible engine and its siren on some occasion, inducing that the sound and the object go together. If children can perceive the siren and engine as related, however, then obviously they already have some capacity to detect intermodal relationships. According to every theory, therefore, humans are able to detect certain intermodal relationships innately, and we use this ability in order to learn spontaneously about further intermodal relationships.

Although the existence of innate and learned capacities to detect intermodal relationships is not in dispute, the nature of these capacities has been debated greatly. Different theories offer very different accounts of the child's initial capacities for detecting intermodal relationships, and of the principles and mechanisms by which the child learns to detect further intermodal relationships.

A. The Sensation-Centered Perspective

According to the first perspective, sensations and a capacity to detect temporal relationships among sensations constitute the primitive basis of intermodal perception, and associative learning processes provide the mechanism for development. The sensation-centered perspective, inherited from empiricist and associationist philosophers, is probably the dominant contemporary view of the development of intermodal perception. This chapter will focus on one of its many variants, derived from the perceptual theory of Hermann von Helmholtz (1885/1962).

To Helmholtz, any meaningful perception depends on the evocation of a set of unconscious sensations and the interpretation of those sensations by an unconscious process akin to inference. Perceivers infer that they are seeing, hearing, or feeling those objects that are the most likely causes of a given pattern of sensation. The sensations themselves are evoked by stimulation directly and innately. The capacity to discover predictable patterns within a stream of sensation is also innately given: children are naturally predisposed to seek and discover contingencies among sensations. Finally, there is an innate tendency to hypothesize that certain predictable patterns of sensation are caused by external objects. All else is learned. Children learn about the predictable patterns of sensation they are likely to encounter. Like experimental scientists, they generate hypotheses about the external objects that are the most likely causes of each pattern, and they test these hypotheses by exploring the world actively and systematically:

> Just how such cognizance of the significance of visual images is first assembled by young children becomes readily apparent when we watch them while they are busy with objects offered to them as toys, how they handle them, look at them from all sides by the hour, turn them around, put them in their mouths, etc., finally throw them down or try to break them, and repeat this each day. One cannot doubt that this is the school where they learn the natural condition of the objects around them . . .
> (Reprinted by permission from von Helmholtz, 1894/1970, pp. 252–253.
> Copyright © 1970 by John Wiley & Sons, Inc.)

This theory can be applied to the problem of intermodal perception. Sensations, for Helmholtz, are modality-specific. When an object is simultaneously seen, heard, and felt, however, sensations in one mode are contingently related to sensations in the other modes. Since children are innately capable of analyzing certain contingencies between sensations, they will come to discover the predictable relations among these visual, auditory, and haptic experiences.

Helmholtz did not describe specifically the kinds of contingencies that children detect or the processes of contingency analysis that they apply. The processes usually discussed within learning theory (see Schwartz,

1978) would *not* seem to be suitable to the task of perceiving a unitary object. Those processes respond not only to relationships among sensations that are produced by one object, but also to relationships among sensations that are produced by several distinct objects. For example, the sound of a doorbell is contingently related to the visual sensation of someone appearing at the door. It would not be desirable, however, for children to treat a person and a doorbell as parts of a single object: children might well learn that the sound of a doorbell predicts the appearance of someone at the door, but they should continue to perceive these events as separate. A major task for any sensation-centered theory of intermodal perception, therefore, is to describe the kinds of contingent relationships that could underlie the perception of unitary objects. No account of contingency analysis within learning theory, to my knowledge, provides a solution to this problem.

Let us suppose, nevertheless, that there are types of contingent relationships among sensations that occur when, and only when, a single object is both seen and heard or seen and felt. If children can detect these relationships through a process of contingency analysis, then they might learn to perceive unitary audible, visible, and tangible objects.

B. The Action-Centered Perspective

According to the second perspective, actions and their structural relationships provide the innate basis for intermodal perception, and development occurs as these actions become appropriately structured. This perspective derives primarily from the developmental theory of Jean Piaget (1952). Piaget proposed that children are born with "reflexes": simple actions that are set in motion by uninterpreted sensory configurations. These actions are independent of one another initially but become coordinated with development because children are also born with tendencies to exercise, extend, and organize their actions into stable structures. Children act spontaneously on the objects that the environment provides, assimilating objects to familiar actions and adjusting these actions to new objects. Thus, a child's activities become articulated and organized. To Piaget, the structuring of action underlies the development of all knowledge. Children come to represent the world of objects in progressively more stable and balanced ways as their actions gain structure and generality.

Piaget's approach to intermodal perception follows from this framework. A reflex action may center on the eyes, hands, mouth, or any other sensitive organ, but there are no reflexes that span separate perceptual systems, and hence no initial capacity for intermodal perception. With development, the senses become coordinated through a process of "reciprocal assimilation": one action (such as looking) is directed to another action (such as moving the fingers), and each is adjusted to the other. When this assimilatory activity has reached equilibrium, sights will evoke reaching and tactile feelings will evoke looking. The diverse actions that can be directed to one object will be fully coordinated eventually, and the child will be able to represent the object as a unitary entity, perceivable through each act and conceptually distinct from them all.[1]

Piaget has described the developing coordinations among actions at a highly abstract level; his description does not clarify *how* the development of structural relationships among actions leads to the apprehension of unitary objects and events. As infants direct different actions to the same object, similar structures are said to develop in the different action systems. Presumably infants perceive unitary objects by detecting these structural relationships. Structural relationships develop among many actions, however, including actions that are *not* directed to the same object. For example, children come to coordinate the act of following a pitched ball with the act of swinging a bat, and the act of beating a drum with the act of marching in a parade. How do children determine whether two coordinated actions are, or are not, directed to the same object? An action-centered theory evidently must propose that there is a special kind of coordination that develops between different actions when, and only when, the actions are directed to a single object. It must propose, moreover, that children have a capacity to detect this special relationship and to recognize it as an indication of a unitary object. Children may perceive unitary objects by looking, listening, and feeling because they can detect a special kind of structure that unites actions that are directed to the same things.

In brief, the action-centered perspective discussed in these pages posits that the reflex actions of newborn infants share no detectable structural relationship, and that actions directed to a single object became structurally related, in a special way, with development. Children are innately

---

[1] In some of his writings (e.g., Piaget, 1969), Piaget states that children and adults have perceptual structures that are only loosely related to action structures. Since he does not directly discuss the perceptual capacities of infants in his principal writings on infancy (Piaget, 1951, 1952, 1954), it is not clear whether he would endow the infant with any innate perceptual structures. Nevertheless, Piaget explicitly states, both in his writings on infancy and in his writings on perceptual development (Piaget, 1969), that knowledge of objects, including knowledge of their multimodal properties, arises from the structuring of action, not from perceptual capacities. In discussing the action-centered approach, accordingly, I will not consider the possibility that purely perceptual structures play a role in intermodal development.

sensitive to these special structural relationships: once the relationships develop, they detect them and perceive unitary objects. Inexperienced infants cannot perceive unitary objects or events, therefore, but they possess some of the central underpinnings of that ability.

C. The Perception-Centered Perspective

According to the third perspective, intermodal perception is rooted in innate mechanisms for perceiving properties of objects, and development occurs as children become able to perceive new object properties. We will focus on the most comprehensive statement of this position, by James J. and Eleanor J. Gibson (E. J. Gibson, 1969, 1982; J. J. Gibson, 1966, 1979).

To the Gibsons, any animal perceives objects, events, and their properties by exploring the environment and detecting invariant relationships in the stimulation it receives. As a person moves her hand around an object, for example, she produces an ever-changing pattern of stimulation on her fingers, but there are relationships in this pattern that are constant. Some of these relationships specify properties of the object, such as its shape and its rigidity. Invariants in stimulation specify properties of events as well. As a person follows an event by looking or listening, her perceptual systems register invariant relationships in light or sound that specify the nature of the event and the things that participate in it. By detecting these relationships, perceivers apprehend properties of the world.

According to the Gibsons, humans and other animals are initially sensitive to certain invariants, and they can perceive the properties of objects and events specified by these invariants. With experience, children become sensitive to new invariant relationships, and thus they come to perceive new aspects of the environment. Learning comes about largely through changes in perceptual selection. Perceivers learn to search for the invariant information that specifies significant properties of the environment. Such learning leads to a progressive differentiation of the perceptual world.

Intermodal perception is possible, according to the Gibsons' theory, because some properties of objects are "amodal": they are specified to more than one perceptual system.

> Unity is the natural effect of multiple specification of invariant properties of things, places, and events.
>
> (E. J. Gibson, 1983, p. 23)

For example, a rough, irregular texture is specified both by invariant relationships in arrays of light at the eye and by invariant relationships in patterns of pressure on the skin. When a perceiver of any age detects an object in two different modes at once, and when the same object properties are perceived in the two modes, she will perceive a unitary object.[2]

Like the sensation-centered and the action-centered perspectives, the perception-centered perspective faces a problem accounting for the development of intermodal perception. Humans perceive the same amodal properties not only when we look at, listen to, and feel a single object, but also when we look at one object while listening to or feeling a second object that is distinct from, but related to, the first. The sound of a violin in an orchestra, for example, has properties in common not only with the visible movements of its bow, but also with the visible movements of the conductor's baton. In order to perceive a unitary object, there must be special amodal properties that unite a visible object only with its own sound, and perceivers must be sensitive to the information that specifies these properties. These properties have not been described in detail (but see E. J. Gibson, 1983, and Spelke, 1983, for further discussion). In the perception-centered perspective discussed in this chapter, it will be assumed that such properties exist and that perceivers detect some of them without learning.

To the Gibsons, in short, the capacity for intermodal perception does not depend on any learned coordination between perceptual modes: humans begin life with capacities to perceive unitary objects by detecting some of their amodal properties. The capacity for intermodal perception does grow, however, as perceivers come to detect further amodal properties. As children explore the environment, they became sensitive to finer and finer distinctions among the properties of events. Furthermore, children come to distinguish among the modalities themselves (Bower, 1979;

---

[2] The perception-centered approach discussed in this chapter roots intermodal coordination in the perception of "distal," amodal properties of objects, not in the detection of amodal invariants in the flow of "proximal" stimulation. According to this approach, one will experience an intermodal relationship whenever the same object property is detected in two modes, whether or not that property is specified by the same invariant stimulus relationship in each of the modes. For example, a child could perceive a relationship between the face and the voice of her father even if she perceives the father's face by detecting its coloring and its spatial structure and perceives his voice by detecting its fundamental frequency and its temporal structure.

The reader should note that both James and Eleanor Gibson have consistently emphasized the amodal character of most stimulus invariants, as well as the amodal character of most object properties. Intermodal perception, on their view, depends both on the detection of amodal stimulus invariants and on the perception of anodal object properties. Their theory of amodal invariants will not be considered in the present chapter, however, for it is not easily distinguished from certain versions of the sensation-centered theory. For a discussion of amodal invariants and their possible role in intermodal perception, see E. J. Gibson (1983) and Spelke (1983).

E. J. Gibson, 1969). A young child may not distinguish between seeing an object and hearing or feeling it; she may simply perceive the object itself and its properties. An older child does distinguish between seeing, hearing, and touching an object, at least in some circumstances.

D. Overview

These are the three perspectives that will guide our inquiry. They offer three contrasting views of the primitive basis of intermodal perception: sensations and mechanisms for detecting temporal contingencies between them, actions and mechanisms for detecting structural relationships among them, and perceptions of amodal properties and mechanisms for detecting stimulus invariants that specify them. The perspectives also propose three kinds of learning process: the analysis of contingencies among sensations and the formation of hypotheses about the likely external causes of these contingencies, the reciprocal assimilation of actions leading to the development of stable action structures and ultimately to the representation of the things that are acted upon; and the abstraction of invariant stimulus relationships leading to the differentiation of the perceptual world.

The rest of this chapter will be concerned with experimental attempts to evaluate these perspectives. This review of research will be selective, for not all research on intermodal functioning in infancy has been undertaken to investigate the child's developing ability to detect relationships among the sight, sound, and feel of an object. Some investigators have focused on the development of levels of coordination between different sensory systems, in order to shed light on the hierarchical development of the nervous system (e.g., Mendelson & Haith, 1976). Some investigators have focused on the development of skills of intermodal exploration, such as the skill of reaching for a visible object, with the goal of understanding skills in general, their acquisition, and their role in cognitive development (e.g., Bruner, 1974). Some investigators have focused on the emergence of abilities to represent an object perceived in one mode and to recognize the object in a second mode, with the ultimate goal of understanding the development of memory, learning, and transfer (e.g., Gottfried, Rose, & Bridger, 1977). The present chapter will not do justice to these efforts. Studies of intermodal development will be discussed only insofar as they shed light on our central concern: the development of knowledge of relationships between auditory, visual, and haptic information about an object or event.

A second caution is in order. Even when an investigation is motivated by the theoretical issues discussed in this chapter, its results are seldom decisive. It is difficult to evaluate these three perspectives experimentally: one cannot simply show, for example, that a relationship between the modalities is, or is not, detected at some particular age in infancy. The primary difference between the three perspectives concerns the *basis* on which intermodal relationships are detected, not the *time* at which the ability to detect such relationships first appears. It is necessary to determine whether the first intersensory coordinations depend on detecting the contingencies of sensations, the structure of actions, or the properties of objects. Similarly, an investigator cannot simply demonstrate that infants learn, or fail to learn, about intermodal relationships at some age. To distinguish among these theoretical perspectives, he or she must investigate the conditions under which learning occurs and the nature of what is learned: whether sensations become associated, actions become structured, or new object properties come to be perceived. It is not surprising, therefore, that psychologists still cannot pass conclusive judgment on any theory of intermodal development.

III. THE FOUNDATIONS OF INTERMODAL PERCEPTION

This section focuses on investigations of the infant's initial capacities to explore objects and events intermodally, to perceive unitary events by looking and listening, and to perceive unitary objects by looking and touching. These investigations should help to reveal whether children begin with abilities to detect temporally related sensations, structured actions, or amodal properties of objects.

A. Intermodal Exploration

Adults tend to look in the direction of a sound and to reach for things they see, especially when these things are unfamiliar and unexpected. In these ways, adults maximize the pickup of information about objects and events. Psychologists have asked whether infants act in these ways as well, and if so, what capacities underlie their actions.

Many observers now agree that newborn infants look reliably toward or away from laterally presented sounds. Newborns have been shown to turn their eyes quickly and briefly toward soft sounds and away from loud sounds (Butterworth & Castillo, 1976; Crassini & Broerse, 1980; Hammer & Turkewitz, 1975; Mendelson & Haith, 1976; Turkewitz, Birch, & Cooper, 1972; Turkewitz, Birch, Moreau, Levy, & Cornwell, 1966; Wertheimer, 1961). Newborn infants have been found to look in the direction of a centrally presented sound—a human voice—as well (Mendelson

& Haith, 1976). Finally, newborn infants turn their heads as well as their eyes toward a sound if it is of long duration and if the infants are properly supported. In several studies, infants were presented with the sound of a rattle, 90° to one side of the head, for 20 sec. After the sound was played for 2 to 3 sec, infants began to turn their heads slowly until they faced the sound directly (Clifton, Morrongiello, Kulig, & Dowd, 1981; Muir & Field, 1979). The same pattern was observed with sounds that were presented very briefly (Clarkson, Clifton, & Morrongiello, 1983). Head turning toward a sound disappears at about 2 months of age and then returns a month later (J. Field, Muir, Pilon, Sinclair & Dodwell, 1980; Muir, Abraham, Forbes, & Harris, 1979).

These observation show newborn infants at their best. In other situations, young infants do not appear to coordinate their looking and listening. For example, visual scanning is not affected by sounds moving continuously across the field of view, either in the presence or in the absence of a visible object (McGurk, Turnure, & Creighton, 1977). Moreover, the tendency to look to a peripherally presented visual display is unaffected by the introduction of an unrelated sound on the same or the opposite side of the visual display (Castillo & Butterworth, in Butterworth, 1981; J. Field, diFranco, Dodwell, & Muir, 1979; McGurk et al., 1977). In these situations, looking is influenced only by the characteristics of the visual display. It appears that the presence of the visual display either distracts attention from the sound or causes infants to localize the sound incorrectly. Both effects are sometimes observed with adults (e.g., Klein, 1977; Radeau & Bertelson, 1977).

Further studies of looking toward a sound reveal that these turns are very inaccurate. In one experiment, for example, infants were presented with a visual or auditory display 10°, 20°, or 40° to the left or right, and their lateral eye movements were observed. With visual displays, the infants looked rapidly in the appropriate direction, turning their eyes further for a more distant stimulus. With auditory displays, infants again looked in the correct direction, but they looked with longer latencies, and the size of their eye movements was unrelated to the distance of the display (Bechtold, Bushnell, & Salapatek, 1979). The failure of infants to scale their looking to the radial distance of a sound may stem from inaccuracies in sound localization. Alternatively, young infants may localize sounds with some accuracy but may fail to calibrate their eye movements to a sound's perceived direction. Bechtold and his collaborators favored the second possibility, and they suggested that infants may need to learn to calibrate visual and auditory systems for localizing objects.

In brief, there is some coordination at birth between auditory localization and systems controlling head and eye movements, but this coordination is far from perfect. The basis for this coordination is not clear. It has been suggested that newborn infants perceive a lateral sound to specify a potentially visible object in the sound's direction: infants turn toward the sound because they expect to see something (Bower, 1979). Failures to look toward a sounding object, on this view, are caused by limits on infant's abilities to deploy attention and to coordinate actions.

Other investigators, in contrast, have concluded that sound-guided head and eye movements are controlled by simple motor programs triggered by uninterpreted sensory patterns (Butterworth, 1981; McGurk et al., 1977). For example, lateral eye movements and head movements might be elicited reflexively by a difference in the intensity or in the time of arrival of a sound at the two ears. Gradual head movements toward an enduring sound may reflect a tropistic tendency to eliminate such interaural differences (J. J. Gibson, 1966, 1976; Muir & Field, 1979). In either case, infants would be able to look systematically toward events without anticipating that they will see an object in any definite spatial position. In support of the second view, it should be noted that infants turn their eyes and heads towards sounds in dark rooms as well as lighted ones (Mendelson & Haith, 1976; Muir et al., 1979), when their eyes are closed as well as when they are open (Turkewitz et al., 1966). These findings cast doubt on the view that infants are "looking for" an event, although they do not rule out that possibility.

If the first interpretation of sound-guided looking could be confirmed, it would support the perception-centered perspective on intermodal development, since auditory–visual exploration would depend on the perception of an amodal property of an object: its position in space. The second interpretation, however, is consistent with all three perspectives. Helmholtz's and Piaget's theories deny that infants innately perceive objects in space by looking and listening, whereas Gibson's theory may be noncommittal as to whether such a perceptual ability guides the earliest acts of orienting. In short, research on auditory–visual localization has not distinguished among theories that offer sensations, actions, and perceptions as the primitive basis of intermodal perception. Future research might be more decisive, as investigators focus on the mechanisms that underlie sound-guided looking (for example, see Morrongiello & Clifton, 1984).

Visual–haptic exploration changes dramatically with development (see Hatwell, in press, for a lucid review). Only at 4 or 5 months of age do infants begin to reach effectively for the things they see (see White, Castle, & Held, 1964). Visually elicited reaching could develop in the manner that Helmholtz described: perhaps infants thrash out at random in the presence of certain visible sensations, observe the consequences of these thrashings, and predict and test these consequences. Alternatively, reaching could develop in the manner described by Piaget, through the reciprocal assimilation and coordination of visual and manual actions. Finally, infants could begin with an ability to perceive some spatial properties of objects by looking and touching, as the Gibsons suggest, but only gradually develop the motor skill that allows them to reach for objects successfully. Studies of the development of effective reaching have investigated these possibilities.

Over the last decade, a number of investigators have focused on the manual activity of newborn infants. Several observers have reported that certain movements of the hands occur when infants are first presented with a visible object, and that the patterning of these movements is similar in some respects to the patterning of movements by older infants who reach for objects. These manual activities have been termed "prereaching" (Trevarthen, 1974).

The nature of prereaching activities has been a subject of controversy. Some investigators have reported that newborn infants' hand and arm movements are adapted to spatial characteristics of an object such as its distance, direction, and solidity (Bower, 1972; Bower, Broughton, & Moore, 1970a; Bower, Dunkeld, & Wishart, 1979; Trevarthen, 1974; see also Butterworth, 1978; de Schonen, 1977; Hofsten, 1982). These investigators have concluded that infants perceive unitary objects by looking and feeling and move so as to apprehend the objects. Other investigations have provided no evidence that the earliest manual activity is guided by visual information for the position and the properties of an object (diFranco, Muir, & Dodwell, 1978; Dodwell, Muir, & DiFranco, 1976, 1979; Rader & Stern, 1982; Ruff & Halton, 1978). These investigations have led to the suggestion that neonatal arm movements do not reflect a capacity to perceive objects but rather a state of excitement or orienting (Bushnell, 1981).

Turning to observations of somewhat older infants, a number of investigators have studied the precursors to reaching, asking if infants learn to reach by trial and error, if they come to reach as they engage in reciprocal assimilatory activity, or if they already perceive the potentially tangible properties of an object by looking and need only learn to control their arms. Most of the evidence supports the last alternative: the manual activity of prereaching infants appears to be guided by visual perception of some of an object's spatial properties. Prereaching infants swipe their arms more frequently when they view an object than when they do not (Twitchell, 1965; White et al., 1964), and they engage in this activity more frequently when viewing an object within reaching distance than when viewing a more distant object (J. Field, 1976a; see also Bower, 1972). Infants tend to swipe in the visible direction of the object (McDonnell,

1979; White et al., 1964), although their swiping may not be affected by the object's three-dimensionality (J. Field, 1976b). Finally, infants engage in activities precursory to reaching more frequently in the presence of an object of graspable size than in the presence of an object too large to grasp (Bruner & Koslowski, 1972). Before infants can reach effectively, they may perceive visually the size and distance of an object, and they may use this information to guide their attempts to manipulate the object.

Once infants begin to reach reliably, their reaching continues to be guided by the visible direction of an object (McDonnell, 1975), its distance as specified by convergence and certain other depth information (Hofsten, 1977; Yonas & Granrud, 1985), its size (Bruner & Koslowski, 1972), and its orientation (Hofsten & Fazel-Zandy, 1984; see also Lockman, Ashmead, & Bushnell, 1984). Most impressively, infants reach appropriately for moving objects. When infants reach for an object that moves across the field of view, they do not aim for the location of the object at the time the arm extension begins but rather for the location that the object will attain once the extension is complete (Hofsten, 1979, 1980; Hofsten & Lindhagen, 1979). These reaches become more successful as infants grow, and they have not been observed at all in infants younger than 4 months. Careful developmental research suggests, however, that the gradual improvement in reaching reflects the growth of the motor system and not the perceptual systems. Infants of all ages aim their reaches for the future position of a moving object, although older infants are better able to execute the intended motor sequence (Hofsten, 1980).

Mature reaching is visually guided in two senses: it is guided by the seen position of the desired object and by the seen position of the hand. By 5 months of age, an infant's reaching is influenced by both kinds of information. Infants of 5 to 8 months adjust their arm movements to accord with the seen position of the hand when the hand is visually displaced by prisms (McDonnell, 1975). The development of this guidance, however, may depend on experience. Lasky (1977) examined reaching to a visual object under circumstances in which infants either could or could not see their hands. When the hands were not visible, reaching was disrupted at $5\frac{1}{2}$ months, but not at earlier ages. In general, however, the younger children showed little reaching, so it is difficult to assess the effect of seeing the hand at that age.

In brief, young infants seem to perceive visually some of the haptically relevant spatial properties of an object: the object's size, distance, and direction. These findings suggest that infants perceive the same spatial properties of objects by looking and by touching, and that suggestion in turn supports the perception-centered perspective on intermodal development.

Strong conclusions cannot be drawn from this research, however, for two reasons. First, the infants in all the noncontroversial studies were at least several months old. Visual–manual coordination could, conceivably, have resulted from earlier visual and manual experience. This possibility seems remote, because the manual exploration of a young infant is very limited (see E. J. Gibson & Spelke, 1983), but it cannot be dismissed.

The second reason for caution in interpreting these studies is that the perceptual basis for visually elicited reaching is not clear, especially at the younger ages. Infants' manual activities toward a visible object may not be guided by implicit knowledge of the graspability of the object but by reflexlike mechanisms triggered by sensory properties of the visual array. For example, a visible object may have more interesting sensory consequences if it is nearby than if it is far away: its surface texture is clearer and its texture elements undergo greater displacements in the visual field as infants move their heads. Infants may swipe more at nearer objects because they are more aroused by these sensory patterns. Similar factors could account for the effects of the size and the radial direction of the object (Bushnell, 1981). Hofsten's studies of reaching for moving objects cast doubt on this suggestion. There is no obvious reason why a rightward moving object on the infant's left should elicit a reach to the right, unless the infant perceived the moving object and anticipated its future position. To evaluate the sensation-centered, action-centered, and perception-centered perspectives; therefore, it would be desirable to conduct experiments such as Hofsten's with younger infants, presenting the infants with visible objects whose spatial properties vary systematically and observing the effects of these variations on both gross and subtle properties of the infants' actions.

In summary, studies of auditory–visual and visual–haptic exploration, while documenting that patterns of intermodal exploration improve with development, provide evidence that infants begin with capacities to perceive amodal properties of objects and to use these properties to guide their actions. In neither set of studies, however, is this evidence conclusive. More decisive experiments may be forthcoming, for investigators are now focusing on the detailed characteristics of infants' exploratory actions and on the visual displays that elicit those actions.

B. Auditory–Visual Perception of Events

We turn now to more direct studies of infants' sensitivity to auditory–visual relationships. A number of experiments have investigated the ability of infants, usually aged 3 to 6 months, to perceive a relationship between the sound and the visible appearance of an event. These studies present infants with events of many kinds, animate or inanimate, repetitive or varied, familiar or novel. In all cases, infants are presented with an array of objects that is moved or deformed, and these object transformations are specified in some manner both in light and in sound.

Many of these studies are based on an interesting exploratory pattern. Infants, like adults, tend to look at the objects that they hear, even if auditory and visual information about an object do not come from the same position in space. This tendency provides psychologists with a means to study infants' perception of auditory–visual relationships. Two visible events can be presented simultaneously or successively, and a sound specific to one of the events can be played from a neutral spatial location. If infants perceive the sound as related to the appropriate event, they should look longer, more frequently, or more rapidly at that event.

In one experiment (Spelke, 1976), 4-month-old infants were presented with motion pictures of a game of peekaboo and of a simple percussion music sequence involving a baton, a tambourine, and a wooden block. The films appeared side by side, while one synchronized sound tract was presented through a central speaker. Infants looked longer at the event that was appropriate to the sound track: they evidently perceived each sound as related to the corresponding visible event. Subsequent research extended this finding (Bahrick, Walker, & Neisser, 1981). Four-month-old infants were shown pairs of events involving objects that moved in synchrony with their sounds, each pair accompanied by one of the two sounds. In one event, a "slinky toy" sprang back and forth between two hands, causing a metallic sound; in a second event, a hand-held baton hit a xylophone, producing a musical sequence; in a third event, two pairs of hands played "pat-a-cake" with appropriate clapping sounds. Infants responded to the sound–object relationships in all three events by looking at the event that corresponded to the sound.

Since these events consisted of natural, possibly familiar objects, infants might have learned about each sound–object relationship. Alternatively, infants might have detected the temporal synchrony of the sound of each object with changes in some of its visible properties. Experiments have now provided evidence that infants are sensitive to auditory–visual synchrony (Allen, Walker, Symonds, & Marcell, 1977; Humphrey, Tees, & Werker, 1979; Mendelson & Ferland, 1982; Spelke, 1979).

For example (Spelke, 1979), 4-month-old infants have been presented with films of two unfamiliar stuffed animals, each paired arbitrarily with a different percussion sound. Each animal was lifted into the air by puppet strings and dropped to the ground repeatedly, and its impacts with the ground were accompanied by one of the sounds. When both objects were shown at once and one sound was played briefly, infants tended to look at the sound-appropriate object. They did this when the sounds and objects were temporally related in several different ways. In one condition, the two objects moved at approximately the same steady tempo but hit the ground at different times. Each sound occurred at the time of one object's impacts and was unrelated to the movements of the other object. In a second condition, the two objects moved at different tempos, and the sound occurred at approximately the same tempo as one object. The sound was not simultaneous with the impacts, or any other consistent spatial position, of either object. Infants detected both temporal relationships; they are sensitive both to the simultaneity and to the similar tempo of sounds and visible movements.

Further experiments provided evidence that infants are sensitive to the synchrony of speech with the visible movements of a face. Infants of 4 to 7 months of age, presented with unfamiliar faces and voices in a preference procedure, looked longer at a voice-synchronized face than at a nonsynchronized face (Spelke and Cortelyou, 1981; Walker, 1982). The same tendency was observed when 3-month-old infants were presented with one face at a time, accompanied by either a synchronized or a nonsynchronized voice (Dodd, 1979). Since many facial movements are synchronized with a voice in the natural speech of adults to infants (Stern, Beebe, Jaffe, & Bennett, 1977), infants might have detected any of a variety of temporal relationships in these events.

Infants of 3 and 4 months, therefore, can detect certain temporal relationships between what they see and what they hear. Can infants detect other auditory–visual relationships? Experiments have addressed this question by presenting infants with temporally related sounds and objects that vary in their nontemporal properties.

One investigation focused on infants' perception of events involving impacts (Spelke, Born, & Chu, 1983). Infants could detect the synchrony of inanimate percussive sounds with the visible impacts of surfaces by relating the sounds to any of three types of visible events: the moment of impact, the moment at which the movement of the object changes, or the moment at which the object passes through a particular spatial position. These sound–object relationships were varied in a series of experiments, and infants' sensitivity to the intermodal relationships was assessed with preferential looking procedures. Infants were found to detect the synchrony of sounds with changes in the movement of an object, irrespective of its spatial position or its impacts with other surfaces. Adults, in contrast, perceived the clearest intermodal relationships when sounds were synchronized with impacts. By 4 months, infants already relate sounds to visible movements; their ability to relate percussive sounds specifically to visible impacts appears to develop after this time.

A second investigation focused on $4\frac{1}{2}$-month-old infants' perception of objects of different substances (Bahrick, 1983). Bahrick hypothesized that infants would detect relationships between the characteristic sounds and visible movements of a rigid versus deformable object. Infants were presented with filmed events involving sponges and wooden blocks. In one film, two wet sponges were squeezed against each other in a manner that would normally produce a "squishing" sound. In the other film, two blocks were made to hit each other so as to produce a "clacking" sound. The squishing sounds were synchronized with the sponges and the clacking sounds with the blocks in one experimental condition; in a second condition, each type of sound was synchronized with the wrong type of object. Infants evidently were sensitive to the relationships between rigid or nonrigid sounds and movements, for they responded to the temporal relationships only when each sound was synchronized with the appropriate visible object. Bahrick proposed that infants perceive the substance of an object by looking and by listening, and that this perception serves as a basis for detecting intermodal relationships. She noted, however, that the infants in her experiment might have responded to further temporal characteristics of the sounds and movements, relating continuous sounds to continuous movements and discrete sounds to discrete movements.

A third experiment investigated infants' perception of expressive behavior by looking and listening (Walker, 1982). Infants of 5 and 7 months were presented with two films of a speaking person, one expressing happiness and one expressing sadness, while tape recordings of the corresponding voices were played. The voices were not synchronized with either of the moving faces. At first, infants showed no preferences between the faces, probably because of the absence of face–voice synchrony. After a few minutes, however, the infants began to look longer at the face that expressed the same mood as the accompanying voice. The infants might have responded to the emotional tenor of each face and voice. Alternatively, they might have responded purely to temporal information, since the happy speech was more rapid and animated than the sad speech. A further experiment supported the first possibility (Walker, 1982). Infants were presented with a happy face and a sad face under conditions in which the faces appeared either right side up or upside down. In both conditions, the faces were accompanied by a voice that was emotionally appropriate to, and synchronized with, one face. The upside-down condition is of interest because it preserves all the temporal relationships present in the right side up condition, yet adults have great difficulty discerning emotional expressions at this orientation. Infants looked at the appropriate face only when it appeared in its canonical orientation. Infants did not respond exclusively to the temporal structure of the visible events, but also to some properties specific to a face, perhaps properties associated with an expression of emotion.

Finally, two series of experiments have focused on intermodal percep-

tion of specific speech sounds (Kuhl & Meltzoff, 1982; MacKain, Studdert-Kennedy, Spieker, & Stern, 1983). Following the preferential looking method, infants were played a series of vowels or simple syllables
while watching two faces. Both faces (on film or videotape) moved in
synchrony with the voice: one face articulated the appropriate speech
sounds, and the other articulated inappropriate speech sounds. The infants looked preferentially to the person whose articulations corresponded to the accompanying speech. By 4 months of age, infants evidently detect relationships between particular speech sounds and
particular facial movements.

In summary, infants are responsive to a variety of auditory–visual relationships. Does their response depend on detecting contingencies between sensations, structural relationships between the acts of looking and
listening, or bimodally specified properties of objects? The action-centered perspective might explain the findings of the face perception and the
speech perception studies. Infants may react emotionally to a happy face
and to a happy voice, and they might respond to similarities between
these two reactions. Moreover, infants may attempt to imitate the speech
gestures they hear and the facial movements they see (see T. Field,
Woodson, Greenberg, & Cohen, 1982; Meltzoff & Moore, 1977), and they
might detect correspondences between these attempts. Similar explanations for the findings of the experiments with inanimate objects are more
difficult to imagine, however, since it is not clear that these events engen-
der any actions. The action-centered perspective seems least promising as
a general account of perception of auditory–visual relationships.

The sensation-centered perspective appears to account well for some of
the experimental findings and less well for other findings. In the experiments in which sounds were temporally synchronized with one of two
moving objects, infants might have detected the intermodal relationships
by analyzing the temporal contingency of certain auditory and visual
sensations. A sensation-based theory cannot account so easily, however,
for infants' detection of relationships between nonsimultaneous sounds
and impacts that occur at the same tempo, between the sounds and the
movements of rigid versus deformable objects, or between auditory and
visual information for specific speech sounds.

Proponents of a sensation-centered theory might propose that infants
learn about the relationship between the sound and movement of a rigid
object, and about the relationship between specific speech sounds and
gestures, over the first 4 months of life: experiments with younger infants
are needed to assess this possibility. To account for infants' perception of
the common tempo of sounds and movements, such theorists might propose that infants do not only detect contingencies between individual

sensations but also detect contingencies between patterns of sensation. To be testable, this hypothesis must include a specification of the kinds of sensory patterns that infants analyze and the contingent relations among these patterns that they detect. Although considerable effort has been devoted to the study of contingency analysis by humans and other animals (see Schwartz, 1978), the ability to detect such higher-order patterns of contingency has not, to my knowledge, been studied. No existing sensation-centered perspective can account for the findings of all the experiments on auditory–visual perception.

The perception-centered perspective appears to provide the simplest account of research on auditory–visual perception. Infants may perceive auditory–visual relationships by detecting amodal properties of objects. They may detect higher-order relationships in light and sound that specify the movements and the substance of an inanimate object and the actions, emotional expressions, and articulatory gestures of a person. Studies of perception within a single modality suggest that infants do perceive the rigidity or deformability of objects (E. J. Gibson, Owsley, & Johnston, 1978), the translatory movements of surfaces (Hofsten, 1979; Kellman & Spelke, 1983), the expressions of emotion of persons (Walker, 1980), and the distinctive sounds of speech (e.g., Eimas, Siqueland, Jusczyk, & Vigorito, 1971). These studies lend credence to the perception-centered theory.

C. Visual–Haptic Perception of Objects and Surfaces

We turn now to infants' perception of a layout that is both visible and tangible. A number of experiments have investigated visual–haptic perception of the shapes, substances, and textures of objects. Other experiments have investigated visual perception of an extended surface and anticipation of its tactile consequences.

By 6 months of age, infants who explore an object manually can subsequently recognize its shape visually. They may demonstrate their recognition by looking at or reaching for the object they have felt in preference to a novel object. For example, 8-month-old infants were allowed to manipulate a noise-making toy that they could not see, and then they were shown that toy and a different toy side by side. The infants reached for the familiar toy (Bryant, Jones, Claxton, & Perkins, 1972). Similarly, infants of 6 months who were allowed to touch an unseen object later looked longer at that object than at a novel object (Ruff & Kohler, 1978). The same patterns have been observed with nonhuman infant primates (Dolgin, Premack, & Spelke, 1980; Gunderson, 1983).

Infants do not always look at an object they have felt. After tactual familiarization with an object of one shape, 1-year-old infants may look longer at an object of a different shape (Gottfried, Rose, & Bridger, 1977), whereas infants who were born prematurely and/or who live in less well-educated families may show no reliable visual preferences (Rose, Gottfried, & Bridger, 1981). In a more recent series of experiments (Streri & Pêcheux, in press), $4\frac{1}{2}$-month-old infants who were familiarized with an object visually were found subsequently to engage in greater haptic exploration of an object with a novel shape, although no consistent preferences were obtained in a symmetrical haptic-to-visual transfer task. Conflicting findings may have been obtained in these experiments, because intermodal transfer tasks elicit two conflicting tendencies: a tendency to explore one object both by looking and by touching, and a tendency to explore something new (Spelke, 1985; see also Rolfe & Day, 1981). In any case, the above studies reveal that 6-month-old infants do detect the relationship between visual and haptic information for an object's shape.

Three experiments suggest the capacity for visual–haptic perception is present earlier in life. Meltzoff and Borton (1979) allowed 1-month-old infants to suck either a smooth sphere or a sphere with nubs without seeing the object. Subsequently, the infants were given a visual preference test between two larger objects with these smooth and rough textures. The infants tended to look at the object with the texture they had felt. This experiment provides evidence that infants can perceive the texture of an object both visually and haptically. Unfortunately, one experiment has failed to replicate this effect (Allen, 1982).

Similar research has focused on visual–haptic perception of substances (E. J. Gibson & Walker, 1984). One-month-old infants were allowed to explore either a rigid or a flexible object in the mouth. After mouthing the object for 60 sec without seeing it, the infants were shown two visible objects, side by side. One object was moved rigidly while the other was subjected to an elastic deformation. The infants looked longer at the object that underwent a *novel* pattern of motion. It is not clear why a novelty preference was observed in this study, rather than a preference for the familiar substance (see E. J. Gibson, 1983, and Spelke, 1985, for discussion). Nevertheless, the experiment provides evidence that 1-month-old infants perceive the substance of an appropriately moving object both visually and haptically.

In another study (Streri, 1985), $2\frac{1}{2}$-month-old infants were allowed to explore an object of a simple shape (a ring or a disk) in one hand, out of the visual field. After a period of haptic habituation (following Streri & Pêcheux, 1986), the infants were given a visual preference test with the two forms. Infants looked longer at the novel form. It appears, therefore, that prereaching infants can perceive the textures, substances, and shapes of certain objects either by touching or by looking, and that they can recognize visually a texture, substance, or shape they have felt.

Visual–haptic perception of extended surfaces has been studied in detail, using techniques that differ considerably from those discussed so far. In all the above studies, infants were presented both with visual and with auditory or haptic information about an object, and their sensitivity to the congruity or incongruity of the two sources of information was assessed. In the studies that follow, infants are presented only with visual information for a surface, but it is a surface with certain affordances (J. J. Gibson, 1979): certain consequences for action. Activity in response to this visual information is observed in order to determine whether infants appreciate, on some level, that the visible surface has certain tactile consequences. The existence of such anticipatory activity is of interest for many reasons: it may shed light on the development of perception, of cognitive processes, and even of emotion (see Campos, Hiatt, Ramsay, Henderson, & Svejda, 1978; E. J. Gibson, 1982). In this chapter, however, infants' anticipatory activity is described only insofar as it sheds light on the capacity for intermodal perception. If an infant, on seeing an object, expects the object to have certain tactile qualities, he or she obviously appreciates the relationship between these visual and tactile qualities.

The most well-known studies of this kind concern infants' behavior on the "visual cliff" (E. J. Gibson & Walk, 1960; Walk & Gibson, 1961). Infants in the second half-year of life often avoid crawling off a support when they face a visually specified drop-off, even when coaxed by a parent: they move forward only in the presence of visual information for a surface of support. Animals of other species such as chickens, goats, and sheep also avoid an optically specified drop-off from birth, as do hooded rats who are reared in darkness and are tested on their first exposure to the light.

Since human infants do not crawl until $6\frac{1}{2}$ months, the development of avoidance of the cliff is not well understood. Investigations of younger infants placed directly on the cliff or placed in walkers that permit independent locomotion suggest that avoidance of the cliff is affected by experience (Campos et al., 1978) and/or maturation (Rader, Bausano, & Richards, 1980). The interactions of these factors are still not clear.

Further evidence for visual–tactual perception of surfaces comes from studies of younger infants. Studies of "looming" have revealed that newborn animals of many species back away from an approaching surface or from a two-dimensional display that simulates the approach of a surface by a pattern of symmetrical expansion (Schiff, 1965). When young human infants are presented with such displays, they have been reported to blink (White et al., 1964; Yonas, 1979), to stiffen (Ball & Tronick, 1971), to withdraw the head (Ball & Tronick, 1971; Ball & Vurpillot, 1976; Bower, Broughton, & Moore, 1970b), and to interpose their arms between their faces and the object (Ball & Tronick, 1971; Bower et al., 1970b; Yonas, Pettersen, Lockman, & Eisenberg, 1980; see Yonas, 1981, for a review).

Are infants' reactions to an approaching surface guided by visual perception of the surface and its approach? One series of experiments (Yonas, Bechtold, Frankel, Gordon, McRoberts, Norcia & Sternfels, 1977) suggested that head withdrawal to a looming display depends only on infants' perception of moving two-dimensional contours: infant withdraw their heads not in order to defend themselves but to follow visually the rising upper contour of the display. Two experiments have cast doubt on this suggestion and provide evidence that a looming display specifies imminent collision for an infant. Bower (comment on Yonas et al., 1977, pp. 281–282) presented infants with a shadow pattern specifying an object about to fall upon them. He reported that infants withdrew their heads from this display as they do from looming displays, even though the falling object had a falling rather than a rising upper contour. Carroll and Gibson (1981) presented 3-month-old infants with two different displays of expanding contours. In one display, a small surface approached the infants on a collision course. In the other display, a large surface with an aperture approached the infants. The aperture occupied the same position as the object in the first display. Infants withdrew their heads sharply from the approaching object, but they leaned back only slightly when the aperture approached them and many infants turned as if to watch this surface go by. This experiment indicates that infants show defensive head withdrawal only to certain kinds of expanding contours. Although approaching obstacles and approaching apertures both have expanding contours, they have different consequences for an infant, and infants appear to appreciate these consequences. These experiments provide evidence that infants can perceive visible surfaces and take account of their tactile consequences.

Finally, experiments reveal that young infants use visible surfaces as information about their own posture. For adults, visual information for an upright stable orientation guides postural stability; we can sometimes be made to lose our balance if the walls of a room move around us (Lishman & Lee, 1975). One-year-old infants who can stand independently can be similarly fooled: they are likely to fall backward, for example, if the walls of the room swing toward them. These infants evidently take the movement of the walls as information that they are falling forward, and they compensate by moving in the opposite direction (Lee & Aronson, 1974). Although 1-year-olds might have learned to use vision as a source of postural information when they learned to stand, recent studies indicate that analogous adjustments are made by infants too young to stand, to sit, or even to reach for objects (Butterworth, 1983; Butterworth & Hicks, 1977; Schonen, personal communication). Once again, a linkage between different perceptual systems is indicated. It is not clear if this linkage results from infants' perception of amodal properties of surfaces and their orientations, or if the response is evoked directly by certain sensory patterns.

In summary, infants of 1 and 2 months can coordinate visual and tactile information about the texture, the substance, and the shape of an object and about the movements of extended surfaces. As infants grow, their active manipulation becomes more effective and new actions come to be guided by visual information. Most infants of 7 months take account of the visually specified distances of surfaces and use this information to guide their locomotion. Younger infants, however, are already sensitive to relationships between how a surface looks and how it feels.

The sensation-centered and action–centered perspectives provide natural accounts for the slow development of haptic exploration and of certain visually-guided actions. These perspectives have more difficulty accounting for the results of experiments showing visual–haptic coordination in young infants. Proponents of these perspectives could propose that the early intermodal coordinations depend on specific linkages between motor patterns and uninterpreted visual sensations. Such explanations are attractive as long as the coordination exhibited by infants is limited and the stimulus displays that evoke a reaction can be simply described. Blinking to a looming object at 3 weeks of age, for example, might well depend on a reflex linkage. Later in infancy, when a looming object evokes a wide range of different adaptive activities, and when these responses occur only when an object (not an aperture) approaches, sensory–motor linkage hypotheses are strained, but then one could propose that the later coordinations develop through experience. Defensive reactions to an approaching object, for example, may result from associative learning or from a process of reciprocal assimilation between acts of visual perception, arm raising, and head withdrawal. If learning does underlie defensive reactions, the speed of this learning is quite remarkable. Three-month-old infants cannot begin to reach for an object, yet they respond appropriately when an object approaches on a collision course.

The sensation-centered and action-centered perspectives would seem to have the greatest difficulty explaining the finding that 1- and 2-month-old infants can perceive an object's texture, substance, and shape intermodally. One might amend a sensation-centered theory by proposing that infants detect contingencies among spatial patterns of sensations, and that the visual and haptic patterns of sensations evoked by an object of a certain texture, shape, or form have something in common. Similarly, one might develop an action-centered theory that postulates innate structural relationships between the actions of looking at and feeling an object of a certain texture, substance, or shape. These amended theories would be very different from Helmholtz's and Piaget's original proposals, however, and they currently have little independent motivation. The sensation-centered and action-centered perspectives offer no straightforward explanation of experiments on visual-haptic perception.

In contrast, the perception-centered perspective could account for all the abilities demonstrated by young infants by proposing that infants perceive certain properties of objects and surfaces both visually and tactually. Adherents to this perspective must offer a separate explanation for developmental changes in responses to a visually specified drop-off, perhaps in terms of the maturation of a visuomotor program controlling crawling (see Rader et al., 1980; Richards & Rader, 1981). Aside from this complication, the perception-centered perspective seems to offer a reasonably simple account of all the studies of visual–haptic perception.

D. Overview

In this author's opinion, studies of the early capacity for intermodal perception lend greatest plausibility to a perception-centered theory of development. Experiments on intermodal exploration, auditory–visual perception, and visual–haptic perception all provide evidence that infants perceive some of the distal properties of objects when they look at, listen to, and manipulate those objects. When infants detect the same object property through two perceptual systems, they appear to perceive an intermodal relationship. No conclusive choice among the three perspectives can be made, however, for no experimental findings directly refute any of the theories. The sensation-centered and action-centered perspectives remain tenable, and each position has contemporary adherents (for example, see Bushnell, 1981; McGurk & MacDonald, 1978). The innate basis of intersensory coordination is still not known.

IV. DEVELOPMENTAL CHANGES IN INTERMODAL PERCEPTION

This discussion will focus first on studies of infants' learning about relationships between the audible and visible properties of objects, and then on studies of developmental changes in infants' reactions to conflicting visual and haptic information. We will consider whether the development of intermodal perception can be explained by processes of hypothesis testing and associative learning, by the structuring of actions, or by the differentiation of perception of object properties.

A. Learning about Auditory–Visual Relationships

Adults perceive many auditory–visual relationships that are quite arbitrary. They relate thunder to lightning, chimes to a grandfather clock, and a friend's voice to her face. These abilities surely depend on acquired knowledge about visible, sound-producing objects. Recent research suggests that the acquisition of such knowledge begins early in life.

The most familiar audible and visible objects in the infant's world are probably his parents. Young infants have been shown to know about the relationship between each parent's face and voice and to use knowledge of this relationship when they explore. In one study (Spelke & Owsley, 1979), infants of $3\frac{1}{2}$, $5\frac{1}{2}$, and $7\frac{1}{2}$ months sat facing between the mother and father and heard the nonsynchronized voice of one parent spatially centered between the parents. Infants of all ages tended to look to the parent whose voice was played. Knowledge of the face–voice relations evidently guided their looking. In a similar study (Cohen, 1974), infants of 8 months were found to look longer to the mother when her own voice was played from her direction than when a female stranger's voice was played from the mother's direction. Infants as young as 2 weeks may exhibit the same pattern, though the results of studies at this age are not fully clear (Carpenter, cited in Bower, 1979, and in Mendelson, 1979; Bigelow, 1977; Spelke & Owsley, 1979). Knowledge of the relationship between each parent's voice and face appears to develop in the first year of life, perhaps quite early in that year.

By 6 months of age, infants have also learned that male faces go with male voices and female faces go with female voices (Francis & McCroy, 1983; see also Miller & Horowitz, 1980). When presented with an unfamiliar voice played between a male and a female face, 6-month-old infants look longer at the face of the same sex. Three-month-old infants show no such tendency. Infants may learn about these intermodal relationships during the first months of life.

Infants also learn about relationships between the sounds and the visible appearance of inanimate objects. Learning can take place over one brief laboratory session in which infants are presented with an unfamiliar, sounding object. For example, Lyons-Ruth (1977) presented 4-month-old infants with a visibly moving toy and a sound that came from the same direction. The toy moved laterally, back and forth, in repeated 10-sec turns, and the sound occurred at the end of each movement. Lyons-Ruth tested whether infants learned about the sound–object relationship by determining if familiarization with the sounding object affected infants' subsequent patterns of looking. In the test, the sound was presented to the baby's right, accompanied by the same object or by a different object. Sounds and objects were not synchronized. Infants looked in the sound's direction for a longer time if they encountered the appropriate visible object.

Lyons-Ruth's study revealed that infants can learn rapidly about auditory–visual relationships. During the familiarization period, the sound and object were related in several ways: they were spatially coincident, the sound was temporally synchronized with the object's movement, and the object was the only thing that moved in the infant's field of view while the sound was played. Subsequent research by Lawson (1980) and Spelke (1981) has attempted to determine which of these conditions of familiarization were critical for learning.

Lawson investigated the effects of spatial and temporal information on infants' learning about sound–object relationships. Six-month-old infants were familiarized with a single inanimate object and an inanimate sound that were spatially coincident, temporally synchronized, or both. After the period of familiarization, the infants received a test in which the familiar object and a novel object were presented side by side, accompanied by the familiar sound or a novel sound. If infants had learned about the sound–object relationship during the familiarization period, they were expected to look at the familiar object when its sound was played.

Lawson's experiments provide evidence that both temporal and spatial information affect infants' learning. The effects of temporal information can be discerned by considering patterns of searching after familiarization with a spatially coincident sound and object that either were or were not temporally synchronized. Infants learned about the auditory–visual relationship when a spatially coincident sound and object were temporally synchronized (Experiment 1). When the object moved together with a continuous, nonsynchronized sound (Experiment 4), significantly less searching occurred: the disruption of this temporal relationship affected infants' learning. Not all disruptions of temporal synchrony disrupted learning, however: when an object moved continuously with the discontinuous sound (Experiment 3), patterns of searching were the same as in the first condition.

The effects of spatial information in Lawson's experiments can be discerned by considering patterns of searching after familiarization with a temporally synchronized sound and object that were, or were not, spatially coincident. As noted, appropriate search occurred when infants were familiarized with a synchronized sound and object that were spatially coincident (Experiment 1). When the synchronized sound and object were widely separated in space (Experiment 2), a nonsignificant drop in appropriate search occurred. This drop suggested that the spatial relationship between the sound and object affected learning about the auditory–visual relationship. Learning may be affected in complex ways both by temporal and by spatial information for a sound–object relationship.

Other experiments indicate that infants learn about the relationship between a sound and a synchronized moving object when the sound and object are spatially separated to a smaller extent (Spelke, 1981). Infants of 4 months were presented with two stuffed animals, side by side, that bounced against a surface at approximately the same steady rate, out of phase with each other. While the animals moved, two percussion sounds were played in succession through a speaker that was centered between the objects. Each sound was synchronized with the bounces of one object.

Learning was tested in two ways. One procedure was similar to the methods of Lyons-Ruth and Lawson. When infants were looking between the two objects, one of the sounds—now out of synchrony with both objects—was played. Infants evidently learned about the sound–object relationship, for they tended to look at whichever object had been formerly synchronized with the sound. Learning was also tested through a habituation and transfer test. One of the sounds was played with no visual accompaniment for an extended period, and it was followed by a silent preference test between the objects. Infants showed a novelty preference for the object not specified by the preceding sound; this effect provides further evidence that they had learned about the intermodal relationship. Appropriate search and novelty preferences were observed in two further experiments in which the lateral positions of the objects were reversed during the test. Infants evidently learned to relate sounds to objects with particular visible characteristics, not to objects in particular spatial positions. These studies provide evidence that infants can learn about an auditory–visual relationship when a sound and a moving object are united only by their temporal synchrony during a period of familiarization.

In summary, infants can learn about a sound–object relationship after very brief exposure to a sounding object: 1 or 2 min of familiarization is sufficient. Infants are most apt to learn about auditory–visual relationships when sounds and objects share a common temporal and spatial structure. Under some conditions, however, it may be sufficient for the objects and sounds to be spatially related (Lawson, 1980) or temporally related (Spelke, 1981). Finally, infants can learn to relate a sound to a synchronized object even if a second, nonsynchronized object is present, and even if the infants spend much of their time looking at the nonsynchronized object while the sound is played. Infants in Spelke's (1981) studies, for example, observed two visible objects at once during the familiarization period, and looking times to the two objects were roughly equal. In some studies, infants actually looked longer at the object that was not synchronized with a sound than at the synchronized object. They learned, however, to relate the sound to the synchronized object. Infants do not come to associate all sounds and objects that they perceive at the same time.

None of the three theoretical perspectives accounts fully for infants' learning in these experiments. In all the studies, infants were familiarized with sounds and objects that were temporally and/or spatially related but which were otherwise paired arbitrarily. Because of the arbitrary nature of these pairings, there would not seem to be any special structural relationship between the acts of looking at a toy and listening to a percussion sound, and it is unlikely that the infant changed his actions so as to construct such a relationship. Similarly, there would not seem to be any amodal object property that unites each animal with each percussion sound. It is unlikely that infants searched for and detected new stimulus invariants that specified such a property. Neither the action-centered nor the perception-centered perspective, therefore, can account easily for learning about these arbitrary intermodal relationships.

The sensation-centered perspective would seem to offer a more natural description of infants' learning about arbitrary sound–object relationships. Infants may have learned to associate each sound to a particular visual object by analyzing the contingent relations between the occurrence of the sound and the movements of the object. It is not clear, however, why learning is affected by the spatial relationship between the sound and object, or why learning is so little affected by the amount of simultaneous exposure to a sound and object. Furthermore, the above experiments indicate only that infants can learn about *certain* arbitrary sound–object relationships; they do not indicate whether infants will learn to connect *any* sound and visible object with equal ease. According to the sensation-centered perspective, a child should apply the same principles of contingency analysis to any patterns of sensation. It is possible, however, that children are more selective. Even newborn infants might resist learning that a visible person produces the sound of a buzzer, however contingent one stimulus is upon the other. This possibility remains untested.

B. Reacting to Discrepant Visual and Haptic Information

The studies reviewed in previous sections provide evidence that infants' manual activity is guided by visual information for the distance, the direction, and some aspects of the size, shape, and texture of an object. These studies appeared to provide evidence that infants are sensitive to certain visual–haptic relationships. Further experiments, however, call that conclusion into question. Young infants have been shown to respond differently than older children when reaching for certain objects that they see or hear. In particular, there are developmental changes in infants' reactions to situations in which visual and haptic information are placed in conflict.

In some studies, infants have been presented with stereoscopic information specifying an object in front of them, under conditions in which no object is actually present. This illusion can be produced with various devices (see Bower, Broughton, & Moore, 1971; J. Field, 1977). From $5\frac{1}{2}$ months of age—and perhaps younger—infants reach for the visible object, and their reaching is adapted, at least grossly, to the object's visually given distance (Gordon & Yonas, 1976). When the infant's hand reaches the empty space where the object is seen, she feels nothing, and her hand is seen to pass through the object. Older children express considerable surprise in these circumstances, and they may test their hands for numbness or search haptically for the object with extensive movements of the fingers, hands, and arms. In most studies (see Bower et al., 1971, for an exception), infants as old as $9\frac{1}{2}$ months show neither of these reactions (J. Field, 1977; Gordon, Lamson, & Yonas, 1978, cited in Yonas, 1979; Gordon & Yonas, 1976).

Similar findings emerge from studies by Bushnell (for a review, see Bushnell, 1981). She presented infants of 8 to 15 months with a solid object that was visible in a definite location within a box. The seen location of the object was displaced from its true location by a mirror arrangement, and a different unseen object was placed where the first object appeared to be. Thus, when infants reached for the visible object, they encountered an object of a different size, shape, and/or texture. They also could not see their hand touch the object. One might expect a person in this situation to be surprised, to explore the object intensely, or to search for the source of the discrepancy. Infants above 9 months of age tended to act in these ways, but 8-month-old infants did not.

How is one to account for these findings? The infant's problem evidently does not stem from an inability to detect a correspondence between the seen and felt shape or texture of an object, for much younger infants can do this in some circumstances (Meltzoff & Borton, 1979; Streri, 1985). It is possible that infants do not react to discrepant visual and haptic information because of an attention limit of some kind: they may be unable to perceive two different shapes or substances at the same moment. Alternatively, it is possible that infants cannot detect discrepant visual and haptic information when they see and feel an object simultaneously because of a "visual capture" effect: the presence of visual information about the object's shape may distort the child's haptic perception of its shape so as to reduce or even eliminate the discrepancy. Visual capture effects of this kind are obtained with adults (e.g., Rock & Victor, 1964; see Welch & Warren, 1980, for a review). Neither of these explanations, however, offers a plausible account for the infant's behavior when she reaches for an object and encounters nothing at all.

At least one potential explanation remains. Young infants may experience an intermodal conflict, but they may fail to show surprise or systematic search because these reactions cannot be set in motion by the detection of such a conflict. According to the latter explanation, the perceptual knowledge of young infants is less *accessible* to them than is the otherwise similar perceptual knowledge of adults. Adults can use knowledge of intermodal relationships to guide any actions or thoughts. Infants, in contrast, may be able to use knowledge of intermodal relationships only in certain restricted ways. Such knowledge may guide their looking at an object they feel, but it may not lead them to search for the causes of discrepant sensory patterns.

In many cognitive domains, psychological capacities may become progressively more accessible with development (Rozin, 1976). Rozin suggested that the development of intelligence, both phylogenetically and ontogenetically, is characterized by the achievement of progressively greater access to abilities that are innate but are initially functional only in quite restricted contexts. On this view, individuals of different ages differ less in the complexity of the systems that govern their actions than in their ability to harness such systems for new purposes. As children grow, they achieve greater access to their intrinsic capacities, and so they become capable of acting and thinking in new ways.

None of the three perspectives on intermodal perception truly captures this kind of change. The accessibility hypothesis, nevertheless, seems to combine insights from the perception-centered and the action-centered perspectives. To propose that the development of intermodal perception reflects the increasing accessibility of intrinsic perceptual capacities is to grant that such intrinsic capacities exist, in accord with the perception-centered theory. To propose that these perceptual capacities are initially restricted in range and become more broadly useful with growth, however, is to describe a kind of development that is central to Piaget's action-centered theory. The entire period of infancy, according to Piaget, is a time when innate action structures are extended, coordinated, and generalized as they are applied to new objects. In different ways, both Gibsonian and Piagetian theories may help to explain the developmental progression that Rozin describes.

C. Overview

The above research suggests, in brief, that developmental changes in intermodal perception spring from several sources. Like older children and adults, infants may learn to relate certain arbitrarily paired sounds and visible objects by analyzing the structure of the events in which those objects participate. Moreover, infants may come to act on objects in new ways as their initial capacities to detect intermodal relationships become more accessible for new purposes. Each of the three perspectives on intermodal perception seems to shed some light on these phenomena. No general account of perceptual learning yet encompasses them all.

V. CONCLUSION

The research that has been discussed provides ample evidence that looking, touching, and listening are coordinated from a very early age, and that learning and development extend and change that initial coordination. The most interesting questions, however, concern not the existence of an innate coordination between the modalities but its basis, not the existence of learning but the nature of the mechanisms that subserve it. We have seen repeatedly that experiments addressing these questions are difficult to devise. Thus, students of intermodal perception find themselves on a terrain furnished with many experimental findings to use as landmarks, but with few unassailable principles to provide an appropriate frame of reference.

We have considered three hypotheses about the innate basis of intermodal perception: sensations and their contingent relationships, actions and their structural relationships, and perceptions of objects and their amodal properties. The third, perception-centered perspective seemed the best-supported account of the origins of intermodal perception. Infants do perceive properties of objects such as their size and substance from a very early age, and they appear to perceive the same object properties by looking, listening, and feeling. It seems likely that infants perceive unitary objects and events by detecting these amodal properties.

We have also considered three accounts of intermodal learning and development, accounts that center on processes of associative learning about relationships among sensations, processes of reciprocal assimilation leading to the structuring of actions, and processes of invariant detection leading to perceptual differentiation. All three processes seem to provide explanations of certain aspects of intermodal development. Associative and invariant-detection processes may partly account for infants' learning about arbitrary auditory–visual relationships; invariant-detection processes and processes for structuring actions may describe certain aspects of the development of reactions to intermodal discrepancies.

These conclusions are tentative. Experiments on intermodal perception in infancy permit one to reject certain specific theoretical proposals, and they highlight ways in which each theoretical perspective might be made more specific. These experiments, however, have not resolved the basic controversy between the sensation-centered, the action-centered, and the perception-centered perspectives on development.

Some aspects of this controversy may be settled by further research on intermodal perception in infancy. It is important, for example, to investigate the capacity for intermodal perception in newborn infants, to investigate more closely the process of learning about intermodal relationships, and to assess the contribution of maturation and learning to the development of intermodal functioning. I believe, however, that the greatest advances in our understanding of the development of intermodal perception will not come from research on intermodal perception specifically, but rather from research of broader scope.

None of the three perspectives guiding this chapter proposes that there is anything special about *intermodal* perception, or about human infants. The same sensations, actions, and mechanisms for perceiving objects that are said to underlie intermodal perception are thought to underlie perceptions of all kinds. For all theorists except possibly Piaget, moreover, the same principles that characterize the development of perception in humans are proposed to characterize the development of perception in other animals. According to all three perspectives, therefore, an understanding of intermodal perception in infancy could grow from investigations of other capacities and even other species.

For example, comparative research could be undertaken to test the central claims of the three perspectives. If the specific sensations, actions, and perceptions of very young animals differ somewhat from species to species, then comparative research could investigate whether species differences in the initial capacity for intermodal perception are best predicted by species differences in what animals can sense, in how they can act, or in what they can perceive. Furthermore, controlled-rearing studies of nonhuman species could probe the effects of early experience on intermodal perception, thereby shedding light on the mechanisms of development. Both methods have been used to investigate responses to looming objects (Schiff, 1965) and to the visual cliff (Walk & Gibson, 1961); studies using these methods appear to support a perception-centered theory. More such experiments, focusing on auditory–visual perception of events and on visual–haptic perception of objects, might be illuminating.

Studies of intermodal development could be broadened in a second way, for the three perspectives on intermodal perception can be tested through other kinds of experiments with human infants. Piaget's experiments with his own infants provide one illustration of the benefits of a broad approach to the study of early perceptual and cognitive development (Piaget, 1952, 1954). Piaget examined his infants' reactions to a variety of problems in a variety of domains. His theory of sensory–motor development is highly compelling, in part, because his interpretation of an infant's performance on one cognitive task is constrained by his interpretations of performance on all other tasks. In particular, Piaget's claims about the development of intermodal perception are bolstered by his studies of the development of concepts of objects, causality, space, and time: all converge on a single description of development in infancy.

A second example of a broad approach to development is provided by E. J. Gibson's research on infants' perception of substances. Gibson and her colleagues propose that infants, like adults (Fieandt & Gibson, 1959), are able to perceive the rigidity or flexibility of a moving object by detecting invariant information specifying the object's characteristic motion. To investigate the development of this sensitivity, Gibson has studied infant's perception of the rigidity or flexibility of a single moving object (E. J. Gibson et al., 1978; Walker, Gibson, Owsley, Megaw-Nyce, & Bahrick, 1980), of a set of different moving objects composed of the same substance (E. J. Gibson, Owsley, Walker, & Negaw-Nyce, 1979), of an object both seen and heard (Bahrick, 1983), of an object both seen and felt (E. J. Gibson & Walker, 1982), and of an extended surface (E. J. Gibson, 1984). These studies all provide evidence that infants can perceive the rigidity or flexibility of a substance and that this perceptual ability can underlie perception of intermodal relationships.

Theoretical progress will be made, I believe, if more investigations follow these examples. Instead of exploring the development of intermodal perception *per se,* investigators might focus more directly on the capacities that serve as the basis of *all* perception and on the principles that underlie all perceptual development. Those working from a sensation-centered perspective could investigate the nature of the unconscious, elementary sensations that, they believe, form the building blocks of perception. They might also investigate the processes of contingency analysis that could lead the child to discover just those contingent relationships that unite the visual sensations evoked by an object to the auditory and tactile sensations the object produces. Those working within an action-centered theory could focus on the nature and structure of the child's initial actions, on the infant's sensitivity to structural relationships uniting actions directed to the same object, and on the principles by which actions become further structured and coordinated. Those working within a perception-centered theory could study the invariant relationships in stimulation that infants detect, the properties of objects and events that infants might thereby perceive, and the principles and mechanisms by which the infants' perceptions undergo differentiation.

By turning in these directions, investigators of infant perception could help to overcome the most serious weakness of each perspective: the central concepts of these theories need to be formulated more precisely. Research is needed to investigate which, if any, of the potential concepts of sensation, action, or invariant should figure in an account of the initial capacity for intermodal perception. Research is also needed to investigate the nature of the processes by which infants analyze contingencies, coordinate actions, and detect new invariants, to determine the roles these processes play in the development of intermodal perception.

It may seem unfair to burden the student of infant perception with these tasks. Physiologists and psychologists have attempted to discover the properties of elementary sensations for over 100 years, with little success (see Hochberg, 1979). Attempts to specify the universal processes of contingency analysis have met with somewhat greater success, but the nature and the generality of those processes are still disputed (Schwartz, 1978). The tasks of defining an elementary unit of action and of specifying the principles by which actions are coordinated have also proved difficult (but see Gallistel, 1980), and the relationship, if any, between the coordination of action and the perception of objects and events has not frequently been studied. Finally, the task of specifying what invariants perceivers detect, and what properties of objects and events these invariants specify, has only begun (J. J. Gibson, 1966, 1979; E. J. Gibson, 1982).

Students of infant perception have made little contribution to these theoretical efforts in the past. They may, however, be especially well suited to this task. One reason the analysis of perception has been so difficult in the past, I believe, is that investigators have focused on subjects whose fundamental processes of perception are hidden under layers of knowledge, skill, and ingenuity. In studies of human adults, any elementary sensations and actions that might exist will surely be cloaked by vast collections of perceptual and motor skills. Mechanisms for perceiving properties of objects and events will also be difficult to discern, amid the adult's many other means for arriving at judgments in perceptual tasks. Finally, basic principles of learning and development will be hidden among the many special learning strategies that adults have discovered through luck, instruction, or insight.

Consider, in contrast, the newborn infant. Infants surely lack most of the knowledge and skills that we enjoy as adults. The most basic and general mechanisms of perception, therefore, are more likely to serve as guides to their actions, and the most basic mechanisms of learning are more likely to provide the means by which they acquire knowledge. Psychologists may glimpse the fundamental basis of perception, and the principles of its development, through studies of human infancy.

ACKNOWLEDGMENTS

I thank Penny Prather, Ulric Neisser, and Wendy Smith Born for their comments and suggestions. Preparation of this chapter was supported by a grant from the National Institute of Child Health and Human Development (HD-13428).

REFERENCES

Allen, T. W. (1982, March). *Oral-oral and oral-visual object discrimination.* Paper presented at the meeting of the International Conference on Infant Studies, Austin, TX.

Allen, T. W., Walker, L., Symonds, L., & Marcell, M. (1977). Intrasensory and intersensory perception of temporal sequences during infancy. *Developmental Psychology, 15,* 225–229.

Bahrick, L. E. (1983). Infants' perception of substance and temporal synchrony in multimodal events. *Infant Behavior and Development, 6,* 429–451.

Bahrick, L. E., Walker, A. S., & Neisser, U. (1981). Selective looking by infants. *Cognitive Psychology, 13,* 377–390.

Ball, W. A., & Tronick, E. (1971). Infant responses to impending collision: Optical and real. *Science, 171,* 818–820.

Ball, W. A., & Vurpillot, E. (1976). Perception of movement in depth in infancy. *Annee Psychologique, 76,* 383–399.

Bechtold, A. G., Bushnell, E. W., & Salapatek, P. (1979, March). *Infants' visual localization of visual and auditory targets.* Paper presented at the meeting of the Society for Research in Child Development, San Francisco, CA.

Bigelow, A. (1977, March). *Infants recognition of the mother.* Paper presented at the meeting of the Society for Research in Child Development, New Orleans, LA.

Bower, T. G. R. (1972). Object perception in infants. *Perception, 1,* 15–30.

Bower, T. G. R. Comment on Yonas et al. Development of sensitivity to information for impending collision. *Perception & Psychophysics,* 1977, *21,* 281–282.

Bower, T. G. R. (1979). *Human development.* San Francisco, CA: Freeman. Bower, T. G. R., Broughton, J. M., & Moore, M. K. (1970a). The coordination of visual and tactual input in infants. *Perception and Psychophysics, 8,* 51–53.

Bower, T. G. R., Broughton, J. M., & Moore, M. K. (1970b). Demonstration of intention in the reaching behavior of neonate humans. *Nature (London), 228,* 679–680.

Bower, T. G. R., Broughton, J. M., & Moore, M. K. (1971). Infant responses to approaching objects: An indication of response to distal variables. *Perception and Psychophysics, 9,* 193–196.

Bower, T. G. R., Dunkeld, J., & Wishart, J. G. (1979). Infant perception of visually presented objects (technical comment). *Science, 203,* 1137–1138.

Bruner, J. S. (1974). The organization of early skilled action. In M. P. M. Richards (Ed.), *The integration of a child into a social world.* London & New York: Cambridge University Press.

Bruner, J. S., & Koslowski, B. (1972). Visually preadapted constituents of manipulatory action. *Perception, 1,* 3–14.

Bryant, P. E., Jones, P., Claxton, V., & Perkins, G. H. (1972). Recognition of shapes across modalities by infants. *Nature (London), 240,* 303–304.

Bushnell, E. W. (1981). The ontogeny of intermodal relations: Vision and touch in infancy. In R. D. Walk & H. L. Pick, Jr. (Eds.), *Intersensory perception and sensory integration.* New York: Plenum.

Butterworth, G. (1978). Review of *A primer of infant development* by T. G. R. Bower. *Perception, 7,* 363–365.

Butterworth, G. (1981). The origins of auditory-visual perception and visual proprioception in human development. In R. D. Walk & H. A. Pick (Eds.), *Intersensory perception and sensory integration.* New York: Plenum.

Butterworth, G. (1983). Structure of mind in infancy. *Advances in infancy research* (Vol. 1). Norwood, NJ: Ablex.

Butterworth, G., & Castillo, M. (1976). Coordination of auditory and visual space in newborn human infants. *Perception, 5,* 155–160.

Butterworth, G., & Hicks, L. (1977). Visual proprioception and postural stability in infancy. A developmental study. *Perception, 6,* 255–262.

Campos, J. J., Hiatt, S., Ramsay, D., Henderson, C., & Svejda, M. (1978). The emergence of fear on the visual cliff. In M. Lewis & L. Rosenblum (Eds.), *The development of affect.* New York: Plenum.

Carroll, O. J., & Gibson, E. J. (1981, April). *Differentiation of an aperture from an obstacle under conditions of motion by three-month-old infants.* Paper presented at the meeting of the Society for Research in Child Development, Boston, MA.

Clarkson, M. G., Clifton, R. K. & Morrongiello, B. M. (1983, April). *Newborns show head orienting toward brief stimuli.* Paper presented at the meeting of the Society for Research in Child Development, Detroit, MI.

Clifton, R. K., Morrongiello, B. M., Kulig, W., & Dowd, J. M. (1981). Newborns' orientation toward sound: Possible implications for cortical development. *Child Development, 52,* 833–841.

Cohen, S. E. (1974). Developmental differences in infants' attentional responses to face-voice incongruity of mother and stranger. *Child Development, 45,* 1155–1158.

Crassini, B., & Broerse, J. (1980). Auditory-visual integration in neonates: A signal detection analysis. *Journal of Experimental Child Psychology, 29,* 144–155.

DiFranco, D., Muir, D., & Dodwell, P. C. (1978). Reaching in very young infants. *Perception, 7,* 385–392.

Dodd, B. (1979). Lip reading in infants: Attention to speech presented in- and out-of-synchrony. *Cognitive Psychology, 11,* 478–484.

Dodwell, P. C., Muir, D., W., & diFranco, D. (1976). Responses of infants to visually presented objects. *Science, 194,* 209–211.

Dodwell, P. C., Muir, D. W., & diFranco, D. (1979). Technical comment: Infant perception of visually presented objects. *Science, 203,* 1138–1139.

Dolgin, K., Premack, D., & Spelke, E. (1980, November). *Evidence of intermodal sensory transfer capacity in infant primates.* Paper presented at the Eastern Regional meeting of the Animal Behavior Society, Binghamton, NY.

Eimas, P. D., Siqueland, E. R., Jusczyk, P., and Vigorito, J. (1971). Speech perception in infants. *Science, 171,* 303–306.

Field, J. (1976a). The adjustment of reaching behavior to object distance in early infancy. *Child Development, 47,* 304–308.

Field, J. (1976b). Relation of young infant's reaching to stimulus distance and solidity. *Developmental Psychology, 12,* 444–448.

Field, J. (1977). Coordination of vision and prehension in young infants. *Child Development, 48,* 97–103.

Field, J., diFranco, D., Dodwell, P., & Muir, D. (1979). Auditory visual coordination in $2\frac{1}{2}$-month-old infants. *Journal of Infant Behavior, 2,* 113–122.

Field, J., Muir, D., Pilon, R., Sinclair, M., & Dodwell, P. (1980). Infants' orientation to lateral sounds from birth to three months. *Child Development, 51,* 295–298.

Field, T., Woodson, R., Greenberg, R., & Cohen, D. (1982). Discrimination and imitation of facial expressions by neonates. *Science, 218,* 179–181.

Francis, P. L., & McCroy, G. (1983, April). *Bimodal recognition of human stimulus configurations.* Paper presented at the meeting of the Society for Research in Child Development, Detroit, MI.

Gallistel, C. R. (1980). *The organization of action: A new synthesis.* Hillsdale, NJ: Erlbaum.

Gibson, E. J. (1969). *Principles of perceptual learning and development.* New York: Appleton.

Gibson, E. J. (1982). The concept of affordances in development: The renascence of functionalism. In W. A. Collins (Ed.), *Minnesota symposia on child psychology: Vol. 15. The concept of development.* Hillsdale, NJ: Erlbaum.

Gibson, E. J. (1983). The development of knowledge about intermodal unity: Two views. In L. S. Liben (Ed.), *Piaget and the foundations of knowledge.* Hillsdale, NJ: Erlbaum.

Gibson, E. J. (1984). Perceptual development from the ecological approach. In A. Brown, M. Lamb, & B. Rogoff (Eds.), *Advances in developmental psychology,* Vol. 30. Hillsdale, NJ: Erlbaum.

Gibson, E. J., Owsley, C. J., & Johnston, J. (1978). Perception of invariants by five-month-old infants: Differentiation of two types of motion. *Developmental Psychology, 14,* 407–415.

Gibson, E. J., Owsley, C. J., Walker, A., & Megaw-Nyce, J. (1979). Development of perception of invariants: Substance and shape. *Perception, 8,* 609–619.

Gibson, E. J., & Spelke, E. S. (1983). The development of perception. In J. H. Flavell & E. M. Markman (Eds.), *Handbook of child psychology: Vol. 3. Cognitive development.* New York: Wiley.

Gibson, E. J., & Walk, R. D. (1960). The "visual cliff." *Scientific American, 202,* 64–71.

Gibson, E. J., & Walker, A. (1984). Development of knowledge of visual and tactual affordances of substance. *Child Development, 55,* 453–460.

Gibson, J. J. (1966). *The senses considered as perceptual systems.* Boston, MA: Houghton-Mifflin.

Gibson, J. J. (1976). Commentary on "The relation between audition and vision in the human newborn," by M. J. Mendelson & M. M. Haith. *Monographs of the Society for Research in Child Development, 41*(Serial No. 167).

Gibson, J. J. (1979). *The ecological approach to visual perception.* Boston, MA: Houghton Mifflin.

Gordon, F. R., & Yonas, A. (1976). Sensitivity to binocular depth information in infants. *Journal of Experimental Child Psychology, 22,* 413–422.

Gottfried, A. W., Rose, S. A., & Bridger, W. H. (1977). Crossmodal transfer in human infants. *Child Development, 48,* 118–123.

Gunderson, V. M. (1983). Development of cross-modal recognition in infant pigtail monkeys (macaca Nemestrina). *Developmental Psychology, 19,* 398–404.

Hammer, M., & Turkewitz, G. (1975). Relationship between effective intensity and directional eye-turns in the human newborn. *Animal Behaviour, 23,* 287–290.

Hatwell, Y. (in press). *La fonction perceptive de la main.* Lille, France: Presses Universitaires de Lille.

Hochberg, J. (1979). Sensation and perception. In E. Hearst (Ed.), *The first century of experimental psychology.* Hillsdale, NJ: Erlbaum.

Humphrey, K., Tees, R. C., & Werker, J. (1979). Auditory-visual integration of temporal relations in infants. *Canadian Journal of Psychology, 33,* 347–352.

Kellman, P. J., & Spelke, E. S. (1983). Perception of partly occluded objects in infancy. *Cognitive Psychology, 15,* 483–524.

Klein, R. M. (1977). Attention and visual dominance: A chronometric analysis. *Journal of Experimental Psychology: Human Perception and Performance, 3,* 365–375.

Kuhl, P., & Meltzoff, A. N. (1982). The bimodal perception of speech in infancy. *Science,* *218,* 1138–1140.

Lasky, R. E. (1977). The effect of visual feedback of the hand on the reaching and retrieval behavior of young infants. *Child Development, 48,* 112–117.

Lawson, K. R. (1980). Spatial and temporal congruity and auditory-visual integration in infants. *Developmental Psychology, 16,* 185–192.

Lee, D. N., & Aronson, E. (1974). Visual proprioceptive control of standing in human infants. *Perception and Psychophysics, 15,* 529–532.

Lishman, T. R., & Lee, D. N. (1975). The autonomy of visual kinesthesis. *Perception, 2,* 287–294.

Lockman, J. J., Ashmead, D. N., & Bushnell, E. W. (1984). The development of anticipatory hand orientation during infancy. *Journal of Experimental Child Psychology, 37,* 176–186.

Lyons-Ruth, K. (1977). Bimodal perception in infancy: Responses to auditory-visual incongruity. *Child Development, 48,* 820–827.

MacKain, K., Studdert-Kennedy, M., Spieker, S., & Stern, D. (1983). Infant intermodal speech perception is a left hemisphere function. *Science, 219,* 1347–1349.

McDonnell, P. M. (1975). The development of visually guided reaching. *Perception and Psychophysics, 19,* 181–185.

McDonnell, P. M. (1979). Patterns of eye-hand coordination in the first year of life. *Canadian Journal of Psychology, 33,* 253–267.

McGurk, H., & MacDonald, J. (1978). Auditory-visual coordination in the first year of life. *Infant Behavior and Development, 1,* 229–240.

McGurk, H., Turnure, C., & Creighton, S. J. (1977). Auditory-visual coordination in neonates. *Child Development, 48,* 138–143.

Meltzoff, A. N., & Borton, R. W. (1979). Intermodal matching by human neonates. *Nature (London), 282,* 403–404.

Meltzoff, A., & Moore, M. K. (1977). Imitation of facial and manual gestures by human neonates. *Science, 198,* 75–78.

Mendelson, M. J. (1979). Acoustic-optical correspondence and auditory-visual coordination in infancy. *Canadian Journal of Psychology, 33,* 334–346.

Mendelson, M. J., & Ferland, M. B. (1982). Auditory-visual transfer in four-month-old infants. *Child Development,* 1022–1027.

Mendelson, M. J., & Haith, M. M. (1976). The relation between audition and vision in the human newborn. *Monographs of the Society for Research in Child Development, 41*(Serial No. 167).

Miller, C. L., & Horowitz, F. D. (1980, April). *Integration of auditory and visual cues in speaker classification by infants.* Paper presented at the International Conference on Infant Studies, New Haven, CT.

Morrongiello, B. A. & Clifton, R. K. (1984). Effects of sound frequency on behavioral and cardiac orienting in newborn and five-month-old infants. *Journal of Experimental Child Psychology, 38,* 429–446.

Muir, D., Abraham, W., Forbes, B., & Harris, L. (1979). The ontogenesis of an auditory localization response from birth to four months of age. *Canadian Journal of Psychology, 33,* 320–333.

Muir, D., & Field, J. (1979). Newborn infants orient to sounds. *Child Development, 50,* 431–436.

Piaget, J. (1951). *Play, dreams and imitation in childhood.* New York: Norton.

Piaget, J. (1952). *The origins of intelligence in children.* New York: Norton.

Piaget, J. (1954). *The construction of reality in the child.* New York: Basic Books.

Piaget, J. (1969). *The mechanisms of perception.* London: Routledge.

Radeau, M., & Bertelson, P. (1977). The aftereffects of ventriloquism. *Quarterly Journal of Experimental Psychology, 26,* 63–71.

Rader, N., Bausano, M., & Richards, T. E. (1980). On the nature of the visual-cliff avoidance response in human infants. *Child Development, 51,* 61–68.

Rader, N., & Stern, J. D. (1982). Visually elicited reaching in neonates. *Child Development, 53,* 1004–1009.

Richards, J. E., & Rader, N. (1981). Crawling onset age predicts visual cliff avoidance in infants. *Journal of Experimental Psychology: Human Perception and Performance, 7,* 382–387.

Rock, I., & Victor, J. (1964). Vision and touch: An experimentally created conflict between the senses. *Science, 143,* 594–596.

Rolfe, S. A., & Day, R. H. (1981). Effects of the similarity and dissimilarity between familiarization and test objects on recognition memory in infants following unimodal and bimodal familiarization. *Child Development, 52,* 1308–1312.

Rose, S. A., Gottfried, A. W., & Bridger, W. H. (1981). Crossmodal transfer in infants: Relationships to prematurity and socio-economic background. *Developmental Psychology, 17,* 90–97.

Rozin, P. (1976). The evolution of intelligence and access to the cognitive unconscious. *Progress in Psychobiology and Physiological Psychology, 6,* 245–279.

Ruff, H. A., & Halton, A. (1978). Is there directed reaching in the human neonate? *Developmental Psychology, 14,* 425–426.

Ruff, H. A., & Kohler, C. J. (1978). Tactual visual transfer in 6-month-old infants. *Infant Behavior and Development, 1,* 259–264.

Schiff, W. (1965). The perception of impending collision: A study of visually directed avoidant behavior. *Psychological Monographs, 79,* No. 604.

Schonen, S. de (1977). Functional asymmetries in the development of bimanual coordination in human infants. *Journal of Human Infant Studies, 3,* 144–156.

Schwartz, B. (1978). *Psychology of learning and behavior.* New York: Norton.

Spelke, E. S. (1976). Infants' intermodal perception of events. *Cognitive Psychology, 8,* 533–560.

Spelke, E. S. (1979). Perceiving bimodally specified events in infancy. *Developmental Psychology, 15,* 626–636.

Spelke, E. S. (1981). The infant's acquisition of knowledge of bimodally specified events. *Journal of Experimental Child Psychology, 31,* 279–299.

Spelke, E. S. (1983). Constraints on the development of intermodal perception. In L. S. Liben (Ed.), *Piaget and the foundations of knowledge.* Hillsdale, NJ: Erlbaum.

Spelke, E. S. (1985). Preferential looking methods as tools for the study of cognition in infancy. In G. Gottlieb & N. Krasnegor (Eds.), *Measurement of audition and vision in human infancy.* Norwood, NJ: Ablex.

Spelke, E. S., Born, W. S., & Chu, F. (1983). Perception of moving, sounding objects in infancy. *Perception, 12,* 719–732.

Spelke, E. S., & Cortelyou, A. (1981). Perceptual aspects of social knowing: Looking and listening in infancy. In M. E. Lamb & L. R. Sherrod (Eds.), *Infant social cognition.* Hillside, NJ: Erlbaum.

Spelke, E. S., & Owsley, C. J. (1979). Intermodal exploration and knowledge in infancy. *Infant Behavior and Development, 2,* 13–28.

Stern, D. N., Beebe, B., Jaffe, J., & Bennett, S. L. (1977). The infants' stimulus world during social interaction: A study of caregiver behaviors with particular reference to repetition and timing. In H. R. Schaffer (Ed.), *Studies in mother-infant interaction.* New York: Academic Press.

Streri, A. (1985, July). *Tactile discrimination of form in 2- to 3-month-old infants: Is cross-modal transfer to vision possible?* Paper presented to the International Society for the Study of Behavioral Development, Tours, France.

Streri, A., & Pêcheux, M.-G. (1986). Tactual habituation and discrimination of form in infancy: A comparison with vision. *Child Development, 57,* 100–104.

Streri, A., & Pêcheux, M.-G. (in press). Vision to touch and touch to vision transfer of form in 5-month-old infants. *British Journal of Developmental Psychology.*

Trevarthen, C. (1974). The psychobiology of speech development. *Neurosciences Research Program Bulletin, 12,* 570–585.

Turkewitz, G., Birch, H. G., & Cooper, K. K. (1972). Responsiveness to simple and complex auditory stimuli in the human newborn. *Developmental Psychology, 5,* 7–19.

Turkewitz, G., Birch, H. G., Moreau, T., Levy, L., & Cornwell, A. C. (1966). Effect of intensity of auditory stimulation on directional eye movements in the human neonate. *Animal Behaviour, 14,* 93–101.

Twitchell, T. E. (1965). The automatic grasping responses of infants. *Neuropsychologia, 3,* 247–259.

von Fieandt, K., & Gibson, J. J. (1959). The sensitivity of the eye to two kinds of continuous transformations of a shadow pattern. *Journal of Experimental Psychology, 57,* 344–347.

von Helmholtz, H. (1962). J. P. C. Southall (Ed.), *Treatise on physiological optics* (Vol. 3). New York: Dover. (Original work published 1885)

von Helmholtz, H. (1970). The origin of the correct interpretation of our sensory impressions. In R. M. Warren & R. P. Warren (Eds.), *Helmholtz on perception: Its physiology and development.* New York: Wiley. (Original work published 1884).

von Hofsten, C. (1977). Binocular convergence as a determinant of reaching behavior in infancy. *Perception, 6,* 139–144.

von Hofsten, C. (1979). Development of visual directed reaching: The approach phase. *Journal of Human Movement Studies, 5,* 160–178.

von Hofsten, C. (1980). Predictive reaching for moving objects by human infants. *Journal of Experimental Child Psychology, 30,* 369–382.

von Hofsten, C. (1982). Eye-hand coordination in newborns. *Developmental Psychology, 18,* 450–461.

von Hofsten, C., & Fazel-Zandy, S. (1984). Development of visually guided hand orientation in reaching. *Journal of Experimental Child Psychology, 38,* 208–219.

von Hofsten, C., & Lindhagen, K. (1979). Observations on the development of reaching for moving objects. *Journal of Experimental Child Psychology, 28,* 158–173.

Walk, R. D., & Gibson, E. J. (1961). A comparative and analytical study of visual depth perception. *Psychological Monographs, 75,* No. 15.

Walker, A. S. (1980). *The perception of facial and vocal expressions by human infants.* Unpublished doctoral thesis, Cornell University, Ithaca, NY.

Walker, A. S. (1982). Intermodal perception of expressive behaviors by human infants. *Journal of Experimental Child Psychology, 33*, 514–535.

Walker, A. S., Gibson, E. J., Owsley, C. J., Megaw-Nyce, J., & Bahrick, L. E. (1980). Detection of elasticity as an invariant property of objects by young infants. *Perception, 9*, 713–718.

Welch, R. B., & Warren, R. H. (1980). Immediate perceptual response to intersensory discrepancy. *Psychological Bulletin, 88*, 638–667.

Wertheimer, M. (1961). Psychomotor coordination of auditory and visual space at birth. *Science, 134*, 1692.

White, B. L., Castle, P., & Held, R. (1964). Observations on the development of visually directed reaching. *Child Development, 35*, 349–364.

Yonas, A. (1979). Studies of spatial perception in infancy. In A. D. Pick (Ed.), *Perception and its development: A tribute to Eleanor J. Gibson.* Hillsdale, NJ: Erlbaum.

Yonas, A. (1981). Infants' responses to optical information for collision. In R. N. Aslin, J. R. Alberts, & M. R. Peterson (Eds.), *The development of perception: Vol. 2. The visual system.* New York: Academic Press.

Yonas, A., Bechtold, A. G., Frankel, D., Gordon, F. R., McRoberts, G., Norcia, A., & Sternfels, S. (1977). Development of sensitivity to information for impending collision. *Perception and Psychophysics, 21*, 97–104.

Yonas, A., & Granrud, C. E. (1985). Development of depth sensitivity in infants. In J. Mehler & R. Fox (Eds.), *Neonate cognition: Beyond the blooming, buzzing confusion.* Hillsdale, NJ: Erlbaum.

Yonas, A., Pettersen, L., Lockman, J., & Eisenberg, P. (1980, April). *The perception of impending collision in three-month-old infants.* Paper presented at the International Conference on Infant Studies, New Haven, CT.

7

Perception of Speech and Sound in Early Infancy

PATRICIA K. KUHL
Department of Speech and Hearing Sciences and
Child Development and Mental Retardation Center
University of Washington
Seattle, Washington 98195

I. INTRODUCTION

There are two characterizations of infants' "initial state" regarding speech perception. One argues that infants enter the world equipped with mechanisms specially evolved for the perception of speech—that they are endowed with an "innate phonetics." By this account, infants are born with a "speech module" (Fodor, 1983), a device specially designed to decode the complex and intricate acoustic signals used by human beings to communicate with one another.

The other characterization of infants' initial state argues that infants begin life without specialized mechanisms dedicated to speech, and that infants' initial responsiveness to speech can be attributed to their more general sensory and cognitive abilities. On this view, infants do not initially process speech in a language-specific way. They only gradually develop a phonetic-level representation of speech, perhaps in attempting to learn the mapping between acoustic cues and word meanings.

Proponents of both positions agree that infants' early responsiveness to speech is quite remarkable. But they differ in the degree to which they believe an infant's demonstration of a particular phenomenon mandates the attribution of "special mechanisms" to infants. Thus, proponents of

HANDBOOK OF INFANT
PERCEPTION, VOLUME 2

the two positions do not differ with regard to the facts about what infants can do, but do differ with regard to their willingness to impute specially evolved mechanisms to infants, based on what they do.

The purpose of this chapter is to explain how these two characterizations came about, and demonstrate how a series of experiments directly bear on our interpretation of infants' behaviors. As I will show, the pendulum has swung between the two alternatives in the 15 years since the initial study was published. The field moved first toward, and then subsequently against, attributing specialized mechanisms to infants. Now new data exist providing different evidence of infants' early sophistication in their perception of speech, once again making it tempting to attribute a "phonetic level" to infants.

Before focusing on this debate there are some preliminaries that are essential. For example, we will need to describe the techniques used to study infant audition, as well as to review briefly what is known about the infant's ability to perceive simple nonspeech sounds. We will examine the data on auditory thresholds for pure tones of various frequencies, and data on the infant's ability to resolve differences in frequency, intensity, and duration. In addition, some understanding of the mechanisms of speech production, of the acoustic events which result from articulatory movements, and of the linguistic nature of speech, must precede any description of the experiments on infants. Speech perception is a technical field, and familiarity with certain terms and concepts in speech production (glottis, laryngeal vibration, vocal tract, resonances, and antiresonances), speech acoustics (spectrogram, fundamental frequency, formant, voice-onset time), and linguistics (phoneme, distinctive feature, prosody, stress, intonation contour), is essential to the arguments; they are briefly discussed.

This is a discipline in which precision makes a difference. A 20-msec change in "voice-onset time" provides an acoustic "cue" that reliably changes perception from "bat" to "pat," and infants respond to this change in a linguistically relevant manner at birth. Perhaps this intriguing fact will motivate the reader to attempt to digest the enormous number of details that necessarily precede the discussion of the issues and the data.

II. BACKGROUND ON THE STUDY OF SPEECH PERCEPTION

A. Speech as an Acoustic Signal

1. The Acoustics of Speech Production

The production of sound by the human vocal tract has been studied extensively (Minifie, 1973; Shoup, Lass, & Kuehn, 1982). Briefly, the vocal tract system functions as a tube with one end closed (the glottis) and the other open (the lips). The source of sound is typically periodic vocal-fold vibration at the glottis. It consists of a pure tone at the fundamental frequency of the talker's voice, and the fundamental's harmonics. A sound source can also be generated within the vocal tract itself. For example, an aperiodic signal (noise) can be created at a point of constriction in the vocal tract, as in the production of a fricative sound like /s/.

Regardless of the type of sound source, the acoustic energy is modified by the shape of the vocal tract. The tract acts as a filter, producing resonances (frequency regions in which the energy is passed freely) and antiresonances (frequencies in which the energy is suppressed). When producing a speech sound, the tract adopts a characteristic shape, thus creating particular concentrations of energy along the frequency scale that correspond to the resonant frequencies of the vocal tract. These regions of high energy concentration are called "formants." When the vocal tract remains steady, as when a particular vowel sound (like the /a/ in "pop") is sustained, these resonances (and thus the formants) remain fairly constant. In ongoing speech, however, the vocal tract shape changes vary rapidly as the tongue darts from target to target. Therefore the formant frequencies almost never remain constant.

Early research on speech perception focused on single syllables, attempting to identify the acoustic information (the "cues") responsible for phonetic perception. Perception was shown to depend on the locations of formants, and particularly on the very rapid (20–100 msec) formant transitions that occur in speech. Formants are represented as dark bands on spectrographic displays and are numbered in sequence from the lowest frequency to the highest frequency. Figure 1 illustrates the vocal tract configuration for the three "point" vowels (/i, a, u/), so named because they represent acoustic and articulatory extremes. A spectrographic (frequency over time) display of each vowel is also shown. The formant frequencies are seen as dark bands in the spectrographic display and they are numbered consecutively starting with the lowest frequency.

These three displays represent the acoustic results of maintaining a static posture while sustaining a vowel sound. If a phrase is produced, the changing formant transitions reflect the altered resonances that are created as the articulators move to and from various target positions. Figure 2 shows a spectrographic display of the author producing the phrase "Handbook of Infant Perception." As shown, the formant frequencies are rarely constant.

2. Acoustic Cues for Segmental Features: Some Examples

Early experiments in the field painstakingly detailed the portions of the acoustic signal that governed the perception of various speech features.

Vocal Tract Configuration

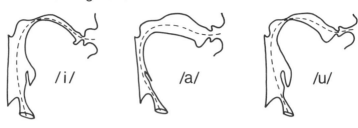

Formant Frequency Configuration

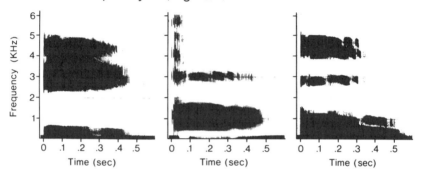

Figure 1. Vocal tract configurations for the three "point" vowels (/i, a, u/). A spectrographic (frequency over time) display of each vowel is shown.

These studies were accomplished in four steps and always involved single isolated syllables. The four steps consisted of: (a) contrasting natural speech utterances differing by one linguistic feature such as /ba/ and /pa/; (b) forming hypotheses, by visual inspection of the spectrograms, concerning the "critical cues" for the particular speech feature; (c) synthesizing the syllables using only the acoustic features hypothesized to be critical; and (d) testing the perception of the newly created syllables. These four steps—analyze, hypothesize, synthesize, test—still form the research plan for work in speech acoustics. The main difference is that each step in the early work was accomplished using fairly crude techniques. Speech was analyzed on a sound spectrograph rather than a digital computer (Potter, Kopp, & Green, 1947). It was "synthesized" by painting on the "Pattern Playback," a machine invented for speech that converted the patterns drawn at various points on the frequency scale into a sound with corresponding frequency components (Delattre, Liberman, Cooper, & Gerstman, 1952). The test phase was accomplished by simply having the investigators judge whether or not the synthesized syllable could be appropriately identified, rather than by conducting a formal study.

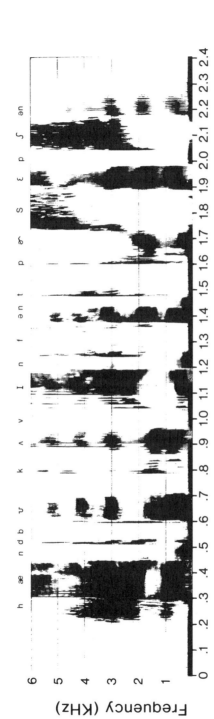

Figure 2. Spectrographic display of a female talker producing the phrase "Handbook of Infant Perception."

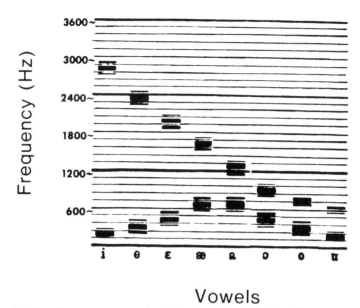

Vowels

Figure 3. Two-formant patterns painted for the "Pattern Playback." When reproduced they are perceived as the English vowels /i/ as in "beat," /e/ as in "bait," /ɛ/ as in "bet," /ae/ as in "bat," /a/ as in "bottle," /ɔ/ as in "bought," /o/ as in "boat," and /u/ as in "boot." (Adapted from Delattre et al., 1952.)

The results of this early work produced valuable descriptions of the acoustic events underlying phonetic perception. For example, early studies showed that the locations of the first two formants were sufficient to distinguish among the vowels (Delattre et al., 1952), even though in natural speech four formants can often be identified. Figure 3 shows two-formant patterns painted on the Pattern Playback. When played, they reproduce eight of the most common English vowels. A comparison of Figures 1 and 3 shows that while as many as four formants can be seen in the natural speech spectrograms, two formants are sufficient to distinguish the vowels.

The acoustic events underlying the perception of consonants were also identified. These studies demonstrated that the perception of individual linguistic features, such as the "place of articulation" and the "manner of articulation," were governed by different aspects of the acoustic signal. Moreover, studies using synthesized utterances showed that even though naturally produced syllables contrasted in a number of ways, single isolated cues were sufficient for indicating a particular feature value. For example, perception of the place feature, which specifies the location of

Natural

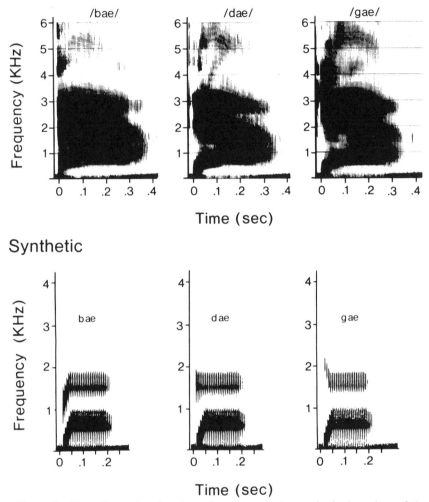

Synthetic

Figure 4. Naturally produced and two-formant computer synthesized versions of the syllables /bae/, /dae/, and /gae/.

the major constriction in the vocal tract, depends primarily on the frequency content of the "burst" and the initial formant transitions (Blumstein & Stevens, 1980). Studies using synthesized speech showed, however, that the second-formant transition was a sufficient cue for distinguishing the place feature (Delattre, Liberman, & Cooper, 1955). In

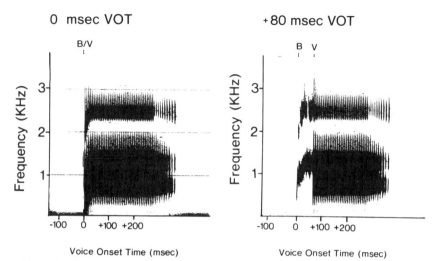

Figure 5.   Computer-synthesized syllables representing /ba/ (0 msec VOT) and /pa/ (+80 msec VOT) in English.

Figure 4, the natural syllables /bae/, /dae/, and /gae/ are contrasted with their two-formant synthesized versions.

Perception of the manner feature, which indicates major distinctions in the ways sounds are produced, was generally associated with changes in the first formant. For example, the distinction between "voiced" and "voiceless" sounds produced with the same place of articulation (e.g., /b/ vs. /p/) were related to an acoustic dimension called "voice-onset time" (VOT). In English, voiced sounds are characterized by the simultaneous occurrence of periodic laryngeal vibration (voicing) and the onset of the syllable; in voiceless stops, voicing is delayed relative to the initiation of the syllable. Measurements of VOT indicate the difference (in msec) between the onset of voicing (seen in the first formant) and the onset of the syllable (seen as a burst of frequency information that occurs when the stop is released).

In Figure 5, two-formant synthetic versions of the syllables /da/ and /ta/ are shown. The onset of voicing (V) and the onset of the burst (B) are marked for each syllable. Notice that the delay of voicing produces a "cut-back" in the first formant of the voiceless sounds relative to their voiced counterparts. This cutback of the first formant produces the timing difference between voiced and voiceless sounds that is measured in msec of VOT. Voiced sounds typically have a VOT of between 0 and +35 msec, depending on the place of articulation. Voiceless sounds have a VOT of between +30 and +150 msec.

Taken together, the spectrograms in Figures 4 and 5 illustrate two points. First, acoustic cues that are sufficient to govern the perception of linguistic features have been identified, and second, the perception of linguistic features is governed by what appear to be independent aspects of the acoustic signal.

To summarize, during the first 30 years of work in the this area, much was learned about the acoustics of speech. For each speech feature a detailed set of acoustic events that were sufficient to govern perception was described. However, as we will discuss in a later section (II.B.2.b), this did not completely solve the problem of listeners' perception of speech. The same acoustic event was shown to be sufficient to govern perception of different phonetic segments, and quite diverse acoustic events were shown to be equivalent in their potential for indicating the same phonetic value. These findings led to arguments suggesting that in order to account for the listener's ability to perceive the phonetic structure of language, it was necessary to posit the existence of special mechanisms that evolved to analyze speech.

3. Acoustic Cues for Prosodic Features

In speech we perceive two distinct aspects of the sound, the phonetic identity of the sound units and the "prosody" of the utterance. As just reviewed, the identities of the sound units are determined by the pattern of formant frequencies over time. Prosody refers to the stress and intonation pattern of speech. The acoustic cues underlying the perception of prosody are also complex. The perception of stress is dictated by the relative values of three parameters—duration, intensity, and fundamental frequency—when compared across syllables. Stressed syllables are typically longer, louder, and higher in pitch (Lehiste, 1976). Figure 6 illus-

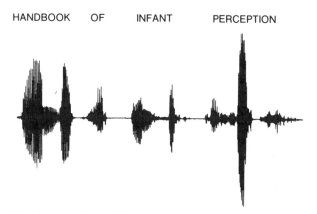

HANDBOOK   OF   INFANT   PERCEPTION

Figure 6. Waveform envelope of the phrase "Handbook of Infant Perception." Each syllable produces an amplitude "burst." As indicated by the increased amplitude, primary stress occurred on the two syllables of "Handbook" and on the second syllable of "Perception."

trates the waveform envelope of the phrase "Handbook of Infant Perception." The waveform envelope provides information about the amplitude contour over time. Each syllable produces an amplitude "burst." The waveform envelope indicates that both syllables in the word "Handbook," and the second syllable in the word "Perception," received primary stress. These syllables were more intense than those surrounding them, and, while this is not shown, were spoken with a higher fundamental frequency.

Another prosodic characteristic of speech is its intonation (pitch) contour. A simple difference in intonation contour differentiates sentences produced with a "declarative" as opposed to an "interrogative" contour. The former is characterized by a rise-fall intonation contour while the latter has a rising intonation contour. The perception of pitch contour is primarily determined by the fundamental frequency, that is, the frequency of glottal vibration. However, higher-level linguistic variables play a role in its perception as well (Lieberman, 1967).

Variations in a sound's identity and its prosody are accomplished by two independent mechanisms in speech production. Changes in the formant frequencies of a sound (which govern the perception of identity) are due solely to alterations in the shape of the upper vocal tract. Changes in the pitch or stress of an utterance are effected by alterations at the level of the glottis. Thus, two different vocal tract postures (resulting in two different vowel sounds, like an /a/ and an /i/, can be produced with identical stress and intonation contour. Similarly, the same vocal-tract posture (vowel sound) can be produced with two different stress patterns and intonation contours. These two distinct parts of the speech production mechanism—the vocal tract and the glottis—produce events that are phenomenally separated in perception. We perceive the identity of the sound as well as the prosody of the sound, and the two are perceived as independent events.

B. Speech as a Linguistic Signal

1. Levels of Processing

Models of speech perception have been strongly influenced by information-processing models of perception (Haber, 1969; Neisser, 1966). These models argue that perception involves hierarchically organized stages in which information is successively transformed, reduced, and stored. At each level, information about the signal is recoded in successively more abstract forms. While these stages in processing must in some way be temporally successive, the data suggest that decisions at higher levels strongly influence processing at earlier stages, so the information must be processed in parallel.

A number of models of speech perception based on information-processing have appeared (Pisoni, 1978; Stevens & Halle, 1967; Studdert-Kennedy, 1976). While differing in some major respects, the models agree that there are distinct processing levels involved in the transformation from an acoustic signal to a perceived message. The levels commonly posited (Studdert-Kennedy, 1976) include: (a) auditory, (b) phonetic, (c) phonological, and (d) higher-order linguistic (lexical, syntactic, and semantic). These levels are schematically represented in Figure 7.

The first level, the auditory level, involves the transformation from an acoustic waveform to a neurally encoded signal. Typically, this level was assumed to produce relatively simple, straightforward, frequency-over-time transformations of acoustic signals—ones that would result in a neural representation that was similar to that shown in the sound spectrogram (Liberman & Studdert-Kennedy, 1977; Pisoni, 1978; Studdert-Kennedy, 1976). More recent studies have examined the neural representation of speech sounds in the VIIIth (auditory) nerve in cats (Delgutte, 1980; Kiang, 1980; Sachs & Young, 1979; Young & Sachs, 1979). These data show that formant-frequency information is preserved in the auditory nerve. However, these studies also strongly suggest that the auditory level of analysis does not actually provide a neural representation exactly equivalent to that shown by the sound spectrograph in several important respects. (See Kuhl, 1982 for discussion.)

A second level assumed to operate in the hierarchy was the phonetic level of processing. The necessity for positing this stage of analysis derived from data suggesting that there was no one-to-one relationship between specific acoustic signals and their percepts. These data had a profound influence on the field and served as the catalyst for models which assumed that the phonetic level of analysis involved mechanisms that evolved especially for speech (Liberman, Cooper, Shankweiler, & Studdert-Kennedy, 1967).

A third level posited was the phonological level. It was at this stage that the phonetic units or segments were converted into language-specific groupings, or phonemes. Phonemes are defined as the abstract categories in a language that serve to mark a change in the meaning of an utterance. They are not particular phones or segments, but abstract groupings whose members are functionally equivalent. Language-specific rules would indicate, for example, that in Japanese the phonetic segment /l/ and the phonetic segment /r/ are both derivations of a single phoneme, and therefore do not change the meaning of a word. In English the two phonetic segments form two distinct phonemic categories, and serve to distinguish words such as "rake" and "lake."

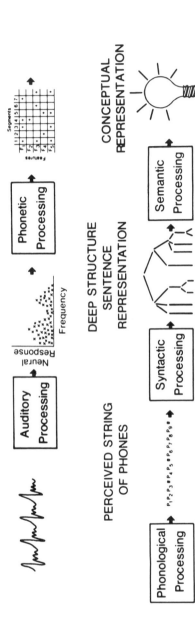

Figure 7. Processing levels commonly posited to exist in the transformation from an acoustic signal to a perceived message. Processing at higher levels is presumed to influence processing at lower levels. (From Kuhl, 1979b.)

A fourth level of analysis included all higher levels of processing such as those involving a lexical search, a syntactic analysis, and a semantic interpretation. Much of the early work on speech perception pointed to the important role that higher-order linguistic constraints played in the perception of speech, both for isolated syllables and for sentences and connected discourse. Numerous studies suggested that information at these higher levels served as knowledge that the listener used to constrain the number of possible messages (e.g., Cole & Jakimik, 1980).

In the first 40 years of speech research on adults most experiments were aimed at the auditory/phonetic level of processing. Moreover, it is at this level that we can direct questions about speech processing toward infants.

2. The Phonetic Level of Processing: A Closer Look

There are several reasons why study at the phonetic level of language seemed a particularly important and scientifically engaging puzzle to work on. First, the phonetic structure of language demonstrated universality. Second, it was amenable to an experimental approach, one which allowed cross-cultural, developmental, and phylogenetic comparisons to be made. Third, the phonetic level demonstrated interesting complexities that paralleled the structure of language at higher levels.

a. *Phonetic Universals.* The phonetic structure of language is diverse but restricted in interesting ways across languages. Certain articulatory maneuvers never appear as phonetic units in the world's languages. Others are very popular. Moreover, the acoustic forms that have been used in the phonetic inventory of language form a restricted set.

Jakobson, Fant, and Halle (1969) described the restrictions and regularities evident in the phonetic structure of language. Consider the "voiced–voiceless" distinction. This distinction is phonemic in most of the world's languages in some form, but its realization illustrates a restricted use of the potential range. This is best illustrated when one examines the acoustic correlates of the voicing feature.

Lisker and Abramson (1964) described a simple acoustic complex, VOT, that adequately separated three voicing categories. Figure 5 displayed synthetic versions of voiced and voiceless syllables as realized in English. Figure 8 shows naturally produced versions of these two plus an example from an additional category used in the world's languages. The additional one exemplifies the "prevoiced" category, and together with the two used in English, the voiceless-unaspirated and voiceless-aspirated categories, comprise the three categories of voicing used nearly universally in the world's languages. For all three, the onset of voicing and the burst of noise produced at the onset of the syllable are marked, and VOT

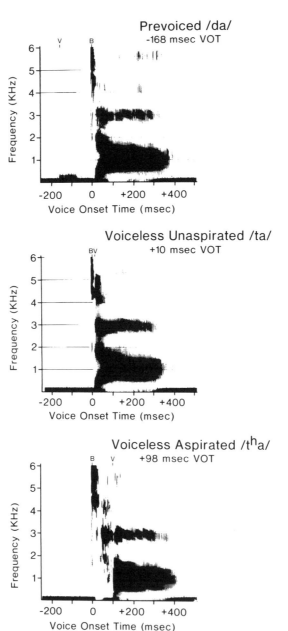

Figure 8. Naturally produced syllables representing three voicing categories commonly used in the world's languages. Most languages use two of the three categories. Spanish and French use the first two, while English and Danish use the last two. The onset of voicing (V) and the onset of the burst (B) are marked.

is indicated. As shown, in prevoiced stops, voicing precedes the onset of the burst. In voiceless-unaspirated stops, voicing and the burst occur nearly simultaneously. In voiceless-aspirated stops, voicing lags the burst considerably.

In most languages, two of these three categories are employed. In English, voiceless-unaspirated and voiceless-aspirated stops are phonemically contrastive, but in French and Spanish, prevoiced stops and voiceless-unaspirated stops are contrastive. In some languages (Thai, for example), all three categories are contrastive. Measurements of VOT in the productions of talkers across 11 different languages revealed a trimodal distribution of VOT's reflecting the average VOT values of the three categories (Lisker & Abramson, 1964). Distributions for the three places of articulation are shown in Figure 9. Notice that the exact location of the peak VOT value shifts slightly with the place of articulation of the stop consonant. The important point here is that speakers across eleven languages do not produce a random distribution of VOT's. Rather, the VOT values are clustered around three points appropriate for the three categories. Thus, the voiced-voiceless distinction is achieved similarly across many different languages and is considered a "phonetic universal."

These restrictions on the articulatory/acoustic events used in the phonetic inventory led to arguments about the nature and origins of the constraints on phonetic structure. What was the nature of the pressure that guided the selection of the phonetic inventory? Were there restrictions in the potential actions performed by the articulators? Or were the constraints auditory in nature? If both played a role, what guided the interactive process? Questions such as these led to the studies that will be described in later sections.

   b. *Characteristics of Speech: A Lack of Linearity and Invariance.* Another aspect motivating research at the phonetic level was its complexity. A simple fact demonstrates the point: Speech cannot be recognized by machine. This is true despite the fact that a great deal of money and efforts by linguists, speech scientists, engineers, psychologists, and psychoacousticians have been devoted to solving the problem. Klatt (1977), writing the final report of a project sponsored by the Department of Defense in which three million dollars a year was spent for five years to provide a breakthrough in speech recognition, shows that limited success was attained only when speech was analyzed within the context of a specific task; that is, tasks in which strong syntactic, semantic, and dialogue constraints were imposed and a limited number of speakers were used. Why is the recognition of speech so difficult?

Chomsky and Miller (1963) described two problems, a lack of "linear-

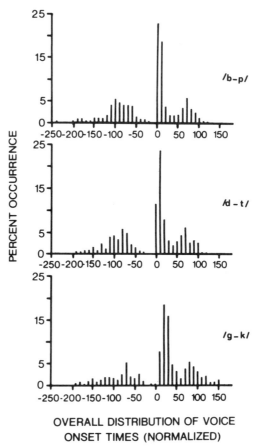

Figure 9. Distributions of VOT values for bilabials (/b-p/), alveolars (/d-t/), and velars (/g-k/) occurring in eleven different languages. VOT is trimodally distributed, reflecting the three voicing categories used throughout the world's languages. (From Lisker and Abramson, 1964.)

ity'' and a lack of ''invariance,'' that account for most of the difficulty in speech recognition. The linearity problem relates to the fact that the sound stream is not temporally segmentable in a way that corresponds to perceived phones. The acoustic events that result in the perception of an ordered string of phones do not occur in a linear, left-to-right order. Reconsider the acoustic representation in Figure 2. The dynamics of articulatory motion are such that while a word must at some level be a preplanned sequence of discrete units, such as a sequence of target articulatory positions, the physiological realization of such a plan results in nearly continuous motion of the articulators with no obvious junctures. Consequently, a continuous time-varying acoustic waveform is produced—one that is not easily segmented into words, syllables, or phonemes using physical criteria. Moreover, the acoustic cues are not organized in a left-to-right manner such that they relate temporally to the perceived string of phones. Acoustic events both preceding and following a phonetic segment may carry information critical to its identity. Studies have shown that information that is remote from a phonetic unit—in fact occurring after the unit—affects its identity (Miller & Liberman, 1979).

Second, a particular acoustic event in speech is not related in a one-to-one fashion to the phonetic percept it invokes. Phonetic units are multiply cued and the cues are highly context dependent. Early research on speech demonstrated that the acoustic information for phonetic units depended on the phonetic context in which the unit appeared (Liberman et al., 1967), its position in a syllable (Ohman, 1966), and the talker who produced it (Peterson & Barney, 1952). More recent experiments demonstrate that "trading relations" exist between acoustic cues (Best, Morrongiello, & Robson, 1981; Fitch, Halwes, Erickson, & Liberman, 1980). That is, an increase in the value along one acoustic dimension necessitates a decrease in the value along a second acoustic dimension, in order to produce the same perceptual effect. Thus, perception of the phonetic units of speech is neither isotemporal nor isomorphic to its acoustic representation.

C. "Special" Mechanisms and the Importance of Data on Infants

There were two discoveries that formed the basis for the "special mechanisms" claim. The first was the problem just discussed, the complexity of the relationship between the acoustic representation of the signal and phonetic perception. The earliest studies in the field, designed to uncover what was expected to be a relatively simple set of rules relating the acoustic properties of speech to its perception, discovered instead an enormously complex mapping between sound and percept. Specific acoustic events ("cues") were shown to underlie the perception of sound—as witnessed by our eventual ability to artificially create ("synthesize") intelligible speech—but rather than finding the expected one-to-one correspondence between acoustic events and phonetic perception, researchers verified time and again that the rules relating the two were extremely complex. This many-to-one relationship between sound and percept, it was argued, mandated a "special mechanism." Moreover, since the acoustic signal did not appear to provide an invariant set of cues that explained perception, the mechanisms underlying speech perception were thought to be based on recognition of another source of potentially invariant information—the motor movements that produced the sound.

Thus, an articulatory representation was argued to mediate the relation between sound and percept (Liberman et al., 1967).

The second finding which supported the existence of specially evolved mechanisms based on articulation was the discovery of "categorical perception," which is here abbreviated as CP (Studdert-Kennedy, Liberman, Harris, & Cooper, 1970). The CP phenomenon was thought to reflect perception in a "speech mode," since it initially appeared to apply only to the perception of sounds perceived as speech. CP involved the following demonstration. A continuum of sounds was created along which an acoustic dimension was altered in small equal steps. The acoustic cue manipulated was one that distinguished two syllables such as /ba/ and /pa/. Tests showed that while the acoustic dimension changed continuously along the continuum, perception was discontinuous. Adults presented with the stimuli perceived a series of /ba/'s that changed abruptly to a series of /pa/'s. Moreover, the ability to discriminate between sounds taken from the continuum was constrained in a curious way. Adults appeared to be incapable of discriminating syllables that were given the same phonetic label. Yet, they were very good at discriminating two syllables that had been given different phonetic labels, even though they were separated by the same physical difference as the within-category pairs had been. Thus, the discrimination of speech sounds from a continuum exhibited "peaks" and "valleys"—regions where discriminability was enhanced and regions in which discriminability was reduced. Enhanced discriminability occurred at the "boundaries" between phonetic categories, while reduced discriminability occurred within phonetic categories.

Figure 10 shows an example of CP for the /ra-la/ contrast (Miyawaki, Strange, Verbrugge, Liberman, Jenkins, & Fujimura, 1975). An additional point was illustrated by this example. CP occurred only for contrasts that were phonemic in an adult speaker's language. Japanese adults, for whom the /ra-la/ distinction is not phonemic, did not produce the characteristic peak in the discrimination function for /ra-la/ stimuli (Fig. 10, bottom) (Miyawaki et al., 1975). Their ability to discriminate the stimuli hovered near chance. This result provided potent evidence that, in adults, CP was strongly tied to one's phonological categories. Thus, it appeared to be a linguistic phenomenon.

These constraints on the ability to discriminate appeared to be unique to speech—when the acoustic cues that differentiated the speech signals were removed from context and presented in isolation, which in this case involved the isolated third-formant transition, the CP effect was not reproduced for either group (Miyawaki et al., 1975). Thus, it was argued that CP reflected the operation of a mechanism that was specific to speech

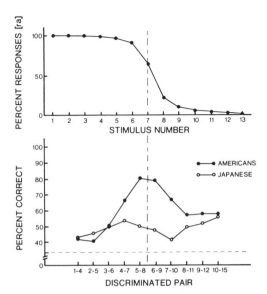

Figure 10. A test of categorical perception in American and Japanese adults. (From Miyawaki et al., 1975.)

rather than one that was associated with general auditory perception. Moreover, since CP was restricted to sounds that could be produced by speakers of a particular language, it was argued to derive from a mechanism based on production (Studdert-Kennedy et al., 1970).

Thus, there was a strong scientific *Zeitgeist* which gave rise to the initial investigation of infant speech perception. In 1971, when the first infant study was published (Eimas, Siqueland, Jusczyk, & Vigorito, 1971), the study of speech perception in adults was only about 20 years old, and the first theory of speech perception integrating these facts—the Motor Theory—had just been described in detail (Liberman et al., 1967). Motor theory made two strong claims about the nature and specificity of the mechanisms involved in the perception of speech. It argued (a) that the perception of speech was accomplished by speech-specific mechanisms—that is, ones that had evolved specifically for the perception of speech, and (b) that these mechanisms were based on an articulatory representation of speech.

It was in this milieu that Eimas et al.'s study was undertaken. Young infants were not yet producing speech. The question was: Do young infants demonstrate CP? Or does it occur only later, after experience in producing (or listening to) speech? The data provided evidence that 1- to 4-month-old infants demonstrated the enhanced discriminability at phonetic boundaries that was typical of CP in adults. As Eimas et al. (1971)

noted, the effect existed ". . . with relatively limited exposure to speech, as well as with virtually no experience in producing these same sounds and certainly with little, if any, differential reinforcement for this form of behavior" (p. 306).

Eimas (1975a) argued that this form of perception was indicative of the infant's biological predisposition to acquire language, and that the effect was attributable to the existence of phonetic feature detectors that were tuned to the acoustic events in speech. He argued that such detectors were part of the biological endowment of the human organism. Later data by Best, Hoffman, and Glanville (1982) revealed that as early as 2 months of age infants demonstrated hemispheric asymmetries for speech signals. The impact of the these abilities was clear. At a very early age, infants partitioned the sound stream in a linguistically relevant way, and processed speech sounds in their right ears better than in their left ears, and this moved theorists toward attributing language-specific mechanisms to infants at birth.

In the decade that followed, many studies were aimed at explaining the basis of CP in adults and infants. Was CP the result of specially evolved mechanisms, or could it be explained in some other way? Renewed attempts to investigate whether or not CP could be explained by more general auditory mechanisms, rather than specially evolved ones, were undertaken.

These tests took two forms. In one, a renewed interest was generated for comparisons between the perception of speech and nonspeech sounds. Previous work had used nonspeech sounds that were not directly analogous to speech, so the new studies attempted to do a better job of mimicking speech sounds while still not allowing them to be perceived as speech. In another set of experiments, the perception of speech by nonhuman animals was examined. Both approaches made contributions to arguments concerning the mechanisms underlying speech perception, but they tested different hypotheses.

Comparisons between speech and nonspeech acoustic signals tested whether or not the mechanisms underlying speech perception were "speech-specific" (e.g., Pisoni, 1977). That is, they tested whether the underlying mechanisms responsible for speech perception were tuned so as to exclude signals that, while mimicking critical acoustic aspects of speech, were not perceived as speech. These experiments will be reviewed in detail in a later section, but the data suggested that the CP effect could be reproduced with nonspeech signals. Thus, whatever the mechanisms underlying phonetic perception, they were not tuned in a sufficiently narrow fashion so as to exclude nonspeech signals that mimicked certain acoustic aspects of speech.

Studies of the perception of speech by nonhuman animals were designed to test a different hypothesis (Kuhl, 1978). These studies posed a new question: Can the CP effect be obtained in the *absence* of specially evolved mechanisms? Animals do not have specially evolved mechanisms for speech. Thus, the argument was that if animals produced the CP effect, then specially evolved mechanisms were not necessary for the effect. Later we will review these data in detail, but they confirmed the hypothesis—the CP effect was reproducible in nonhuman listeners.

These findings had a substantial impact on theory. CP was reproduced in an animal, and this opened up the possibility for the first time that infants might produce the CP effect without access to specially evolved mechanisms. Because animals reproduced CP, theorists began to hesitate before imputing specially evolved mechanisms to human infants solely on the basis of CP. The pendulum began to swing away from the attribution of a "phonetic level" in infants (Eimas & Tartter, 1979; Jusczyk, 1981; Kuhl, 1978; Kuhl & Miller, 1978). There were now two alternative interpretations of infants' responses to speech—infants' responses could be due either to specially evolved mechanisms or simply to infants' general auditory perceptual abilities. Without further data showing that infants were capable of more complex abilities, theorists were left without a strong argument in favor of the idea that mechanisms specially evolved for speech were part of the infant's innate endowment.

In the years that followed, more complex experiments were undertaken with infants in an attempt to test the notion that infants' abilities should be attributed to mechanisms subserving language-specific processes rather than simply to those subserving more general auditory perceptual processes. In the sections that follow we will review the data and arguments in greater detail. We will also examine new findings on infants, ones that go beyond CP and again ask the question: Do any of the abilities demonstrated by infants require special mechanisms? Should we impute a "phonetic level" to infants at birth?

D. Summary

Research on speech has focused largely on perception at the phonetic level. There are three reasons for this. First, the phonetic level provided evidence of linguistic universals. The phonetic units of the world's languages are drawn from a restricted set of articulatory and acoustic types. This suggests that the phonetic level was constrained either by basic articulatory abilities, by auditory abilities, or by an interaction between the two. The fact that the selection of phonetic units is not random prom-

ised to reveal something fairly basic about the kinds of pressures that led
to the evolution of speech and language. Second, the phonetic level involved an apparently complex representation of information, and as such
mirrored higher levels of language. Finally, the phonetic level was experimentally accessible from birth. Thus, it held the potential for revealing
fundamental principles about man's innate preparedness for language.

Early work with adults identified the acoustic information that governed the perception of specific phonetic units, and in the process, discovered that the perception of speech involved complex interactions among
acoustic events. A lack of acoustic invariance was characteristic of
speech, and this, together with the existence of perceptual phenomena
that were initially presumed to be unique to speech, led to the first theory
of speech perception—the Motor Theory—which held that speech perception was the result of a mechanism that evolved especially for speech.
The theory held that the specialized mechanism depended upon an articulatory representation of speech.

This hypothesis placed infant data at the center of attention. If young
infants failed to demonstrate the perceptual proclivities shown by adults,
prior to their production of speech, this would support the argument that
knowledge acquired while learning to produce speech was essential. If, on
the other hand, infants produced such effects initially, before the production of speech, then such a view would not be supported.

The data showed that very young infants demonstrated the CP effect,
thus dissociating CP from experience in producing phonetic units. At the
same time, however, the data suggested that the mechanisms underlying
CP were part of the infant's biological endowment, and this led to the
attribution of "phonetic feature detectors" to infants. However, subsequent findings demonstrating that these effects were not unique to human
listeners or to speech, moved theoreticians away from the attribution of a
"phonetic level" to infants. In subsequent sections, these historical arguments and data will be reviewed in further detail. In addition, new findings
on infants that address the question of infants' abilities will be described.
First, however, we turn to a description of the techniques used to study
infants' perception of speech.

III. METHODS FOR ASSESSING SPEECH PERCEPTION IN INFANCY

Speech-sound discrimination by young infants has been investigated
using a variety of techniques including both behavioral and electrophysiologic approaches. The electrophysiologic techniques, heart-rate decelera-

tion and auditory-evoked response, have not been used as extensively as the behavioral techniques and have produced somewhat equivocal data on speech (Morse, 1978). The behavioral techniques, on the other hand, are responsible for the large data base on infant speech perception that we now have, and the results produced have been remarkably consistent. These behavioral methods will be briefly described.

There are two techniques that are currently in use in most laboratories: the high-amplitude sucking technique (HAS) and the head-turn technique (HT). The HAS has been widely used since 1969 when Siqueland and Delucia described its use for experiments on visual perception with infants. It was adapted by Eimas et al. (1971) for the study of speech. The head-turn technique was developed for auditory threshold experiments in infants (Wilson, Moore, and Thompson, 1976) and then applied to speech-sound discrimination (Eilers, Wilson, & Moore, 1977). The technique was adapted to study the perception of speech categories by Kuhl (1979a, 1980, 1983) and used as a directional localization technique by Trehub, Schneider, and Endman (1980). Two other techniques employing auditory preference and visual preference will be described when studies are reviewed using these techniques. (See Kuhl, 1985a, for detailed descriptions of methods used in the study of infant speech perception.)

A. The High-Amplitude Sucking Technique (HAS)

The HAS technique has been reviewed in detail by Jusczyk (1985). Briefly, a speech sound is presented to infants each time they produce a sucking response whose amplitude exceeds a criterion. That particular speech sound is presented until the infant's sucking rate drops below some decrement criterion (habituation). Then, experimental infants are presented with a novel speech sound while control infants continue to be presented with the first sound.

Figure 11 demonstrates the procedure. The infant sucks on a blind nipple attached to a pressure transducer. The infant's sucking responses produce pressure changes inside the nipple that are monitored with a standard pressure transducer. The resulting pressure waveforms are shown at the bottom of the figure. An amplitude criterion is set for each infant during a no-sound baseline condition. After the baseline level has been established, a speech sound is presented immediately after each response with a maximum repetition rate of one per second.

Typical data from experimental and control infants are shown in Figure 12. The abscissa is labeled in minutes before and after the shift point (the point at which the sound is changed for experimental infants). During the first minute of contingent sound presentation, the response rate typically

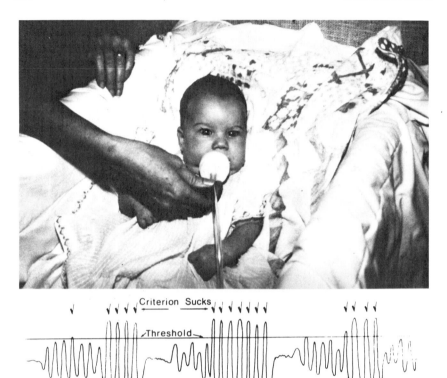

Figure 11. The high-amplitude sucking (HAS) procedure. An eight-week-old infant produces speech sounds by sucking on a nipple. Pressure changes resulting from the infant's sucking responses are monitored. Those exceeding an amplitude criterion trigger the presentation of a speech sound. (From Kuhl, 1976.)

decreases. Most infants appear mildly startled and stop sucking for a moment when the first sounds are presented, as suggested by the decrease in response rate between the baseline minute and the first minute of sound presentation. Eventually, however, the response rate increases and reaches a maximum as infants learn that sucking produces sound. The same speech sound is presented until a 20% decrement in response rate occurs for two consecutive minutes. When this habituation criterion is met, infants in the experimental group are presented with a new sound while infants in the control group continue to hear the first sound. Both the experimental and the control infants are monitored for four minutes after the habituation criterion is met.

Eimas and Miller (1980a) altered the procedure by using a fixed habituation period with all other aspects of the technique identical. Using either

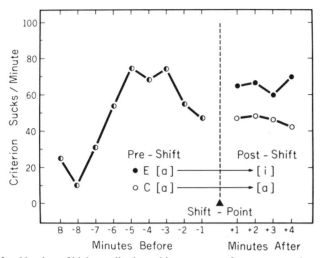

Figure 12. Number of high-amplitude sucking responses from one experimental and one control infant tested in the HAS procedure. Preshift sucking responses for the two infants were averaged. At the shift point, the experimental infant was presented with a new sound. (From Kuhl, 1976.)

of the two habituation rules, the mean response rate for the two minutes immediately preceding the shift is subtracted from the mean response rate for the two or four minutes immediately following the shift to obtain a difference score for each infant. Experimental infants typically increase their response rates when the speech sound is changed (dishabituation) while control infants either continue to decrease or do not change their response rates. Significant differences between the mean difference scores shown by the two groups of infants are taken as evidence that infants of this age can discriminate the two speech sounds.

Two other modifications of the technique have been employed. Spring and Dale (1977) used the same single-stimulus format as that used previously during the preshift period, but alternated the pre- and postshift stimuli during the postshift period. This was done to decrease the memory load in the task. Kuhl (1976; Kuhl & Miller, 1982) also altered the stimulus presentation format, but did so during both the pre- and postshift periods. In this modification, multiple exemplars were presented during both the pre- and postshift phases of the experiment. The purpose of this was to test whether infants could recognize similarity along a particular dimension that the stimuli shared. Such a design allowed other kinds of questions to be answered, such as whether infants were capable of detecting a change in one dimension when a second dimension was constantly varied.

The HAS technique has some limitations (Kuhl, 1985a). The fact that the speech sound serves as the reinforcing stimulus makes it particularly difficult to interpret negative results; one cannot separate infants' inability to discriminate two sounds from a potential lack of interest in them. Second, as currently used, only group data can be obtained. Sucking responses are under the control of diverse factors and, without the no-change control group, increases in sucking responses by the experimental group cannot be interpreted. Third, the high attrition rates (50–60%) prevent one from generalizing the results to all infants at the age under test. Fourth, the technique works best for infants under four months of age. At older ages, infants become restless in infant seats and are not as interested in sucking on a nipple. Nevertheless, most of the early data on infants' perception of speech was obtained using the HAS technique, and the results have proven highly reliable.

B. The Head-Turn Technique (HT)

The Head-Turn Technique (HT) was adapted to study speech-sound discrimination. (See Kuhl, 1985a, for a review of the history of the technique.) In the first speech-discrimination study using HT, Eilers et al. (1977) trained infants to make a head-turn response whenever a speech sound, repeated once every second as a "background" stimulus, was changed to a "comparison" speech sound. A head turn which occurred during the presentation of the comparison stimulus was rewarded with a visual stimulus, a toy monkey that would clap cymbals when activated.

The test situation is shown in Figure 13. Infants are held by a parent so that they face an Assistant located to the infant's right side. The Assistant maintains the infant's attention at midline or directly in front of the Assistant by manipulating a variety of silent toys. A loudspeaker is located at a 90° angle to the Assistant and the visual reinforcer is placed directly in front or on top of the loudspeaker. The visual reinforcer consists of a toy animal housed in a dark plexiglass box so that the animal is not visible until the lights mounted inside the box are illuminated. The Experimenter is in an adjoining control room which also houses equipment (now typically a computer) that presents the stimuli and controls the contingencies.

In the speech-discrimination version of the design, two types of trials, change and control, were run. During a change trial, the stimulus was changed from one speech sound to another speech sound. During control trials, the sound was not changed. For both types of trials, the head turns occurring during a specified observation interval were scored. If a head turn occurred on a change trial, the trial was scored as correct. If a head turn occurred during a control trial, the trial was scored as an error.

The head-turn technique has the advantage of providing individual data; this has been particularly important for clinical application. Its chief

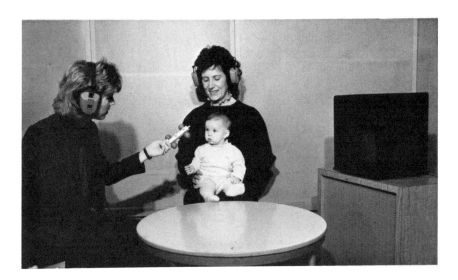

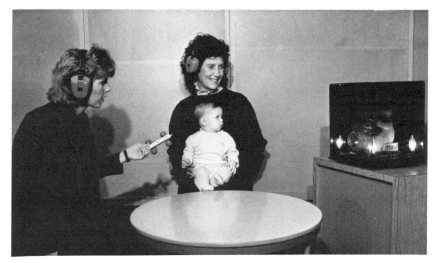

Figure 13. The head-turn technique. Infants are trained to produce a head turn toward a loudspeaker on the infant's left when a "background" sound is changed to a "comparison" sound. If infants do so at the appropriate time, a visual reinforcer (a bear tapping a drum) is lit and activated. (From Kuhl, 1976d.)

limitation is that it has not proven successful with infants under about six months of age. (See Kuhl, 1985a for discussion.) Although it has been used with infants as old as 18 months of age (Eilers et al., 1977), it is ideally suited to infants in the 5.5- to 12-month age range. Beyond this age, infants lose interest in the reinforcer and tend to be increasingly restless. Older infants become interested in other aspects of the situation; they become "object-permanence" wise and seem to expect the monkey to reappear. They sometimes peer in the box when the lights are out looking for the monkey.

Kuhl (1979a) modified the standard HT procedure to study speech-sound categorization in infants. The previous work using HT had focused on infants' abilities to discriminate between two sounds. Kuhl's studies were designed to test infants' recognition of the similarity between discriminably different members representing a phonetic category. Thus, they were designed to test the categorization of speech sounds, the ability to "render discriminably different things equivalent" (Bruner, Goodnow, & Austin, 1956).

The modification involved training infants to respond differentially to two speech tokens, one representing each of two categories. To one stimulus, infants were trained to produce the HT response. To the other, they were trained to inhibit the HT response. Once trained, infants' responses to novel stimuli from both the two speech categories is tested. For example, Kuhl (1979a) tested 6-month-old infants on the discrimination of two vowels, /a/ and /i/, until they met a performance criterion (nine out of 10 consecutive trials correct). Then, novel /a/'s and /i/'s produced by new talkers were introduced. The question was: Would infants categorize the novel /a/'s and /i/'s appropriately? Would they produce head-turn responses to all of the novel members of one of the vowel categories and refrain from producing it to all members of the other vowel category? Using this design, analysis of the infant's response to each novel stimulus the first time it is presented provides data on infants' immediate recognition of category membership for speech sounds.

A different modification of the basic HT procedure was made by Trehub et al. (1980) and Schneider, Trehub, and Bull (1980). This modification was designed to assess auditory thresholds. It involved a directional (left or right) head-turn response. Infants were reinforced for turning towards a sound source, which occurred either to the infant's right or left, whenever they detected it. A trial did not terminate until the infant made a head-turn response of 30° or more either to the left or right. A potential problem associated with this modification as it is applied to threshold measurement is the fact that the ability to localize sound depends in part on the frequency of the signal in adults (Jeffress, 1975). Localization cues are provided by both the signal's differential time of arrival and its differential intensity at the two ears, and use of these two cues is frequency dependent. At low frequencies (below 1500 Hz), timing cues have been shown to be most effective; at high frequencies, intensity differences are most effective. If infants are more sensitive to intensity as opposed to timing cues, they might localize high frequencies better than low frequencies. They would thus respond better to high frequencies in such a test. This may result in lower sensory thresholds at high frequencies that are not attributable to true sensory differences but to infants' ability to localize. This potential confounding of the independent and dependent variables makes the interpretation of such findings more difficult.

C. Summary

Two behavioral techniques, the high-amplitude sucking (HAS) technique and the head-turn (HT) technique (and their adaptations), have been widely used to study infants' responses to speech and sound. The age ranges over which the two techniques can be applied do not overlap. HAS has been used with infants between 1 and 4 months of age; HT has been used with infants between 5.5 and 18 months of age. HAS cannot provide individual data whereas HT can. Negative results are always difficult to interpret, but particularly using the HAS technique because the stimuli under test serve as the reinforcing stimulus.

IV. DEVELOPMENT OF BASIC SENSORY CAPABILITIES

One of the first questions one might ask about the young infant's perception of auditory signals is whether they are capable of detecting the acoustic energy in speech sounds. In other words, do infants demonstrate auditory sensitivity that is sufficient to make speech sounds audible? Given sufficient sensitivity to the acoustic energy in speech, do young infants demonstrate sufficient auditory acuity for frequency, intensity, and duration to differentiate the sounds of speech?

There are very few studies on infant auditory psychophysics, and those that do exist have not always met the minimum criteria for methodological rigor. Our purpose here will be to review exemplary studies in the area, cite the points of disagreement among studies, and highlight the relevance of the findings to the perception of speech.

A. Auditory Sensitivity

1. Pre- and Postnatal Auditory Function

While the precise onset of auditory function *in utero* is unknown, there is evidence that the auditory system is functional before birth. The anatomical and electrophysiologic data (Hecox, 1975) suggest that this is the case, as well as recordings of fetal movements in response to sound. We do not know how fetal responsiveness changes with the intensity and frequency of the sound.

Despite fetal auditory functioning, several factors may limit fetal responsiveness. First, the sounds reaching the fetus are attenuated. The mother's abdominal wall provides considerable attenuation of the sound that is transmitted to the amniotic sac. Walker, Grimwade, and Wood (1971) measured sound transmitted through the abdominal wall and found significant attenuation of frequencies above 1000 Hz. Second, sounds reaching the fetus will be masked by intrauterine noise. Walker et al. (1971) also measured the intensity of intrauterine noise and found it to be approximately 85 dB SPL. This level of ambient noise in the uterine environment would provide significant masking of most sounds, thus potentially precluding stimulation of the fetal auditory system. Third, the fetal auditory system is operating in a fluid-filled environment and the transmission characteristics of such a system are not well understood. Nonetheless, more recent studies (Armitage, Baldwin, & Vince, 1980; Querleu & Renard, 1981) have demonstrated that frequencies under 1000 Hz are transmitted to the amniotic sac with little attenuation. It is possible, then, that the prosodic characteristics of voices might be transmitted to the fetus. This point may be important in explaining the results of experiments which suggest that neonates recognize their mother's voice (Section IX, Voice Recognition).

There are several studies of auditory thresholds in the early postnatal period, though most of the data have been gathered using electrophysiologic techniques. Behavioral studies using good psychophysical techniques have appeared only recently, and involve infants that are 6 months of age or older. These studies have employed either the basic HT procedure or the directional HT technique which is a modification of it (Section III.B).

The threshold sensitivity studies on infants older than 6 months generally support two conclusions. First, infants' thresholds are higher than those of adults. Second, infants' thresholds are less discrepant in the high-frequency region than in the low-frequency region. Regarding the first point, a number of studies report thresholds in infants that are within 10- to 25-dB of adult thresholds (Berg & Smith, 1983; Nozza & Wilson, 1984; Schneider et al., 1980; Sinnott, Pisoni, & Aslin, 1983; Trehub et al., 1980). Furthermore, a number of these studies report that sensitivity to high-frequency signals is better, relative to adult "norms," than sensitivity to low-frequency signals (Nozza & Wilson, 1984; Schneider et al., 1980; Sinnott et al., 1983; Trehub et al., 1980). The latter finding is at variance with earlier data obtained using electrophysiologic techniques and younger infants (Hecox, 1975). These studies suggest that low-frequency hearing is better than high-frequency hearing. No simple explanation can be offered to account for the disagreement concerning differential sensitivity across frequency. The disagreement might be attributed to age differences or to differences inherent in the techniques used at the two ages, or both.

Regarding the behavioral data, Schneider et al. (1980) and Trehub et al. (1980) reported greater sensitivity to high-frequency signals in infants. Schneider et al. reported that infant–adult thresholds were similar at frequencies above 8000 Hz, while the disparity between them at lower frequencies was much greater. Similarly, Trehub et al. (1980) showed that infant-adult discrepancies in sensitivity to octave bands of noise centered at 10,000 Hz and 19,000 Hz were greater for the lower-frequency noise band. Subsequent data on 6-month-olds provided by Nozza and Wilson (1984), and data by Sinnott et al. (1983) on 7- to 11-month-olds, also support this conclusion.

Trehub et al.'s data indicated that thresholds for the low-frequency octave band shown by 6-, 12-, 18-, and 24-month-olds gradually approached those of the adult. This frequency-specific development in sensitivity is in agreement with data provided by Elliott and Katz (1980) and Yoneshige and Elliott (1981), which suggest that auditory sensitivity gradually improves until about 10 years of age, but that low-frequency sensitivity improves to a greater degree.

Trehub et al. (1980) attributed the greater similarity in thresholds at high frequencies to true sensory differences rather than to any other factors. It remains unclear, however, whether infants actually show an improvement in low-frequency sensitivity or whether something else is responsible for the adult–infant differences. One possibility is that the adult "norms" reflect a loss in high-frequency sensitivity. It is well established that high-frequency hearing is fragile. It is first to reflect the damaging effects of exposure to noise in the environment, the effects of ototoxic drugs, and the effects of aging. Bredberg (1968) has reported localized hair-cell loss in the basal turn of the cochlea (responsible for high-frequency hearing) in human adolescents.

Two other nonsensory factors cannot be ruled out in explaining differences between adult and infant thresholds. First, anatomical differences may play a role. Both the size and shape of the pinna and the ear canal, as well as the tympanic membrane and middle-ear cavity, change during early life. These changes alter the resonance characteristics of the outer and inner ear canal and may provide frequency-specific effects. It is possible that the narrower, shorter canal of the infant produces a high-frequency resonance, thus producing more energy in that region and correspondingly lower thresholds.

A second factor is the presence of middle-ear pathology. Only one study (Nozza & Wilson, 1984) used screening procedures (tympanometry) to rule out infants with existing middle-ear infections. Nozza and Wilson tested those infants who failed tympanometry so that he could examine detection thresholds as a function of frequency for infants with middle-ear pathology. He demonstrated that thresholds were considerably higher in infants who failed tympanometry (13 dB higher at 4000 Hz), and also that the infants failing the screening test were more variable as a group than those who passed tympanometry screening. Since middle-ear disease is very common in the first year of life, it is possible that the level of the signal actually reaching the inner ear is attenuated. Whether this accounts for frequency-specific losses is unknown, but the results suggest that infants with middle-ear pathology should be screened out in future studies.

2. Summary

There are no behavioral studies indicating absolute sensitivity as a function of frequency *in utero* or for neonates. Regarding hearing *in utero,* it is clear that infants' auditory systems are functional prior to birth, but the auditory system's ability, in a fluid-filled environment, to transduce frequency and intensity information has not been experimentally examined. In addition, the intrauterine environment is noisy, serving to mask sounds under 85 dB SPL. The abdominal wall provides sufficient attenuation of frequency information above 1000 Hz. For these reasons, it is difficult to estimate the responsiveness of the infant to signals that are likely to reach the fetal auditory system, such as the prosodic characteristics of voices.

In infants 6 months of age and older, the HT technique has been successfully applied to the study of auditory sensitivity as a function of frequency. These studies show that thresholds are generally elevated when compared to adult thresholds, but that the discrepancy is smaller for high frequencies (above 4000 Hz) than for low frequencies. These behavioral results using older infants, which show enhanced high-frequency hearing, differ from the results obtained with electrophysiologic techniques and younger infants, which show enhanced low-frequency hearing. This discrepancy is at present unresolved. Further studies will need to be done before these results can be effectively related.

B. Acuity for Frequency, Intensity, and Duration

There are few data providing estimates of the infant's ability to detect changes in frequency, and no data on their ability to detect changes in intensity or duration. Regarding frequency, two early experiments examined the discrimination of pure-tone signals differing rather substantially in frequency, both using the HAS procedures. Trehub (1973a) tested 5- to 16-week-olds on three contrasts involving frequency differences: a 100 Hz versus 200 Hz square wave, a 1000 Hz versus 2000 Hz square wave, and a 200 Hz versus 1000 Hz sine wave. She found no evidence of discrimination for these contrasts. Two factors may account for this failure to show discrimination. Each of Trehub's contrasts involved octaves, and octave generalization (the perception of a common pitch for signals that involve doubling in frequency) is a well-established phenomenon in musical perception for adult listeners. More recent data are consistent with the notion that infants demonstrate octave generalization (Demany & Armand, 1984). It is possible, then, that the infants did not react to the change in frequency because they too perceived the similarity among signals in octave relationship with one another.

A second possibility is that a change in a pure-tone stimulus, while discriminable, is not sufficiently interesting to provoke the infant's renewed willingness to suck after habituation in the HAS technique. As previously mentioned, negative results are particularly difficult to interpret using this technique, because infants have to not only detect the novel stimulus but be sufficiently interested in it to produce criterion sucking responses. A later study by Wormith, Pankhurst, and Moffitt (1975), again using the HAS technique, makes this latter interpretation less likely. They examined the discrimination of pure tones differing by 200 and 500 Hz (not an octave) in 1-month-olds and provided evidence of discrimination.

More recently, Olsho, Schoon, Sakai, Turpin, and Sperduto (1982a,b) used the HT procedure to estimate difference limens between 1000 and 3000 Hz in 5- to 8-month-olds. They used an adaptive staircase procedure in which infants listened to a pure tone at a particular frequency and were reinforced for making a head-turn when the pure tone changed in frequency. The frequency difference between the two tones was initially 96 Hz. This difference was gradually reduced using a staircase algorithm. The difference limen (dl) was estimated such that it represented the 70% correct point. While the data for individual infants varied considerably, infants reliably detected a 2% change in frequency. Adults generally detect a 1% change in frequency.

In a later study, Olsho (1984) examined infants' difference limens for a greater range of frequencies (250–8000 Hz), using the same procedure. She examined whether infants' difference limens differed for low versus high frequency sounds, just as infants' thresholds do. The results showed that infants' dl's between 200 and 2000 Hz were nearly twice as large as adults' dl's, but at 4000 and 8000 Hz, there was no statistical difference in the Weber fractions (F/F) produced by the two groups. In fact, infants performed better than adults at high frequencies.

As yet, there is no clear explanation of these differences in sensitivity to specific frequencies, nor in the differences in resolution at specific frequencies between infants and adults. For both detection and resolution measures, high-frequency responsiveness is better than low-frequency responsiveness. It is possible that there are true sensory differences between infants and adults, owing perhaps to the fact that the differentiation of cochlear ,structures proceeds from the basal (high-frequency) to the apical (low-frequency) end of the cochlea (Bredberg, 1968). Other possibilities cannot be ruled out, however, such as effects related to the relative "salience" or ability to remember low- versus high-frequency tones. Infants appear to be highly alerted to high-frequency information (IX. Voice Recognition), and this may play a role in tasks such as HT in which infants have to remember the frequency of the stimulus that they are initially trained to respond to. Studies varying the memory load involved in the task may help resolve these issues.

It is clear that there are few studies on infant auditory psychophysics. We are just beginning to see data on infants' abilities to resolve differences in frequency. Studies on infants' resolution of intensity and duration have yet to appear. These studies will make valuable contributions to our knowledge of infant auditory development.

V.   THE DISCRIMINATION OF SPEECH BY INFANTS

A.   Discrimination of Phonetic Contrasts: Single-Syllable Units

One of the first questions one might ask about young infants' speech perception abilities is whether or not they can hear the differences between syllables differing in a single phonetic feature, such as in the words "bat" and "pat." These distinctions are cued by what in physical terms appear to be subtle changes in frequency, intensity, and duration. One might suppose that infants at first require large acoustic differences to evidence discrimination, and only gradually come to rely upon the finer differences which adults are capable of using.

A large number of studies have examined this point. These studies are aimed at determining whether young infants are capable of discriminating two syllables that differ with respect to a single phonetic feature, when the distinction is cued by a single acoustic feature. The attempt to manipulate one acoustic feature while controlling all other acoustic features has been accomplished in one of two ways: either the stimuli are generated by computer, allowing one to isolate and manipulate the acoustic features of each stimulus, or the experimental stimuli are chosen from a large number of naturally produced exemplars such that the noncritical acoustic dimensions are matched as closely as possible.

Each approach has advantages and disadvantages. The use of natural speech is desirable because it contains all of the information critical to its identification, but it is difficult to match two naturally produced syllables on all of the noncritical acoustic dimensions such as duration, loudness, and fundamental frequency. An adult listener's judgment that the two stimuli are matched on all noncritical dimensions is no guarantee that the stimuli are perceptually equivalent on all noncritical dimensions for the infant. In addition, natural speech does not allow the investigator to manipulate the target dimension in small steps; nor does the use of natural speech allow the investigator to control systematically the acoustic cues that are contained in the phonetic unit being examined. In contrast, computer-synthesized stimuli can be perfectly controlled, but they are sometimes of poor quality, making it difficult for untrained listeners to identify them. This problem restricts generalization of the findings from synthetic stimuli to natural ones. Recent progress in speech synthesizers (Klatt, 1980) has led to an ability to produce sounds that older ones could not, such as fricatives and nasals, and also the ability to vary additional parameters and produce speech that sounds more natural. Both approaches can be legitimately used. The choice depends upon the specific question being asked.

In the first study published in the area (Eimas et al., 1971), computer-generated stimuli were used because the question was whether or not 1- and 4-month-old infants discriminated stimuli from a /ba/ - /pa/ continuum that differed by only 20 ms (+20 ms VOT vs. +40 ms VOT). The stimuli were chosen such that adults perceived the stimuli as /ba/ and /pa/, respectively. The results showed that infants demonstrated this ability. The fact that they did so at such an early age was surprising and gave rise to a series of experiments exploring the extent and range of the infant's discriminative capacities. Before the end of the first decade of research, some 30 published studies appeared, involving over 50 different speech contrasts (Kuhl, 1979b).

Studies demonstrated infants' abilities to discriminate between synthetic stop consonants differing in their place of articulation (Eimas, 1974; Morse, 1974), in which the acoustic cue manipulated was the direction and extent of the second and third formant transitions. Infants were shown to discriminate syllables whose second-formant starting frequencies differed by only 230 Hz when the two syllables were labeled by adult listeners as /ba/ and /da/, respectively. Other experiments demonstrated that infants discriminated naturally produced isolated vowels (/a/ vs. /i/ and /i/ vs. /u/) (Trehub, 1973a). Later studies of vowel discrimination provided evidence that infants discriminate synthetically produced vowels that are spectrally similar, such as /i/ versus /ɪ/ (Swoboda, Morse, and Leavitt, 1976).

Studies published by Eimas (1975b) demonstrated that infants discriminate differences in the third-formant transitions of syllables, differences that distinguish the liquids /r/ and /l/ by adult listeners. Discrimination of the duration of the first-formant, an acoustic cue sufficient to change an adult's percept of a syllable from /ba/ to /wa/, was demonstrated by infants (Hillenbrand, Minifie, & Edwards, 1979). The acoustic cues for nasal resonance, sufficient to change an adult's percept from /ba/ to /ma/, was also discriminated by infants under 4 months of age (Eimas & Miller, 1980b). Taken as a whole, these studies suggest that infants between the ages of one and four months are capable of discriminating speech contrasts that involve fine differences in frequency, intensity, and duration, when those acoustic differences underlie the distinctions between phonetic units.

Very few studies reported failures to discriminate, and those that did contained methodological problems that weakened the impact of the studies. Fricative sounds differing in the place of articulation feature (/sa/ vs. /za/ and /fa/ vs. /θa/ were not discriminated by 3-month-olds (Eilers & Minifie, 1975; Eilers et al., 1977). Eilers et al. reported that 6-month-olds and 12-month-olds discriminated the /sa-za/ pair, but not the /fa-θa/ pair. The authors interpreted these results as indicating developmental changes in speech perception. A number of authors, however, disagreed with the conclusion. One objection was related to the clarity of the naturally produced stimuli used in the experiment (Jusczyk, 1981). Adult listeners identified the /fa/ and /θa/ tokens correctly only 70% and 60% of the time, respectively. Also, the method used to obtain the difference scores in the HAS procedure was questioned. It involved comparing the last 4 minutes of the preshift phase with the last 4 minutes of the postshift phase, rather than the last 2 minutes in both instances. Eimas and Tartter (1979) argued that using the last 4 minutes of the preshift would tend to increase the variability, thus potentially obscuring significant differences between the experimental and control groups after the shift point. Independent attempts to replicate Eilers et al.'s result have not been undertaken for the /sa-za/ pair, but Jusczyk, Murray, and Bayly (1979) demonstrated the discrimination of synthesized /fa/ and /θa/ by 2- to 3-month-olds.

In summary, tests of the discrimination of syllables differing by a single phonetic unit by young infants suggest they are capable of discriminating among minimally paired syllables. They do so on the basis of acoustic cues that are sufficient to allow the differentiation of those same syllables by adult listeners. The number and diversity of contrasts that have been successfully discriminated by infants has led to the conclusion that infants under the age of 4 months can discriminate many, perhaps all, of the phonetic distinctions relevant in English (Eilers, 1980; Eimas & Tartter, 1979; Kuhl, 1979b; Morse, 1978). That they are capable of doing so at a very early age, prior to the systematic production of these units, and without the benefit of extensive exposure to these phonetic units, is impressive.

Yet, one should not assume that this ability is generalized to natural environments, in which the phonetic units appear in longer and more complex contexts, or are produced by voices that have more irrelevant (and distracting) acoustic characteristics than the computer's "voice." It would also be incorrect to assume that the abilities demonstrated by infants are the sum total of those required to master English phonology. The data demonstrate only that infants are sensitive to the acoustic differences that are sufficient to distinguish phonetic units in an isolated context. Putting the results in this light is not meant to underplay their importance in language learning but simply to remind the reader that much more than the ability to discriminate sound is required for adultlike speech perception.

B. Discrimination of Phonetic Contrasts: Multisyllabic Units

Tests of infants' abilities to discriminate speech in multisyllable contexts were an attempt to duplicate more natural (and more difficult) listening conditions. In fact, one of the first reported failures to discriminate in the infant speech perception literature was a study involving multisyllabic contrasts (Trehub, 1973b). In this study, infants did not evidence discrimination of the /b-p/ contrast in a three-syllable context, /ataba/ versus /atapa/. Trehub's infants also failed to discriminate a two-syllable contrast in which the temporal order of the syllables was reversed (/mapa/ versus /pama/), but did discriminate another two-syllable contrast, /aba/ versus /apa/. This led to the suggestion that infants may find it much more difficult to discriminate contrasts in longer contexts.

Since that time, a number of studies have examined phonetic contrasts in 2- and 3-syllable contexts. The work on two-syllable contrasts has in each case provided evidence of discrimination. For example, Jusczyk and Thompson (1978) tested discrimination in 8-week-olds using the HAS technique and synthetic stimuli. They showed that infants discriminated two-syllable contrasts such as /daba/ versus /daga/ and /bada/ versus

/gada/. Jusczyk, Copan, and Thompson (1978) extended these two-syllable tests to stimuli containing semivowels, such as /dawa/ versus /daga/
and /wada/ versus /gada/. These studies were important not only from the
standpoint of showing discrimination in a longer context, but because
they showed infants' abilities to discriminate contrasts in medial position.
Since the acoustic cues used to differentiate phonetic contrasts are not
identical in the initial, medial, and final positions of syllables, these studies provided new information on this point as well. Three studies have
now verified the discrimination of phonetic contrasts in even longer contexts, ones typical of multisyllabic words. More importantly, these studies reveal some of the parameters that may be important in enhancing the
discriminability of a phonetic contrast in a longer context.

Goodsitt, Morse, Ver Hoeve, and Cowan (1984) examined two factors
that may affect an infant's ability to detect a change in a longer string of
syllables: (a) the degree of redundancy in the context in which the target
syllable is embedded, and (b) the serial position of the target syllable.
They examined discrimination of the syllables /ba/ and /du/ using the HT
technique with 6.5-month-old infants. The syllables were put in a three-
syllable context. In the "redundant" context, the two nontarget syllables
were identical. For example, infants hearing the trisyllable /kokodu/ as
the background stimulus, were reinforced for making a head-turn response when the stimulus was changed to /kokoba/. In addition, the infants were tested with trisyllable stimuli in which the target syllables /ba/
and /du/ were placed in the medial or initial position, as in /kobako/ and
/bakoko/, respectively. In the "mixed" context, the two nontarget syllables were themselves different. In this condition, infants heard the background trisyllable /kotiba/, and were reinforced for detecting a change to
/kotidu/. As before, the position of the target syllable was randomly altered so that it also occurred in the medial and initial positions, as in
/kobati/ and /bakoti/.

The results demonstrated that infants in the redundant condition performed at about 75% correct on the average, while infants in the mixed
group performed at about 66% correct on the average. Performance was
reliably above the 50% chance level for both groups, but the difference
between conditions was also significant. This suggests that redundancy in
the surrounding context enhances the infant's ability to detect a new
syllable. The more diverse the context, the more difficult it is for the
infant to pick out the target syllable. Recognition of the target syllable did
not, however, depend upon its serial position in the trisyllable context.

Another factor influencing the discrimination of target syllables in multisyllabic contexts is their accompanying prosodic features. The exact
way in which certain accompanying prosodic features might enhance the
perception of phonetic units occurring in multisyllable strings has been

documented (Karzon, 1985). Karzon was interested in the extent to which syllables, such as /ra/ and /la/, shown to be discriminated by 2- to 3-months-olds when presented in isolation (Eimas, 1975b), would be discriminated in longer strings, such as in the trisyllable strings /marana/ versus /malana/. She argued that certain prosodic features, such as those typical of the stress and intonation contours used by caretakers when directing speech towards their infants ("Motherese"), when applied to the contrastive syllable, might serve to highlight it.

Karzon reported six experiments. In each, she tested 1- to 4-month-olds using the HAS technique. The stimuli were computer-synthesized with the voice of a female talker. The critical acoustic features differentiating /ra/ and /la/ were the starting frequencies of the second and third formants. In the first experiment, the isolated /ra/ and /la/ syllables were shown to be discriminated. In the second experiment, these same /ra/ and /la/ syllables were placed in the trisyllable context, /marana/ - /malana/. For this experiment, the amplitudes and durations of the three syllables were held constant, and the /ra/ and /la/ syllables were given only a slight increase in the fundamental frequency (10 Hz) to make the trisyllables sound more natural. This slight increase in the fundamental was not sufficient to produce the perception of differential stress across the three syllables; adult listeners perceived the three-syllable word as having equal stress on all three syllables. The results of this experiment provided no evidence that infants could discriminate /marana/ from /malana/.

A third experiment was designed to examine the effect of acoustically highlighting the two syllables. Karzon argued that perhaps the exaggerated fundamental-frequency contours typical of "Motherese" would enhance the two syllables, thus making them more discriminable. The two three-syllable strings were resynthesized using a "bell-shaped" fundamental-frequency contour typical of those reported for infant-directed speech (Fernald & Simon, 1984; Grieser & Kuhl, in press). The peak in the fundamental frequency occurred on the two target syllables. The contour changed from 180 Hz to 350 Hz, a change of about 11 semitones, again typical of those reported to occur in "Motherese" (Fernald & Simon, 1984; Grieser & Kuhl, in press). Once again, however, the results provided no evidence of discrimination.

To enhance the two syllables even more, again in a way typical of Motherese, Karzon placed additional acoustic cues for stress on the syllable. She increased the intensity (5 dB) and the duration (70 msec) of the two target syllables when compared to their surrounding syllables to provide exaggerated stress. Infants did provide evidence of discriminating these two multisyllables. The effects of intensity and duration were not isolated from the effects of the exaggerated pitch contour. To test whether this acoustic highlighting effect was directed toward the syllable on which the stress occurred, rather than to the entire word, she did a fifth experiment in which the exaggerated stress and intonation was placed on the first (nontarget) syllable, /ma/. Her results showed that this was insufficient. No evidence of discrimination was obtained.

In a final experiment, the effects of stress and intonation more typical of the speech directed by adults to one other (nonexaggerated) was examined. The target syllables /ra/ and /la/ were now synthesized to be only 2 dB more intense (as opposed to 5 dB). They were only 48 ms longer (as opposed to 70 ms), and the change in fundamental frequency from onset to the peak was 35 Hz, or 3 semitones (as opposed to 170 Hz, 11 semitones). The results suggested that these stress and intonation changes were not sufficient to produce discrimination.

In summary, the studies by Goodsitt et al. (1984) and Karzon (1985) provide evidence to suggest that infants are capable of detecting phonetic changes that occur in three-syllable strings. Their ability to do so, however, depends upon at least two things: (a) the extent to which the context is redundant (Goodsitt et al., 1984), and (b) the degree to which the target syllable receives exaggerated stress and intonation (Karzon, 1985). Apparently, an interaction between segmental and suprasegmental acoustic cues occurs in speech perception. The extreme exaggeration of prosodic cues enhances the discriminability of the cues underlying segmental contrasts. Karzon's fifth experiment suggested that exaggerated stress and intonation affects perception not by calling attention to the word as a whole, but by calling attention to the specific stressed syllable. It is particularly noteworthy that the effective prosodic cues were those typically produced by caretakers when speaking to their infants.

Further studies will be required before we can specify the exact prosodic components that are necessary to obtain discrimination. In Karzon's (1985) study, exaggerated intonation on both syllables was insufficient. Discrimination was not evidenced until intensity and duration were also exaggerated. The effects of intensity and duration alone were not assessed. Perhaps more than a single indicator of stress must be present in order for discrimination to be evidenced, but the three cues underlying stress—exaggerated intonation, intensity, and duration—have not yet been studied singly in these three-syllable utterances, and then in combination, to demonstrate the components that are sufficient and necessary to obtain discrimination.

These experiments extend our knowledge of infant speech perception in important ways. They extend our tests of discrimination to longer utterances, ones more representative of speech in natural settings. They also reveal interesting interactions between the processing of segmental and nonsegmental (prosodic) dimensions in speech. Most importantly, the data indicate that the exaggeration in intonation and stress that is typical of infant-directed speech enhances the discrimination of multisyllabic syllables.

C. Discrimination of Prosodic Information

While the last section reviewed studies suggesting that certain kinds of prosodic information can enhance the perception of phonetic units, there are only a few studies aimed specifically at investigating the discrimination of the acoustic cues responsible for the perception of prosodic information itself. In an early study involving a heart-rate measure, Kaplan (1969) investigated 4- and 8-month-olds' abilities to discriminate stress and intonation contour in the phrase "See the cat." The phrase was naturally spoken with one of two nonexaggerated intonation contours, either a terminal rise (indicating a question) or a terminal fall (indicating a statement). In addition, one set of stimuli was spoken with concomitant stress on the final word, the other without.

Kaplan's results suggested that both age groups showed a reliable change in heart-rate variability (either an increase or a decrease) to a pitch change in the presence of concomitant stress. Neither group provided evidence of discriminating the pitch contours in the absence of stress. But Kaplan argued that infants should show an increase in heart-rate variability, and since only the 8-month-old infants did so (4-month-olds demonstrated a decrease), she concluded that the ability to discriminate intonation contours with concomitant stress develops between the ages of 4 and 8 months. Since both groups had shown a reliable change in heart-rate variability, it seems reasonable to conclude that both groups discriminated pitch-contour changes.

Later experiments support this conclusion. Morse (1972), using the HAS technique, also tested discrimination for rising as opposed to falling intonation contours. Two identical syllables differing only in their terminal fundamental frequencies were used. The rising contour changed from 120 Hz to 194 Hz and the falling contour changed from 120 Hz to 70 Hz; the stimulus change occured during the last 150 msec of the syllable /ba/. Six- to 8-week-old infants were tested. The results provided evidence that infants could discriminate these pitch contour differences.

Spring and Dale (1977) examined discrimination of the acoustic cues underlying adults' perception of stress. They tested 4- to 17-week-old infants using HAS and synthetically generated syllables. In their first experiment, the disyllables /ba'ba/ and /baba'/ were synthesized such that the stressed syllable contained all three acoustic cues known to be related to stress perception by adults—increased fundamental frequency, intensity, and duration. They demonstrated that infants could discriminate the syllables. In a second experiment, duration was the only cue for stress. The stressed syllable was 23 msec longer than the unstressed syllable. Again, infants evidenced discrimination.

The studies by Jusczyk and Thompson (1978) involving disyllables that were previously mentioned were also aimed at the infant's discrimination of the location of primary stress. These authors tested contrasts such as /da'ga/ versus /daga'/ and /wa'da/ versus /wada'/. The acoustic cues for stress involved all three parameters underlying stress perception—fundamental frequency, intensity, and duration. Their results suggested that infants discriminated each of the contrasts tested. No independent manipulations of the three underlying acoustic cues were attempted.

A study by Kuhl and Miller (1982) also investigated the discrimination of intonation contour and potential interactions between the discrimination of prosodic and phonetic distinctions. The study examined whether 4- to 16-week-old infants could detect a change in a target dimension if an irrelevant dimension was randomly varied throughout the experiment, serving as a distractor. The HAS paradigm was employed. A change in the target dimension occurred at the "shift-point"; the irrelevant dimension was randomly varied throughout both the pre- and postshift periods.

In one condition, the target dimension was a change in the vowel and the irrelevant dimension was the pitch contour of the vowel. In a second condition, the target dimension was the pitch contour of the vowel and the irrelevant dimension was the vowel's identity. The stimuli were two /a/'s and two /i/'s synthesized such that one /a/ and one /i/ had identical monotone pitch contours and one /a/ and one /i/ had identical rise-fall pitch contours. Discrimination of vowel identity and pitch contour were tested with and without irrelevant variation in the second dimension.

Kuhl and Miller's data (Figure 14) showed that when either a change in vowel identity or in pitch contour occurred in the absence of variation in a second dimension, infants discriminated that change. That is, sucking responses reliably increased after the shift point when compared to their control groups. On the other hand, when a change in a target dimension occurred against a background of random change in a second dimension, performance depended upon the specific dimension that served as the target. When vowel identity was the target dimension and pitch contour served as the second dimension, infants provided evidence of discrimination by demonstrating an increase in sucking scores after the shift point. However, when pitch contour was the target dimension and vowel identity served as the second dimension, no evidence of sucking recovery, and thus no evidence of discrimination, was obtained.

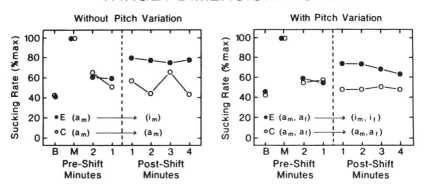

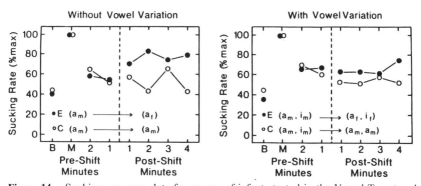

Figure 14. Sucking-recovery data for groups of infants tested in the Vowel Target and Pitch Target conditions. In both conditions, detection of a change in the target dimension was tested with an without variation in the second dimension. Data for experimental (sound change) infants are shown with closed circles; data for control (no sound change) infants are shown with open circles (From Kuhl and Miller, 1982.)

The results supported the notion that infants are capable of making a phonetic discrimination in the presence of irrelevant variation along a prosodic dimension. Regarding the asymmetric nature of the effect, the authors interpreted the data to mean that for these particular stimuli, the vowel dimension was more salient than the pitch dimension. Infants listening to a vowel such as /a/, which changed in pitch, found it easy to detect a new vowel such as /i/, which also changed in pitch. But they found it difficult to focus on pitch when the vowel was constantly changed, and failed to detect a dramatic change in pitch when a constant change in the vowel occurred throughout. Kuhl and Miller argued that infants readily detect the similarity between vowels whose pitch contours change, but do not readily detect the similarity in the pitch contours of two stimuli whose vowels were different. Thus, they argued, vowel "constancy" might be easier than pitch "constancy." Systematic manipulation of the acoustic cues representing the two levels of each dimension would need to be undertaken before the data could be interpreted in terms of a general precedence for the acoustic cues underlying vowel identity over the acoustic cues underlying pitch perception, but this initial result showing the detection of similarities among speech sounds sharing a particular dimension were intriguing. These results led to further studies on category recognition that are described in Section VI.B.

In summary, relatively few studies have addressed the discrimination of prosodic cues by infants. Yet, the data available confirm that infants under 4 months are (a) capable of discriminating changes in intonation contour when they occur in the absence of variation in other dimensions, and (b) that they discriminate changes in stress when they are cued either by duration alone or by concomitant changes in intonation contour, intensity, and duration. Future studies will need to address the issue of cue interaction in the perception of segmental and prosodic acoustic features.

VI. PERCEPTUAL ORGANIZATION IN SPEECH
PERCEPTION: TWO APPROACHES

The acquisition of language obviously requires that infants distinguish the smallest entities that convey meaning—the phonetic units of the language. In the previous sections we have reviewed numerous studies suggesting that young infants are capable of making these discriminations. But the perception of speech requires more than this. It requires that infants perceptually group sounds that are phonetically equivalent. This seemingly straightforward requirement is complicated by the complexity of the relationship between phonetic percept and sound. As we have reviewed, the two are not related in a simple one-to-one fashion. Thus, it is important to determine whether infants demonstrate an ability to categorize sounds—to "render discriminably different things equivalent" (Bruner et al., 1956).

Attempts to study speech-sound categorization in infancy have focused on two phenomena. An early approach was the extensive work on categorical perception (Eimas, 1974, 1975b; Eimas & Miller, 1980b; Eimas et al., 1971); a more recent approach is the work on equivalence classification (Hillenbrand, 1983, 1984; Kuhl, 1979a, 1980, 1983, 1985b). Both of these approaches tap the infant's ability to perceive categories. Categorical perception experiments focused on the infant's ability to perceive a *difference* between stimuli taken from a continuum that were perceived by adults to be members of the same or of different phonetic categories. In order to demonstrate the phenomenon, infants had to show enhanced discriminability for stimuli from different (as opposed to the same) adult-defined phonetic categories. Equivalence classification studies are aimed at demonstrating the infant's ability to perceive the *similarity* among discriminably different stimuli based on their phonetic equivalence. These studies were designed to examine whether infants perceive a common identity among sounds that are acoustically diverse but phonetically equivalent. Thus, categorical perception studies focus on the perception of differences for stimuli that vary along a single dimension, while equivalence-classification studies focus on the perception of similarity for discriminably different stimuli that vary along many dimensions.

A. Categorical Perception

1. Introductory Remarks

Among the perceptual phenomena exhibited in speech, none received more attention than "categorical perception" (CP) (Liberman et al., 1967). Its initial discovery was taken as strong evidence for the existence of specially evolved mechanisms for speech perception. The CP phenomenon could not be predicted by known psychophysical laws or by known perceptual principles. The early data suggested that CP was unique to speech. As we will review, more recent data suggest it is not unique to speech, nor, it appears, to human listeners. The impact of the data on nonspeech and the data on nonhuman listeners on the interpretation of CP has been considerable. We will therefore review both the original findings and these more recent results.

The original definition of CP in adults was as follows: It was said to occur when the ability to discriminate two stimuli was predicted by the ability to label them differently (Studdert-Kennedy et al., 1970). This was unusual, since it is a classic finding in psychology that far more stimuli can be discriminated than can be distinctly labeled (Miller, 1956). To demonstrate CP, two tasks were compared. In one, listeners "labeled" each of the stimuli from an acoustic continuum that was designed to manipulate an acoustic cue that differentiates two consonants in small steps. In another, listeners attempted to discriminate pairs of stimuli taken from the continuum. The definition stipulated that the discrimination of any two stimuli on the continuum should be exactly predicted by the extent to which those two stimuli were given different phonetic labels.

Thus, CP was demonstrated when the listener's discrimination performance was near chance for phonetically equivalent stimuli, but very good for phonetically different stimuli. The data from early adult studies met these criteria (Liberman, Harris, Eimas, Lisker, & Bastian, 1961; Liberman, Harris, Hoffman, & Griffith, 1957; Liberman, Harris, Kinney, & Lane, 1961). Each of the studies demonstrated chance performance for within-category contrasts and excellent performance for between-category contrasts.

More recently, investigators have pointed out that the degree to which results following the strict CP model will be obtained depends upon the psychophysical procedure used, the step-size chosen for discrimination testing, and the degree of stimulus uncertainty involved in the task (Ades, 1977; Kuhl, 1978, 1979c, 1982; Pastore, 1976). Studies demonstrated that adults were capable of producing better than chance performance on within-category contrasts when the discrimination procedure was altered or training was used (Carney, Widin, & Viemeister, 1977; Pisoni & Lazarus, 1974). Wood (1976) advocated the separation of the strict definition of categorical perception, which required that discrimination be predicted by labeling, from the simpler phenomenon related to the discrimination "peaks" in the functions. He proposed that the peaks in discrimination be termed the "phoneme-boundary effect" instead of "categorical perception." As Wood explained,

> the phoneme boundary effect implies only (a) that there exist a relatively abrupt increase in discriminability at some location(s) along a stimulus continuum between phonetic categories, and (b) that the location(s) of such increases in discriminability correspond closely to the locations of category boundaries as determined from absolute identification experiments. (p. 1388)

As Wood pointed out, this change in emphasis removed the requirement that the absolute level of discrimination be predicted by the labeling data, and also removed the theoretical interpretation—that discriminability increases were the direct result of phonetic categorization—inherent in the original conceptualization of CP.

Thus, the "phoneme-boundary effect" simply indicates that significant increases in discriminability occur in the region of the phonetic boundary. It does not predict the precise level of performance that will be obtained at any place along the continuum. In examining the infant and animal data, the effect we are looking for is this enhanced discriminability typical of CP in adults.

2.   Infant Data for Speech Stimuli

   a.   *Evidence for Enhanced Discriminability.* Four studies on infants provide evidence that the enhanced discriminability typical of CP exists in young infants (Eimas, 1974, 1975b; Eimas & Miller, 1980b; Eimas et al., 1971). In each of these experiments infants under 4 months of age were tested with pairs of stimuli taken from a computer-generated continuum. For example, Eimas et al. (1971) chose three pairs of stimuli from a /ba-pa/ continuum varying in voice-onset time. The three pairs of stimuli all differed by 20 msec VOT (−20 msec VOT vs. 0 msec VOT, +20 msec VOT vs. +40 msec VOT, +60 msec VOT vs. +80 msec VOT). Since the phonetic boundary on this continuum falls at about +25 msec VOT, adult listeners perceived the first pair as /ba/, the last pair as /pa/ and the second pair as /ba/ and /pa/.

Eimas et al. (1971) argued that if infants perceived the stimuli categorically they would demonstrate the ability to discriminate only the +20 ms VOT versus +40 msec VOT pair, since these two stimuli straddled the phonetic boundary and were perceived as different by adult subjects. The sucking recovery data, displayed in Figure 15, showed that infants did not demonstrate the ability to discriminate the −20 msec VOT versus 0 msec VOT pair nor the +60 msec VOT versus +80 msec VOT pair, but did demonstrate the ability to discriminate the +20 msec VOT versus +40 msec VOT pair. Similar results have since been obtained for a place of

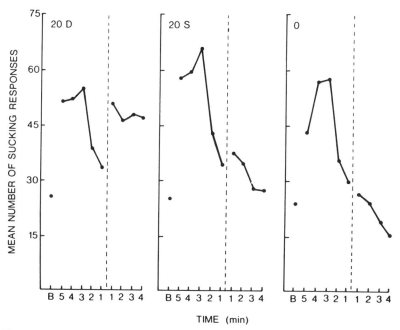

Figure 15. Sucking-recovery data for infants tested in the first categorical perception experiment on infants which was conducted using a /ba-pa/ continuum. The condition marked "20D" involved the between-category contrast. (From Eimas et al., 1971.)

articulation (/bae-dae-gae/) continuum (Eimas, 1974), a liquid (/ra-la/) continuum (Eimas, 1975b), and a manner of articulation (/ba-ma/) continuum (Eimas & Miller, 1980b).

   b. *Evidence for Context and Cue-Trading Effects in Categorical Perception.* Other more complex effects were also investigated using the CP design. Context and cue-trading effects are examples of these. We will first consider context effects. Recall that speech perception studies showed that the acoustic cues underlying phonetic perception were context dependent. The phonetic units surrounding a target unit, the specific talker who produced it, the rate at which it was spoken, and its position in a syllable altered the acoustic cues necessary for the perception of a particular target. Studies of CP in adults confirm the effects of context by showing that the exact location of enhanced discriminability on a continuum is altered by the context in which the phonetic unit appears (e.g., Miller & Liberman, 1979). Thus, adult listeners take contextual information into account when evaluating the acoustic cues for speech, suggesting at the very least mechanisms that are sensitive to context-dependent rather than absolute cues.
   Cue-trading effects are similar, but take the argument one step further. In these cases, the cues that are necessary to achieve a particular phonetic percept not only change with the context, but in a specific compensatory way. The value along one acoustic dimension determines the value that is required along a second dimension. The effects of the two dimensions appear to be additive, such that an increased value on the first dimension must be accompanied by a decreased value on the second dimension.
   Both context and cue-trading effects are important to theoretical accounts of speech perception because they suggest the possibility that the perceived equivalence between disparate acoustic events derives from their association in production. That is, the acoustic cues that perceptually trade with one another are argued to do so because they are a natural concomitant of the act of producing the sound. This would suggest that the perceptual system is driven by a representation that is specified in speech-motor terms, such that a listener's "knowledge" of articulation produces perceived equivalence. This view is favored by the investigators who have produced cue-trading effects in adult listeners (Best et al., 1981; Fitch et al., 1980; see Liberman, 1982 for review). An alternative view is that these compensatory effects are the result of the functional characteristics of the auditory system. That is to say, the perceptual trading relations derive from the way in which the auditory system combines acoustic information in perception, irrespective of it's status as speech.

The two points of view differ in their predictions about the outcomes of species-comparative, developmental, and nonspeech experiments. The articulatory account argues that the effects are exclusive to human listeners since they derive from knowledge of articulation. Regarding developmental data, a strong version of the articulatory account (see Liberman, 1957; Liberman, Cooper, Harris, & MacNeilage, 1963) argues that infants will not demonstrate these effects until after they can produce the sounds, and that the effects should not obtain for nonspeech sounds. The auditory account predicts that such effects will be present in nonhuman animals who do not have speechlike articulatory skills, but whose auditory capabilities are similar to those of man's. It further predicts that infants will demonstrate the effects and that the effects could be mimicked with nonspeech signals that duplicate the effective acoustic parameters.

(1) Context Effects. One example of a context effect is that provided by a change in the rate of speech. Recent studies suggest that adult listeners may take rate-of-articulation information into account when making decisions about the phonetic identity of a particular target unit, even when the information about the rate of articulation is remote from the target and occurs after the target unit.

Miller and Liberman (1979) demonstrated that the location of a syllable-initial /b-w/ boundary changed as a function of the duration (and thus the perceived rate) of the syllable. In their first experiment, the syllable was lengthened to indicate slower speech by increasing the duration of the vowel. Miller and Liberman demonstrated that for this "long" syllable continuum, the boundary was located at a longer transition duration than it was for the "short" syllable continuum. In a second experiment, they showed that if the syllable was lengthened in a different way, one not associated with a slower rate of articulation, the effect was reversed. In this case, the authors lengthened the syllable by adding formant transitions to the end of the original vowel. This created the perception of a final consonant on the syllables but did not signal a slowed rate of speaking. The continuum was perceived as ranging from /bad/ to /wad/. In this case, the perceptual boundary moved toward shorter transition durations.

Eimas and Miller (1980a) showed that 2- to 3-month-old infants demonstrate one part of this effect. Using the same stimuli used by Miller and Liberman (1979), these authors selected syllables from the "long" and "short" /ba-wa/ continua. Syllables were chosen to create four stimulus pairs, including both within-category pairs and between-category pairs from each continuum. Infants were tested using the HAS technique. The results demonstrated that infants discriminated only the between-category pairs on both continua. Eimas and Miller interpreted the data to suggest that infants are sensitive to contextual information, and that they perceive duration information relationally. They did not, however, examine the second effect—that of lengthening the syllable in a way that did not indicate a slowed rate of speech. We can say, therefore, that infants perceive duration information in a relative fashion, but we cannot as yet tie this to the perception of a phonetic unit's rate of articulation, as is indicated in adults. Nevertheless, these results were an important step forward in showing the level of sophistication in infants' responses to speech.

(2) Cue-Trading Effects. Cue-trading effects are similar to context effects. In cases of cue-trading, two very different types of acoustic information are equivalent with regard to their potential for indicating a particular phonetic value. Moreover, the acoustic cues are additive, in that an increase in the value along one dimension necessitates a decrease in the value along a second dimension in order to produce the same perceptual effect.

The first example of cue-trading in infants supports the claim that they are sensitive to compensatory effects. This particular case involves the voiced-voiceless distinction in plosive consonants. Research has shown that a cue-trading relation exists between the duration of the first formant and the VOT required to perceive a voiceless stop (Summerfield & Haggard, 1977).

Miller and Eimas (1983) tested this trading relation for transition duration and VOT on 2- to 3-month-olds using the HAS technique. They created two continua varying in VOT from 5 msec to 55 msec. This variation in VOT is sufficient to change an adult's percept from /ba/ to /pa/. One continuum was constructed with short (25 ms) transitions and the other with long (85 ms) transitions. For adults, the boundary value between voiced and voiceless stops varied on the two continua. On the short continuum the boundary occurred at about 25 ms while on the long continuum the boundary occurred at about 45 msec. The infants were tested with four pairs of stimuli: 5 msec versus 35 msec "short" (perceived as /b/ and /p/ respectively by adults); 35 msec versus 55 msec "short" (both perceived as /p/ by adults); 5 msec versus 35 msec "long" (both perceived as /b/ by adults); 35 msec versus 55 msec "long" (perceived as /b/ and /p/ respectively by adults). The infants provided evidence of discriminating only the 5 msec versus 35 msec-"short" pair and the 35 msec versus 55 msec-"long" pair. Thus, the data suggest that the location of enhanced discriminability on these two continua occurs at different places for infants as well. The authors concluded that the data provided evidence of "trading relations" in infants.

Context and cue-trading effects in adults imply a perceived equivalence between sounds that are differentially cued. For example, we know that adults perceive the /b/ in the short-syllable context (created with short transitions) as equivalent to the /b/ in the long-syllable context (created with long transitions). The data collected on infants, however, do not ask this question directly. They determine whether the location of enhanced discriminability occurs in different places on the short and long continua. They do not address the question of the perceived equivalence of syllables across context. In order to do so, tests would have to be conducted in which infants were trained to respond to a stimulus synthesized with one set of cues (the /b/ stimuli on the "short" continuum), and then tested for generalization to stimuli synthesized with a different set of cues (the /b/ stimuli on the "long" continuum). Such tests have not been conducted using these kinds of stimuli, but Kuhl (1979a, 1980, 1983, 1985b) has employed this technique to test equivalence classification for certain phonetic categories in 6-month-olds (Section VI.B.). Shifts in the location of the boundary on the two continua demonstrate a perceptual context effect, but do not directly test the perceived equivalence between phonetically identical stimuli that are represented by different acoustic events.

Another example of cue-trading that has been tested with infants involves the perception of silence as a phonetic cue. It involves the contrast "slit" versus "split" (Fitch et al., 1980). Many studies have shown that inserting or lengthening the silent gap between two syllables is sufficient to change perception from a voiced to a voiceless stop. Increasing the silent gap between syllables changes words like "rabid" to "rapid" and "ruby" to "rupee." In single syllables or between words, the perception of a voiceless stop can be created by adding silence: "see" changes to "ski" and "sue" to "spu"; "say shop" changes to "say chop" and "gray ship" to "great ship" (Dorman, Raphael, & Liberman, 1979; Repp, Liberman, Eccardt, & Pesetsky, 1978).

Studies have shown that the length of the silent gap inserted in these situations interacts with the spectral aspects of the remainder of the syllable. The duration of the silent gap necessary to indicate the presence of a voiceless stop is not constant. It depends upon the degree to which the spectral cues in the remainder of the syllable suggest the presence of the voiceless stop. Optimizing the spectral cue necessitates de-emphasizing the temporal cue.

For example, Fitch et al. (1980) synthesized two versions of "lit," one with bilabial formant transitions and one without. Frication noise appropriate to the perception of "s" was appended to the beginning of these syllables to create "slit." Then, two continua were created in which a silent gap, varied in 10-ms steps, was inserted between "s" and "lit." For both continua, the continued addition of a greater silent gap eventually produced the percept "split." Of greater interest, however, was the fact that the required silent duration varied for the two versions of "lit." When the spectral information for "p" was more complete, less silence was required to produce "split" than when the spectral information for "p" was less well specified. Fitch et al. (1980) argued that the convergence of two such diverse acoustic cues as silence and formant transitions in perception was tied to a listener's knowledge of their common articulatory origin.

In two experiments, Morse, Eilers, and Gavin (1982) provided some evidence that infants were also sensitive to trading relations. They employed the operant head-turn procedure and 6- to 8-month-old infants to test the discrimination of three contrasts: (1) naturally produced "slit" versus "split," (2) naturally produced "slit" versus the syllable "split" created by inserting silence between "s" and "lit" ("slit" + s) and (3) naturally produced "split" versus "slit" + s. They found evidence of discrimination in the first two conditions, but not in the third. In other words, their results parallel an adult's perception of naturally produced "split" and "slit" + silence as equivalent exemplars of "split." Morse et al. conclude that since infants are capable of discriminating "slit" from "slit" + silence, when silence is the only cue distinguishing them, and fail to discriminate naturally produced "split" from "slit" + silence, that they also are sensitive to trading relations. These results are important, but would be strengthened by the use of a procedure that directly measured the infant's perception of similarity for the two acoustically different versions of "split." Should infants demonstrate generalization from one version of "split" to an acoustically different version of it, the conclusion that infants were sensitive to "trading relations" would be quite strong.

In summary, only limited data are available on context and cue-trading effects in infants, but the data that are available provide support for the notion that infants are sensitive to these effects. One example of a context effect and two examples of cue-trading effects have been demonstrated in infants. In the following section, nonspeech correlates to these effects will be reviewed. The data suggest that neither the simple cases of CP, nor those fashioned after these more complex effects, are specific to speech.

3. Nonspeech Correlates of Categorical Perception

a. Adult Data for Nonspeech Stimuli. The studies reviewed in this section provide comparisons between the perception of speech and the perception of nonspeech sounds that mimic the acoustic cues in speech without being identified as speech. These comparisons contribute to the special mechanisms debate in a specific way. Tests using nonspeech sounds address the "tuning" of the mechanisms that underlie speech perception (Kuhl, 1978, 1979c, 1986a, 1986b). That is, they test whether the mechanisms underlying speech perception are so narrowly tuned as to exclude nonspeech signals. They test whether the mechanisms are responsive *only* to speech sounds. If, for example, CP effects could not be obtained using nonspeech sounds, and this was originally the case (see, e.g., Mattingly, Liberman, Syrdal, & Halwes, 1971), then one could safely conclude that the mechanisms underlying speech perception are "speech-specific." However, if nonspeech results mimic those seen in speech, as they have more recently, then the conclusion with regard to the underlying mechanisms is less clear.

The confusion regarding the interpretation of nonspeech tests when they match those obtained with speech is due, at least in part, to the interchangeable use of two terms (Kuhl, 1986b,d). The claim that mechanisms evolved "especially for speech" was originally equated with the claim that the mechanisms were "speech-specific." While existence of the latter ("speech-specific mechanisms") necessitates the former (the evolution of "special mechanisms"), the reverse is not true. The evolution of special mechanisms does not necessitate mechanisms that are speech-specific. Mechanisms may have evolved especially for the perception of speech, but not be designed so as to exclude nonspeech signals mimicking the critical features in speech. If such special mechanisms exist, they would be described as having evolved "especially for the perception of speech," but they would not be "speech-specific" because nonspeech signals are sufficient to trigger them.

Thus, it is possible that nonspeech stimuli, mimicking certain aspects of the spectral information in speech, work because they "fool" the relevant feature-detecting mechanisms (Kuhl, 1978, 1986b,d). By this argument, experiments which reproduce speech effects using nonspeech signals can not lead unambiguously to the conclusion that special mechanisms, evolved to detect the information in speech, do not exist. They can only suggest that the mechanisms which underlie the perception of speech, regardless of their nature and origins, are not so narrowly tuned that they *exclude* nonspeech signals. Demonstrating that CP can be replicated with nonspeech signals suggests that speech and nonspeech are tied to a common processing mechanism. But that mechanism could either be one that evolved especially for speech, or more general auditory processing mechanisms.

While the first attempts to demonstrate CP for a nonspeech continuum failed (Liberman et al., 1961; Mattingly et al., 1971), two clear cases of CP for nonspeech stimuli, each of which is designed to mimic the acoustic cues underlying the voicing distinction, have been published.

The two experiments demonstrate CP for stimuli designed to mimic certain aspects of voiced and voiceless consonant-vowel syllables without being perceived as speech. Miller, Wier, Pastore, Kelly, and Dooling (1976) used noise-buzz sequences designed to simulate the gross spectral characteristics of stimuli varying in VOT. More recently, Pisoni (1977) varied the onset times of two pure tones (500 Hz and 1500 Hz) to create a tone-onset-time (TOT) continuum which encompassed the location of both the Spanish and the English boundary. Pisoni's results demonstrated that discrimination was best in the region where the two tones were staggered by 20 msec in either direction of simultaneous onset, that is, when the high tone preceded the low tone by 20 msec or followed the low tone by 20 msec. Pisoni (1977) concluded that the perception of the voicing feature in speech may reflect a basic limitation on the auditory system's ability to process temporal-order information.[1]

In addition to these experiments, studies have been done to determine whether the more complex context effects can be replicated with non-speech stimuli. Pisoni, Carrell, and Gans (1983) replicated the context effect involving rate of speech using nonspeech stimuli in adults. They synthesized pure-tone patterns whose frequencies were identical to the center frequencies of the formants in the stimuli employed by Miller and Liberman (1979). They created stimuli comparable to the "long" and "short" CV syllables as well as ones comparable to the CVC stimuli used by Miller and Liberman. A continuum was created for the simulated CV and CVC patterns in which the transition durations were comparably varied. Listeners labeled these stimuli as having abrupt versus gradual onsets, and the perceptual boundary between the two categories was determined. The results demonstrated that the nonspeech data were identical to those produced in speech. That is, the location of the boundary for nonspeech stimuli mimicking the short CV stimuli was displaced toward shorter transition durations when compared to the boundary for the nonspeech stimuli mimicking the long CV stimuli. Moreover, the adult data showed that when the stimulus was lengthened by adding a final transitional element, comparable to Miller and Liberman's CVC stimuli, the boundary value shifted toward shorter transition durations.

The fact that these nonspeech patterns mimic the results found for speech shows that the duration of nonspeech auditory events are also processed in relation to the context in which they appear. Pisoni et al.

---

[1] While a temporal-order hypothesis makes general predictions about the locations of perceptual boundaries, it has not to date been able to account for the fact that the location of the boundary shifts with the first-formant's onset frequency (Lisker, 1975; Summerfield and Haggard, 1977) or with the frequency of the second formant (Kuhl, 1982; Summerfield, 1982).

interpreted their results as refuting the hypothesis put forward by Miller and Liberman (1979) which was that the effects for speech depended on a mechanism that took "rate of articulation" information into account. Pisoni et al. (1983) argued that rather than attribute the speech results to special mechanisms, both the speech and nonspeech effects should be attributed to general auditory processing mechanisms. The position taken by this author is that both Miller and Liberman's and Pisoni et al.'s interpretation can account for the data. Miller and Liberman's position can account for both the speech and the nonspeech data by claiming that specially evolved mechanisms exist but that they are not so narrowly tuned so as to exclude nonspeech signals. Similarly, the position of Pisoni et al. can account for both the speech and nonspeech data by claiming that general auditory mechanisms are responsible for both effects. Thus, when speech and nonspeech tests produce similar results, no definitive conclusions about the origins of the underlying mechanisms can be made (Kuhl, 1978, 1986a,b).

b. *Infant Data for Nonspeech Stimuli.* The agreement between the speech and nonspeech data for adult listeners naturally led to a strong interest in the performance of infants in discrimination tasks involving nonspeech stimuli. Of those cited for adults, two have been examined in young infants, the relatively simple one involving tone-onset-time (TOT), and the more complex one involving the context effect of rate. Jusczyk, Pisoni, Walley, and Murray (1980) tested the discrimination of sounds varying in TOT. The stimuli were synthesized to duplicate those used by Pisoni (1977). Jusczyk et al. predicted that infants, like adults, would discriminate only those stimuli that straddled the −20 msec or +20 msec TOT boundaries. They tested a number of stimulus pairs: −70 msec versus −40sec; −40 msec versus −10 msec; −30 msec versus 0 msec; −20 msec versus +10 msec; −10 msec versus +20 msec; 0 msec versus +30 msec; +10 msec versus +40 msec; and +40 msec versus +70 msec.

Contrary to their prediction, the sucking recovery scores indicated that only the −70 msec versus −40 msec and +40 msec versus +70 msec contrasts were discriminated. The data provided support for the notion that infants perceive three categories on the TOT continuum, but the data suggested that the boundaries for these categories were located in different places for infants than for adults. The fact that discrimination was symmetrical, that on both sides of the continuum discrimination was not evidenced until the tones were temporally offset by at least 40 msec, suggests that infants may require a longer interval between the onsets of two tones before perceiving them as nonsimultaneous. The perception of simultaneity may develop such that progressively shorter offsets are required to perceive nonsimultaneity for two auditory signals. If so, one cannot argue, as Pisoni (1977) did for adults, that temporal-order perception underlies the voiced-voiceless distinction in infants. Perhaps infants are responding to speech stimuli on the basis of a different acoustic feature than that used by adults. This TOT result in infants needs to be replicated, since its outcome is theoretically important.

Jusczyk, Pisoni, Reed, Fernald, and Myers (1983) replicated the context effect involving rate, using nonspeech stimuli, with infants. The results demonstrated that, just as when listening to speech, infants needed a shorter transition duration to detect a change in ''short'' stimuli, and a longer transition duration for detecting a change in ''long'' stimuli. This means that infants are sensitive to overall duration in nonspeech as well as in speech, and that transition duration is processed relationally for both signals. As in the Eimas and Miller (1980a) study involving speech, the authors tested only the first effect, the one in which nonspeech patterns mimic vowel lengthening in CV syllables. They did not test the effect of lengthening the syllable by adding a consonant (the CVC study) using nonspeech stimuli. We cannot push the argument further, therefore, for either speech or nonspeech, and claim that infants take some more complex information into account unless we dissociate rate and overall duration. This dissociation has yet to be done in the infant tests involving speech or nonspeech.

To summarize, the adult studies now show a close correspondence between a listener's ability to discriminate similar acoustic features in speech and nonspeech stimuli, and this provides valuable information about the mechanisms underlying phonetic perception. For adults performing in these tasks, speech and nonspeech patterns may be processed by a common mechanism. We do not know, however, whether both are processed by a mechanism that evolved for speech, or whether both are processed by general auditory mechanisms. The results for infant listeners are mixed, with one study (Jusczyk et al., 1983) supporting a close agreement between speech and nonspeech, and a second one (Jusczyk et al., 1980) failing to do so. Thus, a strong conclusion about the agreement between speech and nonspeech data by infants is not possible at this time, and the whole issue of a common mechanism underlying speech and nonspeech processing for these tasks in infants is less well resolved. Further experiments addressing this issue need to be done.

4. The Perception of Speech by Nonhuman Animals

The logic underlying the initial attribution of special mechanisms to infants rested on one critical assumption. The assumption was that CP required specialized phonetic mechanisms and could not be accounted for in any other way. As long as this assumption held, it was reasonable to impute specialized phonetic mechanisms to infants. There was no alternative explanation. General auditory mechanisms were not thought to be sufficient to explain CP because at the time tests of CP for nonspeech sounds had failed to reproduce the effect (cf. Mattingly et al., 1971).

Yet the question remained: Were specialized phonetic processing mechanisms necessary to produce CP or were general auditory mechanisms sufficient? The argument for using an animal model to test this question was fairly straightforward (Kuhl 1979c; 1986b). Humans' response to speech stimuli probably involves both auditory and phonetic levels of processing. The commonly held expectation is that at some point in the processing of speech, general auditory mechanisms give way and more specialized phonetic ones take over. The question is: How do we pull the two levels apart? Where does auditory-level processing end and phonetic processing begin? An animal model helps to answer these questions. If the animal species is chosen so that it displays auditory abilities that are similar to man's, then the animal provides a model of man's auditory level of processing, and does so in the absence of any processing that is specifically linguistic. The advantage of this is that the animal reflects what is "natural" for the auditory-processing system when phonetic-level influences have been stripped away and only auditory-level influences remain.

An important implication follows this reasoning. Theory holds that CP requires a specialized phonetic mechanism and that more general auditory mechanisms cannot account for it. A nonhuman animal is not equipped with the specialized phonetic machinery. If the animal succeeds, it is due to auditory-level processing. Stated simply, then, the hypothesis under test in animal experiments involving speech is this: Is auditory-level processing sufficient to reproduce the phenomenon? Or is phonetic-level processing necessary? If animals and humans behave similarly we can then conclude that the phenomenon can exist in the absence of specialized mechanisms. As we have already stated, this claim cannot be unambiguously supported by the results of tests involving nonspeech signals.

There is another reason why these studies are important. The study of speech-sound perception by animals may lead to an understanding of the constraints placed by the auditory system on the selection of the phonetic contrasts used in language. Studies demonstrating that the acoustic cues which differentiate phonetic categories are well matched to the basic sensitivities of the auditory system provide information concerning the role that hearing played in the evolution of the acoustics of language (Kuhl & Padden, 1982, 1983). In short, then, there are two reasons to pose the question: Do animals produce CP? We want to know whether the phenomenon can exist in the absence of special mechanisms—that is, with mechanisms based purely on the auditory-level. And second, we want to understand the evolution of the sound system of language; specifically, we want to know whether the phonetic units of speech were chosen to exploit man's basic auditory sensitivities (Kuhl, 1986b).

While the research completed on animals' perception of speech is at present quite extensive (Kuhl, 1986b), two examples will be cited here to illustrate the findings. The first data are from the original study (Kuhl & Miller, 1975), which examined an animal's ability to categorize sounds from a speech–sound continuum. This test focused on the characteristic labeling functions obtained in speech. The question for animals was whether the boundary between the two categories on the continuum coincided with the phonetic one, or appeared someplace else. The second data are more recent and focus directly on tests of the "phoneme boundary effect" (Kuhl & Padden, 1982, 1983). The question here is whether or not in the absence of any experience in "labeling" the stimuli on the continuum, an animal will demonstrate enhanced discriminability at the boundaries between phonetic categories.

The Kuhl and Miller (1975) study resembled an adult categorization experiment, only with animals. The question was: Where would an animal place the boundary on a phonetic continuum? Chinchillas were used in this first experiment because they were mammals whose basic auditory abilities are similar to man's (Kuhl, 1979c). They were trained, using an avoidance conditioning procedure, to distinguish computer-synthesized versions of the syllables /da/ and /ta/. Recall that Figure 5 displayed computer-synthesized stimuli varying in VOT.

The animals were trained to discriminate the two "endpoint" stimuli on a /da-ta/ continuum, 0 msec VOT and +80 msec VOT. During training, they were not given any exposure to the rest of the test continuum. To one of the endpoint stimuli (either 0 or +80 depending upon random assignment), animals were trained to cross a midline barrier in a cage to avoid a mild shock and the sounding of a buzzer. To the other stimulus the animal was trained to inhibit the crossing response, and this behavior was rewarded with water. When performance on these endpoint stimuli was near perfect, a generalization paradigm was used to test the intermediate stimuli, those between /da/ and /ta/ on the continuum (+10 msec VOT to +70 msec VOT, in 10-msec steps). The design of the experiment was that during generalization testing, half of the trials would involve the endpoint stimuli. On these trials, all of the appropriate feedback was given, just as it had been during the training phase. On the other half of the trials, the intermediate stimuli were presented in random order.

The intermediate trials were those most critical for theory. On trials involving intermediate stimuli, the feedback was arranged to indicate that the animal was always correct, no matter what the response. There was no "training" on these stimuli, and thus no clue was provided to the animal telling him where to place the boundary on the continuum.

The data are shown in Figure 16 (top). The mean percentage of /da/ responses to each stimulus on the continuum are plotted for chinchillas and human adults. The curves were generated by a least-squares method. The resulting phonetic boundaries, located at 35.2 msec VOT for humans and 33.3 msec VOT for animals, did not differ significantly. A subsequent study using a totally different procedure and monkeys rather than chinchillas demonstrated that the location of the boundary on a /da-ta/ continuum was located at +28 msec, in good agreement with the chinchilla data (Waters & Wilson, 1976).

Kuhl and Miller (1978) extended these tests to continua involving other voiced–voiceless pairs, namely bilabial (/ba-pa/) and velar (/ga-ka/) contrasts. These stimuli were of interest because human listeners' boundaries differ with the place of articulation specified by the particular voiced-voiceless pair. The new tests involving the bilabial and velar stimuli were run exactly as the previous ones. The endpoint VOT values were 0 and +80 msec. The intermediate stimuli (+10 to +70 msec in 10-msec steps) were presented with feedback indicating that the animal was correct regardless of his performance. Thus, no training occurred on these stimuli. The results again demonstrated excellent agreement between the human and animal categorization data. The boundary values for the bilabial stimuli were 26.8 msec VOT for humans and 23.3 msec VOT for animals (Figure 16, middle), which are not significantly different. The boundary values for the velar stimuli were 42.3 msec VOT for humans and 42.5 msec VOT for animals (Figure 16, bottom). Again, the values did not differ significantly.

Kuhl and Miller (1978) note that the individual categorization functions for the three places of articulation showed that each human and animal subject had ordered their boundary values similarly. For every subject, the lowest boundary value occurred when listening to the bilabial series, the highest boundary value occurred for the velar stimuli, with the alveolar boundary between these two.

The data suggested that animals' natural boundaries coincided with humans' phonetic ones. These findings raised the intriguing possibility that phonetic boundaries in human language were designed to exploit auditorially natural ones in the first place (Kuhl, 1978, 1979c; Kuhl & Miller, 1975, 1978). But while these possibilities had been newly raised by the data, more detailed questions about animals' abilities still remained. Animals' categorization functions had been examined, but to this point no studies had been done on animals' discrimination of specific pairs of

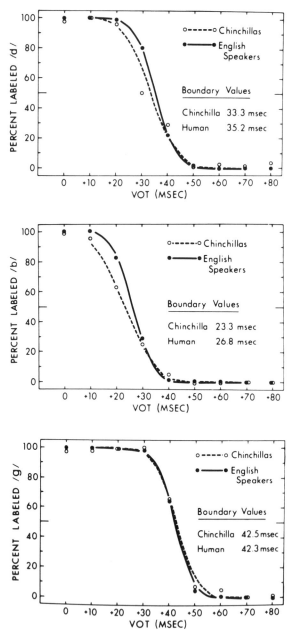

Figure 16. Categorization of sounds from speech continua by animals (chinchillas) and human adults tested on stimuli from three voiced–voiceless continua, /d-t/ (top), /b-p/ (middle), /g-k/ (bottom). In each case, animals were trained to respond differentially to the two endpoint stimuli (0 msec VOT and +80 msec VOT). Then, the intermediate stimuli were presented in the absence of any training. The locations of the boundaries for the two groups did not differ significantly. (From Kuhl and Miller, 1978.)

stimuli from the continuum. Since it is the enhanced discriminability between categories—the "phoneme boundary effect"—that sets speech apart from other phenomena in psychophysics and in cognitive psychology, and since infants appear to demonstrate this effect without learning or experience (Eimas et al., 1971) discrimination tests were considered important.

Three studies directly addressed discriminability of stimulus pairs from a speech-sound continuum. (See also Kuhl, 1981a and Sinnott, Beecher, Moody, & Stebbins, 1976, for different types of discrimination tests on animals). Morse and Snowden (1975) used a heart-rate procedure to examine discrimination of stimuli from a synthetic /bae-dae-gae/ continuum in rhesus monkeys. Results demonstrated that the rhesus monkey discriminated both the within-and between-category pairs, since both groups demonstrated significantly more dishabituation than the control group, which was presented with a single stimulus. However, the degree of dishabituation was significantly greater for those animals presented with between-category comparisons—with stimuli falling on opposite sides of the human boundary—than for those subjects presented with within-category pairs, thus suggesting that discrimination of between-category pairs was enhanced in rhesus monkeys.

Two additional studies have examined macaques on the discrimination of speech-sound pairs (Kuhl & Padden, 1982, 1983). The technique involved training a monkey to initiate a trial by depressing a telegraph key. The animal was taught to lift the telegraph key when the two stimuli were *different,* and was rewarded with a squirt of applesauce for doing so. If the stimuli were the *same,* the monkey was rewarded with applesauce for holding the key down until the end of the trial. During training, stimuli that were easily discriminable like a tone versus a noise or a click versus a buzz, were used. Eventually the monkey had to discriminate various vowel sounds, some of which differed only in intensity or pitch.

The design of the experiment was to choose stimulus pairs from a speech sound continuum, just as is done in tests on infants, and examine their discriminability. The CP model predicts differential discriminability across the continuum, with pairs that straddle the phonetic boundary being most discriminable. Using this procedure, two studies were conducted, one using stimuli from three different voicing continua (Kuhl & Padden, 1982), and the other using stimuli from a place continuum (Kuhl & Padden, 1983). The results of the two experiments were identical—in both cases animals demonstrated the discrimination typical of CP.

The case will be illustrated using the example involving a continuum varying in place (/bae-dae-gae/) (Kuhl & Padden, 1983). Recall that a change in the place of articulation from bilabial (/b/) to alveolar (/d/) to velar (/g/) can be governed by a change in the starting frequency of the second formant transition (Figure 4). The aim of the experiment on animals was to test whether there were any locations along a two-formant /bae-dae-gae/ continuum where discriminability was enhanced, and if so, whether those particular locations coincided with the locations of human phonetic boundaries. Animals' discrimination of these sounds was tested for seven pairs of stimuli, each separated by two steps on a 15-step continuum (stimulus pairs 1 vs. 3, 3 vs. 5, 5 vs. 7, and so on).

The results are shown in Figure 17. The average percent correct discrimination score is given for each pair. The locations of the human phonetic boundaries are marked by dashed vertical lines. As shown, the best performance occurred on stimulus pairs 3 versus 5, 9 versus 11, and 11 versus 13. These are the only pairs that differ significantly from chance, and involve stimuli from different phonetic categories for humans. Thus, while stimulus pairs were always separated by an equal physical distance on the continuum, their perceived differences were not equivalent. Discriminability was poor when the stimuli involved pairs taken from the same phonetic category, but discriminability was very good when the stimuli involved pairs taken from different phonetic categories.

Taken as a whole, these data lend support to the notion that enhanced discrimination near phonetic boundaries can be demonstrated in mammals other than man. Kuhl (1986b,d; Kuhl & Padden, 1983) argues that this finding supports two conclusions. First, that in the evolution of language, the choice of the particular phonetic units used in communication was strongly influenced by the extent to which the units were ideally suited to the auditory system. It has been argued (Kuhl, 1979c, 1981a; Kuhl & Padden, 1983; Stevens, 1972, 1981) that the perception of certain

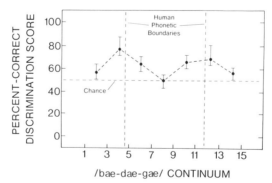

Figure 17. Discrimination performance for animals tested on pairs of stimuli from a place of articulation (/b-d-g/) continuum. Discriminability is significantly enhanced at the /b-d/ and the /d-g/ boundaries. (From Kuhl and Padden, 1983.)

auditory properties, such as spectral shape, direction of formant change, and temporal order, served as a set of constraints on the acoustics of language. The second conclusion is that since animals demonstrate these phenomena, the fact that infants do so is not sufficient evidence *by itself* to support the notion that the underlying mechanisms responsible for the effects in infants are ones that evolved especially for speech. While not ruling out such a conclusion, these data do not allow us to accept it without additional converging evidence.

B. Equivalence Classification for Speech in Infancy

1. Introduction

The section on categorical perception described experiments showing that infants demonstrate enhanced discriminability for stimuli located at the phonetic boundaries between speech categories. Infants were shown to discriminate stimuli that straddled the adult-defined phonetic boundaries, while they failed to discriminate stimuli belonging to the same phonetic category. Moreover, the results showed that infants' boundaries changed when the context was altered, again replicating effects seen in adults. What do these findings tell us about the infant's ability to perceive the similarity among diverse instances representing a phonetic category? Do the data provide evidence of categorization—of the ability to render discriminably different things equivalent?

Using the CP test paradigm, evidence of categorization is derived from performance on within-category contrasts, and the data showed that within-category differences were not detected by infants. But this null result has two possible interpretations. Either infants fail to discriminate the stimuli because they recognize category equivalence, or they fail because they are simply not capable of discriminating the stimuli. The strength of the evidence for categorization is thus limited.

Categorization requires that discriminably different stimuli be perceived as equivalent. In speech, this means that infants must recognize the similarity among phonetically equivalent events that are represented by very diverse acoustic cues. We want to know whether infants recognize phonetic equivalence in the sounds produced by different talkers, and if they recognize a phonetic unit's identity when it occurs in different contexts. This necessitates two things: (a) that infants recognize phonetic equivalence when the values of the critical dimensions underlying the perception of the phonetic unit are altered; and (b) when additional dimensions that are acoustically prominent, but irrelevant to the task of phonetic categorization, are introduced.

When we ask whether infants can categorize we want to know if they can sort a variety of instances into "Type A" and "Type B" events, even though the various A's (or B's) are clearly differentiable. To perform such a task requires that infants recognize the similarity among discriminably different instances representing a category, while at the same time recognizing the essential difference that separates the two categories. Thus, categorization requires a process in which the perceiver recognizes equivalence.

An approach to the study of speech-sound categorization was developed by Kuhl (1979a, 1980, 1983, 1985b for discussion). The tests involved an adaptation of the head-turn technique (Section III.B). The experiments were designed to assess the degree to which training an infant to discriminate two speech sounds, each representing a different phonetic category, would result in the correct categorization of novel instances from those same two phonetic categories. If infants demonstrate equivalent treatment of the training stimuli and the novel stimuli in this design one can argue that infants recognized the training and novel stimuli as members of the same category.

Two main features distinguish this approach from the CP approach. First, the nature and the diversity of the stimuli representing the categories distinguish these experiments from ones of CP. Second, the technique requires the infant to produce an equivalent response to stimuli that are perceived to be equivalent, rather than to produce a response based on the detection of a difference between two stimuli.

Regarding the first, rather than differing on a single acoustic parameter, as in the studies involving discrimination of sounds drawn from a physical continuum, the stimuli varied along a number of dimensions. For example, in the first experiment using this design, Kuhl (1979a) examined infants' discrimination of two vowel categories, /a/ (as in "pop") and /i/ (as in "peep"). The stimuli used in the experiment varied along three dimensions, phonetic identity (/a/ vs. /i/), pitch contour (interrogative vs. declarative), and talker identity (male, female, or child). Stimuli belonging to the same category (all /a/'s for example) were shown to be easily discriminable from one another by infants. The question was: Can infants perceptually group ("sort") the sounds along any one of these dimensions?

Each of the three dimensions is physically represented in the stimulus in a complex way. In no case can the acoustic rules for sorting along any of these dimensions be stated in a simple, frequency-specific way. Furthermore, each dimension is physically represented by cues that are acoustically prominent. Thus when attempting to organize the stimuli along any one particular dimension, the variations along the other dimensions provide potential distraction. Categorization along the phonetic dimension in this example requires that the diverse acoustic events underlying identity be recognized as equivalent, while the acoustically prominent but irrelevant acoustic events associated with changes in the pitch contour and talker be ignored.

Regarding the second, infants produced an equivalent response to stimuli that, while discriminably different, were perceived as equivalent. This provided a measure of infants' ability to categorize the sounds. Infants were trained to make a head-turn response when an /a/ vowel, produced by a male voice with a falling pitch contour, was changed to an /i/ vowel. The two stimuli were acoustically matched in every other detail. After this initial training, infants were tested with novel stimuli representing the two categories, ones produced by female and child talkers, with either rising or falling pitch contours. The extent to which infants demonstrated the correct response to novel stimuli from both categories was measured. If, for example, an infant had been trained to produce a head-turn response to the male's /i/ vowel, but not to his /a/ vowel, the prediction was that the infant would produce a head-turn response to a novel /i/ (one produced by a female or child), but not to an equally novel /a/.

This kind of task to presents quite a different set of problems for the infant than the typical speech discrimination experiment. Two differences are noteworthy (Kuhl, 1981b, 1985b). First, an infant must discover and focus on the acoustic dimension relevant to the particular phonetic distinction under test. This may be relatively easy when the phonetic context and the talker are held constant, as in the categorical perception experiments described above, in which single stimuli from each of two phonetic categories were to be discriminated. But when a variety of stimuli representing a phonetic distinction are used, the critical cues vary and the listener must somehow "take into account" the complex mapping between acoustic cues and percepts that is brought about by contextual variation.

The second process related to categorization is a concomitant of the first. When the phonetic context and the talker are varied, acoustically prominent but phonetically irrelevant acoustic dimensions are introduced. To recognize that /di/ and /du/ are similar, the infant must ignore the most prominent difference between them, their vowels. In addition, other dimensions such as voice pitch, as well as the timbre differences between the voices of different talkers, are other prominent acoustic characteristics that a listener must ignore when categorizing phonetically, since these dimensions do not provide critical information concerning the phonetic identity of the stimulus.

In summary, these experiments are distinguished by both stimulus considerations and by response considerations. On the stimulus side the design included (a) substantial variation in the criterial cues underlying pho-netic identity. This was done by varying the context, position or talker factors, and (b) substantial variation in dimensions that were irrelevant to phonetic identity. In some cases, these irrelevant variations were con-comitant with variation in the criterial dimensions. For example, varying the talker alters the locations of the formant frequencies (the criterial dimension), but also introduces irrelevant variation in the fundamental frequency, and in the spectral differences that help identify the voices of particular talkers.

On the response side, two factors distinguish the experiments. First, the design requires the infant to form two categories. Second, in these experiments infants produce a response to indicate the detection of simi-larity, and thus the ability to categorize. Infants cannot succeed in these experiments without correctly sorting each novel stimulus into one of the two categories. Thus, the use of an active response to code the perceived similarity between percepts provides strong evidence of the ability to categorize (Kuhl, 1985b).

Equivalence classification experiments have now been completed for categories based on vowels, consonants, and for certain other dimen-sions. Experiments in each category will be used to illustrate the ap-proach and detail some of the findings (see Kuhl, 1985b for full review).

2.   Equivalence Classification for Vowel Categories

When vowels are produced by talkers whose vocal tracts have different overall dimensions, as when the identical vowel is produced by a male, a female, and a child, the formant frequencies are very different (Peterson & Barney, 1952). This is due to the fact that the overall dimensions of the vocal tracts of men, women, and children are not proportional to one another (Fant, 1973), so the resulting resonances (and therefore formant frequencies) are not related as ratio transforms. This means that when even simple vowels such as /a/ are spoken by a group of different people, they cannot be classified correctly by a computer. These vowels are fre-quently confused with neighboring vowels such as /ae/ and /ɔ/.

The question is: Can infants categorize vowels correctly? Can the same vowel spoken by different people be equated by infants? If infants cannot relate the sounds spoken by one talker to those same sounds spoken by another, it would be difficult indeed to learn language. The name of an object would sound different each time a new person named it. Thus, this perceptual ''normalization'' for the speech of different talkers is critical for language.

Such an ability is also critical to infants' abilities to produce speech themselves. That is, talker normalization is a prerequisite for vocal imitation. Why is this the case? The infant's vocal tract is not capable of producing the absolute formant frequencies produced by adults (Lieberman, 1980). Their vocal tracts cannot produce such low frequency resonances. If infants attempted to imitate adult speech by producing the exact frequencies produced by an adult, they would soon find that it is not possible. But they do not attempt this exact frequency match. Their ability to normalize the vowels produced by different talkers must reveal a similar "pattern" in vowels spoken by different talkers. When attempting to imitate a vowel or pitch contour produced by an adult, infants mimic the "pattern" rather than the absolute formant frequencies of the adult. This can be seen in the infant's imitation of pitch contour observed in studies on cross-modal speech perception (Kuhl & Meltzoff, 1982; Section VIII).

The study by Kuhl and Miller (1982) previously described (Section V.C) provided the first results relevant to the issue of vowel categorization. Recall that the study examined whether 4- to 16-week-old infants could detect a stimulus change at the shift point in an HAS experiment if a second dimension was randomly varied throughout the experiment. The two dimensions were vowel identity and pitch contour. The design of the experiment was to present infants with two different exemplars during the pre- and postshift periods. The two stimuli shared either the vowel dimension (and varied in pitch), shared the pitch dimension (and varied in vowel identity) or neither. Kuhl and Miller argued that evidence in support of infants' detection of vowel similarity might be found in the amount of time taken to habituate across conditions during the preshift phase of the experiment.

Models of habituation (Cohen, 1973, McCall & McGhee, 1977) assume that in order to demonstrate habituation, the infant must store a composite description of ("remember") the stimulus presented during the preshift period, and eventually recognize that the stimulus being presented again and again matches the stored representation. Recognition of the similarity between the stimulus being presented and the stored representation reduces the infant's interest in that stimulus and this results in a decrease in the response being measured (habituation). Kuhl and Miller reasoned that habituation to multiple stimuli was particularly interesting because it might reveal the infant's perception of similarity. They argued that sets of stimuli that shared a particular dimension should be perceived as more similar than sets that did not. They argued further that the perception of similarity would serve as an aid to memory. Thus, if infants were capable of detecting similarity, then the time it took to reach the habituation criterion should decrease.

The habituation data are shown in Figure 18. Time-to-habituation (TH)

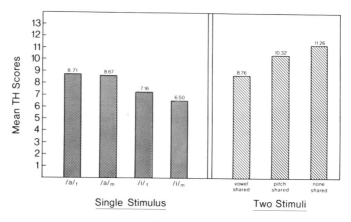

Figure 18. Time-to-habituation (TH) data for infants listening to either a single stimulus or pairs of stimuli sharing different features. The subscripts refer to monotone (m) and falling (f) pitch contours. (From Kuhl and Miller, 1982.)

was defined as the number of minutes spent in the preshift phase of the experiment, excluding the baseline minute. The TH scores for all groups presented with a single sound during preshift are shown as well as for those groups presented with two stimuli. Comparisons between the two-stimulus groups and the single-stimulus groups revealed that infants took significantly longer to meet the habituation criterion when two sounds were presented during the preshift period rather than one. However, this result was also shown to be asymmetric. It was dependent upon the specific dimension that the two sounds had in common. When the two sounds shared the vowel identity, TH was not significantly greater than it was in any condition in which a single sound was presented. In contrast, when the two sounds shared pitch or shared neither of the two dimensions, TH was signficantly longer than when a single sound was presented or when two sounds that shared vowel identity were presented.

The data were interpreted in support of the notion that infants recognized the similarity among stimuli sharing the vowel dimension and that this reduced the memory load during the habituation phase of the experiment. A shared dimension did not always make two stimuli easier to remember since, when the two stimuli shared pitch, a significant increase in TH scores were obtained. In fact, it took almost as long to habituate when the stimuli shared pitch as it did when they had no features in common. Kuhl and Miller argued, therefore, that infants did not recognize similarity along the pitch dimension, perhaps because they were distracted by a constant change in the second more salient dimension, vowel identity.

While the Kuhl and Miller (1982) study demonstrated the infant's ability to tolerate variation in irrelevant dimensions and perceive the similarity among vowels, it did not examine the infant's ability to recognize phonetic similarity among vowel stimuli as diverse as those produced by different talkers. To extend these results to such a situation, Kuhl (1979a) adapted the HT technique to examine the perception of vowel categories.

In the first experiment using an equivalence classification design, the vowels /a/ and /i/ were used. Six-month-old infants were trained to produce a head-turn response for a visual reinforcer (Figure 13) when the vowel produced by a male talker (with a falling pitch contour) changed from /a/ to /i/. Then, infants' response to novel vowels produced by a women and children was tested.

The results of two experiments provided evidence that 6-month-old infants perceptually equate the vowels spoken by different talkers. One employed a design in which the novel stimuli were gradually introduced in a series of stages. Another employed a design in which the novel stimuli were introduced in a single stage, and first-trial data were examined. The latter data were most important for theory. Since infants had not been previously exposed to the novel vowels, their response on the first trial in which it was presented show whether or not they "categorized" it correctly. The results showed that infants produced near-perfect performance on each of the novel vowels on the first trial during which it was presented (Figure 19). Thus, infants appear to correctly categorize /a/ and /i/ vowels regardless of the talker producing them.

In another study (Kuhl, 1983), these results were extended to vowel categories that are much more similar from an acoustic standpoint and therefore much more difficult to categorize. The vowels were /a/ (as in "cot") versus /ɔ/ (as in "caught"). In naturally produced words containing these vowels, the overlap in the formant frequencies is so extensive that the two categories cannot be separated on this acoustic dimension (Peterson and Barney, 1952). Moreover, in most dialects used in the United States, talkers do not distinguish between the two vowels. The experiment was run just as before. Infants were trained on the /a/ and /ɔ/ vowels spoken by a male talker. Then, novel vowels spoken by female and child talkers, with additional random changes in the pitch contours of these vowels, were introduced. Results of the /a–ɔ/ study again showed correct performance on the novel vowels on the first trial (Kuhl, 1983).

Thus, studies of both spectrally dissimilar and spectrally similar vowel categories show that by 6 months of age infants recognize equivalence classes that conform to the vowel categories of English. Given the demon-

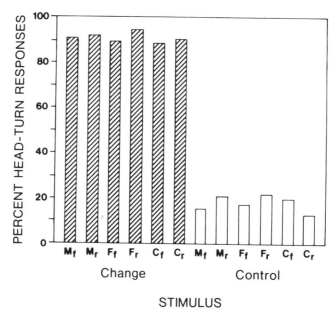

Figure 19. Group data for the /a-i/ vowel categorization experiment. Percent head-turn responses to each individual stimulus in the reinforced (Change trials) and nonreinforced (Control trials) classes are shown. Infants were trained to produce a head-turn response to a vowel (either /a/ or /i/) spoken by a male with a falling pitch contour, and to refrain from turning to the male's production of the opposite vowel. The training stimuli represent the far left "Change" stimulus and the far left "Control" stimulus. After training, novel /a/ and /i/ vowels produced by female and child talkers with either a rising or a falling pitch contour were introduced. The data show near perfect responding to the novel vowels. (Adapted from Kuhl, 1979a.)

stration that infants categorize variants for an easily discriminably contrast (/a-i/), as well as for a difficult contrast (/a–ɔ/), Kuhl (1983) suggested that infants probably demonstrate this vowel "constancy" for all vowel categories in English.

3. Equivalence Classification for Consonant Categories

Research reviewed in earlier sections emphasized the extreme context-dependency of the cues for consonant categories. Thus, studies of equivalence classification for consonant categories in infants are of great interest theoretically. Consonant studies have been reported by Kuhl and her colleagues (Hillenbrand, 1983, 1984, Kuhl, 1980). These experiments use the same basic design as the tests on vowels just described. Infants are trained to differentiate two CV syllables, whose initial consonants differ. In Kuhl (1980) experiments on fricatives are described in which syllables beginning with /s/ as in "sell," are contrasted with syllables beginning with /ʃ/, as in "shell." During training the consonants were spoken by a female talker and they appeared in an /a/ vowel context (/sa/ vs. /ʃ/. Once training on these syllables were complete, novel /s/ and /ʃ/ syllables were introduced. These new syllables differed both in the talker who produced them (2 male and 2 female talkers) and the vowel context in which the consonants appeared (/a/, /i/, and /u/). In all, 22 novel syllables were introduced. The infant's task was to categorize the novel syllables by producing a head-turn response to those beginning with one of the consonants (either /s/ or /ʃ/) and to inhibit the head-turn response to the opposite category.

It was a challenging task, more difficult than the vowel categorization tests in which the within-category variation was not as extreme. Yet infants performed well in the task with some of them producing a near errorless performance (Kuhl, 1980). We will illustrate the results of consonant tests with another example provided by Hillenbrand (1983, 1984), who worked on consonant categorization in the same laboratory. Hillenbrand ran two experiments. In one, categorization was based on the /m/ versus /n/ consonant distinction. In the other, two classes of consonants were distinguished on a featural basis. In both experiments two groups of infants were tested so that the experiment involved a comparison of the performance of these two groups. The two groups differed with respect to the relationship among the stimuli assigned to the reinforced category. For a "phonetic" group, the stimuli were assigned to the reinforced and the unreinforced categories on the basis of their linguistic classification, just as it had been in previous studies. But a second "random" group was tested, and for this group the same stimuli were assigned to either the reinforced or the unreinforced group on a random basis.

A comparison between two groups can be beneficial because it empirically tests the hypothesis that infants perform well in categorization tests by memorizing which stimuli appear in the reinforced class. The "memory" hypothesis can be put forward whenever first-trial data are not used because once the infant has feedback concerning his performance, one could argue that the stimuli are remembered as belonging to the reinforced as opposed to the non-reinforced class of sounds. It is important in these cases to test the hypothesis directly. First-trial data, such as those reported for the vowel categorization studies (Kuhl, 1979a, 1983) cannot be explained by the memory hypothesis, since the infant has no previous experience with the stimulus. In the vowel studies, therefore, control groups testing the memory hypothesis were not necessary.

In the feature-level experiment (Hillenbrand, 1983), a set of stop-plosives (/b/, /d/, and /g/) was contrasted with a set of nasals (/m/, /n/, and ŋ). In order to perform in the task, infants had to recognize properties common to stops but not to nasals, while disregarding the differences among stops and among nasals. Both the experiment involving the phoneme-level (/m/ vs. /n/) contrast and the experiment involving the feature-level contrast employed the two group (phonetic-random) design. In each study, two groups, a phonetic and a random group, were initially trained to discriminate single exemplars from each of the two categories. Then, additional exemplars were progressively introduced. Finally, when all of the stimuli had been introduced, each group was given 75 trials. The data obtained during these last 75 trials were compared for the two groups.

In the feature-level experiment, the phonetic group was initially trained on the /ma-ba/ contrast. Stimuli were then gradually added until the final stage in which the nasal syllables /ma, na, ŋa/ each produced by a male and a female talker, were contrasted with the plosive syllables /ba, da, ga/ produced by the same male and female talkers. Infants in the random group were initially trained on the contrast between the syllable /na/ produced by a male voice and the syllable /ba/ produced by a female voice. Stimuli were added to each category in stages analogous to those for the phonetic group with the exception that the stimuli in each category could not be perceptually organized along a phonetic, or any other, dimension.

In the nasal experiment, the infants in the phonetic group were tested on the /m-n/ contrast. The final stage of the experiment contrasted the syllables /ma, mi, mu/ produced by a male and a female with the syllables /na, ni, nu/ produced by the same two talkers. In the random version of the experiment, the same 12 stimuli were used but they were assigned to the reinforced and nonreinforced categories such that they could not be perceptually organized along any single dimension.

In both experiments, infants in the phonetic group performed significantly better than infants in the random group. Percent correct scores for the phonetic and random groups tested in the feature-level task are shown in Figure 20. The main effects of Trial Type (Change vs. Control) and Group (Phonetic vs. Random) were both significant, as well as the Trial Type × Group interaction, indicating the superior performance by infants in the phonetic group. Infants produced more correct head-turn responses during change trials when the reinforcement contingency was tied to a dimension on which the sounds could be perceptually sorted.

Analysis of the responses to individual stimuli showed that infants in the phonetic group responded correctly to all of the individual stimuli in the category, while infants in the random group tended to respond primarily to the first stimulus in the reinforced category. Figure 21 illustrates this by providing the data for individual stimuli in Hillenbrand's (1983) feature-level experiment. As shown, infants in the phonetic group produced

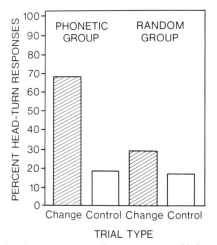

Figure 20.   Percent head-turn responses for two groups of infants tested in a consonant categorization experiment. The "phonetic" group was reinforced for sorting sounds based on phonetic feature. The "random" group was reinforced for sorting sounds based on their arbitrary assignment to one of two groups. Only the phonetic group produced significantly more head-turn respnoses during Change as opposed to Control trials. The subscripts refer to male (m) and female (f) talkers. (From Hillenbrand, 1983.)

head-turn responses to all stimuli representing the reinforced category, and refrained from making head-turn responses to all of the stimuli in the non-reinforced category. In contrast, infants in the random group had to learn which stimuli were reinforced simply by memorizing them. They could not be perceived as a category. These infants produced head-turn responses only to the initial stimulus in the reinforced category that was first paired with reinforcement.

The results were similar for the phoneme-level experiment (Hillenbrand, 1984). The results showed that infants in the phonetic group produced head-turn responses to all stimuli representing the reinforced category, while refraining from responding to all members of the nonreinforced category. In contrast, infants in the random category did not perform well. They had to try and memorize which stimuli were reinforced, and apparently could not do this. They responded reliably only to the first stimulus that was presented from the reinforced category.

These experiments provide strong evidence that infants recognize the similarity among syllables that share their initial consonants, or that share a phonetic feature. They also demonstrate that infants perform very poorly when the reinforcement contingency is not tied to a dimension that allows the perceptual organization of the sounds into two categories. Obviously, infants do not solve these categorization tests by simply mem-

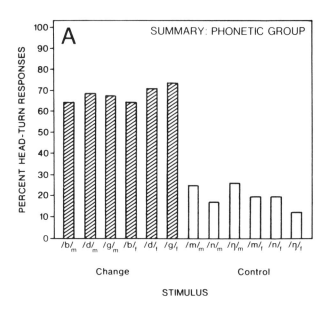

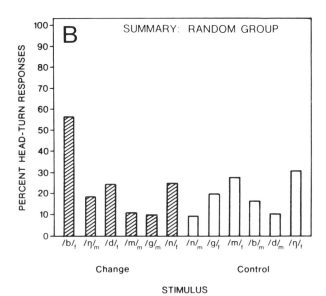

Figure 21. Percent head-turn responses to individual stimuli for infants tested in the "phonetic" and "random" groups of the feature-level categorization experiment. (From Hillenbrand, 1983.)

orizing which stimuli are reinforced. To succeed in these tasks, infants have to recognize similarity among the syllables in the reinforced class.

4. Equivalence Classification for Categories Based on
   Other Features

Categories in speech can also be based on prosodic cues, such as pitch (rising vs. falling), or on voice identification (male vs. female). The literature on phonological development has provided many examples in which children accurately replicate the intonation contour or stress pattern of utterances while failing to accurately produce the phonetic-level elements. These data have been taken in support of the idea that prosodic cues are particularly salient to young infants. Similarly, one would expect that infants might be good at recognizing the differences between male and female voices, since they have early exposure to both their mother's and father's voices.

There are only two experiments using pitch contour as a sorting rule in an equivalence classification experiment. The previously reviewed experiment by Kuhl and Miller (1982) using HAS did not demonstrate that very young infants (4 to 16 weeks) were capable of recognizing a pitch-contour change in the presence of random variation in the vowel (recall that infants in this experiment were shown to be capable of detecting the change in the absence of random variation in the vowel). Kuhl and Miller argued that young infants would find it easier to attend to the pitch dimension if either (a) the perceptual difference between the two levels of the pitch dimension were increased or (b) the perceptual difference between the two levels of the competing dimension, vowel identity, were decreased. Categorization studies on adult listeners demonstrate that reaction time when classifying stimuli on the pitch dimension decreases under both conditions listed above (Carrell, Smith, and Pisoni, 1981).

To test this using an equivalence classification design, Kuhl and Hillenbrand (1979) employed the same set of vowel stimuli used in the /a-i/ and /a-ɔ/ studies. The stimuli consisted of the vowels /a/, /i/, and /ɔ/, each computer synthesized to represent productions by a man, a woman, and a child, and each produced with both a rising and a falling intonation contour. The set of stimuli could thus be sorted perceptually on the basis of either vowel identity, pitch contour, or talker. Kuhl and Hillenbrand were interested in determining, first, whether infants were capable of performing on the head-turn task when reinforcement was dictated by the pitch dimension rather than on the vowel dimension and second, whether infants sorting on the basis of pitch performed more accurately when the perceptual difference between the levels of the competing dimension (vowel identity) was smaller. They predicted that infants would perform more accurately when the levels of the vowel dimension were represented by /a/ and /ɔ/ rather than when they were represented by /a/ and /i/.

Two groups of 6-month-olds were run in experiments identical to the ones previously described on vowel identity. The results confirmed that the 6-month-olds were capable of sorting these stimuli using the pitch-contour dimension, but the second prediction was not confirmed. Infants performed with equal facility in the two experiments. Thus, while young infants (4 to 16 weeks) have not been shown to organize stimuli into categories based on pitch, 6-month-olds can do so.

Another set of experiments tested whether 6-month-old infants could sort sounds based upon the sex of the talker. Miller, Younger, and Morse (1982) tested infants in an equivalence classification experiment in which the reinforcement contingency was based on the difference between male and female voices. They had the male and female talkers produce "Hi." Infants were reinforced for producing a head-turn response when a change from a male to a female voice occurred but not when one female voice changed to a different female voice. These authors also tested infants in a random condition to which the stimuli were randomly assigned to the reinforced and unreinforced categories. The results of the experiment showed that infants tested in the condition in which the male–female distinction dictated the reinforcement contingency performed significantly above chance. Infants tested in the condition in which the stimuli were randomly assigned to the reinforced and nonreinforced categories did not.

In a second experiment, Miller et al. examined infants' use of another sorting rule. This time the reinforcement contingency was based on the fundamental frequency (high vs. low) that occurred in the productions of "Hi." This acoustic variable would normally be highly correlated with the perception of sex differences in voices. However, in this case the acoustic measurement resulted in the assignment of both male and female voices to the high- and low-fundamental frequency categories. The reason for this is that the authors used the "peak" in the fundamental rather than a measure of the "average" fundamental. The results showed that infants could not learn this contingency.

The authors concluded that the infants must have been using an acoustic dimension other than the fundamental frequency to sort male and female voices. However, since the measure of fundamental frequency for the male and female voices was the peak fundamental frequency, rather than the average, the possibility remains that if the measure of the fundamental had been something closer to the average fundamental frequency, infants may have succeeded at the task. Nevertheless, the experiments demonstrate that infants are capable of sorting sounds based on the differences between male and female voices. They also suggest that sorting is not based on the peak frequency in the fundamental.

5. Summary

These experiments demonstrate that infants can indeed "sort" sounds. Infants detect equivalences between auditory events that differ dramatically, and do so with apparent ease. They perceive similarities between speech sounds that have undergone various transformations due to the talker who produced the sound and the context in which it appeared. At the segment level, the experiments show that infants perceive the similarity among vowels produced by different talkers, and among syllables containing the same consonant. In the latter case, infants have been shown to recognize the similarity among consonants even when they appear in different vowel contexts. Categorization is not restricted to the segment level, since the data show that infants perceive the equivalence among sounds sharing a phonetic feature. Moreover, infants recognize similarity among sounds whose prosodic features are similar, and among sounds produced by male as opposed to female talkers. In each of these cases, infants treat discriminably different sounds as equivalent, while maintaining a distinction between two categories. By 6 months of age, infants appear to be "natural" categorizers.

6. Issues Related to Equivalence Classification

The existence of these perceptual categories in 6-month-old infants has important theoretical implications for the development of speech. Without the ability to recognize that the sounds produced by different talkers are equivalent, infants would have to learn sound–meaning correspondences independently for each talker. Moreover, preserving a "constancy" for speech uttered by different talkers is fundamental to the infant's own production of speech. Infants learn to produce sounds by imitating those produced by another, and imitation depends on the ability to equate the sounds produced by others with ones infants themselves produce. That infants do indeed preserve phonetic identity for vowels spoken by different talkers is thus important to the acquisition of speech and language.

The value of preserving phonetic identity across context and position at the segment or feature level is more complex. Theorists argue that detailed knowledge of segmental phonology exists in adults and is highly rule-governed (Chomsky & Halle, 1968). Do infants' abilities to perceive the similarities among syllables sharing a particular speech sound reflect a rule-governed phonology wherein segments consisting of consonants and vowels are represented? Kuhl (1985b) has addressed this question. It has two parts. One part focuses on the size of the unit that category member-ship is based on, that is, the "unit-of-analysis." The other part focuses on the nature of the information involved, whether it is speech information, per se, that is specified.

The first has to do with the representation of speech. Specifically, do infants' abilities to recognize similarities among syllables whose initial consonants are identical mandate a segmental representation of speech? Stated differently, when infants perceive the similarity among syllables such as /ma/, /mi/, and /mu/, and distinguish them from /na/, /ni/, and /nu/, does it mean that infants represent these syllables as being comprised of two phonetic segments—/C/ and /V/? Furthermore, does the recognition of equivalence derive from the specification that syllables such as /ma/, /mi/, and /mu/ share the common consonantal segment /m/?

The data are consistent with the claim that infants have access to a seg-ment-level analysis. In fact, the data presented in these studies (Hillen-brand, 1983, 1984; Kuhl, 1979a, 1980, 1983) provide the first evidence allowing one to advance such a claim. Nevertheless, while infants' abili-ties can be explained by a phonetic-segment representation, the data do not necessitate this explanation (Kuhl, 1985b, 1986a). Consider the /ma, mi, mu/ case. The claim that the perception of similarity is based on the recognition of a common phonetic segment (/m/) in each of the syllables depends upon a number of factors. First, we need to establish the fact that perceptual grouping is not due to a failure to discriminate. If infants cannot hear the difference between /ma/, /mi/, and /mu/, then we have no evidence of "categorization," much less of "segmentation."

We do, in fact, have evidence that this is not the case. Infants' percep-tion of similarity does not result from a failure to discriminate—these infants readily perceive the differences between the syllables. Yet, they perceive their similarities. We know, then, that infants' representation of these syllables allows them to break the syllables down into some kind of "parts"—ones that allow them to detect similarity at the beginnings of the syllables in spite of differences at the ends of syllables. At the very least, then, this ability must rely on a representation of units that allows *portions of syllables* to be isolated and compared across syllables.

Experiments have also shown that infants are capable of categorizing at a featural level. Hillenbrand (1983) demonstrated that infants detect the similarity among a group of plosives (/b, d, g/) and distinguish them from a group of nasals (/m, n, ŋ/). The representation must therefore allow simi-larity to be detected at a featural level. So the representation must allow these *portions of syllables* to be isolated and compared as well. We con-clude, therefore, that infants can break syllables down into some kind of "parts." But we do not as yet know what the "parts" consist of, phonetic segments, phonetic features, or "something else." (See Kuhl, 1985b, 1986a for further discussion.)

Other experiments have focused on the "unit-of-analysis" issue. Mehler and Bertoncini (1978) argued in favor of the syllable, but their experiment cannot be interpreted unequivocally. In another relevant experiment, Miller and Eimas (1979) presented 2- to 4-month-olds with a random sequence of the syllables /ba/ and /dae/ during the preshift phase of an HAS experiment and the syllables /bae/ and /da/ during the postshift phase. The sucking-recovery scores demonstrated that infants were capable of detecting the change when it involved the recombination of consonants and vowels to form two new syllables. In a second experiment, Miller and Eimas extended these findings to a situation in which the infants were required to detect a recombination at the feature-level. Infants were presented with the syllables /ba/ and /ta/ prior to the shift-point and the syllables /da/ and /pa/ after, thus requiring the infants to detect a change in the combination of the levels of the voicing and place features. Again, discrimination was evidenced.

These outcomes could support either one of two conclusions. The results are consistent with the idea that infants recognized recombinations of segments, thus suggesting that they rely on a segment-level representation. This is the explanation preferred by the authors. But it is also possible that infants recognized that a new "whole-syllable" was presented and this would not require a segment-level representation. Additional experiments will be needed to provide data on the "unit-of-analysis" question.

A second issue raised by the equivalence classification studies is the specific nature of the information represented. When infants recognize that vowels spoken by different talkers are similar, or that plosive consonants such as /b/, /d/, and /g/ are similar, what kind of information is the recognition of equivalence based on? Can one assume that what is recognized as similar is speech information per se? Or is some other information, wholly independent of speech, responsible? The answer depends on whether or not some property can be identified that allows one to group sounds within a category together, while at the same time serving to separate the two categories. Once the property is specified, its status as "phonetic" information can be assessed.

Consider the vowel example. Kuhl (1979a) argued that the categories /a/ and /i/ might have been distinguished on the basis of the diffuse-compact feature (Jakobson, Fant, and Halle, 1969). The vowel /a/ is "compact," with one mid-frequency peak in the spectrum, while /i/ vowels are "diffuse," with two or more widely spaced spectral peaks. This feature would be present regardless of the talker producing the vowel. Thus, infants could have sorted the vowels produced by different talkers on this basis. If we had evidence that the vowels /a/ and /i/ were separated on the basis of the diffuse-compact feature, could we claim that the categorization involved speech information, per se? Stating that categorization was based on a distinctive feature such as compact-diffuse suggests that it is speech information, but it does not have to be. The feature can be described in purely acoustic terms. Compact spectra have a single prominent spectral peak while diffuse spectra have more than one. Therefore, categorization could presumably have occurred without recognizing the information's status as a feature of speech.

The same argument can be made for Hillenbrand's (1983) feature-level experiments. Infants in that experiment separated consonant categories that differed with regard to their feature specification. But did categorization depend upon the recognition of a common featural specification of the sounds, or on an acoustic property that underlies featural specification? Recognizing this, Hillenbrand (1983) argued that infants in his feature-level experiment may have separated the categories based on a simple property of their overall spectra—their rise-time characteristics. Plosives, as the term implies, have rapid onsets. Their amplitudes grow faster than those of nasals, whose rise-times are comparatively slow. In addition, nasals have a low-frequency resonance associated with them. Infants could have used these relatively simple properties in distinguishing the plosive category from the nasal category.

One approach to this general question would be to test infants' responses to nonspeech sounds whose spectral shapes mimic the formant patterns of the sounds without sounding like speech. Sine-wave analogs of plosive and nasals would capture their rise-time differences without being identified as speech, and might be perceptually grouped with their speech counterparts. Let us argue, for the moment, that nonspeech sounds are categorized with their speech-sound counterparts. What could we claim? Unfortunately, while it would indeed be an interesting finding, such results would not allow one to claim that categorization occurs "wholly independently of speech." These nonspeech analogs mimic the critical features in speech and may be detected solely because of this. That is, the mechanisms underlying speech perception may be designed to detect these properties, and stimuli mimicking these properties may "fool" them (Kuhl, 1986b).

The only way to dissociate the "phonetic" account from the "wholly independent" account (Kuhl, 1986a, 1986b) is either to: (a) construct a case in which the two accounts lead to opposite predictions, that is, construct categories in which categorization using the acoustic property does not correlate with categorization by phonetic identity; or (b) show that a nonhuman species perceives the same categories. In the former, the two are effectively dissociated because the predictions are opposite one another. Depending on the outcome, infants are either using acoustic or phonetic information to categorize. In the latter, the two are dissociated because animals have no phonetic representation. If animals succeed, they do so using a purely auditory strategy. Their success indicates that categorization can be accomplished without the recognition of the information's status as speech, per se. At this point, we do not know whether the information used to categorize sounds in these experiments involves a phonetic representation of speech. Future experiments will be necessary to determine this.

VII.   CROSS-LANGUAGE STUDIES OF SPEECH PERCEPTION

Experiments on adults from different linguistic environments and on infants being reared in those environments offer a unique opportunity to observe the potential effects of specific kinds of experience on perception. Cross-language comparisons provide a way to test the hypothesis that effects such as categorical perception are attributable to language-specific processes. If CP reflects a language-specific process by which phonetic units are categorized, then listeners tested on nonnative phonetic contrasts should not show CP. Conversely, speakers for whom the phonetic contrast is one used in their language should produce the effect.

A.   Cross-Language Studies on Adults

The earliest studies on the perception of voicing by adults confirmed the fact that there were differences in the perception of voiced and voiceless stimuli that could be attributed to the language of the listener. Studies of English, Spanish, and Thai adults showed that the three groups partitioned the same VOT continuum differently. English listeners partitioned the continuum at VOT's that separated voiceless-unaspirated and voiceless-aspirated categories, while Spanish listeners partitioned it between the prevoiced and voiceless-unaspirated categories (Abramson & Lisker, 1979; Williams, 1977). Thai adults partitioned the continuum into three categories. In all instances, adult listeners showed enhanced discriminability in the vicinity of their respective phoneme boundaries, but not elsewhere.

This pattern of results is clearly illustrated in the study by Miyawaki et al. (1975) previously discussed. Recall that they compared discrimination performance using a continuum ranging from /ra/ to /la/ in Japanese and

American monolingual speakers. The results demonstrated that while the American listeners produced a clear peak in the discrimination function at the phonetic boundary between /r/ and /l/, discrimination performance for Japanese monolinguals was near chance across the entire continuum (Figure 10). Other studies examined English adults' abilities to discriminate Czech contrasts (Trehub, 1976) and Hindi contrasts (Werker, Gilbert, Humphrey, and Tees, 1981). Both studies reported a failure to provide evidence of discrimination.

These studies provide clear evidence that linguistic experience exerts a major influence on the perception of phonetic distinctions. It would appear that accurate discrimination of small differences in the acoustic cues underlying phonetic distinctions is restricted to instances in which the acoustic cues are phonemically contrastive for the adult listener. This is qualified only in the instance in which nonnative English-speaking adults are tested on the English voicing contrast (Streeter, 1976; Williams, 1977). In this case, discrimination has been shown, although performance is not as good as that produced by English-speaking adults.

While the data as a whole suggest that it is difficult to discriminate contrasts that are not phonemic in an adult's linguistic environment, they do not assess the degree to which specific kinds of training or feedback might improve an adult's ability to discriminate nonphonemic contrasts. Three studies have examined the effects of training. Strange (1972) attempted to train American college-age students to discriminate stimuli in the region of the Spanish boundary on a VOT continuum. Results showed a broadening of the discrimination peak, but this improved discrimination did not generalize to a VOT series with a different place of articulation (alveolar as opposed to bilabial). Werker et al. (1981) tested Hindi and American adults on two Hindi contrasts. One group of Americans was given training, another was not. Werker et al. showed that without training, American adults provided no evidence of discriminating either Hindi contrast, but that with training, one of the two Hindi contrasts showed a little improvement.

More positive results on the effects of training have been obtained in a study by Pisoni, Aslin, Perey, and Hennessy (1982). These authors showed that English-speaking adults can be trained to identify three categories on the VOT continuum. Moreover, the subjects demonstrated two discrimination peaks which corresponded to the locations of the Spanish and English phonetic boundaries, regardless of whether they were trained to identify the stimuli or not. Two things may have accounted for these more positive results. First, Pisoni et al. resynthesized the VOT stimuli so as to improve the detectability of the prevoicing, and make it more similar to the sounds produced by native-speaking Spanish speakers (Williams,

1977). This factor alone, or its combination with feedback on the discrimination test, may have accounted for their success.

Two factors need to be examined more carefully in adult cross-language studies. First, investigators have not optimized discriminability by altering the psychophysical procedure used or the degree of stimulus uncertainty involved in the task. The absence of enhanced discriminability may be due to the difficutly in performing in certain kinds of discrimination tasks. Cross-language differences will be particularly obvious when the procedure used to test the adult listener requires the retention of the stimulus for a longer period of time, such that the listener must rely on "labels" for the stimuli. Second, the stimuli used in some of these experiments may fail to capture the acoustic cues necessary to produce "good exemplars" of the contrasts, particularly when nonnative speakers synthesize the stimuli. Nonetheless, it appears to be quite difficult for adults to produce the enhanced discriminability at phonetic boundaries for nonnative contrasts that is so evident when listening to their native contrasts. How early are these cross-language differences evidenced?

B. Cross-Language Studies on Infants

As we have reviewed, adults demonstrate profound cross-language differences. Infant studies can thus provide information concerning the development of these differences. Do infants initially discriminate all phonetic contrasts and then gradually acquire language-specific phonological rules which effectively require them to collapse some of the categories? If so, is the change brought about by experience in producing and/or listening to the sounds or by some other factor?

Attempts to discover the age at which infants demonstrate differences in their perception of native and nonnative phonetic contrasts, and what those differences can be attributed to, has received a considerable amount of attention. The first experiments asked whether young infants could discriminate contrasts that are not phonemic in the linguistic environment in which they are being reared. For example, the evidence is fairly convincing that infants reared in non-English environments are capable of discriminating at least one contrast that is phonemic in English but not in the infant's native language. Streeter (1976) demonstrated that 2-month-old Kikuyu infants discriminated the English voicing contrast in addition to the voicing contrast that is phonemic in Kikuyu but not in English (prevoiced vs. voiceless-unaspirated stops.) Lasky, Syrdal-Lasky, and Klein (1975) demonstrated similar results for Spanish infants.

Other experiments have also provided evidence that infants discriminate nonnative contrasts, and directly compared infants' and adults' discrimination of these nonnative contrasts. Trehub (1976) showed that American infants (but not American adults tested with the same stimuli in the same laboratory) discriminated a Czech contrast. In a more recent study, Werker et al. (1981) tested American infants, American adults, and Hindi adults on the discrimination of two Hindi contrasts. In both instances, the performances of American infants tested using the HT technique were indistinguishable from that of Hindi adults. American adults, however, even with training, failed to perform significantly above chance.

Discrimination of the Spanish contrast by American infants has been more difficult to establish, suggesting that it may be more difficult to discriminate. Eimas (1975a), using the HAS technique, failed to find evidence for the discrimination of small differences in VOT in the region of the Spanish boundary by 2- to 3-month-old American infants. He did, however, provide some evidence for the discrimination of large differences in the prevoiced region of the VOT continuum (-10 ms VOT vs. -70 ms VOT). Similarly, Eilers, Gavin, and Wilson (1979) tested 6-month-old American and Spanish infants using the HT technique and demonstrated that American infants failed to provide evidence of discrimination of stimuli straddling the Spanish boundary, while Spanish infants did discriminate the stimuli. In contrast, Aslin, Pisoni, Hennessey, and Perey (1981) provide the clearest evidence to date that American infants are capable of discriminating prevoiced stimuli. They used a new set of stimuli, the same as those used by Pisoni et al. (1982), which were synthesized to enhance the perception of prevoicing. Aslin et al. (1981) also used a technique that minimized stimulus uncertainty and memory constraints. Their results demonstrated that 6- to 11-month-old American infants are capable of discriminating closely-spaced stimuli in the prevoiced region of the VOT continuum. Whether these more positive results should be attributed to the new stimuli, the testing procedure, or both, is not known.

In the aggregate, these studies support the notion that young infants discriminate many, if not all, phonetic contrasts regardless of the linguistic environment in which they are reared. But when is it that infants begin to reflect language-specific perceptual biases? When would Japanese infants fail to discriminate /r/ from /l/ like their elders do? In the first developmental study on infants' cross-language abilities, Werker and Tees (1984) provide important data suggesting that infants' loss of a discriminative capacity they once had for nonnative contrasts occurs prior to one year of age. Their data suggest that between 10 and 12 months of age infants fail to discriminate nonnative contrasts that they successfully discriminated earlier. These authors provide cross-sectional and longitudinal data on the discrimination of a Hindi contrast and a Salish contrast by infants reared in an English-speaking environment. Infants in three age groups were tested, 6–8 months, 8–10 months, and 10–12 months of age. The HT technique was used and infants were given up to 45 trials to meet a performance criterion. In each case in which a failure to discriminate was obtained, infants were shown to discriminate an English contrast both before and after testing on the nonnative contrast. This demonstrated that the failure to discriminate was not due to fatigue or other factors.

Results of both the cross-sectional and longitudinal samples demonstrated a gradual decline in infants' abilities with increasing age. Most of the 6- to 8-month-olds met criterion on both contrasts. In the 8–10 month group, a smaller proportion, but still a majority of the infants, met criterion on both contrasts. But by 10 to 12 months of age virtually none of the infants met the criterion. These data are shown in Figure 22. Statistical

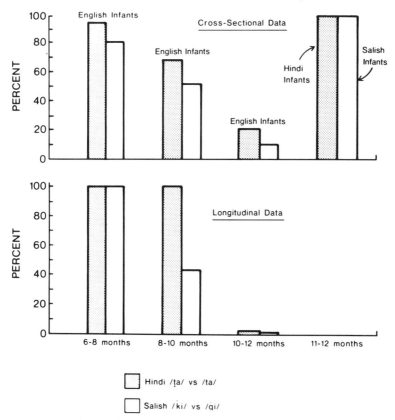

Figure 22. Number of infants meeting a performance criterion on the discrimination of nonnative contrasts at three different ages. (From Werker and Tees, 1984.)

comparisons demonstrated that performance by the oldest group differed significantly from performance by the two younger groups. Further tests confirmed the fact that 10- to 12-month-old Hindi infants could still discriminate the Hindi contrast.

These data provide the first strong evidence supporting the claim that infants initially discriminate all contrasts and then eventually fail to discriminate ones that are not phonemic in their language. Moreover, the comparison between the 12-month-old English and Hindi children allows one to assert that the difference between them is attributable to language experience of some kind. What accounts for this developmental change?

Eimas (1975a) addressed the question early on. He hypothesized that because of a lack of exposure to certain phonetic units during development the infant lost the ability to distinguish them from contrastive units. He attributed this to the potential need for innately specified phonetic-feature detectors to be stimulated in order to remain functional. The problem with this interpretation is that it argues that auditory experience with the contrasts, per se, is the critical factor that accounts for the differences eventually seen in adults. This account fails to explain all of the differences in cross-language abilities because in certain instances the particular phonetic unit actually occurs in the speech of the adults of the language. It does not occur contrastively, but it is produced by the adult speakers of the language. For example, Japanese adults produce exemplars of /ra/ and /la/ (Goto, 1971), and American adults produce exemplars of the Spanish prevoiced /ba/ (Lisker & Abramson, 1964), even though in both instances their usage is not phonemically contrastive. It does not appear to be the case, therefore, that the mere presence or absence of auditory experience with a particular phonetic unit could explain all of the cross-language differences between adult speakers.

Another account of the eventual disintegration of discriminative ability is that it occurs at another level, one less affected by sensory factors and more sensitive to cognitive and linguistic factors. Japanese infants may eventually collapse the /r/ vs. /l/ categories because they recognize that the two phonetic units are used interchangeably when referencing a particular object or event. They recognize that the distinction does not change the meaning of a word. This requires, of course, that infants (a) recognize that objects and events in the world are named, and (b) that they correlate a specific acoustic signal with a specific object or event. Only then could the infant recognize that different acoustic signals are equivalent in naming a particular event. When might these linguistic/cognitive abilities be expected to emerge in the child? The language-acquisition literature is not at all clear on this question. By 18 months children clearly demonstrate the knowledge that things in the world have names by their productive naming of certain objects, people, and events. But when comprehension can be said to be "productive," that is, not specific to a given instance of the category, is not well established.

In summary, then, whether this eventual failure to discriminate nonnative constrasts is a sensory-level phenomenon, due to a lack of exposure to certain sounds, or a linguistic/cognitive level phenomenon, attributable to a reorganization of sounds into phonologically relevant categories, is as yet undetermined, but these new data are an important step in relating infants' early speech perception abilities to the acquisition of language.

VIII. THE COGNITIVE REPRESENTATION OF SPEECH: STUDIES ON INTERMODAL SPEECH PERCEPTION

The studies reviewed to this point have examined infant speech perception as a purely auditory phenomenon. These studies have amply illustrated the exquisite skill which infants demonstrate when perceiving speech auditorially. They show that very young infants discriminate and categorize sounds in ways that conform to the linguistic classification of the sounds. But is speech a purely auditory phenomenon for the infant? We turn now to an examination of infants' cross-modal perception of speech.

Kuhl and Meltzoff (1982) posed an auditory–visual cross-modal mapping problem to infants. They examined infants' recognition of the correspondence between mouth movements presented visually and auditorially. Infants were shown two filmed images, side by side, of a talker producing two different vowel sounds, /a/ and /i/ (Figure 23). The two mouths moved in perfect synchrony. (See Kuhl and Meltzoff, 1984 for details.) The sound track corresponding to one of the two faces (either /a/ or /i/) was presented through a loudspeaker midway between the visual images, so there were no spatial clues concerning which of the two faces produced the sound. The hypothesis was that if infants were capable of detecting the correspondence between the auditorially and visually presented speech information, they would look longer at the face that "matched" the sound.

Infants were placed in an infant seat within a three-sided cubicle. The infants were video- and audio-recorded. The experimental procedure involved a familiarization and test phase (Figure 24). During the familiarization phase, an infant was shown each face separately for 10 sec without sound. Following this 20-sec period, the faces were briefly covered until the infant's gaze returned to midline. Then, the sound was turned on and both faces were presented for the 2-minute test phase. The sound pre-

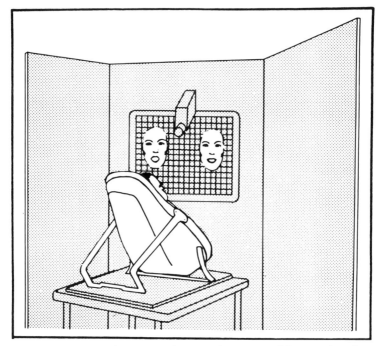

Figure 23. Experimental set-up used to test the cross-modal perception of speech in infants. Infants see two faces producing the vowels /a/ and /i/ while a single sound (either /a/ or /i/) is presented from a loudspeaker located midway between the two facial images. (From Kuhl and Meltzoff, 1982.)

sented to the infants, the left–right positioning of the two faces, the order of familiarization, and the sex of the infant were counterbalanced. Infants' visual fixations were scored by an independent observer who could neither hear the sound nor see the faces presented to the infant. The observer recorded the amount of time the infant spent fixating the left and right facial images.

	FAMILIARIZATION PHASE			TEST PHASE
VISUAL STIMULI	FACE 1	FACE 2	midline gaze	BOTH FACES
AUDITORY STIMULI	...	...		/a/.../a/.../a/.../a/...
TIME	10 sec.	10 sec.		2 min.

Figure 24. Procedure used to test cross-modal speech perception in infants. (From Kuhl and Meltzoff, 1982.)

The results of the experiment clearly supported the hypothesis that infants detected a match between "visual" and "auditory" speech. The percentage of total fixation time devoted to the matched versus mismatched face was calculated for each infant. A significant proportion of the infants (24 of 32) looked longer at the face matching the sound than at the mismatched face ($p < 0.01$). The mean percentage fixation time devoted to the matching face was 73.63% which is significantly different from the 50% chance level ($p < 0.01$). There were no significant left–right preferences, face preferences, or familiarization order effects. MacKain, Studdert-Kennedy, Spieker, and Stern (1983) replicated this basic cross-modal effect using di-syllables varying in both the consonant and the vowel, such as "mama" and "lulu," although there were also some interesting interactions with the side the matched face appeared on in that study.

In a second experiment, Kuhl and Meltzoff (1982) examined the nature of the auditory information that was critical to the detection of these auditory–visual correspondences. They altered the original auditory stimuli (the sets of /a/ and /i/ vowels) so as to remove the spectral information necessary to identify the vowels (formant frequencies) while preserving their temporal characteristics (amplitude and duration). The stimuli were computer-generated pure-tone signals centered at the average fundamental frequency of the female talker (200 Hz). Their onset and offset characteristics, and overall amplitude envelopes, were synthesized to duplicate those of the original vowels. Kuhl and Meltzoff argued that if the ability to detect auditory–visual correspondences was based on knowledge of the relationship between a particular articulatory movement and its concomitant speech sound, then the effect should not obtain when the auditory information provided the infant was not sufficient to identify the speech sound. Since the signals used in the second experiment did not contain information sufficient to identify the sound, they predicted that the effect would not be reproduced.

Kuhl and Meltzoff's second experiment also served as a test of an alternative hypothesis, namely that infants in their first experiment might not be relying on spectral information, but on temporal information to link particular face–voice pairs. Other experiments on infants suggest that they can detect gross temporal misalignment between mouth movements and sound (Dodd, 1979). While Kuhl and Meltzoff argued that the technique they employed to align the sound and film tracks made such a temporal hypothesis an unlikely explanation for the outcome of their first experiment, the second experiment addressed the issue directly. Thus, if infants in the first experiment were relying on temporal information to link particular face-voice pairs, then they should still look longer at the "matched" face, even though the vowels were now represented only by

their sine-wave amplitude envelopes. Alternatively, if the spectral information contained in the vowels was necessary for the detection of these
auditory–visual correspondences, performance should drop to chance.

Another group of 32 infants between 18 and 20 weeks were tested using
the exact same procedure and the new stimuli. Infants looked at the same
/a/ and /i/ faces, but instead of listening to vowels they heard pure tones.
The pure tones matched the temporal and amplitude characteristics of the
original vowels so that they grew louder as the mouths opened wider, and
became softer as the mouths closed. The results showed that the mean per
cent fixation time to the "matched" face dropped to chance. Thus, the
study demonstrated that some aspect of the spectral information contained in the original vowels was critical to the detection of the cross-
modal match.

The recognition of auditory–visual correspondences for speech suggests that by four months of age the infant possesses some knowledge of
the relationship between the auditory and articulatory correlates of
speech. They appear to recognize that the vowel /a/ "goes with" an open
mouth, while the vowel /i/ "goes with" spread lips. What accounts for
infants' cross-modal speech perception abilities? Have infants simply
learned to associate an open mouth with the sound pattern /a/ and re-
tracted lips with /i/? If so, then the interpretation is not complicated; it is
simple association learning. We do not favor this explanation, whereby an
arbitrary pairing was forged by associative learning (Kuhl & Meltzoff,
1984). But if not this, then on what basis is the match between sound
pattern and facial configuration made?

Kuhl and Meltzoff discussed two possibilities. The first suggests that
the effect derives from a phonetic representation of speech, the second
that the effect occurs wholly independently of speech. Both accounts are
fairly complicated and are taken up in detail elsewhere (Kuhl & Meltzoff,
1984; in press).

The main postulate of the "phonetic account" is that the perceived
match between the acoustic and optic information is based on infants'
knowledge of phonetics—in this case, their knowledge about the auditory
and visual realizations of phonetic information, and the equivalence of
this information when perceived by eye and by ear. The second account
argues very differently. It holds that the detection of a match is based on
something else, something "wholly independent of speech." By this account, the auditory and visual byproducts of speech are related by some
other property, one directed by simple physics.

A current experiment aimed at separating the phonetics and physics
explanations is underway. The test involves using nonspeech auditory
analogs of the three-formant vowels. If these nonspeech analogs, when

presented with the same facial images, result in a replication of the cross-modal effect, it is consistent with the notion that a physical property, independent of speech, relates particular mouth configurations to particular kinds of auditory signals. If not, infants' abilities to detect these auditory-visual correspondences for speech may reflect an intermodal representation of speech information, per se.

Kuhl and Meltzoff (1982; in press) advocate the latter interpretation. They relied, in part, on another observation made during the cross-modal experiments, one also suggestive of knowledge of intermodal relations for speech. The observation was that infants demonstrated differential vocal imitation of the speech and nonspeech stimuli (Kuhl and Meltzoff, 1982). Infants tested in their first experiment (who listened to the vowels) produced vocalizations themselves. These infants appeared to imitate the vowels they heard, particularly their prosodic characteristics. Figure 25 provides an example of an infant's imitation of the fundamental frequency (pitch) contours of the adult's vowels (Kuhl & Meltzoff, 1982). The adult produced a rise-fall intonation contour. The infant, whose vocal folds are shorter, produces a higher absolute frequency when compared to the adult, but mimics the rise-fall pattern in his own production of the sound. As shown, the infant alternated his productions with hers, taking turns in the exchange. These findings suggest that infants are capable of vocal imitation. They can direct their articulators to produce an auditory signal that is perceived as similar to the sound produced by another.

The imitative responses produced by the infants listening to speech were not equaled by the infants who listened to the nonspeech sounds. In comparison to the ten infants who babbled in response to hearing the speech sounds (Experiment 1), only one infant who heard the nonspeech tones (Experiment 2) did so. The infants listening to nonspeech were curiously silent. These infants watched the same faces producing speech sounds, and looked just as long at them as infants in the speech condition

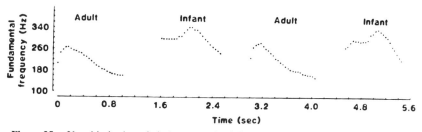

Figure 25. Vocal imitation of pitch contour by infants. (From Kuhl and Meltzoff, 1982.)

did (Kuhl and Meltzoff, 1984), but they did not vocalize. Apparently, speech sounds are more effective elicitors of infant babbling than non-speech sounds are (Kuhl, 1986c).

There is no question that imitation and cross-modal perception exist in a domain independent of speech. Results showing that newborns imitate facial gestures are a powerful demonstration of this (Meltzoff & Moore, 1977, 1983). The finding that speech is intermodally represented in infants complements other work on cross-modal perception by infants. It has been suggested that young infants have a general ability to detect and utilize intermodal equivalences (Meltzoff, 1985; Meltzoff & Borton, 1979; Meltzoff & Moore, 1977, 1983; Spelke, 1979). The present experiment extends this previous work by providing another example of young infants' cross-modal abilities. The degree to which these speech effects uniquely differ from, or are a special case of, more general intermodal abilities is yet to be determined. The recognition of cross-modal correspondences for speech provides a particularly rich and detailed set of examples with which to examine the nature and bases of infants' abilities to relate information picked up through different modalities.

Further work will either suggest that speech is a "special" case of intermodal representation, or alternatively that it is part of a more general cognitive proclivity to represent information in this way. In either case, any characterization of the infant's initial state has to account for the infant's apparent ability, at 4 months of age, to match the sound produced by another with a vocal tract it cannot see, articulators (like the larynx responsible for the matched pitch contours shown in Figure 25) it cannot feel, and without inordinate numbers of attempts to do so. The infant appears capable of vocal imitation. Any theory of infants' initial state will have to account for this (Kuhl, 1986c).

Work in this same laboratory is now being directed toward exploring the relationship between the detection of auditory–visual correspondences and vocal imitation, and the extent to which either or both depend on "babbling" or other specific kinds of experience (Kuhl & Meltzoff, 1984; Meltzoff & Kuhl, in press). Moreover, further tests will be aimed at examining whether the basis of the effect is the intermodal representation of speech information per se, or whether some other, more general knowledge relating faces to sounds, wholly independently of speech, could account for it (Kuhl & Meltzoff, 1984, in press). This demonstration of auditory-visual speech perception in 4-month-old infants provides information on the acquisition of knowledge of the relationship between audition and articulation in infancy, and represents a first step in exploring the intermodal representation of speech in infants.

IX. SPEECH AS A SOCIAL SIGNAL: VOICE RECOGNITION

Research on the infant's perception of speech has been primarily aimed at questions related to its linguistic significance. In the past, little attention has been paid to the social significance of speech for infants. Recently, however, research has focused on two aspects of research on voice recognition by infants. As might be expected, work in this area began with the question of infants' detection and preference for the voices of their caretakers, auditory signals that have obvious social significance for the young infant.

A. Recognition of Mother's Voice

Research on voice recognition initially focused on the recognition of mother's voice vs. that of a strange female voice. In the first of these studies, Mills and Melhuish (1974) tested 20- to 30-day-old infants using a modified HAS procedure. Infants were presented with a tape-recorded sample of a stranger's voice contingent on their high-amplitude sucking responses during the preshift phase. Then, two 3-minute test periods followed during which high-amplitude sucking responses were reinforced by either the mother's voice or the stranger's voice. The results indicated that the infants produced significantly more high-amplitude sucking responses during the postshift phase in which mother's voice was presented. However, the interpretation of the study is confounded by the fact that mother's voice was presented live while the stranger's voice was tape recorded.

A subsequent study by Mehler, Bertoncini, Barriere, and Jassik-Gerschenfeld (1978), also using the HAS procedure, avoided this problem. They presented 4- to 6-week-old infants with speech produced by the infant's mother or another mother. Mehler et al. recorded all utterances and had each woman produce speech segments that were highly intonated (typical of "Motherese") and others that were monotone. They could then test the effects of mother vs. stranger and highly intonated vs. monotone voice on the infant's preference. The results indicated that infants preferred their mother's voice, but only when it was highly intonated. The authors concluded that 1-month-olds are capable of recognizing and actually prefer mother's voice, but that recognition and preference may depend upon the mother's production of highly-intonated utterances.

More recently, DeCasper and Fifer (1980) provided evidence of a preference for mother's voice in even younger infants, 3-day-olds. A modified version of the HAS was used. DeCasper and Fifer made the presentation of tape-recorded voice signals contingent on the duration of the interval between sucking bursts (the IBI). For half the infants, mother's voice was presented contingent on IBI's that were shorter than the median IBI obtained during baseline; for the other half, mother's voice was contingent on the occurrence of IBI's that were longer than the median IBI. For both groups, another mother's voice was presented in the opposite condition. DeCasper and Fifer showed that the infants responded in such a way so as to turn on their mother's voice as opposed to another mother's voice. For half the infants, they then reversed the conditions for producing their own mother's voice and showed that the infants again adapted their sucking patterns to turn on the voice of their own mother.

Since these infants only had about 12 hours postnatal contact with their mothers, DeCasper and Fifer (1980) raised the possibility that the effect was due to intrauterine exposure to certain aspects of the mother's voice. Recall that two studies, one with sheep (Armitage et al., 1980) and the other with humans (Querleu & Renard, 1981) recorded within the amniotic sac using a hydrophone. Both studies suggest that sounds with frequencies under 1000 Hz were transmitted through the abdominal wall with little attenuation, whereas sounds with higher frequencies were greatly attenuated. As suggested earlier, however (Section IV.A.1), almost nothing is known about the fetal auditory system's transduction of frequency and intensity information, so we cannot state conclusively that neonates' preferences for their mother's voice is brought about by *in utero* exposure to it.

B. Infant Preference for "Motherese"

Research has demonstrated that the speech directed toward young infants by adults is considerably simplified in its syntactic form and semantic content when compared to that directed toward adults (see Snow and Ferguson, 1977 for review). This modification of the speech directed toward infants has been termed "Motherese." More recent research on the acoustic aspects of Motherese shows that it involves the use of a higher overall fundamental frequency, exaggerated intonation contours, and a slower tempo (Fernald & Simon, 1984; Grieser & Kuhl, in press; Stern, 1977). This alteration of the linguistic and prosodic aspects of the speech directed towards infants is apparently universal, having been measured in languages such as German (Fernald & Simon, 1984) and even in tone languages such as Chinese Mandarin (Grieser & Kuhl, in press).

Despite the suggestion that Motherese is spoken universally, and suggestions about the potential effects of these signals on infants (Stern, 1977), few studies have been directed toward demonstrating the significance of these speech patterns for infants. Until recently, in fact, studies had not attempted to examine the extent to which the infant discriminated Motherese from other kinds of speech, nor had studies been directed toward the infant's potential "preference" for these speech patterns.

One set of experiments has addressed these issues. Fernald (in press) examined whether infants demonstrated a "preference" for Motherese when presented with a choice between infant-directed and adult-directed speech. Follow-up experiments by Fernald and Kuhl (1981) examined the acoustic determinants of that preference.

Fernald (in press) developed a technique to test the auditory preferences of 4-month-olds. Briefly, infants sat on a parent's lap, facing a three-sided enclosure. A loudspeaker was mounted in the right and left panels of the enclosure. The experiment was designed to give the infant a choice between listening to infant-directed and adult-directed speech. Head-turns to one side or the other determined which of the two kinds of signals the infant was presented with. For half of the infants, Motherese was presented following right head-turns while adult-directed speech was presented following left head-turns. For the other half of the infants, this left–right positioning was reversed. The procedure involved familiarizing the infants, in counter-balanced order, with the signals presented from their left and right sides. Then, each infant was tested until 15 head-turn responses occurred. Each head-turn response was followed by the presentation of an eight-sec sample of either infant- or adult-directed speech, depending on the direction of the turn. The measure of the infant's performance was the total number of trials, out of 15, that the infant turned in the direction required to produce Motherese.

The stimuli consisted of the speech of four adult women, recorded as they talked to their 4-month-olds and to an adult. None of the infants of these four women participated in the experiment. One 8-sec phrase was exerpted from the infant- and adult-directed utterances of each of the talkers. The results showed that 33 of the 48 infants turned more often towards Motherese than towards adult-directed speech. This is significantly different from the 50% chance level of responding. Group measures contrasting the total number of head-turns towards the two types of signals also produced significant results.

In a series of additional experiments, Fernald and Kuhl (1981) isolated certain acoustic characteristics of the adult-directed and infant-directed utterances to identify the acoustic determinants of the preference for Motherese. Since the most dramatic acoustic difference between Motherese and adult-directed speech is its prosodic character, the fundamental frequency was isolated for study. In three studies, the pitch, intensity, and durational characteristics of the fundamental were isolated. In the first of these experiments, the two types of speech samples were represented by pure-tones that followed the pitch contours of the speech samples. The signals were presented at a constant amplitude, but were designed to follow the original signal's temporal characteristics. In a second experiment, the pure-tone signals were designed to follow the exact amplitude characteristics of the signals, while holding frequency constant. Again, the signals followed the durational characteristics of the original signals. Since these two experiments did not allow the separation of frequency or amplitude from temporal patterning, a third experiment was designed to examine the effect of the temporal characteristics in isolation. In this experiment, the pure-tone signals were of constant frequency and amplitude. The tones simply followed the on–off characteristics of the original signals. The procedure followed in each of these experiments was identical to the original Motherese preference experiment.

The data demonstrated that the preference for Motherese shown in the first study was maintained in the second, when the two types of signals were represented only by their fundamental frequency contours. However, in the third and fourth studies when the signals differed only in the amplitude of the fundamental frequency, or only in the temporal (on–off) characteristics of the signals (with frequency and amplitude held constant), no preference was obtained.

The results of these experiments demonstrate two things. First, they demonstrate that infants given a choice produce responses required to hear Motherese, suggesting that these signals are particularly attention-getting for infants (Fernald, in press). Second, the studies show that this attention-getting quality is preserved when the signals are represented only by their fundamental-frequency variations (Fernald & Kuhl, 1981). The results suggest that one of the more compelling differences between infant-directed and adult-directed speech—their fundamental-frequency differences—may be a highly slaient auditory characteristic for infants.

These signals have both a higher average frequency as well as an extended range. Which of these two characteristics is primarily responsible for the infant's preference cannot be specified, since in the second experiment both aspects of the fundamental-frequency were present. Further research will need to be directed at the independent effects of pitch movement per se, versus absolute pitch, as determinants of auditory preference.

In summary, the data on voice recognition suggest three things: (a) that infants recognize their mother's voices at birth or very shortly thereafter, (b) they prefer to listen to Motherese, even when it is spoken to them by women other than their own mothers, and (c) infants' preference for Motherese appears to be governed by the frequency characteristics of the signal rather than by other acoustic factors such as amplitude or temporal factors. Whether these proclivities on the part of very young infants are developed *in utero* are the result of early parent–infant interaction, or, in the case of infant preference for Motherese, derive from an inherent attraction towards signals that are high in frequency, or extremely variable, must be determined by future experiments. Regardless of their origins, these abilities have obvious advantages for infants. Being attracted to the voices of caretakers who are addressing you probably aids in establishing social bonds between caretakers and infants.

X. GENERAL SUMMARY

There are two characteristics of infants' initial state regarding speech perception. Both hold that infants demonstrate phenomena that are highly conducive to the acquisition of speech at a very young age. But one attributes these abilities to predispositions that are specifically linguistic in nature. This account argues that infants are born with a "speech module," a device specially designed to decode speech signals. The alternative account holds that while infants' abilities are conducive to language learning, they are not due to language-specific mechanisms. On this view infants' abilities are attributable to their more general sensory skills and cognitive strategies.

This chapter provided a review of the data and arguments presented in the 15 years of research on the perception of speech by infants. It attempted to unravel an historical account which highlighted the initial discovery and the scientific *Zeitgeist* which surrounded it. This discovery, the demonstration that one-month-old infants demonstrated categorical perception, had an enormous impact on the field. The finding demonstrated that young infants partition the auditory stream in linguistically appropriate ways, prior to producing speech and prior to a protracted period of listening to it.

One-month-olds are prearticulate infants and the finding caused problems for Motor Theory, which claimed that categorical perception derived from specific knowledge of articulation. Yet the finding suggested that the mechanisms underlying speech perception were innate, and this added support to the characterization specifying that infants come into the world equipped with "special mechanisms" that evolved for speech. Renewed attempts ensued to uncover the basis of categorical perception. The question was: Is the categorical perception effect due to mechanisms that evolved for speech, or are other more general sensory mechanisms responsible?

The issue was addressed by examining categorical perception's specificity—to human listeners and to speech. The data showed that the categorical perception effect could be replicated with nonspeech auditory signals, suggesting that whatever mechanisms were responsible, they were not so narrowly tuned as to exclude nonspeech sounds that mimicked speech. More importantly for theory, the effect was replicated in animals. Animals do not have mechanisms specialized for language or speech. Whatever phenomena they reproduce can be handled by a purely auditory-level mechanism. Thus, finding categorical perception in animals meant that the existence of the phenomenon did not necessitate the existence of specially evolved mechanisms. This raised, for the first time, the possibility that infants might have produced these effects using purely auditory-level mechanisms.

This caused theorists to move away from attributing a "phonetic-level" competence to infants. Since animals reproduced these effects, theorists hesitated to impute "special mechanisms" to infants based solely on the demonstration of categorical perception.

In the decade the followed, tests of other more complex phenomena in infants were undertaken. Were there other behaviors demonstrated by infants that might lead us to attribute a phonetic competency to infants? As reviewed here, there are indeed new phenomena suggesting an even more sophisticated responsiveness to speech by infants. These new phenomena focus on infants' detection of complex equivalences in speech information, and show that very young infants are aware of complex mappings for the information underlying phonetic categories.

Three cases of equivalence detection are particularly noteworthy. First, infants detect similarities between discriminably different auditory events that signal the same phonetic unit (equivalence classification), demonstrating the detection of complex auditory–auditory "matches," or equivalence classes. Second, infants relate speech information presented by eye to that presented by ear (cross-modal speech perception), thus demonstrating knowledge of auditory–visual equivalence classes. Third, they match the productions of others with productions of their own (vocal imitation), thus providing evidence of a knowledge of auditory–motor equivalence classes.

One could easily account for the detection of these complex equivalences by imputing a phonetic level competence to infants. A representation of phonetic units would entail a specification of the equivalences between diverse representations of phonetic units—between different acoustic events, between the auditory and visual concomitants of speech, and between the auditory representation of a sound and its motor equivalent.

Yet, the alternative account cannot be rejected. Categorization, cross-modal perception, and imitation are competencies that have been demonstrated to exist in infants outside of the world of language and speech. They are not specific to speech, and thus, even complex behaviors such as these may not be due to a domain-specific "speech-module." It appears, then, that even if speech is intermodally represented in infants, speech may not require "special mechanisms" to be organized in that way. Rather, speech may draw upon a natural cognitive proclivity to represent information intermodally.

Regardless of the outcome of this debate, the importance of the findings for infants should not be overlooked. Whether infants categorize, cross-modally match, and imitate the sounds of language becuase they possess a "speech module," or whether they do so because they have a natural propensity to do so matters little to the infant. What matters is that very young infants do indeed respond to speech as though the categories are already complexly mapped—representing them as a set of auditory, visual, and motor equivalents. While debates about the nature and origins of these phenomena must continue, we should not overlook the fact that infants' abilities, whatever their origins, are highly conducive to language learning.

ACKNOWLEDGMENTS

During the preparation of the manuscript, the author was supported by grants from the National Science Foundation (BNS 8316318 and BNS 8103581), and from the National Institutes of Health (HD-18286). The author thanks Andrew N. Meltzoff for helpful comments on drafts of the manuscript and DiAnne L. Grieser for valuable assistance in every phase of the preparation of the manuscript.

REFERENCES

Abramson, G., & Lisker, L. (1970). Discriminability along the voicing continuum: Cross-language tests. *Proceedings of the Sixth International Congress of Phonetic Sciences.* Prague: Academia, pp. 569–573.

Ades, A. E. (1977). Theoretical notes: Vowels, consonants, speech, and nonspeech. *Psychological Review, 84,* 524–530.

Armitage, S. E., Baldwin, B. A., & Vince, M. A. (1980). The fetal sound environment of sheep. *Science, 208,* 1173–1174.

Aslin, R. N., Pisoni, D. B., Hennessey, B. L., & Perey, A. J. (1981). Discrimination of voice onset time by human infants: New findings and implications for the effects of early experience. *Child Development, 52,* 1135–1145.

Berg, K. M., & Smith, M. C. (1983). Behavioral thresholds for tones during infancy. *Journal of Experimental Child Psychology, 35,* 409–425.

Best, C. T., Hoffman, H., & Glanville, B. B. (1982). Development of infant ear asymmetries for speech and music. *Perception and Psychophysics, 31,* 75–85.

Best, C. T., Morrongiello, B., & Robson, R. (1981). Perceptual equivalence of acoustic cues in speech and nonspeech perception. *Perception and Psychophysics, 29,* 191–211.

Blumstein, S. E., & Stevens, K. N. (1980). Perceptual invariance and onset spectra for stop consonants in different vowel environments. *Journal of the Acoustical Society of America, 67,* 648–662.

Bredberg, G. (1968). Cellular pattern and nerve supply of the human organ of Corti. *Acta Otolaryngologica, 236*(suppl.).

Bruner, J. S., Goodnow, J. J., & Austin, G. A. (1956). *A Study of Thinking.* New York: Wiley and Sons.

Carney, A. E., Widin, G. P. & Viemeister, N. F. (1977). Noncategorical perception of stop consonants differing in VOT. *Journal of the Acoustical Society of America, 62,* 961–970.

Carrell, T. D., Smith, L. B., & Pisoni, D. B. (1981). Some perceptual dependencies in speeded classification of vowel color and pitch. *Perception and Psychophysics, 29,* 1–10.

Chomsky, N., & Halle, M. (1968). *The Sound Pattern of English.* New York: Harper and Row.

Chomsky, N., & Miller, G. A. (1963). Introduction to the formal analysis of natural languages. In R. D. Luce, R. R. Bush, & E. Galanter (Eds.), *Handbook of Mathematical Psychology (Vol. 2).* New York: Wiley and Sons, pp. 269–321.

Cohen, L. B. (1973). A two process model of infant visual attention. *Merrill Palmer Quarterly, 19,* 157–180.

Cole, R. A., & Jakimik, J. (1980). A model of speech perception. In R. A. Cole (Ed.), *Perception and Production of Fluent Speech.* Hillsdale, N.J.: Erlbaum, pp. 133–163.

DeCasper, A. J., & Fifer, W. P. (1980). Of human bonding: Newborns prefer their mothers' voices. *Science, 208,* 1174–1176.

Delattre, P., Liberman, A. M., & Cooper, F. S. (1955). Acoustic loci and transitional cues for consonants. *Journal of the Acoustical Society of America, 27,* 769–773.

Delattre, P., Liberman, A. M., Cooper, F. S. & Gerstman, L. J. (1952). An experimental study of the acoustic determinants of vowel color: Observations on one- and two-formant vowels synthesized from spectrographic patterns. *Word, 8,* 195–210.

Delgutte, B. (1980). Representation of speech-like sounds in the discharge patterns of auditory-nerve fibers. *Journal of the Acoustical Society of America, 68,* 843–857.

Demany, L., & Armand, F. (1984). The perceptual reality of tone chroma in early infancy. *Journal of the Acoustical Society of America, 76,* 57–66.

Dodd, B. (1979). Lip reading in infants: Attention to speech presented in-and out-of-synchrony. *Cognitive Psychology, 11,* 478–484.

Dorman, M. F., Raphael, L. J., & Liberman, A. M. (1979). Some experiments on the sound of silence in phonetic perception. *Journal of the Acoustical Society of America, 65,* 1518–1532.

Eilers, R. E. (1980). Infant speech perception: History and mystery. In G. H. Yeni-Komshian, J. F. Kavanagh and C. A. Ferguson (Eds.), *Child Phonology, Vol. 2: Perception.* New York: Academic Press, pp. 23–40.

Eilers, R. E., Gavin, W., & Wilson, W. R. (1979). Linguistic experience and phonemic perception in infancy: A cross linguistic study. *Child Development, 50,* 14–18.

Eilers, R. E., & Minifie, F. D. (1975). Fricative discrimination in early infancy. *Journal of Speech and Hearing Research, 18,* 158–167.

Eilers, R. E., Wilson, W. R., & Moore, J. M. (1977). Developmental changes in speech discrimination in infants. *Journal of Speech and Hearing Research, 20,* 766–780.

Eimas, P. D. (1974). Auditory and linguistic processing of cues for place of articulation by infants. *Perception and Psychophysics, 16,* 513–521.

Eimas, P. D. (1975a). Speech perception in early infancy. In L. B. Cohen and P. Salapatek (Eds.), *Infant Perception: From Sensation to Cognition, Vol. II.* New York: Academic Press, pp. 193–231.

Eimas, P. D. (1975b). Auditory and phonetic coding of the cues for speech: Discrimination of the /r-l/ distinction by young infants. *Perception and Psychophysics, 18,* 341–347.

Eimas, P. D., & Miller, J. L. (1980a). Contextual effects in infant speech perception. *Science, 209,* 1140–1141.

Eimas, P. D., & Miller, J. L. (1980b). Discrimination of the information for manner of articulation by young infants. *Infant Behavior and Development, 3,* 367–375.

Eimas, P. D., Siqueland, E. R., Jusczyk, P., & Vigorito, J. (1971). Speech perception in infants. *Science, 171,* 303–306.

Eimas, P. D., & Tartter, V. C. (1979). On the development of speech perception: Mechanisms and analogies. In H. W. Reese and L. P. Lipsitt (Eds.), *Advances in Child Development and Behavior, Vol. 13.* New York: Academic Press, pp. 155–193.

Elliott, L. L. & Katz, D. R. (1980). Children's pure tone detection. *Journal of the Acoustical Society of America, 67,* 343–344.

Fant, G. (1973). *Speech Sounds and Features.* Cambridge, Mass.: MIT Press.

Fernald, A. (in press). Four-month-olds prefer to listen to "Motherese." *Infant Behavior and Development.*

Fernald, A., & Kuhl, P. K. (1981). Fundamental frequency as an acoustic determinant of infant preference for "Motherese." Paper presented at the Biennial Meeting of the Society for Research in Child Development, Boston.

Fernald, A., & Simon, T. (1984). Expanded intonation contours in mothers' speech to newborns. *Developmental Psychology, 20,* 104–113.

Fitch, H. L., Halwes, T., Erickson, D. M., & Liberman, A. M. (1980). Perceptual equivalence of two acoustic cues for stop-consonant manner. *Perception and Psychophysics, 27,* 343–350.

Fodor, J. A. (1983). *The Modularity of Mind.* Cambridge, Mass.: MIT Press.

Goodsitt, J. V., Morse, P. A., Ver Hoeve, J. N., & Cowan, N. (1984). Infant speech recognition in multisyllablic contexts. *Child Development, 55,* 903–910.

Goto, H. (1971). Auditory perception by normal Japanese adults of the sounds "l" and "r." *Neuropsychologia, 9,* 317–323.

Grieser, D., & Kuhl, P. K. (in press). The acoustic characteristics of "Motherese" in a tonal language. *Child Development.*

Haber, R. N. (1969). *Information-Processing Approaches to Visual Perception.* New York: Holt, Rinehart and Winston.

Hecox, K. (1975). Electrophysiological correlates of human auditory development. In L. B. Cohen and P. Salapatek (Eds.), *Infant Perception: From Sensation to Cognition, Vol. 2.* New York: Academic Press, pp. 151–191.

Hillenbrand, J. (1983). Perceptual organization of speech sounds by infants. *Journal of Speech and Hearing Research, 26,* 268–282.

Hillenbrand, J. (1984). Speech perception by infants: Categorization based on nasal consonant place of articulation. *Journal of Acoustical Society of America, 75,* 1613–1622.

Hillenbrand, J., Minifie, F. D., & Edwards, T. J. (1979). Tempo of spectrum change as a cue in speech-sound discrimination by infants. *Journal of Speech and Hearing Research, 22,* 147–165.

Jakobson, R., Fant, C. G. M., & Halle, M. (1969). *Preliminaries to Speech Analysis: The Distinctive Features and Their Correlates*. Cambridge, Mass.: MIT Press.

Jeffress, L. A. (1975). Localization of sound. In W. D. Keidel and W. D. Neff (Eds.), *Handbook of Sensory Physiology, Vol. 5*. Berlin: Springer-Verlag.

Jusczyk, P. W. (1981). Infant speech perception: A critical appraisal. In P. D. Eimas and J. L. Miller (Eds.), *Perspectives on the Study of Speech*. Hillsdale, N.J.: Erlbaum, pp. 113–164.

Jusczyk, P. W. (1985). The high amplitude sucking technique as a methodological tool in speech perception research. In G. Gottlieb and N. A. Krasnegor (Eds.), *Measurement of Audition and Vision in the First Year of Postnatal Life: A Methodological Overview*. Norwood, N.J.: Ablex, pp. 195–221.

Jusczyk, P. W., Copan, H., & Thompson, E. (1978). Perception by 2-month-old infants of glide contrasts in multisyllabic utterances. *Perception and Psychophysics, 24*, 515–520.

Jusczyk, P. W., Murray, J., & Bayly, J. (1979, March). Perception of place of articulation in fricatives and stops by infants. Paper presented at Biennial Meeting of Society for Research in Child Development, San Francisco.

Jusczyk, P. W., Pisoni, D. B., Reed, M. A., Fernald, A., & Myers, M. (1983). Infants' discrimination of the duration of a rapid spectrum change in nonspeech signals. *Science, 222*, 175–177.

Jusczyk, P. W., Pisoni, D. B., Walley, A., & Murray, J. (1980). Discrimination of relative onset time of two-component tones by infants. *Journal of the Acoustical Society of America, 67*, 262–270.

Jusczyk, P. W., & Thompson, E. (1978). Perception of a phonetic contrast in multisyllabic utterances by 2-month-old infants. *Perception and Psychophysics, 23*, 105–109.

Kaplan, E. L. (1969). The role of intonation in the acquisition of language. Unpublished doctoral dissertation, Cornell University.

Karzon, R. G. (1985). Discrimination of polysyllabic sequences by one- to four-month-old infants. *Journal of Experimental Child Psychology, 39*, 326–342.

Kiang, N. Y. S. (1980). Processing of speech by the auditory nervous system. *Journal of the Acoustical Society of America, 68*, 830–835.

Klatt, D. H. (1977). Review of the ARPA Speech Understanding Project. *Journal of the Acoustical Society of America, 62*, 1345–1366.

Klatt, D. H. (1980). Software for a cascade/parallel formant synthesizer. *Journal of the Acoustical Society of America, 67*, 971–995.

Kuhl, P. K. (1976). Speech perception in early infancy: The acquisition of speech-sound categories. In S. K. Hirsh, D. H. Eldredge, I. J. Hirsh, S. R. Silverman (Eds.), *Hearing and Davis: Essays Honoring Hallowell Davis*, St. Louis: Washington University Press, pp. 265–280.

Kuhl, P. K. (1978). Predispositions for the perception of speech-sound categories: A species-specific phenomenon? In F. D. Minifie & L. L. Lloyd (Eds.), *Communicative and Cognitive Abilities—Early Behavioral Assessment*. Baltimore: University Park Press, pp. 229–255.

Kuhl, P. K. (1979a). Speech perception in early infancy: Perceptual constancy for spectrally dissimilar vowel categories. *Journal of the Acoustical Society of America, 66*, 1668–1679.

Kuhl, P. K. (1979b). The perception of speech in early infancy. In N. J. Lass (Ed.), *Speech and Language: Advances in Basic Research and Practice*, New York: Academic Press, pp. 1–47.

Kuhl, P. K. (1979c). Models and mechanisms in speech perception: Species comparisons provide further contributions. *Brain, Behavior and Evolution, 16*, 374–408.

Kuhl, P. K. (1980). Perceptual constancy for speech-sound categories in early infancy. In G. H. Yeni-Komshian, J. F. Kavanagh, & C. A. Ferguson (Eds.), *Child Phonology, Vol. 2, Perception*. New York: Academic Press, pp. 41–66.

Kuhl, P. K. (1981a). Discrimination of speech by nonhuman animals: Basic auditory sensitivities conducive to the perception of speech-sound categories. *Journal of the Acoustical Society of America, 70*, 340–349.

Kuhl, P. K. (1981b). Auditory category formation and developmental speech perception. In R. E. Stark (Ed.), *Language Behavior in Infancy and Early Childhood*. Elsevier: North Holland, pp. 165–181.

Kuhl, P. K. (1982). Speech perception: An overview of current issues. In N. J. Lass, L. V. McReynolds, J. L. Northern, & D. E. Yoder (Eds.), *Speech, Language, and Hearing, Vol. I: Normal Processes*. Philadelphia: W. B. Saunders, pp. 286–322.

Kuhl, P. K. (1983). Perception of auditory equivalence classes for speech in early infancy. *Infant Behavior and Development, 6*, 263–285.

Kuhl, P. K. (1985a). Methods in the study of infant speech perception. In G. Gottlieb & N. A. Krasnegor (Eds.), *Measurement of Audition and Vision in the First Year of Postnatal Life: A Methodological Overview*. Norwood, N. J.: Ablex, pp. 223–251.

Kuhl, P. K. (1985b). Categorization of speech by infants. In J. Mehler & R. Fox (Eds.), *Neonate Cognition: Beyond the Blooming, Buzzing Confusion*. Hillsdale, N. J.: Erlbaum, pp. 231–262.

Kuhl, P. K. (1986a). Reflections on infants' perception and representation of speech. In J. S. Perkell & D. H. Klatt (Eds.), *Invariance and Variability of Speech Processes*. Hillsdale, N.J.: Erlbaum, pp. 19–30.

Kuhl, P. K. (1986b). Theoretical contributions of tests on animals to the special-mechanisms debate in speech. *Experimental Biology, 45*, 233–265.

Kuhl, P. K. (1986c). Infants' perception of speech: Constraints on characterizations of the initial state. In B. Lindblom & R. Zetterstrom (Eds.), *Precursors of Early Speech*. New York: Stockton Press, pp. 219–244.

Kuhl, P. K. (1986d). The special-mechanisms debate in speech: Contributions of tests on animals (and their relation to tests using nonspeech signals). In S. Harnad (Ed.), *Categorical Perception*. Cambridge, MA: Cambridge University Press (in press).

Kuhl, P. K. & Hillenbrand, J. (1979). Speech perception by young infants: Perceptual constancy for categories based on pitch contour. Paper presented at the Society for Research on Child Development, San Francisco.

Kuhl, P. K., & Meltzoff, A. N. (1982). The bimodal perception of speech in infancy. *Science, 218*, 1138–1141.

Kuhl, P. K., & Meltzoff, A. N. (1984). The intermodal representation of speech in infants. *Infant Behavior and Development, 7*, 361–381.

Kuhl, P. K., & Meltzoff, A. N. (in press). Speech sounds as intermodal objects of perception. In A. Yonas (Ed.), *Minnesota Symposia on Child Psychology: The Development of Perception*. Hillsdale, N.J.: Erlbaum.

Kuhl, P. K., & Miller J. D. (1975). Speech perception by the chinchilla: Voiced-voiceless distinction in alveolar plosive consonants. *Science, 190*, 69–72.

Kuhl, P. K., & Miller, J. D. (1978). Speech perception by the chinchilla: Identification functions for synthetic VOT stimuli. *Journal of the Acoustical Society of America, 63*, 905–917.

Kuhl, P. K., & Miller, J. D. (1982). Discrimination of auditory target dimensions in the presence or absence of variation in a second dimension by infants. *Perception and Psychophysics, 31*, 279–292.

Kuhl, P. K., & Padden, D. M. (1982). Enhanced discriminability at the phonetic boundaries for the voicing feature in macaques. *Perception and Psychophysics, 32*, 542–550.

Kuhl, P. K., & Padden, D. M. (1983). Enhanced discriminability at the phonetic boundaries for the place feature in macaques. *Journal of the Acoustical Society of America, 73,* 1003–1010.

Lasky, R. E., Syrdal-Lasky, A., & Klein, R. E. (1975). V O T discrimination by four to six and a half month old infants from Spanish environments. *Journal of Experimental Child Psychology, 20,* 215–225.

Lehiste, I. (1976). Suprasegmental features of speech. In N. J. Lass (Ed.), *Contemporary Issues in Experimental Phonetics.* New York: Academic Press, 225–239.

Liberman, A. M. (1957). Some results of research on speech perception. *Journal of the Acoustical Society of America, 29,* 117–123.

Liberman, A. M. (1982). On finding that speech is special. *American Psychologist, 37,* 148–167.

Liberman, A. M., Cooper, F. S., Harris, K. S., & MacNeilage, P. F. (1963). A motor theory of speech perception. In C. G. M. Fant (Ed.), *Proceedings of the Speech Communication Seminar,* Stockholm, 1962. Stockholm: Royal Institute of Technology, Speech Transmission Laboratory.

Liberman, A. M., Cooper, F. S., Shankweiler, D. P., & Studdert-Kennedy, M. (1967). Perception of the speech code. *Psychological Review, 74,* 431–461.

Liberman, A., Harris, K. S., Eimas, P., Lisker, L., & Bastian, J. (1961). An effect of learning on speech perception: The discrimination of durations of silence with and without phonemic significance. *Language and Speech, 4,* 175–195.

Liberman, A. M., Harris, K. S., Hoffman, H. S., & Griffith, B. C. (1957). The discrimination of speech sounds within and across phoneme boundaries. *Journal of Experimental Psychology, 54,* 358–368.

Liberman, A. M., Harris, K. S., Kinney, J. A., & Lane, H. (1961). The discrimination of relative onset-time of the components of certain speech and nonspeech patterns. *Journal of Experimental Psychology, 61,* 379–388.

Liberman, A. M., & Studdert-Kennedy, M. (1978). Phonetic perception. In R. Held, H. Liebowitz, and H. L. Teuber (Eds.), *Handbook of Sensory Physiology, Vol. 8, Perception.* Heidelberg: Springer-Verlag, pp. 143–178.

Lieberman, P. (1967). *Intonation, Perception, and Language.* Cambridge, Mass.: MIT Press.

Lieberman, P. (1980). On the development of vowel production in young children. In G. Yeni-Komshian, J. Kavanagh, & C. Ferguson (Eds.), *Child Phonology, Vol. I Production.* New York: Academic Press, pp. 113–142.

Lisker, L. (1975). Is it VOT or a first-formant transition detector? *Journal of the Acoustical Society of America, 57,* 1547–1551.

Lisker, L., & Abramson, A. S. (1964). A cross-language study of voicing in initial stops: Acoustical measurements, *Word, 20,* 384–422.

MacKain, K., Studdert-Kennedy, M., Spieker, S., & Stern, D. (1983). Infant intermodal speech perception is a left-hemisphere function. *Science, 219,* 1347–1349.

Mattingly, I. G., Liberman, A. M., Syrdal, A. K., & Halwes, T. (1971). Discrimination in speech and nonspeech modes. *Cognitive Psychology, 2,* 131–157.

McCall, R. B., & McGhee, P. E. (1977). The discrepancy hypothesis of attention and affect in infants. In F. Weizman and I. C. Uzgiris (Eds.), *The Structuring of Experience.* New York: Plenum Press, pp. 179–210.

Mehler, J., & Bertoncini, J. (1978). Infants' perception of speech and other acoustic stimuli. In J. Morton & J. C. Marshall (Eds.), *Psycholinguistics 2: Structures and Processes.* Cambridge: MIT Press, pp. 67–105.

Mehler, J., Bertoncini, J., Barriere, M., & Jassik-Gerschenfeld, D. (1978). Infant recognition of mother's voice. *Perception, 7,* 491–497.

Meltzoff, A. N. (1985). The roots of social and cognitive development: Models of man's original nature. T. M. Field & N. Fox (Eds.), *Social Perception in Infants*. Norwood, N.J.: Ablex, pp. 1–30.

Meltzoff, A. N., & Borton, R. W. (1979). Intermodal matching by human neonates. *Nature, 282,* 403–404.

Meltzoff, A. N., & Kuhl, P. K. (in press). Infants' perception of faces and speech sounds: Challenges to theory. In P. Zelazo (Ed.), *Challenges to Developmental Paradigms*. Hillsdale, N.J.: Erlbaum.

Meltzoff, A. N., & Moore, M. K. (1977). Imitation of facial and manual gestures by human neonates. *Science, 198,* 75–78.

Meltzoff, A. N., & Moore, M. K. (1983). Newborn infants imitate adult facial gestures. *Child Development, 54,* 702–709.

Miller, C. L., Younger, B. A., & Morse, P. A. (1982). The categorization of male and female voices in infancy. *Infant Behavior and Development, 5,* 143–159.

Miller, G. A. (1956). The magical number seven, plus or minus two: Some limits on our capacity for processing information. *Psychological Review, 63,* 81–97.

Miller, J. D., Wier, C. C., Pastore, R. E., Kelly, W. J., & Dooling, R. J. (1976). Discrimination and labeling of noise-buzz sequences with varying noise-lead times: An example of categorical perception. *Journal of the Acoustical Society of America, 60,* 410–417.

Miller, J. L., & Eimas, P. D. (1979). Organization in infant speech perception. *Canadian Journal of Psychology, 33,* 353–367.

Miller, J. L., & Eimas, P. D. (1983). Studies on the categorization of speech by infants. *Cognition, 13,* 135–165.

Miller, J. L. & Liberman, A. M. (1979). Some effects of later-occurring information on the perception of stop consonant and semivowel. *Perception and Psychophysics, 25,* 457–465.

Mills, M., & Melhuish, E. (1974). Recognition of mother's voice in early infancy. *Nature, 252,* 123–124.

Minifie, F. D. (1973). Speech acoustics. In F. D. Minifie, T. J. Hixon, and F. Williams (Eds.), *Normal Aspects of Speech, Hearing, and Language*. Englewood Cliffs, N.J.: Prentice-Hall, pp. 235–284.

Miyawaki, K., Strange, W., Verbrugge, R., Liberman, A. M., Jenkins, J. J., & Fujimura, O. (1975). An effect of linguistic experience: The discrimination of /r/ and /l/ by native speakers of Japanese and English. *Perception and Psychophysics, 18,* 331–340.

Morse, P. A. (1972). The discrimination of speech and nonspeech stimuli in early infancy. *Journal of Experimental Child Psychology, 14,* 477–492.

Morse, P. A. (1974). Infant speech perception: A preliminary model and review of the literature. In R. L. Schiefelbusch & L. L. Lloyd (Eds.), *Language Perspectives-Acquisition, Retardation, and Intervention*. Baltimore: University Park Press, pp. 19–53.

Morse, P. A. (1978). Infant speech perception: Origins, processes, and alpha centauri. In F. D. Minifie & L. L. Lloyd (Eds.), *Communicative and Cognitive Abilities–Early Behavioral Assessment*. Baltimore: University Park Press, pp. 195–227.

Morse, P. A., Eilers, R. E., & Gavin, W. J. (1982). The perception of the sound of silence in early infancy. *Child Development, 53,* 189–195.

Morse, P. A., & Snowdon, C. T. (1975). An investigation of categorical speech discrimination by rhesus monkeys. *Perception and Psychophysics, 17,* 9–16.

Neisser, U. (1966). *Cognitive Psychology*. New York: Appleton-Century-Crofts.

Nozza, R. J., & Wilson, W. R. (1984). Masked and unmasked pure-tone thresholds of infants and adults: Development of auditory frequency selectivity and sensitivity. *Journal of Speech and Hearing Research, 27,* 613–622.

Ohman, S. E. G. (1966). Coarticulation in V C V utterances: Spectrographic measurements. *Journal of the Acoustical Society of America, 39,* 151–168.

Olsho, L. W. (1984). Infant frequency discrimination. *Infant Behavior and Development, 7,* 27–35.

Olsho, L. W., Schoon, C., Sakai, R., Turpin, R., & Sperduto, V. (1982a). Auditory frequency discrimination in infancy. *Developmental Psychology, 18,* 721–726.

Olsho, L. W., Schoon, C., Sakai, R., Turpin, R., & Sperduto, V. (1982b). Preliminary data on frequency discrimination in infancy. *Journal of the Acoustical Society of America, 71,* 509–511.

Pastore, R. E. (1976). Categorical perception: A critical re-evaluation. In S. K. Hirsh, D. H. Eldredge, I. J. Hirsh, & S. R. Silverman (Eds.), *Hearing and Davis: Essays Honoring Hallowell Davis.* St. Louis: Washington University Press, pp. 253–264.

Peterson, G. E., & Barney, H. L. (1952). Control methods used in a study of the vowels. *Journal of the Acoustical Society of America, 24,* 175–184.

Pisoni, D. B. (1977). Identification and discrimination of the relative onset time of two component tones: Implications for voicing perception in stops. *Journal of the Acoustical Society of America, 61,* 1352–1361.

Pisoni, D. B. (1978). Speech perception. In W. K. Estes (Ed.), *Handbook of Learning and Cognitive Processes, Vol. 6.* Hillsdale, N.J.: Erlbaum, pp. 167–233.

Pisoni, D. B., Aslin, R. N., Perey, A. J., & Hennessy, B. L. (1982). Some effects of laboratory training on identification and discrimination of voicing contrasts in stop consonants. *Journal of Experimental Psychology: Human Perception and Performance, 8,* 297–314.

Pisoni, D. B., Carrell, T. D., & Gans, S. J. (1983). Perception of the duration of rapid spectrum changes in speech and nonspeech signals. *Perception and Psychophysics, 34,* 314–322.

Pisoni, D. B., & Lazarus, J. H. (1974). Categorical and noncategorical modes of speech perception along the voicing continuum. *Journal of the Acoustical Society of America, 55,* 328–333.

Potter, R. K., Kopp, G. A., & Green, H. C. (1947). *Visible Speech.* New York: D van Nostrand.

Querleu, D., & Renard, K. (1981). Les perceptions auditives du feotus humain. *Medicine et Hygiene, 39,* 2102–2110.

Repp, B. H., Liberman, A. M., Eccardt, T., & Pesetsky, D. (1978). Perceptual integration of acoustic cues for stop, fricative, and affricate manner. *Journal of Experimental Psychology: Human Perception and Performance, 4,* 621–637.

Sachs, M. B., & Young, E. D. (1979). Encoding of steady-state vowels in the auditory nerve: Representation in terms of discharge rates. *Journal of the Acoustical Society of America, 66,* 470–479.

Schneider, B., Trehub, S. E., & Bull, D. (1980) High-frequency sensitivity in infants, *Science, 207,* 1003–1004.

Shoup, J. E., Lass, N. J., & Kuehn, D. P. (1982). Acoustics of speech. In N. J. Lass, L. V. McReynolds, J. L. Northern, & D. E. Yoder (Eds.), *Speech, Language, and Hearing, Vol. I: Normal Processes.* Phildadelphia: W. B. Saunders, pp. 193–218.

Sinnott, J. M., Beecher, M. D., Moody, D. B., & Stebbins, W. C. (1976). Speech sound discrimination by monkeys and humans. *Journal of the Acoustical Society of America, 60,* 687–695.

Sinnott, J. M., Pisoni, D. B., & Aslin, R. N. (1983). A comparison of pure tone auditory thresholds in human infants and adults. *Infant Behavior and Development, 6,* 3–17.

Siqueland, E. R., & DeLucia, C. A. (1969). Visual reinforcement of nonnutritive sucking in human infants. *Science, 165,* 1144–1146.

Snow, C. E., & Ferguson, C. A. (1977). *Talking to Children: Language Input and Acquisition.* Cambridge: Cambridge University Press.

Spelke, E. S. (1979). Perceiving bimodally specified events in infancy. *Developmental Psychology, 15,* 626–636.

Spring, D. R., & Dale, P. S. (1977). Discrimination of linguistic stress in early infancy. *Journal of Speech and Hearing Research, 20,* 224–232.

Stern, D. (1977). *The First Relationship: Infant and Mother.* Cambridge, Mass.: Harvard University Press.

Stevens, K. N. (1972). The quantal nature of speech: Evidence from articulatory-acoustic data. In E. E. David, Jr., & P. B. Denes (Eds.), *Human Communication: A Unified View.* New York: McGraw-Hill, pp. 51–66.

Stevens, K. N. (1981). Constraints imposed by the auditory system on the properties used to classify speech sounds: Evidence from phonology, acoustics, and psychoacoustics. In T. Myers, J. Laver, & J. Anderson (Eds.), *Advances in Psychology: The Cognitive Representation of Speech.* Amsterdam: North-Holland.

Stevens, K. N., & Halle, M. (1967). Remarks on analysis by synthesis and distinctive features. In W. Wathen-Dunn (Ed.), *Models for the Perception of Speech and Visual Form.* Cambridge, Mass.: MIT Press, pp. 88–102.

Strange, W. (1972). The effects of training on the perception of synthetic speech sounds: Voice onset time. Unpublished doctoral dissertation, University of Minnesota.

Streeter, L. A. (1976). Language perception of 2-month-old infants shows effects of both innate mechanisms and experience. *Nature, 259,* 39–41.

Studdert-Kennedy, M. (1976). Speech perception. In N. J. Lass (Ed.), *Contemporary Issues in Experimental Phonetics.* New York: Academic Press, pp. 243–293.

Studdert-Kennedy, M., Liberman, A. M., Harris, K. S., & Cooper, F. S. (1970). Motor theory of speech perception: A reply to Lane's critical review. *Psychological Review, 77,* 234–249.

Summerfield, Q. (1982). Differences between spectral dependencies in auditory and phonetic temporal processing: Relevance to the perception of voicing in initial stops. *Journal of the Acoustical Society of America, 72,* 51–61.

Summerfield, Q., & Haggard, M. (1977). On the dissociation of spectral and temporal cues to the voicing distinction in initial stop consonants. *Journal of the Acoustical Society of America, 62,* 435–448.

Swoboda, P. J., Morse, P. A., & Leavitt, L. A. (1976). Continuous vowel discrimination in normal and at risk infants. *Child Development, 47,* 459–465.

Trehub, S. E. (1973a). Infants' sensitivity to vowel and tonal contrasts. *Developmental Psychology, 9,* 91–96.

Trehub, S. E. (1973b). Auditory-linguistic sensitivity in infants. Unpublished doctoral dissertation, McGill University, Montreal.

Trehub, S. E. (1976). The discrimination of foreign speech contrasts by infants and adults. *Child Development, 47,* 466–472.

Trehub, S. E., Schneider, B. A., & Endman, M. (1980). Developmental changes in infants' sensitivity to octave-band noises. *Journal of Experimental Child Psychology, 29,* 282–293.

Walker, D., Grimwade, J., & Wood, C. (1971). Intrauterine noise: A component of the fetal environment. *American Journal of Obstetrics and Gynecology, 109,* 91–95.

Waters, R. S., & Wilson, W. A., Jr. (1976). Speech perception by rhesus monkeys: The voicing distinction in synthesized labial and velar stop consonants. *Perception and Psychophysics, 19,* 285–289.

Werker, J. F., Gilbert, J. H. V., Humphrey, K., & Tees, R. C. (1981). Developmental aspects of cross-language speech perception. *Child Development, 52,* 349–355.

Werker, J. F., & Tees, R. C. (1984). Cross-language speech perception: Evidence for perceptual reorganization during the first year of life. *Infant Behavior and Development, 7*, 49–63.

Williams, L. (1977). The voicing contrast in Spanish. *Journal of Phonetics, 5*, 169–184.

Wilson, W. R., Moore, J. M., & Thompson, G. (1976). Soundfield auditory thresholds of infants utilizing visual reinforcement audiometry (VRA). Paper presented to the annual convention of the American Speech and Hearing Association, Houston, Texas.

Wood, C. C. (1976). Discriminability, response bias, and phoneme categories in discrimination of voice onset time. *Journal of the Acoustical Society of America, 60*, 1381–1389.

Wormith, S. J., Pankhurst, D., & Moffitt, A. R. (1975). Frequency discrimination by young infants. *Child Development, 46*, 272–275.

Yoneshige, Y., & Elliott, L. L. (1981). Pure-tone sensitivity and ear canal pressure at threshold in children and adults. *Journal of the Acoustical Society of America, 70*, 1272–1276.

Young, E. D., & Sachs, M. B. (1979). Representation of steady-state vowels in the temporal aspects of the discharge patterns of populations of auditory-nerve fibers. *Journal of the Acoustical Society of America, 66*, 1381–1403.

Index